pondon Hill

slawill

Black ditch

slawill moor

This place w^ t ye pistoll was fired from wth ye hooper rod to give ye Allarme to ye camp

Sutton Moor

stipshernts

Sutton malt

Langmar Lake

M: Army marched Left from wte

Sutton Mill

Sedgmoor Lake

Kings - Sedge-Moor

m^r Guns

Scotts Kings

Kings Troop

lower plung bou.

Gun Troop

W: slin.

Bridgwater road over ye moors to Glaston

Midlezy

How part of ye Militia belonging to ye Kings army was quartered Sunday July 5: 1685

Captain-General and
Rebel Chief

James, Duke of Monmouth in Garter robes, by Sir Peter Lely

CAPTAIN-GENERAL AND REBEL CHIEF

The Life of James, Duke of Monmouth

By
J. N. P. WATSON

Foreword by His Grace the Duke of Buccleuch and
Queensberry, K.T.

London
GEORGE ALLEN & UNWIN
Boston   Sydney

First published in 1979

GEORGE ALLEN & UNWIN LTD
40 Museum Street, London WC1A 1LU

© J. N. P. Watson, 1979

Foreword © 1979 The Duke of Buccleuch and Queensberry

British Library Cataloguing in Publication Data

Watson, J. N. P.
  Captain-General and rebel chief
  1. Monmouth, James Scott, *Duke of*
  I. Title
  942.06′6′0924   DA448.9   78–41158

  ISBN 0-04-920058-5

Typeset in 11 on 12 point Baskerville by Trade Linotype Limited, Birmingham
and printed in Great Britain
by Billing & Sons Limited, Guildford, London and Worcester

FOREWORD

by His Grace the Duke of Buccleuch and Queensberry, K.T.

Many great men have unwittingly ˌbelieved that history would prove the correctness of their actions or the rightness of their cause. It is surprising how many, particularly those on the losing side of a dispute, underrated the long-term influence of current chroniclers. So often it is the writers or reporters on the winning side whose words are most eagerly sought and repeated by subsequent historians. As a result, lies, if such they be, become ever more firmly established.

In the case of Monmouth's downfall it was clearly in the best interests of King James II and the establishment to discredit him in the eyes of his supporters. As the author says, 'The King wanted the greatest possible audience to see the national hero die' and there follows a moving description of Monmouth's courageous resistance to the pressures of the Holy men around him to extract a public apology for his actions. The very fact that he did so resist, even at the risk of the future of his wife and children, whom he loved, exposes the falseness of those official descriptions of his cowardly begging for forgiveness.

It is always refreshing to find authors who do take the trouble to research into the 'minority reports' and in consequence make a really positive contribution to the history of our country. For obvious personal reasons I am grateful to the author for portraying my great (x 8) grandfather in a far truer and more fascinating light than has so often been the case.

Bowhill,
Selkirk.
January 1979.

AUTHOR'S ACKNOWLEDGEMENTS

My most grateful thanks are due to Her Majesty the Queen, who graciously allowed me to reproduce Samuel Cooper's portrait of Monmouth as a boy. I am deeply grateful to the Duke of Buccleuch for his help and encouragement generally and for permitting me to use his portraits of the Duke and Duchess of Monmouth; and to his Grace's personal secretary, Miss Lorna MacEchern, for much valuable assistance. I am also indebted: to Captain Michael and Lady Victoria Wemyss for allowing me to visit Wemyss Castle and peruse their family documents; to Colonel Claud Scott, who placed the (unpublished) biography of Monmouth by his father, Lord George Scott, at my disposal; to the Marquess of Bath; and to his Librarian, Miss B. M. Austin, who put the relevant Coventry and Portland Papers at my disposal; to the Duke of Roxburghe for consenting to the reproduction of his painting of the Horse Guards, Whitehall, in the time of Charles II; and to the Duke of Argyll, for allowing the Inveraray portrait of the 9th Earl of Argyll to be reproduced.

I would like to record my gratitude also to the staffs of the Public Record Office; the British Library (and in particular the Departments of Western Manuscripts and of Printed Books); the Bodleian Library (especially Miss Albinia de la Mare); the Royal United Services Institute (especially Miss S. M. Gullick), and the Royal Commission on Historical Manuscripts and the London Library. And, finally, to my wife, Lavinia, who typed the final draft, for her support throughout the writing and preparation of this biography.

I would also like to thank Lieutenant-Colonel W. F. N. Watson for his work on the maps.

AUTHOR'S PREFACE

It was after I was invited to contribute a short history to a regimental series and was studying the Sedgemoor campaign that I became more and more fascinated with the background of the Western Rising, with the story of the Old Cause against arbitrary kingship and religion, with the early Whigs, and above all with the question of why Charles II's eldest son was the Rebellion's *sine qua non*. Having read the three larger biographies – the *Life, Progresses and Rebellion of James, Duke of Monmouth* by George Roberts (1844), *King Monmouth* by Allan Fea (1902), and *James, Duke of Monmouth* by Elizabeth D'Oyley (1938) – I concluded that, excellent as all of them are in many respects, none is sufficiently well balanced to emphasise why the Protestant Duke's services were in such strong demand.

Time and again Monmouth has been described as a weak man. That is as true as it has been for many heroes before and since his day. He was vain, immoral, irresponsible and too easily swayed. And when things went very badly for him, just when his inspiration was most needed, his judgement failed him; he would not take decisions, he gave in to orgies of self-pity, he put his mistress before his duty and self-preservation before honour, while the flexibility, which was one of his greatest assets as Captain-General, became his greatest liability as rebel chief. But he was by no means the shallow personality which has so often been depicted.

His claim to the throne was potentially strong: proof that his father was married to his mother, Lucy Barlow, though most vigilantly suppressed by the Duke of York and his party, was almost conclusive, yet tantalisingly elusive. (Right up to the moment that the 5th Duke of Buccleuch found the marriage certificate in the muniments room at Dalkeith a century ago, and burned it to save embarrassment, the evidence appears to have been there in the background.)

But not one rebel leader, not a single West Country dissident, would have risen for Monmouth on that account alone. What has been consistently underrated by historians and biographers is his reputation for military leadership, the germ of which showed in the naval Battle of Lowestoft, when he was sixteen, and which blossomed as a commander in five capaigns, four on the Continent and one in Scotland, and at home as a military administrator and director of internal security. Roberts and Fea made only brief mention of the Protestant Duke's military career, and although Mrs D'Oyley gave it more attention her analysis remained cursory. Finding no comprehensive accounts of the siege of Maastricht (1673), the campaign that culminated in the Battle of St Denis (1678), or the Battle of Bothwell Bridge (1679), in all of which Monmouth played a distinguished part as senior commander, I have now pieced their stories together (mostly from manuscript accounts in the Public Record Office).

The qualities required of senior officers in the seventeenth century were the aristocrat's stature and self-confidence and physical courage, accompanied if possible by tact, charm, a practical approach and some tactical sense. If fine horsemanship and swordsmanship could be added to a reputation for gallantry, so much the better, for leadership by example was the key to success. That Monmouth owned all these attributes in strong measures and could apply them convincingly was endorsed by all who knew him, and he was judged by all his associates (none of them blind to his faults) as a 'greate generall'. The outstanding qualities that won him this accolade were his stimulating personality, kindness, sincere affability, engaging manner and appreciation of people in all walks of life, which gave him an almost universal capacity for exciting admiration and affection.

His father, who was the first to be charmed by him, exploited Monmouth's gifts for his own comfort and convenience. Although he never wanted to see his son by Lucy Barlow as his heir, Charles used the young Duke's prestige and popularity as a foil for York's growing ambition, frequently reminding his brother of the 'popular candidate's' strength. Monmouth, who believed so strongly in predestination, was placed in a false position from the start, and gained not the glorious fate he envisaged for himself but the role of a dupe, an instrument in the power game. And, since his talents deserved a better fate, perhaps we should follow his career's melancholy end with affection and compassion, not condemnation.

After he turned rebel, his inspiration in the planning and organisation of the projected uprising of 1683 was generally recognised by his companions; and when Shaftesbury, the Whig leader, died shortly before the exposure of the conspiracy, and the rebel cabal was deciding who should succeed him, no less tough and able a soldier and republican politician than Colonel Algernon Sidney echoed all their opinions when he said: 'I know of but one general we can have and that is the Duke of Monmouth, whose conduct and integrity I do not doubt.' Without attempting to understate his shortcomings, that is the Monmouth I hope to have revealed in these pages.

Monmouth's mother, who was born Lucy Walter, assumed the name 'Barlow' when she crossed to the Continent in 1648; I therefore refer to her in the text as Lucy Barlow. Also, because in the narrative I mainly call Monmouth 'James', I have, in order to avoid misunderstanding, referred to James, Duke of York, before he becomes King James II, as 'York'.

J. N. P. WATSON
Pannett's Shipley
Horsham
Sussex
November 1977

CONTENTS

Foreword by His Grace the Duke of Buccleuch and
    Queensberry, K.T.   *page* vii
Author's Acknowledgements   ix
Author's Preface   xi
List of Illustrations   xvii
List of Maps and Diagrams   xix
Prologue   xxi

Book I CAPTAIN-GENERAL   1

1	1649–1662	Boy of Contention	3
2	1662–1665	Baptism of Fire	9
3	1665–1667	First Command	19
4	1667–1670	The Secret Treaty of Dover	25
5	1670–1671	Horseplay and Murder	37
6	1671–1672	Instruction from the Sun King	41
7	1673	Hero of Maastricht	53
8	1673–1677	Protestant Duke in Ascendancy	67
9	1677–1678	Lord-General of the Land Forces	77
10	1678–1679	Counter-Insurgency Commander	89
11	1679	To Scotland with a Velvet Fist	96
12	1679	Zenith and Eclipse	107
13	1679	Recalcitrant Son	113

Book II REBEL CHIEF

14	1680–1681	The Campaign to Win Hearts	125
15	1681	The Oxford Parliament	133
16	1681–1682	Under Arrest	139
17	1682	A *Coup d'État* is Planned	146
18	1683	The Plot that Failed	156
19	1683	Toddington	162
20	1683	Reconciliation	168
21	1683–1684	Thwarted by the Duke of York	172
22	1684–1685	'The King is Dead, God Save the King'	180
23	March–May 1685	Plot of Invasion	192

24   May–June 1685   Beach-head at Lyme Regis   *page* 207
25   13–21 June 1685   'Our Lawful and Rightful
     Sovereign'   215
26   21–25 June 1685   The Race for Bristol   225
27   25–30 June 1685   Hit and Run   232
28   1–6 July 1685   The Path to Sedgemoor   237
29   6–8 July 1685   Disaster   245
30   8–13 July 1685   The King's Prisoner   252
31   13–15 July 1685   Martyr for the People?   258
Postscript : Those He Left Behind   267

Appendix A   Circumstantial Evidence on Allegations that
             Charles II married Lucy Barlow   275
Appendix B   Monmouth's Proclamation from Taunton on
             20 June 1685   278
Appendix C   Notes and Sources   279
Appendix D   Bibliography   294
Index   299

LIST OF ILLUSTRATIONS

PLATES

James, Duke of Monmouth in Garter robes, by Sir Peter Lely (*by permission of His Grace the Duke of Buccleuch*)   *Frontispiece*

Lucy Barlow (*nèe* Walter) by Sir Peter Lely
Charles II, studio of J. M. Wright (*National Portrait Gallery*)
Monmouth as a child, by Samuel Cooper (*by gracious permission of Her Majesty the Queen*)   *Facing page*   8

Monmouth aged about seventeen, artist unknown
Anna, Duchess of Monmouth, by William Wissing (*by permission of His Grace the Duke of Buccleuch*)   *Facing page*   9

The saddle presented to Monmouth by his father on his appointment as Captain-Commandant of the Life Guards (*by permission of His Grace the Duke of Buccleuch*)
A horse match, *c.* 1680, from Richard Blome's *Gentlemen's Recreation*   *Facing page*   40

Monmouth as Military Commander by Henri Gascars (*by permission of His Grace the Duke of Buccleuch*)
Fortress warfare, *c.* 1670: Dutch engineers building a bastion salient   *Facing page*   41

English soldiers at the time of Monmouth's Royal Service, by Colonel Clifford Walton
(a) Grenadiers, *c.* 1678; (b) a Private Gentleman of the 1st (King's) Troop of the Life Guards at about the time Monmouth assumed command of that Corps (1669); (c) a General Officer, *c.* 1678 (*The Royal United Services Institute*)   *Facing page*   72

The Horse Guards, Whitehall, at the time of Monmouth's Captain-Generalcy (*by permission of His Grace the Duke of Roxburghe*)
The Battle of Bothwell Bridge, 1679, artist unknown   *Facing page*   73

James, Duke of York, by Sir Godfrey Kneller (*National Portrait Gallery*)
Princess Mary of Orange, afterwards Mary II of England, after Wissing (*National Portrait Gallery*)
Prince William of Orange, afterwards William III, after Lely (*National Portrait Gallery*)   *Facing page* 104

Opposition Leaders : (a) George Villiers, Duke of Buckingham, by
Sir Peter Lely (*National Portrait Gallery*); (b) William Lord Russell,
artist unknown (*British Museum*); (c) Anthony Ashley Cooper,
Earl of Shaftesbury, after J. Greenhill (*National Portrait Gallery*);
(d) Colonel Algernon Sidney, by Justus van Egmont (*Nottingham
General Hospital*)   *Facing page* 105

The bas-relief memorial commemorating his murder, to Thomas
Thynne, in Westminster Abbey (*Dean and Chapter of Westminster*)
Robert Spencer, Earl of Sunderland, after Johannes Mytens (*British
Museum*)
The Marquess of Halifax, *c.* 1675, attributed to Mary Beale
                                                     Facing page 136

King's Men : (a) Louis Duras, Marquis of Blanquefort, afterwards
Earl of Feversham, by J. Riley (*British Museum*); (b) Judge
Jeffreys, attributed to W. Claret (*National Portrait Gallery*); (c) 1st
Duke of Lauderdale, by J. Huysmans (*National Portrait Gallery*);
(d) Christopher Monck, Duke of Albemarle (*British Museum*)
                                                     Facing page 137

Monmouth's Pocket Book : (a) a page of verses; (b) Monmouth's
horoscope (*British Museum*, Egerton MS, 1527)   *Facing page* 168

Monmouth, an engraving after Lely (*from the collection at Parham
House, West Sussex*)
A photographic restoration of the monument in Toddington Church,
Bedfordshire, to Henrietta, Baroness Wentworth of Nettleside
The 9th Earl of Argyle, artist unknown (*by permission of His Grace
the Duke of Argyll*)   *Facing page* 169

Ford, Baron Grey of Werke, *c.* 1675, by Sir Peter Lely (*Department
of the Environment*)
The 4th Earl of Salisbury whose portrait, by William Wissing, was
painted on top of one of Monmouth (*by permission of The
Marquess of Salisbury*). The 3rd Earl had been a Monmouthite
                                                     Facing page 232

The Dutch 5th-rate, 32-gun man-of-war, on the left of the picture,
by G. L. Backhuisen, would be similar to the *Helderenberg* in which
Monmouth sailed to Lyme Regis in 1685   *Facing page* 233

Four of the Monmouth playing cards : (a) The skirmish at
Keynsham; (b) Ferguson preaching the day before the battle of
Sedgemoor; (c) The rout of the rebels at Sedgemoor; (d) The
taking of the Duke of Monmouth (*British Museum*)   *Facing page* 264

Monmouth, after decapitation. Artist unknown (*National Portrait
Gallery*)   *Facing page* 265

ILLUSTRATIONS IN TEXT

Titus Oates before the Council (*British Museum*)   *page* 90
Protestant Flails (*British Museum*)   92

ENDPAPERS

Facsimile of a contemparary plan of Monmouth's night march across Sedgemoor, drawn by the Rev. Andrew Paschall, Rector of Chedzoy. Paschall sent it to the Earl of Sunderland with the folllowing message : 'In the want I am at present of a skilful hand that might enable me to serve your lordship with an exact draught [*sic*] of this place (to which God be praised we are returned in safety) I have employed some of my neighbours to measure the distances according to the enclosed paper, and I make no doubt but they have done it with care.'

MAPS AND DIAGRAMS

1	Stuart Family Tree	*page* 2
2	Theatre of Operations, Anglo–French invasions of the Netherlands, 1672–3	50
3	The author's impression of the Fortress of Maastricht, 1673	59
4	Monmouth's route to St Denis in August 1678	86
5	The Battle of St Denis	87
6	The author's impression of the main deployment for the Battle of Bothwell Bridge, June 1679	103
7	Monmouth's journey in the West Country, 1680	131
8	The author's impression of the plan for the seizure of London, 1682–3	152
9	Invasion Plans, 1685; and Monmouth's area of activity in the Netherlands, March–May 1685	197
10	The Campaign in the West	223
11	The Fight at Philips Norton, 27 June 1685	234
12	Monmouth's Night March, 5–6 July, and the Battle of Sedgemoor, 6 July 1685	249

This book is dedicated
to the Household Cavalry which Monmouth
commanded from 1668 to 1679

PROLOGUE

Bridgwater, 4 July 1685. After attending the Rev. Mr Ferguson's Matins, James Duke of Monmouth, resplendent still in princely purple, Garter star and neatly combed periwig, climbed the stumpy tower supporting St Mary's Church spire – as you can still climb it today – and pointed his glass eastwards. The view, now obstructed by industrial chimneys, trees and houses, then opened clear across the King's Sedgemoor to Westonzoyland. To see the white tents and, around them, the scarlet dots of the men he had once commanded, and to know his half-brother, Grafton, and the comrade deputy commanders of his youth – Feversham, the two Churchills, Kirke, Douglas, Sackville and Villiers – were at their head, must have roused some strange sensations in him. There, three miles away, was the memory of his illustrious Captain-Generalcy, while here below, in Castlefield, was all he represented now, a ragged, ill-armed host of revolutionaries with their backs to the wall, a host which had marched all of 200 miles with him, which had lured him, with loving respect, to this fatal Bridgwater.

Ranging his spyglass along the Royalist lines, he noted that the horse were widely separated from the foot, and an idea began to form in his mind. It might be possible to circumvent their artillery, to infiltrate the enemy lines in full strength by night, take the cavalry and infantry by two distinct and simultaneous assaults, and so 'prevent their arms coming together'. Why not attack Feversham by stealth, before further reinforcements reached him; then, having routed him, proceed with the current plan and ride to Cheshire?

He had climbed that church tower in a state of utter despair, for everything had gone against him during the past week. He had been forced into ignominious retreat; his ally, Argyle, had been defeated in the Lowlands; William of Orange was poised to support the enemy; and James's own army, dishevelled and ill equipped, was reduced to 4,000, and there were desertions on every hand.

But now he was stimulated by this splendid chance to defeat his uncle, seize the throne vacated by his father of beloved memory, and fulfil the wish of England's common people, who loved him.

When he climbed down from the tower, he was told that a

Sedgemoor peasant sought an interview. He listened eagerly to Godfrey. The Royalists appeared to have posted no guards or pickets, the herdsman reported, and many of them were drunk, or sleeping, their scarlet coats laid out as blankets. The horse were indeed some distance from the foot. Godfrey knew the way across Sedgemoor like the back of his hand, and the paths to Weston. James called a council of war and put his plan to them : to surprise the enemy in dead of night, avoiding the guns on the Bridgwater road and any standing patrols that might be watching in that direction by making a detour north of Chedzoy. Godfrey would guide them across Sedgemoor.

At 11.30 p.m., with Wade's vanguard to set the pace and his own lifeguard of horse riding close around him, James gave the signal for his army to begin its furtive march north-east. An hour later they turned onto the moor. The unschooled horses were his greatest liability : the darkness, the nerviness of their inexperienced riders, straining to hear whispered orders, the swirling marsh mist, and the inevitable continuous concertinaing of the column, would all have contributed to shake the temper of the ill-broken, ill-assorted nags, kicking and shying, often stopping dead in their tracks, and transmitting fear to the troopers, who relayed back their own nervousness. But, considering the whole force numbered more than 600 horses and 3,000 men, all raw levies in a single force, their order and discipline spoke much for James's leadership.

Strange, inopportune thoughts come into men's minds during periods of silent tension and crisis. As he rode on to the King's Sedgemoor that night, did the Duke of Monmouth's thoughts return fleetingly to his early boyhood in the Netherlands, and his beautiful Welsh mother, Lucy Barlow, who had told him over and over that he should be Prince of Wales ('for I was married to your father by a bishop at Liège')? Or did he remember for a moment his father's oft-repeated account of the Battle of Worcester in 1651; how he had climbed the cathedral tower to observe the enemy's movements; and how, when Cromwell began to deploy, Charles had taken command of the Royalist horse and attacked uphill under artillery cover; and how the foot, coming up behind, ran out of ammunition, but stood their ground with pike and sword, and after a long, brave struggle, were inched back into the city. His father had quit his horse by then, and only when Worcester's walls were stormed did he fly. But memories of his father's defeat were not appropriate to this midnight of 4 July 1685.

Well on to the open moor now, the smell of peat marsh in their nostrils, the silent army came to the next channel called the Lang-moor Rhine, whose best crossing was marked by a great boulder, the Devil's Upping Stock, or Langmoor Stone. That night the rock was hidden by fog, and Godfrey steered too far east of it. But, after a long agony of suspense, with much blind casting up and down (any moment one of Compton's outposts might have tumbled on the great column), eventually the plungeon was found, and over they tramped. They were only three-quarters of a mile from the Royalist camp now, and the clock on Chedzoy steeple struck one. At this point James sent Grey, accompanied by Godfrey, to the front of the column with the eight troops of cavalry. But no sooner was the march resumed than the stillness of Sedgemoor was broken by a single shot. One of Compton's blue-coated troopers, glimpsing them through the fog, had raised the alarm.

Spurs hard on, Compton's man galloped back across the Bussex upper plungeon, then down the Royalist battalions' front with a breathless 'Beat the drums, the enemy is come! For the Lord's sake, beat the drums!' Moments later came the drummers' rat-tat-tat.

Monmouth must take advantage of such surprise as he had gained.

Book 1
CAPTAIN-GENERAL

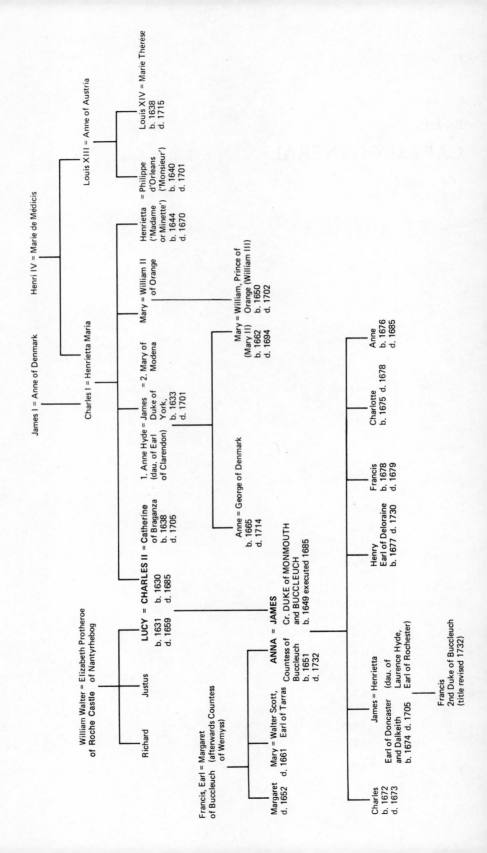

James I = Anne of Denmark

Henri IV = Marie de Médicis

Charles I = Henrietta Maria

Louis XIII = Anne of Austria

William Walter = Elizabeth Protheroe of Roche Castle of Nantyrhebog

Henrietta ('Madame or Minette') b. 1644 d. 1670 = Philippe d'Orleans ('Monsieur') b. 1640 d. 1701

Louis XIV = Marie Therese b. 1638 d. 1715

Mary = William II of Orange

Richard

Justus

LUCY = CHARLES II = Catherine b. 1631 b. 1630 of Braganza d. 1659 d. 1685 b. 1638 d. 1705

1. Anne Hyde (dau. of Earl of Clarendon) = James Duke of York, b. 1633 d. 1701 = 2. Mary of Modena

Mary = William, Prince of (Mary II) Orange (William III) b. 1662 b. 1650 d. 1694 d. 1702

Anne = George of Denmark b. 1665 d. 1714

Francis, Earl = Margaret of Buccleuch (afterwards Countess of Wemyss)

ANNA = JAMES Countess of Cr. DUKE of MONMOUTH Buccleuch and BUCCLEUCH b. 1651 b. 1649 executed 1685 d. 1732

Margaret d. 1652

Mary = Walter Scott, d. 1661 Earl of Tarras

Charles b. 1672 d. 1673

James = Henrietta Earl of Doncaster (dau. of and Dalkeith Laurence Hyde, b. 1674 d. 1705 Earl of Rochester)

Francis 2nd Duke of Buccleuch (title revised 1732)

Henry Earl of Deloraine b. 1677 d. 1730

Francis b. 1678 d. 1679

Charlotte b. 1675 d. 1678

Anne b. 1676 d. 1685

1

BOY OF CONTENTION

If no other verdict on Lucy Barlow – Charles II's first paramour, who was to be posthumously famous as Monmouth's mother – can be relied upon, at least all agreed as to her good looks. 'Bold, brown and beautiful,' said John Evelyn. 'She was very handsome,' the Duke of York concurred, and certainly it was a lovely face that both Lely and Kneller painted. Baronne D'Aulnoy wrote in her *Memoirs of the Court in England* that 'Her beauty was so perfect that, when the King saw her, he was so charmed and ravished and enamoured that . . . he knew no other sweetness or joy than to love her, and be loved by her.'

Mrs Barlow was a pseudonym, a cover supplied by Lucy's cousin, John Barlow, of Barlow Hall, Colchester, Master of Ordnance and Justice of the Peace, under whose protection she travelled to the Hague as a Royalist spy in the summer of 1648. No sooner was she safely out of England than her maternal aunt, Mrs Gosfritt, was arrested and 'put in prison about her said niece Mrs Barlow's going beyond the sea'.[1] Lucy was eighteen then, and only nine years more, years with few rays of happiness, were left to her. Indeed her time in Charles's company was perhaps the most rapturous of her life, for her childhood had been turbulent and insecure.

Her father was William Walter, lord of Roche Castle, over-looking St Bride's Bay, in Pembrokeshire, 'a very considerable place', as it was described in 1640, 'with a body of 500 head of oxen and 2,000 sheep'. Lucy's mother was also from the Welsh squirearchy; she was Elizabeth, daughter of John Protheroe, of the Manor of Hawksbrook, in Carmarthenshire. The Walters were for ever quarrelling and taking legal action against one another, the case *Walter* v. *Walter* being first heard in 1641 when Lucy was eleven. Elizabeth petitioned that Walter failed to support her. Walter made counter-petitions to the effect that his father-in-law, John Protheroe, had failed to produce a promised £600 dowry, and that Elizabeth was unfaithful. On 18 February, 1647, judgement was given that 'William Walter shall have his children sent home to him for their keeping and education'. They did not go; but William was a Parliamentarian, Elizabeth a staunch Royalist, and for this reason, although not a shred of evidence was raised against his wife, Walter eventually had the better of the case.

Roche Castle was garrisoned for the King by Elizabeth Walters's uncle, Lord Carbery, up to 1644, when it was stormed and burned to the ground by Cromwell's men. Walter moved to another Welsh property, while Elizabeth took her children to a house 'at the Back side of Kinge Street, Covent Garden'. Lucy and her brothers, Richard and Justus, spent nearly all their childhood either here or with their grandmother, Mrs Elenor Protheroe, a widow. In spite of their unsettled existence and the shadow of their parents' rows they were well educated. Richard, a Parliamentarian like his father, became High Sheriff of Pembrokeshire, and Justus studied successfully for the bar.

It is possible that Lucy knew Charles before their Dutch encounter. For, on her mother's side, she was usefully connected, being a cousin of the Percys, the children of the 'Wizard Earl' of Northumberland, and the Sidneys, those of the 2nd Earl of Leicester, all friends of the young prince. Countess Dunois, a contemporary, wrote in her *Memoirs* that Charles 'first saw Mrs Barlow in Wales', in 1646, and Baronne D'Aulnoy agrees that he 'first saw her in Wales where she then was'. Soon after Edward Hyde (later Chancellor and Earl of Clarendon) landed in France, with his exiled prince, he wrote, 'I am far from being secure that the intelligence from London of the Prince's marriage may not be true. We were apprehensive of it before he went, and spoke freely to him our opinions of the fatal consequences of it.'[2]

What was he like, the nineteen-year-old Prince-in-exile, the heir to England's throne, whom Lucy loved? Charles had a swarthy face and a coarse mouth, which earned him the nickname 'Black Boy', and prompted the oft-quoted 'odd's fish, I am an ugly fellow'. But he was tall, broad, of fine physique and great charm. Robert Baillie, reporting to the Scots from the Hague in 1649, wrote: 'His Majesty is of a very sweet and courteous disposition . . . He is one of the most gentle, innocent, well-inclined Princes, so far as yet appears, that lives in the world; understands pretty well; speaks not much . . . If God would send him among us, without some of his present counsellors, I think he might make, by God's blessing, as good a King as Britain saw these hundred years. . . .'[3]

Soon after Lucy arrived at the Hague, some of Cromwell's ships, having mutinied and declared for the King, put their officers ashore at Deal, and sailed for Holland to contact the fifteen-year-old Duke of York, the titular Lord High Admiral, who, with the aid of Colonel Bampfylde, had recently escaped from his Roundhead warders at St James's Palace and taken refuge with his sister, the Princess of Orange. When the sailors sent a deputation requesting that he should lead them, the Dutch Prince and Princess suspected a trap. This was Charles's moment; he immediately left St Germain, journeying via Calais for his sister's castle at Helvoetsluys. There he dismissed York to the Hague, and took command of the ships. It was during the fortnight before his raids up the Thames that Charles and Lucy fell in love, were probably married and certainly lived together as man and wife, a relationship which was resumed on his return. Their only child, James, was born on 9 April 1649, just ten weeks after the execution of Charles I.

The question whether his mother was formally married to the King overshadowed James, Duke of Monmouth's whole life. It was the most significant factor of his career. And although all proof of the marriage appears to have been destroyed the inferences that such a marriage did take place are so convincing as to be almost conclusive.*

Charles was nominally King of England, Scotland and Ireland at the time James was born, and it was Dr Stephen Goffe – who, some years later was to be appointed the boy's tutor – who had broken the news by addressing him as 'Your Majesty'. Soon after the birth, father, mother and child went to stay with the Princess of Orange, who was then Lucy's firm friend. They remained at St Germain as guests of Henrietta Maria, Charles's mother, until the end of the month when Charles committed himself to the Scots. And, 'upon his Majesty's going for Scotland in 1650', wrote Ferguson, 'he [James] was committed by his Majesty to the care of his Illustrious Grandmother who lived then at the Par-le-roy in Paris'.[4]

The best hope for the Restoration seemed to lie in an influential marriage for the King. There were those, therefore, who were determined to divide Charles and Lucy, and their first action was to vilify her by pretending she was living a degenerate life. The Princess of Orange, who, up to the middle of 1655, had received Lucy *en belle-sœur*, was also persuaded that her brother must abandon his wife and that the only method was to blacken her name: 'Your wife is resolving whether she will write or no,' she

*See Appendix A.

wrote to Charles from the Hague on 2 May, 1655; 'therefore I am
to say nothing to you from her; but will keep open my letter as
long as the post will permit, to expect what good nature will work,
which I find now does not at all; for 'tis eleven of the clock, and
no letter comes.' On 21 June, Lucy was still with the Princess, who
wrote again to the King: 'Your wife desires me to present her
humble duty to you which is all she can say. I tell her it is because
she thinks of another husband and does not follow your example
as being as faithful a wife as you are a husband. . . .'[5]

Charles's scurrilous Groom of the Bedchamber, Daniel O'Neile,
sarcastically known as 'Infallible Subtle', now entered the lists against
Lucy. In a letter written from the Hague to the King in March
1655, he made no complaint against her. He expressed his sympathy
that if some travelling arrangements had not gone wrong, and thus
delayed Charles, 'in all likelihood you might have been at home
with your wife and children now peaceably'. (Lucy gave birth to
a second child, a daughter, Mary, in 1651).

The following February, however, 'Infallible Subtle' took pen
and paper with more sinister intent: 'I have hitherto forborn giving
your Majesty any account of your commands concerning Mrs
Barlow, because those that I employed to her, brought me
assurances from her, she would obey your Majesty's commands.
Of late I am told she intends nothing less, and that she is assured
from Collen your Majesty would not have her son from her. I am
much troubled to see the prejudice her being here does your
Majesty; for every idle action of hers brings your Majesty upon
the stage.'

Notwithstanding this malice, Lucy remained a Royalist agent and,
in 1656, she travelled to London in the King's service, taking her
two children with her. Ostensibly – 'for Cromwell's information' –
her mission was to collect her share of her mother's estate, but the
visit was really a political one. Charles met her at Antwerp, whither
he had travelled for an interview with the Governor of the Spanish
Netherlands, regarding his impending pact with Spain. He gave her
a present of a pearl necklace, worth £1,500, and he and Lucy were
'a day and a night together'. For her mission, Lucy was escorted by
Colonel Thomas Howard, brother of the Earl of Suffolk and Master
of the Horse to the Princess of Orange, a double-dealing character,
who later transpired to be at once an agent for Cromwell, Charles
and the Dutch. To avoid a compromising position with Howard,
Lucy persuaded her brother Justus (of the Temple) to accompany
her.*

*Her eldest brother, a Commonwealth man, had just completed his year as
High Sheriff of Pembrokeshire.

England was about as difficult of entry and egress at this time as a moated castle, and, inside, Cromwell's police were everywhere. But, under the aegis of his Dutch diplomatic authority, the cunning Howard steered them through to 'a barber's shop near Somerset House', to which Lucy's maid, Ann Hill, had travelled three weeks earlier to prepare for them. Lucy was soon in touch with her fellow agents, who supplied her with a coach and approached her as though she was the Queen: 'during her abode about London,' says the *Heroick Life*, 'the cavaliers, as the loyalists were then called, carried themselves towards her with a profound reverence and awful respect, treating her as a sacred person and serving her on the knee.' Ann Hill, the first to arouse suspicion, was arrested on 26 June. Lucy and the children followed her into the Tower a few days later, but were soon released. They left on Thursday 16 July 1656, St Swithin's day, which, at the end of Monmouth's life was to prove a strange coincidence.

The remainder of the Lucy Barlow saga is all tragedy, for the King had wearied of her – as he was to weary of all his women; and, backed by his counsellors, he was determined to remove the boy from her (he was not interested in Mary), along with any evidence Lucy might possess of the royal marriage. She was now subjected to a rising campaign of persecution and terror. She was helpless in the face of Charles's desertion; she was reviled and betrayed; she was deprived of her promised allowance and constantly under the threat of losing her beloved James.

The counsellors well knew that while Lucy kept her Royal child Charles would be bound, if tenuously, to his wife, and society's memory of his marriage would thus be kept alive. The campaign to abduct James was therefore stepped up. Soon after Lucy returned from London to the Netherlands, a Colonel Slingsby undertook to kidnap James by having Lucy imprisoned for debt. Saved from that, Lucy retaliated by threatening to 'post up certain letters', including the marriage certificate. 'Infallible Subtle' O'Neile then suggested that Charles 'should write a kind letter to the Spanish Viceroy desiring that her trunks may be searched in Slingsby's presence for some suspicious papers'.[6] Meanwhile a desperate Lucy had agreed to surrender James, provided neither of her arch-enemies, O'Neile or Slingsby, should have care of him. But Charles wanted those papers, and the raid on Lucy's rooms was duly carried out. According to William Disney (giving evidence in 1680), 'Mr Prodgers went for him who is now the Duke of Monmouth and took him away from his mother while she was seeking a paper . . . when she missed him she immediately went in quest of him'.[7]

The King gave James a new tutor to replace Dr Goff, a Scottish poet and scholar called Thomas Ross. In April 1658, Ross was writing (to whom we do not know): 'It is a great pity so pretty a child should be in such hands as hitherto have neglected to teach him to read or tell twenty though he hath a great deal of wit and a great desire to learn.'[8]

After some months' searching, Lucy discovered that the Queen Mother had placed James in the Oratorian College of Notre Dame des Verlus, at Colombes, seven miles from Paris, and that the boy was living with William Crofts, whose name he had assumed. She then knew that he was being brought up as a Catholic. Lucy went to Paris to be near her son, but, so far as we know, was never again to influence his life. But she was still fighting. On 26 August 1658 Cromwell's spy, Blank Marshall, wrote of 'another combat between Madam Barlow who bore Charles Stuart two children, and Doctor Floid.[9] He got the worse, and is gone for Holland. He was one of C. Stuart's his chaplains.'[10] About ten months after her deprivation, poor Lucy was dead, at the age of twenty-seven, and the King sent William Erskine, brother of the Earl of Mar (and uncle of the little Countess of Buccleuch, who was to become James's child-bride) to superintend at her funeral at the Huguenot cemetery in the Faubourg St Germain. James Crofts was then nine years of age.

Lucy Barlow (née Walter) by Sir Peter Lely

Charles II, studio of J. M. Wright

Monmouth as a child, by Samuel Cooper

Monmouth aged about seventeen artist unknown

Anna, Duchess of Monmouth, by William Wissing

2

1662–1665

BAPTISM OF FIRE

The characteristics to which nearly all contemporary observers of Charles II's eldest son referred, from boyhood upwards, were his strikingly handsome face, fine figure, debonair presence and physical energy. He radiated beauty like an animal and exulted in being alive. That self-confident animation – the 'boldness' which Evelyn saw in Lucy Barlow – clearly came through very strongly in James.

He revelled in physical activity. His guardian and tutors at Colombes and Paris taught him to ride, fence and dance, and there were few boys of his age who could perform those exercises better. He loved the deer-chase, the sound of hounds and of those great circular French hunting horns; hawking, and shooting with the bow; and risking great leaps with his pony. He was alertly curious about everything. Thomas Ross was trying to fill the gaps in his education. *He hath a great deal of witt and a great desire to learn . . .*

'You are the King's son and the King was married to your mother.' Thomas Ross told him that, and his mother had said it, too.

James was fond of his father, though he had not seen much of him. How he must have enjoyed being taken on his knee and told of the naval skirmishes by the Downs just before he, James, was born. And of the Worcester fight : how his father had climbed the cathedral tower to observe the enemy's movements; and how, when Cromwell began to deploy, he had taken command of the Royalist horse and attacked uphill under artillery cover; and how the foot, coming up behind, ran out of ammunition, but stood their ground with pike and sword and musket-butt, and, after a long brave struggle, were pushed back, inch by inch, into the city. His father had quit his horse by then, and only when Worcester's walls were stormed did he fly. And afterwards there was the hiding in cupboards and priest-holes and tree-tops, the disguises and footsore escape.

In December 1659 his father came down from Brussels to Colombes and told James he thought he might soon be in London with a crown on his head. He stayed twelve days. James had a footman now, a maidservant, a page, a coach with four horses, a coachman and postilions. In the first few months of 1660, scraps of news came through: old General Monck marching on London, Lambert ousted. In April his father wrote exultantly from Breda, from the palace of Mary of Orange, that he had won his throne; and again in May, from London, with descriptions of bonfires and bells ringing and guns firing salutes from the ramparts of the Tower.

James's father ruled the three kingdoms now, as his grandfather had done. Would he himself not soon be summoned? The months crept by and he was not summoned. In September he was in the Palais Royal to see his aunt, sixteen-year-old Minette, married to Monsieur – the Duc d'Orléans and brother of King Louis – with a ceremonial brilliance that much appealed to James; and again he was in Paris the following May, to witness the tournament celebrating the birth of Madame's daughter. Then, at last, two months later, he and the Queen Mother took a coach to the Hague and sailed for the Downs. 'July 22, 1662. The Queen Mother to Greenwich her house,' wrote the Earl of Wemyss. 'I did see her land there that day, and with her Majesty comes James . . . son to this King Charles the second, begotten in Breda on Mistress Walters, one of the Princess of Orange's maids.'[1] Charles's first action was to have James converted to the Church of England.

He was then only thirteen, but so tall that Pepys took him for two years more: 'I also saw . . . which pleased me most, Mr Crofts, the King's bastard, a most pretty spark of about fifteen years old.' 'What great faction there is at Court,' the diarist confided a little later, 'and above all what is whispered, that young Crofts is lawful son to the King, the King being married to his mother. How true this is, God knows; but I believe the Duke of York will not be fooled in this of three crowns.'

Queen Catherine's quaint clothes, convent manners and dull maids of honour may have been the laughing-stock of most of the Court, but she was a very kind young woman, and James, since his mother had died five years earlier, had known little of the warmth and friendship of young women. Seeing how her husband loved him, Catherine of Braganza naturally returned the boy's love. She did not seem to mind in the least Lucy Barlow's son being thrust into her presence. What she abhorred was her husband's continuing preoccupation with Lady Castlemaine and his insistence that the woman should be among her ladies of the bedchamber.

The eyes of an ambitious older woman, a Scot, were now turned on James. This was the Countess of Wemyss, whose first husband, Francis, Earl of Buccleuch, had given her three girls. In that age, when children succumbed easily to disease, two of these had died, leaving only Anna, who was now at the age of eleven, Countess of Buccleuch in her own right and one of the greatest heiresses in the three kingdoms. Charles's Scottish confidante, the Earl of Lauderdale, suggested to Lady Wemyss that she should propose Anna as wife for the King's bastard, the boy being sure to receive a title and to take high precedence. Charles, who was always lured by money and wanted nothing better than the advancement of his beloved son, accepted the offer willingly: 'I . . . am very sensible of the affection which you show me in the offer you make concerning the Countess of Buccleuch', he wrote; 'which I do accept most willingly, and the rather for the relation she hath to you'.[2] The ecstatic Lady Wemyss wrote back: 'Most Sacred Sovereign, I received your Majesty's most gracious letter, and by expressions thereof account myself more happy than any thing else in the world could have made me'.[3]

The King could scarcely do less than raise James Crofts to a marquisate, Lady Wemyss thought; there was even the possibility of the Principality of Wales. Charles, who considered everything done at the Court of his cousin, Louis, to be perfect, saw every reason why James should be made a duke. The high-principled Chancellor, Edward Hyde, Earl of Clarendon, pointed out that, in the case of the French illegitimates, the paramours have been 'women of great quality who had never been tainted with any other familiarity'.[4] Anyway, the boy would become Earl of Buccleuch by Scottish law; why not be content with that? When Clarendon saw certain words in the marriage contract, 'Filio nostro naturali et illegitimo', he was equally forthright. The Chancellor was quick to point out that the term would not go down well with his majesty's subjects.

As might be expected, York was also opposed to Charles on this issue. He posted a note to the Chancellor: 'my brother hath spoken with the Queen-Mother concerning the owning of his son, and in much passion she told him that from the time he did any such thing she would never see his face more. I would be glad to see you before you go to the Parliament that I may advise with you what is to be done, for my brother tells me he will do whatever I please.'[5]

Charles, who rarely if ever did other than what pleased himself, argued that since Anna would bring all the estates into the marriage it was only right that James should give her the higher rank. He preferred to listen to Lady Castlemaine, to Clarendon's deadly enemy, the volatile Earl of Bristol (whose secretary, Slingsby, had taken James from his mother in 1657) and to Lady Wemyss, who was of course pressing hard for the dukedom.[6] Accordingly, on 10 November 1662 a warrant for a grant was issued with the titles of Duke of Monmouth, Earl of Doncaster and Baron Fotheringay. But the King, remembering the associations of that last name with James's Scottish great-great-grandmother, replaced it with Baron Tynedale. And, not content with all that, on the wedding day he added Earl of Dalkeith and Lord Scott, and gave James precedence before all except the Duke of York and Prince Rupert. The boy's surname would be Scott.

Pepys is full of vignettes of James's debut:

December 29, 1662. I spent a little while walking up and down the gallery seeing the ladies, the two Queens, and the Duke of Monmouth with his little mistress . . . December 30. Thence to White Hall, where I carried my wife to see the Queen in her presence-chamber; and the maids of honour and the young Duke of Monmouth playing at cards. Some of them, and but a few, were very pretty; though all well dressed in velvet gowns . . . December 31 . . . to White Hall . . . into the ball this night before the King . . . Of the ladies that danced, the Duke of Monmouth's mistress, and my Lady Castlemaine, and a daughter of Sir Harry de Vic's,* were the best. The Duke of Monmouth is in so great splendour at Court, and so dandled by the King, that some doubt that, if the King should have no child by the Queen, which there is yet no appearance of, whether he should not be acknowledged for a lawful son; and that there will be a difference follow upon it between the Duke of York and him; which God prevent . . .

James and Anna must have appeared a very imposing couple as they stood before the archbishop and made their marriage vows in the panelled, high-ceilinged King's Chamber of Whitehall Palace on the morning of 20 April 1663, he with his athletic figure and his dazzling good looks, flanked by dark chestnut curls, and his Duchess, handsome, wise-eyed and statuesque ('a lively tall young lady of her age').[7] The King wrote that afternoon to one he loved as well as James, his sister 'Minette', the Duchess of Orleans: 'You must not by this post expect a long letter from me, this being James's marriage day, and I am going to sup with them and see them abed together, but the ceremony shall stop there. . . .'[8] Lord Wemyss provides the sequel: 'They did bed for form's sake that night, but did not stay together, being young, he of thirteen years

---

*Chancellor of the Order of the Garter, and sometime H. M. Resident at Brussels, at which time he paid court to Lucy Barlow.

and she of twelve years . . . On the 9th of February, 1664 . . . these two noble persons did bed together at Whitehall and so do they continue since, but not before.'⁹ Pepys, too, made a note of that spring morning: 'This day the little Duke of Monmouth was married at White Hall, in the King's Chamber; and tonight is a great supper and dancing at his lodgings, near Charing Cross. I observed his coat at the tail of his coach: he gives the arms of England, Scotland and France quartered upon some other fields; but what it is that speaks his being a bastard I know not.'¹⁰

Those arms evoking the diarist's cynicism were designed just in time for James's banner to be hung above his seat in St George's Chapel, Windsor, for his installation three days later as a Knight of the Garter, the King's highest favour. Despite his scant education James also received MA degrees from Oxford and Cambridge. 'Here – at Whitehall – I also saw the Duke of Monmouth with his Order of the Garter, the first time I ever saw it,' Pepys went on. 'I hear that the University of Cambridge did treat him a little while since with all the honour possible, with a comedy at Trinity College, and banquet; and made him Master of Arts there, all of which, they say, the King took very well.'

The young duke drew an allowance of £8,000 a year, but, notwithstanding this and his child-bride's fat income from the Buccleuch rents, he was soon in debt. No wonder, with expenses like these: 'Money paid for furniture for their graces chamber, £1,563 10s. 2d . . . for a pair of ear rings set with diamonds for her Grace the Duchess of Monmouth, £1,200 . . . £10 for Hats, £9 for perry wiggs, £15 10s. for a gold fringe, £11 11s. for a privy seal'.¹¹ To play the part of a prince as the King encouraged, with the extravagant Ross to steer him along, James spared no expense on the spacious new lodgings which had been built for him on the shell of the Old Tennis Court at Whitehall. And there were horses and coaches to be maintained and servants to be clothed and paid: pages, footmen, postilions, grooms, gardeners, housemaids, laundry maids, a valet and a barber.¹² James was soon summoned before the Court of Westminster for non-payment of £300–£400 due for paving the street 'before his doore'.¹³ So, within two years of their wedding day, these children were so deeply in debt that a commission, consisting of Lords Arlington, Crofts (James's old guardian), and Lauderdale, and a genuine expert in economics, Sir Thomas Clifford,* was appointed to manage their affairs.

But all the expenditure in the world could never buy harmony for the Monmouths. She was a serious girl, intellectual, and rather

*Three of these, Arlington, Clifford and Lauderdale, were, five years later, to be members of Charles's ruling Cabal.

cold; whereas he loved the gallantry, glitter and frivolity of the Court, of which he was such a star, and the spirit of wild nature and the hunting-field. He sought achievement in physical and practical pursuits. However many times an archbishop might solemnise their union in the King's presence, this was not 'a marriage of God'. But they did share one joy: both, having a sharp ear for music, loved dancing and excelled at it. Charles, who himself cut a very fine figure on the ballroom floor, found his son's step enchanting, and Pepys gives an instance of how – watching him with approving eyes one evening – the King took another opportunity to show his guests the lofty plane on which he would have his son: '. . . The Queen, which I did not know, it seems, was at Windsor at the late St George's feast there; and the Duke of Monmouth dancing with her, with his hat in his hand, the King came in and kissed him and made him put on his hat, which everybody took notice of. . . .'[14] How many of them remarked that Charles was on his way to spoiling the youth beyond redemption?

The King and his son were close and kindred spirits, and they were constantly together in diversion. Pepys, who sat near them on a river trip one July day in 1665, obeserved that 'the Duke of Monmouth is the most skittish leaping gallant that I ever saw, always in action, vaulting, or leaping, or clambering'.[15] Charles was of similar vitality, and it is not difficult to envisage him in his shirt-sleeves at Newmarket (as Francis Barlow portrayed him) introducing James to his favourite recreation, the 'horse-match'. It was Charles who led the revival of this sport, which had become moribund during the Commonwealth. He sent his experts to Barbary, where the best eastern strains could be found, began to record the pedigrees, and established a stud farm and a racing stable. Charles taught James what he had learned from the old Duke of Newcastle: the fundamentals of horsemastership and equestrianism and how to break and school a potential racehorse and hunter. By the mid-1660s everyone noticed what an effective jockey James had become, what a true Stuart he was, loving the feel of a thoroughbred's stride between his long thighs and spending almost as extravagantly on horses as his father, and how they loved to race against each other. Charles determined that his son should be a soldier. But it was at sea that Monmouth first showed his imperturbability under fire; and it was under the uncle who one day was to become his bitter rival and enemy that the boys's first test as a warrior was set.

The Duke of York's appointment as Lord High Admiral, held from the age of five, was no sinecure now. Since boyhood he had held the firm conviction that the first unavoidable responsibility of a prince was to win the reputation of a gallant and successful military commander. In 1652, with the deliberate intention of making a martial name for himself, at the age of eighteen and opposed by his mother, York had ridden penniless out from Paris to offer himself as an officer in the French Army in their war against the Frondeurs. In eight years' rigorous campaigning, first as a cavalry commander and staff officer under the greatest seventeenth-century soldier and military instructor of them all, Turenne; then, temporarily, as commander-in-chief of the French and subsequently of the Spanish army, he won the experience and prestige he sought.

As Lord High Admiral, York now applied Turenne's teaching and his own experience of land tactics and logistics in his leadership of the English fleet. And he had great resolution and courage, as well as expertise. There was no doubt in anyone's mind who commanded the Navy in the Dutch war of 1665; it was the Duke of York. And, as York had once been to Turenne, so Monmouth was now protégé to York. It was from York that he learned the political situation.

The United Dutch Provinces comprised a rich trading alliance, whose ambitions clashed head-on with England's. They had now gained most of the possessions formally divided between Spain and Portugal; they were going all out to exploit the Spice islands and Guinea slave trade and to extend their plantations in America. England's North Atlantic colonies were divided by Holland's acquisition of the New Netherlands; her African and East Indian companies were scarcely able to compete, and Dutch men-of-war were simply taking our merchantmen without legitimate pretence.

Nevertheless, the Hollanders were desperately afraid of the threat posed by Charles's England. They were bitterly annoyed when he obtained Bombay and Tangier with Catherine's dowry, when the English took a large share of the African trade and, most of all, when they snatched New Amsterdam (renaming it New York after the Lord High Admiral). In spite of their wealth and strength, the Dutch were envious and afraid of the fleet which Charles inherited from the Commonwealth, and they were all too well aware that the reputation for ability and dash of York's second-in-command, Prince Rupert, stood only a little below that of their own de Ruyter.

James would have known, too, that his father and his father's principal ministers – Clarendon, Ormonde and the Lord Treasurer, Southampton – were opposed to war with Holland (more on account of her alliance with Louis XIV than for reasons of her naval strength); but that the Duke of York (for whom the word 'republic' was anathema), with an influential group of younger men and the majority in both the Lords and the Commons, was spoiling for battle and revenge.

That October Prince Rupert was all set to lead a fleet against de Ruyter off the Guinea coast when intelligence came through that Holland was preparing an all-out offensive in European waters. Charles was voted £2½ million; 1,200 soldiers were seconded to supplement the naval strength; County Justices hurried in lists of those men in every parish with sea experience; contingency accommodation was set aside at St Bartholemew's and St Thomas's Hospital for the wounded and sick, and the Fleet was duly mobilised. Although reluctant to go to war, Charles was at least anxious that 'his owne deare Sonne' should take the chance to win his spurs and qualify for high command, and so James, accompanied by the aspiring factotum, Ross, was dispatched to Portsmouth to do as his uncle bade him.

What did the Lord High Admiral think of his brother's sixteen-year-old son being thrust upon his staff on the threshold of war with the Dutch? The Queen's difficulty in having children, coupled with continued murmurings of the legitimacy, did not help to endear him to the boy. Nor did rumours and incidents like these recorded by the scandal-loving Pepys: 'February 22, 1664. He (the King) loves not the Queen at all, but is rather sullen with her; and she, by all reports, incapable of children. He is so fond of the Duke of Monmouth, that everybody admires it; and . . . the Duke [of Monmouth] hath said that he would be the death of any man that says the King was not married to his mother. . . .'

At Portsmouth one can imagine the naturally curious James (who had none of his father's indolence) asking endless questions, learning how a fleet of warships was organised and, by imitating the older officers, contriving to make himself useful. Ross was determined that 'his little lord' should keep up of an evening with the other 'young Hectors'. A letter written by the factotum shows that he had invested unhappily for James in wool and how his 'little lord' lost what he had at the tables: 'His Grace [Monmouth] has lost most of their stock [wool shares bought for him by Ross] at play; there being no other diversion, the Guinea gold rolls freely. Cannot wish my little lord to be singular and sit by whilst others lose 5 1. with cheerful satisfaction. His Grace intends to write to the King for money.'[16]

On 23 March Charles declared war, and six weeks later, when the wind was well in the west, with a fleet of 98 ships and James as an aide-de-camp, York put out to sea, making east for Holland. The appearance of the English ships outside Texel harbour, where the enemy fleet lay at anchor, caused a sudden alarm, and James saw the line of beacons fired along the coast. Patiently, York stood off 10 leagues, challenging the enemy, but it seemed they were not yet

James's horoscope, and it must have been a very favourable one for James not only spoke enthusiastically of the abbé to his father but urged Charles to invite him to England. Louis, thinking Pregnani could be prevailed upon to make astrological forecasts which would impress upon the English King the advantage of the Anglo-French alliance, encouraged the idea. But Charles, less gullible than his son, gave 'little credit to such kind of cattle',[20] as he wrote to Madame on 7 March. A fortnight later he told her: 'I came from Newmarket the day before yesterday where we had as fine weather as we could wish, which added much both to the horse-matches as well as to hunting. L'abbé Pregnani was there most part of the time, and I believe will give you some account of it, but not that he lost his money upon confidence that the stars could tell which horse would win, for he had the ill luck to foretell three times wrong together, and James believed him so much as he lost his money upon the same score . . .'[21]

But, in an age of superstition widespread among all classes, it is little wonder that James, in particular, put his faith in predestination. For all the outward *savoir-faire* and self-assurance he displayed, and his promise that he would 'kill any man who says my mother was not married to the King', there can have been few in the world upon whom, subconsciously, the questions who am I? why am I here? which way am I going? pressed more urgently than upon the Duke of Monmouth. For was he not the King's eldest with all the honours of the King's eldest, but without the Principality of Wales and without the proud distinction of being heir to the three Kingdoms?

Feeding his son's ambition, the King only provoked the false position in which he had placed him. James yearned to be loved; he was loved; but since love – from both men and women – came largely in the form of admiration and adulation, he mistook it for permanent devotion. Everyone paid homage to him. ('I please his Majesty greatly', wrote Piero Mocenigo, the Venetian envoy, 'by following the example of the ambassadors in visiting the Duke of Monmouth with such promptitude, as he rejoices at every act of regard shown to his son.') The King indulged James more lavishly with honours than he ever indulged a mistress. By the end of 1669, when he was twenty, he held the appointments of Lord Lieutenant of the East Riding of Yorkshire, Colonel of the Life Guard of Horse, Vice-Chancellor of the University of Cambridge and Knight of the Garter. But he still craved more responsibility, greater honours, higher distinction. Pregnani had promised them.

England longed for her King to present her with a Protestant heir, who would eclipse the Duke of York. If the Queen proved childless, why not handsome, popular Monmouth? many suggested. Rumours and counter-rumours persisted: '. . . I met with Mr Povy who tells me that this discourse which I told him, of the Duke of Monmouth being made Prince of Wales, hath nothing in it,' Pepys recorded in November 1668, 'though he thinks there are all the endeavours in the world to overthrow the Duke of York.'[22]

At a secret meeting at the Duke of York's lodgings shortly before Pregnani's visit, on 25 January 1669, Charles revealed to his brother, and to Lords Arlington and Arundell of Wardour and Sir Thomas Clifford, his intention of becoming a Catholic convert. He said he had called them together to discuss 'the ways and methods fittest for the settling of the Catholic religion in his kingdoms and to consider of the time most proper to declare himself. This he spake with great earnestness, and even with tears in his eyes,' said York; 'and added that they were to go about it as wise men and good Catholics ought to do.'[23] Thus four more were brought into the secret treaty. Madame's brother, York, would very soon declare his religious faith. Charles repeated his promise to convert. The treaty upon which she had set her heart – 'Le Traité de Madame', as it was known – would shortly, so she realised, be a fact. So these should have been joyous and triumphant times for Madame. But it is doubtful whether she lived a happy day between James's departure and her visit to England to complete the treaty in the summer of 1670.

In September 1669 her mother, James's grandmother, Henrietta Maria, whom Madame probably loved better than anyone else in the world, died in dreadful pain. Monsieur, who had become more spiteful and vicious than ever, was constantly accusing her of having an affair with James. Yet she continued to play to the full her mediating role for the secret treaty. Louis overruled Monsieur's objections to her sailing to England to see its fulfilment. And when Monsieur insisted that James be banished to Holland for the duration of the talks, that too was refused. The only compromise allowed him was that the talks should be at Dover and not so much as a mile farther inland. As Madame's ship neared the cliffs it was met by the royal brothers with Prince Rupert and James in the yacht.

During the next few days, under the cover of celebrating the royal reunion, unknown to the rest of England, the treaty, which indirectly was to have such an effect on James's life, was drawn up and signed. Both kings had bargained hard. Ultimately, Louis was to pay Charles £200,000 for entering the Catholic fold and £300,000 as an annual subsidy for joining in the French war against Holland. The following December an 'alternative treaty' was signed on behalf of France by de Croissy, and for England by all the members of the Cabal; its terms were identical with those of the secret treaty, except that the clause relating to Charles's conversion was omitted. That conversion never took place.

Most of this scheming diplomacy, of course, important as it may have been to his life, passed over James's head. The meeting at Dover was veiled by frivolity, and James was good at frivolity. How much he was alone with his young aunt is not on record, but we do have one brief glimpse of the young Life Guards Colonel teasing the French by unfastening his sword at the theatre; and, in his laughing, debonair way, hooking it on to the waist of one of the actors. The witness is the dramatic producer, John Downes:

> . . . This play, *The Impertinents*, or *Sullen Lovers*, had wonderful success, when our company were commanded to Dover . . . the French court wearing their excessive short, laced coats. Mr Nokes, having at that time one shorter than the French fashion, to act Sir Addle in, the Duke of Monmouth gave Mr Nokes his sword and belt from his side and buckled it on himself, on purpose to ape the French. That Mr Nokes looked more like a dressed-up ape than a Sir Arthur: which upon his first entrance upon the stage, put the King and Court into excessive laughter; at which the French looked very chagrin to see themselves aped by such a buffoon as Sir Arthur: Mr Nokes kept the Duke's sword to his dying day . . .[24]

That may have been the last time spontaneous laughter escaped Madame's lips, for within a month of her return to Paris she died with all the agony of her mother's death. Many believed that Monsieur, because of his jealousy of James, had poisoned her. Certainly he so desperately wanted to see James's letters to Madame that he took them from a drawer and had them read to him in French by the husband of his widow's nurse.[25] Rumours of James and Madame were strong in England: 'It was said that she was in love with the Duke of Monmouth while at Dover,' said Sir John Reresby; 'things had been so represented to the Duke her husband, that she died very suddenly after her return to Paris, and not without serious suspicion of having been poisoned.'[26]

Charles was inconsolable. The messenger who rode home with the news did not conceal the rumours that Madame had been poisoned; Charles gave way to an outburst of rage and grief and swore against Monsieur. But, realising there was still no concrete evidence, he then said: 'Monsieur is a villain, but I beg you, Sir Thomas, do not say a word of this.' He then took to his bed, and several days elapsed before he appeared in public again.

Who was 'Sir Thomas'? He was a former member of the Sealed Knot and held a captaincy in Lord Oxford's Regiment of Horse (the Blues); and he was one of those older men who was to exercise a strong influence over James, and to play a tragic part in the Monmouth story – Sir Thomas Armstrong.

5

1670–1671

HORSEPLAY AND MURDER

After George Monk, Duke of Albemarle, died in 1670, the King decided not to appoint any officer to succeed him as Captain-General of the Land Forces, and that, because of the small size of the army, it would be unnecessary to appoint generals in peacetime. Regiments and their supporting arms were not grouped in formations, and the largest single unit was not above 2,400 men. Over this regimentally piecemeal army, in all but name Charles himself was commander-in-chief. In the event of insurrection, it was recognised that the Colonel of the Life Guards would co-ordinate any internal security measures as should be thought necessary, and lead the Household troops, which, apart from the independent garrison companies, comprised the regular army. Technically, therefore, from the age of twenty-one James was the senior military commander, under his father, in the country.[1] But it was in a strange way that he was first to employ his cavaliers against a rebel, against one who dared to insult the King in the House of Commons.

It started when the King objected to the existing tax on play-houses, which, in Burnet's words, 'in so dissolute a time were become nests of prostitution'.[2] Charles reasoned that 'the players are my servants, and a part of my pleasure'. When this was related in the Commons, the outspoken Sir John Coventry – with Moll Davis and Nell Gwyn positively in mind – inquired 'whether did the King's pleasure lie, among the men or the women that acted?' Charles was furious, and suggested to his son that he should deal with Sir John Coventry.

On the night of 8 January 1671, at the end of that session of Parliament, as Coventry was making his way from the Cock tavern in Bow Street to his house in Suffolk Street, by the Haymarket, he was ambushed by a party of the Life Guards. The moment the M.P. spotted the figures lurking in the shadows, he realised what was afoot. Snatching the flambeau from his servant's hand, he put his back to the wall, drew his sword and defended himself bravely, wounding several of the soldiers – Charles O'Brien, Lord Inchiquin's son, being severely stabbed in the arm. But Coventry was soon overpowered and pinned to the ground; whereupon one of the Household Cavalrymen slit his nose to the bone with a penknife. It was to James's rented house in Hedge Lane that the Life Guardsmen retired after the attack, and there O'Brien's wound was dressed. The scandal was out immediately, and *The Haymarket Hectors*, by Andrew Marvell, the Member for Hull, was soon in daring circulation from the printing presses :

> . . . O ye Hay-Market Hectors, how came you thus charm'd
> To be the dissectors of one poor Nose unarm'd
> Unfit to wear Sword, or follow a Trumpet
> That would brandish your knives at the word of a Strumpet.
>
> But was't not ungrateful in Monmouth, ap Sidney, ap Carlo
> To contrive an act so harmful, O Prince of Wales by Barlow.
> For since the kind world has dispens'd with his Mother,
> Might he now well have spared the Nose of John Brother?

It has been said that men-at-arms are of little value unless there is a demon deep inside them spoiling for a fight. If young soldiers are not given a battle, or if their natural aggressiveness is not otherwise channelled continuously into tests of endurance or sport, or they do not have frequent opportunities to raise laughs – by hanging their swords on the waist-belts of short-coated actors, to ridicule the French, for example – the violence will out. James was spoiling for a fight – 'I will kill any man who says the King was not married to my mother' – and his father had virtually given him the power of life and death. Next time it was a matter of death.

Ten weeks after the Coventry affair, in company with his father, York and Rupert, James attended a reception at Lincoln's Inn Hall. But, instead of leaving for home when they did, James proceeded to Whetstone Park, a disreputable street on the north side of Lincoln's Inn Fields. With him were the young Dukes of Albemarle and Richmond, the Earl of Rochester, Viscount Dunbar, Edward Griffin, Lord Annesley and half a dozen more. They had all been drinking and they made such a clamour that the parish officers went to quieten them.[3] 'Drawing their swords', went one account, 'they put the guards to flight, but one named Peter Virnill was seized and, in spite of his plea for mercy, they ran him through the body.'[4]

While street brawling, practical joking and duels, at all hours of the day and night, were run-of-the-mill among the young nobility, killing innocents in cold blood was another matter. Rumour had it that it was Monmouth's sword. Whoever owned the guilty weapon, the whole party was forgiven.[5] James's reprieve was thus drawn up, on Charles's instructions, by the faithful Arlington: 'Gracious pardon to our dear son, James, Duke of Monmouth, of all murders, homicides, felonies, whatsoever at any time, on or before the 28th day of February last past, committed either by himself alone or together with any other person or persons.'[6]

To issue this, Charles needed a good excuse, and he had it ready. Parliament had just voted him a large sum of money, and, on these occasions, by way of gratitude, he was entitled to proclaim an amnesty for certain offences. The Venetian Secretary in London, Girolamo Alberti, followed the royal schemings, and explained them to the Doge and Senate: '. . . He [the King] was proposing to issue a general pardon for all offences, such as is usual when the crown has received large contributions. The people will not find out,' Alberti continues (in cipher), 'and but few others will understand the secret of this generous demonstration, which is . . . intended to save two great nobles at court [Monmouth and Richmond] for the murder of a guard; but chiefly to nullify the force of an act of parliament against those concerned in the Coventry affair, as the King is anxious for them not to be exiled, to the diminution of his authority, seeing that it is well known that the order came from him . . .'

What was Monmouth like at this time? Anthony Hamilton said of him at twenty: 'His face and the exterior graces of his person were such as nature has, perhaps, never bettered. His countenance was all charm; but it was a man's face and in no way insipid or effeminate. Still, every separate feature had its own attraction and its own particular delicacy. He had great natural disposition for all forms of exercise, a winning manner of approach, an air of mightiness; in fact all the physical advantages spoke on his behalf, though in this concert the qualities of his mind were absolutely silent . . .'[7]

Hamilton was fond of making sweepingly derogatory remarks about people's mental qualities: the perfectly sensible Duke of Norfolk was 'stupid as an ox'; when you heard the able and distinguished Earl of Oxford talk, according to Hamilton, 'you realised that he was nobody'; and 'beneath the shelter of Arlington's countenance . . . composed an impenetrable stupidity which passed for the power to keep a secret'. Hamilton was inclined to be superficial in his judgements and assessed courtiers by the calibre of their repartee. Monmouth may have been simple, may have lacked the education to match his position, but he had plenty of common sense, was adept and painstaking in practical matters, and had a jocular, engagingly persuasive approach to carry others along in his endeavours. But however silly and impulsive he was at this age, however gullible and thoughtless, the King remained immensely proud of his prepossessing qualities: see this elegant boy, the fruit of my loins, he seemed to be saying, how dazzling, how stimulating he is. And he liked to show him off as often as he could.

Louis XIV was preparing for his invasion of Holland and in April 1671 Charles dispatched his son to the Spanish Netherlands, to Dunkirk, to attend the lavish review staged by the French King of the 30,000 troops which were the nucleus of the expeditionary force. James 'was entertained with all the respect and kindness imaginable'.[8] Later, with his father, York and Rupert, he travelled from Windsor to inspect the new quay and citadel at Plymouth, diverting from there to make a tour of Portsmouth and Exeter. In October they journeyed as usual to Newmarket races, where 'the plate, being a flagon of 32 price, was run . . . which his Majesty won, there riding beside him the Duke of Monmouth, Mr Thynne* and Mr Eliot'.[9]

On then to Lord Arlington's seat, Euston Hall, Thetford; and from there to Yarmouth and Norwich; Blickling Hall, the Hobarts' home; Oxnead, where the Pastons lived; and Lord Townshends' Raynham Hall (where 'Monmouth's room' is still on view). And back to Euston. The attraction there was Louise de Keroualle, who was entertained by Arlington to bolster his position with Charles, for Charles had become infatuated with her when she was in Madame's suite at Dover in 1670, and Louis realised that no one was more likely to hold him to the French Alliance than she.

The royal party then returned to Newmarket, where James as usual was leader of the fun, and Evelyn found 'the jolly blades racing, dancing, feasting and revelling, more resembling a luxurious and abandoned rout than a Christian court. The Duke of Buckingham was now in mighty favour, and had with him that impudent woman, the Countess of Shrewsbury, with his band of fiddlers, etc. . . .'[10]

Underneath the revelry and abandon, however, stirred the lust for power and glory. Louise de Keroualle's alluring face and figure served to remind Englishmen that their King was deeply beholden to Louis XIV. As for James, it was not long before Charles found a war to bridle his boundless energy and wild ways. To the ambitious Duke of Buckingham's disgust, Monmouth, not he, was to command the British contingent in Louis's army.

*A close friend of Monmouth's, Thynne ('Tom o' Ten Thousand') was soon to be known as 'the Protestant Squire'.

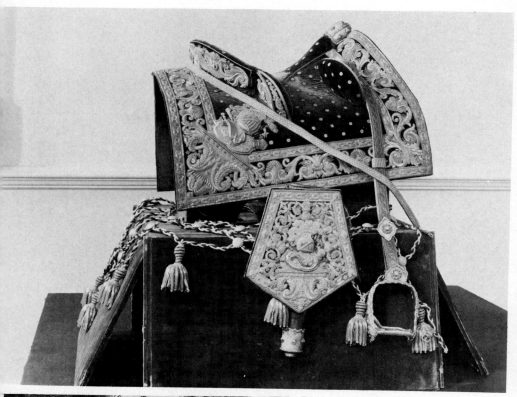

The saddle presented to Monmouth by his father on his appointment as Colonel of the Life Guards, now at Bowhill, Selkirkshire, home of the Duke of Buccleuch

A horse match, *c.* 1680, from Richard Blome's *Gentlemen's Recreation*

Monmouth as Military Commander, by Henri Gascars

Fortress warfare, c. 1670:
Dutch engineers building a
bastion salient

6

INSTRUCTION FROM THE SUN KING

The Third Dutch War, which was to make James a national hero, was a manifestation of his father's dishonourable foreign policy. Charles had 'Madame's Treaty' of 1670 covered by a sham alternative in which his promise of conversion to Catholicism was not mentioned. Foreign policy remained in his hands. While he had French money, he could commit his three Kingdoms, without reference to Parliament, as he liked. The Cabal was his tool, and he and the Cabal decided that the time was now ripe for the treaty with Holland and Sweden, the Triple Alliance, to be revoked as soon as possible; then England, subsidised by Louis, would join France in the destruction of the United Provinces.

The Catholic members of the Cabal put on an act of hesitating in signing the sham treaty; but the Protestants Ashley, Buckingham and Lauderdale, the dupes, were all impatience with their signatures. The King chuckled to himself as he fooled Ashley (and, in 1672, would mockingly thank him for it with the Earldom of Shaftesbury). In his volte-face, Charles not only betrayed the Triple Alliance, and – worse still – worked against the interests of his people by aligning them with their natural enemies, but he tricked Parliament too. At around the same time that the Houses voted him £800,000 to re-equip the Fleet – ostensibly to play its part in the Triple Alliance – a dozen wagons, guarded by an escort of Monmouth's Household Cavalrymen, rolled along the highway from Rye to London with the first instalment of the French secret subsidies. Marvell, the lampooning M.P., who had satirised James for his wild ways, now censured Parliament for its lack of vigilance:

> The senate, which should headstrong princes stay
> Let loose the reins and gave the realm away.

But Dutch insolence, Charles's jealousy of Dutch trade and naval power, and the need, however desperate, for French money, were not his only reasons for seeking war with Holland. He had a family quarrel with the oligarchic republic of De Witt, who denied William of Orange – Charles's nephew, the son of that English princess who had befriended Lucy Barlow twenty years before – the throne that was his by hereditary right, the quasimonarchical stadtholderate. Louis wanted Charles to be the first to declare war. He, Louis, would pay.

Monmouth would have his own regiment of foot, 2,400 strong, the Royal English; and Louis would pay for that as well. 'Last night in the French ambassador's packet came the Duke of Monmouth's commission for a regiment,' wrote Sir Henry Inglesby on 10 February 1671; 'each company is to have two lieutenants, three sergeants, three corporals, besides captain and ensign. Some say there are bills of exchange for money, too.'[1] But James's command was not confined to the Royal English. He would be titular head of a brigade of 6,000, loosely composed of four regiments of foot and one of horse : Lord George Douglas's* Scots, Sir George Hamilton's† Irish, Lord Roscommon's Irish,[2] the Royal English, and Sir Harry Jones's 500 English Horse.[3]

Two company commanders in the Royal English, both volunteers from Lord Oxford's Regiment of Horse, were to fill notable roles in the Monmouth saga : Sir Thomas Armstrong, the knight who brought Charles the news of Madame's death, and Percy Kirke, one day to play butcher in the aftermath of Sedgemoor. The rank and file of all the companies of the regiment was based on volunteers from the Foot Guards – ten from each company[4] – but the bulk were raw recruits, and very raw they were.

And what of James himself? Did it arouse no jealousy, no resentment, that a youth of twenty-three, with scant knowledge of war, and one who had quite recently been indicted on a murder charge, should have the command? Well earned military rank counted for little in the near feudal British army. What mattered was social status. It hurt the dignity of an earl, for example, to take orders from a baronet, or for a baron to defer, whether in camp or in battle, to a knight. On this score no British officer, however

---

*Second son of William, 1st Marquess of Douglas; created Earl of Dumbarton in 1675.

†Elder brother of Anthony Hamilton, author of *The Memoirs of the Comte de Grammont*.

well qualified by experience and reputation, could complain of James's appointment; he was a duke, next in civil seniority after Prince Rupert; and, with his dashing style, charm, practical ability and energy, he had already proved a successful commander of the Life Guards.

Who else might have been appointed? Not Prince Rupert, who for his anti-French attitude and unsolicited criticism was out of favour with the King at this time.[5] Besides, his services would be required on the naval front. Nor Oxford, or Craven, or Russell, the other Guards regimental commanders: their stature was insufficient to impress Louis and the French generals, or the officers of the expeditionary force. York, the Lord High Admiral, was unreservedly in favour of the King's choice, for all Monmouth's sympathies at this time were beyond question, and York imagined he could exert much influence in an army led by his apparently easy nephew.

The only man with whom the appointment appears to have really rankled was a friend of Monmouth's, albeit a contemporary of his father's, a vain and dissolute if clever and articulate nobleman, an amateur in all things, yet ever in search of power – the Duke of Buckingham, royal favourite, member of the Cabal and Master of the Horse.[6] (Very soon Buckingham would have another command, an army to be mustered on Blackheath for the invasion of Holland from the sea, an appointment which would itself cause resentment.) Nearly everyone agreed that James would fill the Dutch assignment well. A note to Charles from Ralph Montagu, Ambassador in Paris, shows that one of James's chief qualifications was as the firmly established leader of the officer corps:

I told him [Louis] . . . that I believed it was natural for your Majesty, if the Duke of Buckingham did not command the forces that were to come into France, to desire it might be the Duke of Monmouth, who would be followed by all the young nobility of England, and did therefore conceive that his Christian Majesty would do you a kindness not to engage to anyone for the command of those English he should raise till he first knew whether you cared to have it for the Duke of Monmouth . . .[7]

All the details of the concentration and embarkation, march and logistics, would be handled on behalf of the Secretary of State by Matthew Lock, the Secretary at War, and his clerks, the Lords of the Treasury, the Commissaries-General of the Musters and the Victuals, and the regimental commanders themselves, all of whom were competent men. And, as regards the Royal English, James would be well served by his experienced lieutenant-colonel, Sir Samuel Clarke. Once in France, the regiments would, for the most part, each take their orders from the French command.

Alberti to the Doge, 25 March : 'The Duke of Monmouth, only two evenings ago, sent his steward to France for the actual preparation of his equipage, a clear sign that his departure is caused by some fresh resolve. But when conversing with me last week he said he did not know when he should move in that direction.' By the time that note was written, a *casus belli* was effected. Charles had sent his ships to prick the Dutch and draw their fire; without any provocation Admiral Holmes attacked their homecoming Smyrna fleet as it passed the Isle of Wight, and got badly mauled in the process. That was enough for the King and the Cabal : an envoy was rushed to Sweden, announcing England's withdrawal from the Triple Alliance and bribing the Swedes to attack any German state that moved in to help Holland. And, without reference to Parliament, Charles declared war.

Louis, who had already accused the Republican Dutch of 'debauching my allies and soliciting my Royal cousins to enter into defensive leagues against me', now simply announced that he was 'dissatisfied' with De Witt's government, and followed suit. The French army, which James visited at Dunkirk in 1671, might require the full summer to complete its occupation of the United Provinces. It had swollen to 119,000, including 8,000 *troupes d'élite* of the Guards (the Maison du Roy); 46 foot regiments of the line, amounting to 56,000 men; 25,000 cavalry; and 30,000 conscripts from the French vassal nations of Switzerland and Italy. It was an army four times the size of any seen in Europe since the days of Rome. 'Jamais', wrote Voltaire, 'on n'avait vu une armée si magnifique et en même temps mieux disciplinée.' In all things its standards were appreciably higher than those of James's motley contingent.

At this time the British army closely emulated the French, who would be Monmouth's chief military influence. Louis and his ambitious young Minister for War, François-Michel Louvois had firstly reorganised, re-equipped and revitalised the Maison du Roy (on which Charles's Household Cavalry and Foot Guards had been modelled) as the prototype for all the regiments; while Colonel Martinet – whose name was soon synonymous with stern discipline – and other Maison du Roy officers, were appointed inspectors of the line regiments.

The French pattern of tactics, which was now followed by all the armies of Europe, was based on the organisation of the infantry, who fought six deep, with the pikemen in the centre and the musketeers on the flank. The spear-headed pike, fourteen feet long, was the defensive arm and the officer's personal weapon. The musket[8] in general use was the heavy wheel-type matchlock, ignited with a slow match or smouldering fuse and fired from a forked rest. But some regiments, those of fusiliers,[9] were already partly issued with the newly invented flintlock or snaphaunce,[10] whose powder was ignited on the principle of flint and steel, a weapon of much greater accuracy and rate of fire and much more easily handled. At its muzzle was fixed the bayonet, a brainchild of Martinet's. (Eventually the flintlock and musket would become the universal weapons for the infantry.) Musketeers and fusiliers also carried swords. A typical company might be composed of 50 matchlock men, 20 fusiliers and 50 pikemen.

Louis's army also included regiments of dragoons, mounted infantry, equipped with the firelock carbine. The sword was still the primary weapon of the shock troops, the cavalry, who also holstered a pair of pistols. The artillery, which had been a separate civilian force until 1669, was then incorporated in the army by regiments. Louis boasted 97 pieces of cannon, divided into culverins, or heavy siege guns (24- and 18-pounders), and quarter cannon (16- and 12-pounders).

Served by instructors like Martinet, Louis and Louvois had their army trained to a high degree, and kept it so. Preoccupation with the social hierarchy was as rife in the French as well as any other European army, but Louis, urged by the bullying, bourgeois Louvois, was beginning to resist it. There was only one acceptable standard for officers of the *Grande Armée*, and, if the discipline and fighting efficiency of their regiments, squadrons and companies failed to reflect and endorse that standard, they found themselves replaced.

No one understood better than Louis the importance of morale: he insisted that good and plentiful rations were always available; he instituted portable kitchens; he ensured that new equipment was always echeloned to replace worn equipment, and, beginning with the Maison du Roy, in 1665, he gave his regiments distinctive uniforms and encouraged inter-unit rivalry. In this new French army there were bands to sing to, of pipe, hautbois and drum, playing stirring tunes, mostly composed by Jean-Baptiste Lully, and convincing promises of *la gloire*, while, in their home towns, the soldiers' families were granted special and honourable status.

It was by the standard of this awe-inspiring and enlightened administration and leadership that James's brigade was judged by Louis, Turenne, Condé, Louvois and the French army. Louis's own anxiety about the English is reflected in a letter from Montagu to the King: '. . . One more thing that I was desired to recommend to you, that, in case the French King should make any levies in England, that you would mingle amongst the new-raised men some old soldiers, that they may be the sooner disciplined and in order for service . . .'[11]

As for the Dutch, no one had watched them more closely than ex-ambassador Temple. 'The States were in disorder, and irresolute what to do,' he wrote in his *Memoirs*. 'The troops were without a general and, which is worse, without heart . . .'[12] They had systematically neglected their army in favour of their marine forces, and they were ringed by enemies, their neighbours, Cologne and Munster, making offensive treaties with France. Louis never doubted that Holland would fall like a plum into his hand before the autumn. Without mentioning the matter to Madrid, he would march with his main army north-east through the Spanish Netherlands, follow the Sambre and the Meuse, cross the Dutch frontier where it intersected with the Rhine, then strike directly for Amsterdam.

The Royal English perhaps to 'shake them down' with an initially unopposed march, were allotted a different route: they were to march due east, crossing the French border at Verdun, and then, travelling by river transport from Metz on the Moselle, north-east through the friendly Archbishopric of Cologne, thence down the Rhine to join the French army in Holland's vassal state, the Duchy of Cleves. Louis was scheduled to leave Paris at the end of April, so James must have his force concentrated at the capital for his regiments to be reviewed and to receive his marching orders well in advance.

It had not been easy to find the full complement for the Royal English: 'The Duke of Monmouth has not completed his regiment to its full number of 2,400 men, having still to raise 300,' wrote one observer, 'whereas the King easily obtained recruits for two supernumerary infantry regiments, because the men will have the advantage of remaining in England.'[13] Below strength or not, James was very proud of Monmouth's Own. His mind's eye saw them in uniforms of yellow. But it was not permitted. Ralph Montagu contacted Arlington on 9 March: 'Mr Digby tells me that the Duke of Monmouth intends to clothe his regiment in yellow. I have sent a suit just as the King here would have them clothed; he must follow that pattern, or it will be ill taken here.'[14] They wore scarlet with James's yellow for facings. The whole brigade was well under strength, but it could not be helped. On 8 April it was reported to Williamson that 'yesterday the Duke of Monmouth, Mr Godolphin*

*Sidney Godolphin, Groom of the Bedchamber and Envoy Extraordinary, and one day to be the Lord High Treasurer of England.

and Sir Thomas Armstrong, and several others went on board the *Monmouth* yacht at 7.30 p.m. with a very fair wind at NE. The *Guernsey* frigate sailed as convoy, but 'tis said she left the yacht because she spied 3 sail, suspected to be Hollanders, and pursued them.'[15]

'The Duke of Monmouth has hastened from Dieppe to Paris by the posts,' wrote the Venetian ambassador in Paris on 27 April; 'the day before yesterday he presented himself to the King and was received with particular marks of kindness by the Queen as well.'[16] Madame de Sévigné, who had pleasant memories of him from his stays with Madame, now enjoyed a glimpse of him at a dinner : 'The assembly, though large, was orderly,' she enthused in a letter to her daughter on 6 May; 'I was sitting in the proximity of M. de Tulle, M. de Colbert and M. de Monmouth, who is as handsome as in the days of the Palais Royal and who, by the way, is joining the King's Army.'[17]

By this time Louis had reached his main force at Charleroi, informed Monteroy, Governor of the Spanish Netherlands, that he proposed to march across his territory to invade the Dutch republic, brushed aside Monteroy's objections, and, on 17 May, reached Visé, a town on the Meuse, in the Dutch enclave of Maastricht. There he awaited the arrival of Condé, who was leading his division in from Lorraine. The fortress of Maastricht, built in considerable depth, containing a garrison of 8,500 and, dominating the river, was the greatest of the Dutch bastions. Should we attempt to take it now, Louis wondered, or cordon it, to be dealt with later? These were the days when warfare – conducted only during the summer months – consisted of little more than sieges and of the passage of canals and rivers, when commanders surrounded themselves with great continued lines, designed to defend a frontier or bar the progress of an adversary.

The investment of a fortress implied carefully constructed circumvallations (a ring of seige works to hold off relief armies) and contravallations (earthworks facing the fortress). The French had succeeded the Dutch as the masters of siege warfare, and there was no greater technical expert in the world than Louis's engineer, Sébastien de Vauban, who had recently modernised the French forts, and who was with the army now. Condé advised his King to besiege Maastricht; Turenne said to leave it to be dealt with later, as a quite separate operation. Louis's instinct told him Turenne was right : he must waste neither time nor resources but must make for the principal objective – Amsterdam. Leaving a brigade to surround the garrison city, he sent Condé directly east to the Rhine, which he crossed at Kaiserwerth on 28 May (the same day that, 200 miles away, York and Rupert, with scant help from their French allies, were fighting De Ruyter in the bloody drawn battle of Solebay). Condé would work his way north, up the Rhine's right bank, through the hostile Duchy of Cleves, while Louis and Turenne moved over the Duchy's western frontier. Between them they would reduce the Cleves fortresses before broaching the main Dutch line of defence on the river Ijssel.

Meanwhile, the Royal English were making reasonable progress through Cologne. James, with Sidney Godolphin,[18] was seen leaving Paris for Metz on 11 May in his usual smart and glittering style. Perwych, Secretary at the English embassy, commented that 'His Grace's equipage was the most *magnifique* I ever saw in France.'[19] He caught up with his main guard at Rheims on the 13th, crossed the Maas at Verdun on the 19th, embarked his troops on the Moselle at Metz on the 20th, and was at Thionville on the 24th, and Trier (Trèves) on 1 June.

For his assault crossing of the Rhine, the French King chose Tolhuis, a customs post for river traffic, where in this very dry summer of 1672 the water was only three or four feet deep. Louis described the operation as 'hardi, vigoureux, plein d'éclat, et glorieux pour la nation'. Catching up at Emmerich, the Royal English were now given a place in Louis's personal brigade, while Godolphin kept Arlington informed as to James's career: 'The King uses the Duke of Monmouth with all the kindness imaginable and has placed his regiment in his own brigade . . . He bids me assure the King my Master that he would have particular care to instruct [him] and commended him extremely for both his diligence and application.'[20]

Another onlooker who watched James's leadership at the sieges of Zutphen and Doesberg noted fulsomely that 'such was his courage and resolution, that though the Duke of Monmouth was sent out with parties much inferior to the enemy in number, yet he charged with such gallantry that the sallies were beaten back, being often pursued by him even to their lines and trenches, when the besieged cannons played most furiously in their defence, and shot like hail sung round his warlike head.'[21]

When the allies broke and took the line of the Ijssel, the States General sued for peace. Louis's humiliating terms, drafted by Louvois, included demands for the Dutch withdrawal to the Waal and a huge war indemnity. The De Witt government hesitated, but the Dutch people, refusing to surrender, turned against the States General. De Witt and his brother were assassinated, and James's first cousin, William of Orange, who had already been appointed Captain- and Admiral-General, was now declared Stadtholder.

Except that this young half-Stuart had courage and ability of leadership, he could not have been much less like James; for he was only five feet tall, stoop-shouldered, ungraceful and ugly, cold, unsympathetic and humourless; he suffered from anaemia and asthma, while the only real loves of his whole life appear to have been Holland and Protestantism. But the paths of William of Orange and James of Monmouth would cross often in the years ahead, and rarely less than amicably.

Holland to James looked much as it did when he walked there at his mother's side in the 1650s, a vivid, green, hedgeless plain, divided by canals and ditches, with roads following the dykes and running along the walls that separated the polders, a flat landscape interspersed with villages and windmills, raised above the general level. Long before Louis approached the frontier, the Dutch were preparing to save their low-lying land from the French by flooding it, as the new Stadtholder's great-grandfather, William the Silent, had done, by piercing the walls and dykes along selected reservoirs. The water courses, thus emptied, would be filled again by opening the sluices into one of the tidal rivers at high tide, or, in some districts, by simply opening the sea-sluices or breaching the dykes. By this procedure they could inundate the whole 20–30 square miles lying below sea level from the coast inwards, between the Zuider Zee and Zeeland. William had this plan put into operation about the middle of June.

Louis, with Monmouth close by him, marched west, took Naarden on 20 June, and occupied Utrecht, which was already abandoned by the Dutch army, on 23 June. Now he was master of the provinces of Gelderland, Utrecht and Overijssel; Amsterdam lay only twenty miles, and, in dry conditions, two days' march away. But it was a water-filled country that lay ahead; the allied army could advance no further. Louis offered to guarantee to the Stadtholder the sovereignty of what remained of Holland – under the protection of France and England. But William was much too proud and tough for that : 'I will never betray a trust', he replied solemnly, 'nor sell the liberties of my country, which my forefathers have so long defended.' It was stalemate.

As for the English at home, the rapidity and force of the French advance alarmed rather than encouraged them. They feared Louis might next steer across the Channel and, in league with Charles, impose Catholicism on them by force of arms. Then (some of them were asking) how long would it be before England became, like the Spanish Netherlands, a mere vassal of France? But they misjudged their King. The overthrow of De Witt and the elevation of William of Orange opened fresh political possibilities for Charles, who felt

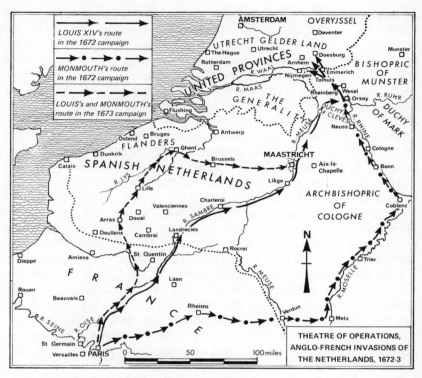

THEATRE OF OPERATIONS,
ANGLO-FRENCH INVASIONS OF
THE NETHERLANDS, 1672-3

he might negotiate separately with William on terms that would be
acceptable to Louis, at the same time allaying his own people's fears.
He offered William the alternatives of sovereignty under Anglo-
French patronage, with a number of difficult conditions, or
annihilation. Bluntly turned down, the English envoys, Arlington
and Buckingham, drove on to Antwerp to negotiate with the Spanish
viceroy, and thence to Louis's camp, where they joined James.

'This day', ran the dispatch at Utrecht for 27 June,[22] 'their
Lordships, His Grace the Duke of Monmouth, and the Duke of
Buckingham and the Earl of Arlington, His Majesty's ambassadors
extraordinary and plenipotentiaries, had their public audience of the
Most Christian King in the afternoon in his quarters in the camp,
which is about a league and a half from hence. They were carried
in two of the King's coaches, conducted by the Duke of
Vendôme . . .' In company with the French commissioners, Louvois
and Pomponne, they drafted a joint policy agreement and a letter,
'couched in very peremptory language', warning William that unless
the bearers returned shortly with a favourable answer 'the Embassy
will be forced to return home by the way of Flanders to offer new
measures and far different'.[23]

Meanwhile, having been alerted by the French Ambassador in London as to Charles's independent overtures to William, Louvois and Pomponne had a second document drawn up, the Treaty of Heeswick, whereby England and France undertook not to treat with the Dutch except on the conditions already rejected by William. The Venetian Envoy, Michiel, explained James's position, as head of the English signatories, to the Doge:

The thing which has aroused most interest at Court is the arrival here with the king of the duke of Buchengham and the Secretary Amelton [sic] with the title of ambassadors. Joined with this is the duke of Mommut [sic], who is already with the army. The king, his father, has chosen to decorate him with letters directed to the king, which entitle him, and beg the king to receive him, as his ambassador extraordinary. From this he emerges as the principal figure of the embassy . . .[24]

Charles, still very much aware of his country's reluctance in the French alliance, and disturbed himself by the magnitude of Louis's military success, gave orders for the British troops to go into winter quarters and for his son's return to London. But James had some private business to complete first; He had to replace the loss, in a fire,[25] of nearly all that 'magnifique équipage'; so, ahead of him to Dover, among other things, came '14 cases of bedding, a silver table, a silver looking-glass, 2 silver stands and 2 silver hearth-irons . . . imported from Calais'. Nor was the King's son exempt from import duty, for these were 'to be brought without search to Whitehall and there opened by one of their officers in his presence'.[26] He arrived at 4 in the morning of 9 August, and 'about six o'clock took horse for London', while 'the 100 men with him . . . went up in the yacht and another vessel'. He reached London in time for the arrival of his first child. Anna gave birth to a son, Charles Scott, Earl of Doncaster, and James was soon devoted to this baby. As his father loved him, so James was to love all his children.

But what were his feelings about his first campaign? It is clear from his later comments that the low standards of the English regiments, compared with the French, depressed him ('nor is anything talked about', wrote Alberti, 'except the Most Christian's dissatisfaction over the slight service rendered by the English, who are undisciplined, and their commanders lack experience'[27]). He was consoled, however, to hear himself praised '. . . for his great application to his business', as the official report put it, 'which has already in this short time made him, in the opinion of all the old experienced officers of this army, a very able commander, and is

like in a little time to equal those of the first rank'.[28] His reward
from Louis for 'that most distinguished service' was a magnificent
diamond ring valued at '17,500 livres tournois', together with a
jewelled box inset with a miniature of the King and 'worth 10,500
livres tournois', while his English reward, according to *The Heroick
Life*, was 'to be joyfully received, with abundance of honour and
respect by his Royal father, and the whole court'.

7

1673

HERO OF MAASTRICHT

The most precious thing in the world to James, the cornerstone of his life, was his father's love and favour. The measure of his success, under the King's patronage, was his position at court. As Privy Councillor and Captain-Commandant of the Household Cavalry, that position was very strong, and, coupled with his vitality and charm and sense of fun, secured for him much of the admiration he coveted. But he was far from being the most powerful courtier; York, Rupert, Ormonde and Buckingham remained ahead of him. Nor – in spite of his father's indulgence, his social position as 'fourth gentleman in the three Kingdoms', his peacetime precedence as Commander of the Life Guards, and his success in the recent campaign – was he yet, except in theory, at the top of the army. York and Rupert were still stronger influences in military, as well as naval, affairs.

The most important English venture in this Third Dutch War (although eventually abandoned), was to be the invasion of Zeeland. Meanwhile Rupert would supersede Buckingham in command of the proposed expeditionary force, and there was now talk of the great soldier of fortune, the German Count Schomberg, going as lieutenant-general on a level with Buckingham. James, still inexperienced, would remain under the French command.

Nor among the King's bastards, even if James stood first, did he stand alone in the King's love. There was Charles Fitz-Charles, otherwise known as Don Carlos, the son of Lucy's successor, Catherine Pegge, soon to be Earl of Plymouth, and described in 1672 as 'a finely bred youth with a great deal of witt'.[1] And there were the Castlemaine children. Southampton, the first of them, would be a duke; so would his brothers, Northumberland and Grafton. And there was de Keroualle's son, destined to be Duke of

Richmond, not to mention Nell Gwyn's St Albans. Inevitably, as his half-brothers grew up, they posed a threat to James's position. At any time a different son might claim Charles's chief affection. Yet in these years the King remained proudly infatuated with his handsome eldest, still described as his 'dearest and *most* entirely beloved son'. While the others would be addressed as 'Plymouth', 'Southampton', 'Richmond', etc., Monmouth to his father was always 'James'. The King was delighted with Louis's reports on his son's conduct in the war, and additional marks of his love and appreciation were never wanting.

In November he was made 'Chief Justice in Eyre of all our Royal Hunting grounds this side of the Trent',[2] and in February, 1673, 'Lord High Chamberlain of Scotland for life'.[3] As an extensive landowner[4] his revenues grew as well as his power: there was no more relying on Anna's money to supplement his own allowance. And these offices furthered his position at Court, the Court at which he dazzled, and which dazzled back at him. This brave and able player, impeccable horseman and field sportsman, master of every game, was filled with a desire to be England's victor ludorum. But by this time it must have been clear to him that the supremacy he desired could be won only by genuine personal achievement, and that, within the limitations of his intellect, such prestige might only be acquired by outstandingly successful leadership in war. And, by chance, the currents of these turbulent and factious times were running relentlessly to the advantage of his aspirations.

Some of those currents, flowing and twisting for James, bore religious labels. Catholicism, as understood by his father, was not so much a system of personal beliefs as a theory of government, founded on the concept of absolutism and unquestioned central control. Charles tried to insinuate Catholicism into England with the compromise of universal religious toleration. On 15 March, 1673, he issued his Declaration of Indulgence for Tender Consciences, by which the penal laws against dissenters were suspended, places of public worship promised to Protestant non-conformists, and freedom of worship, in their own houses, to Catholics. But only the Catholics were grateful for their benefits. From the moment the Declaration was announced, the non-conformists, along with the Anglicans, became convinced that the Dutch war was a cloak to introduce 'Popery and arbitrary government', to confiscate the liberty they had – sealed with the blood of Charles's father. Already it was widely rumoured and would soon be publicly revealed that York was a secret 'papist', and that it was only a matter of days before the King would accept the faith himself. No wonder Louis's army, sweeping across the Netherlands in that

June of 1672, with James's French-supplied contingent under command, filled the English people with fear. They wondered how soon it would embark for English coasts.

Shaftesbury, the militant Protestant, whom Charles had secretly mocked for being taken in over the Catholic clause of the Secret Treaty, was now furious at discovering that Charles was (as Lauderdale told him) a secret Catholic and (as Arlington told him) irrevocably pledged to Louis. Shaftesbury – soon to steer Monmouth down a dangerous path – was emerging as the leader of the liberal Country Party, which now attacked the policy of the Cabal. His principal aims were to have the Declaration revoked and the standing army disbanded. Charles began to hate this scholarly, artful politician, whom he had raised from Ashley Cooper to Shaftesbury and now called 'Little Sincerity'.

On 8 March, 1673, swayed by Chancellor Shaftesbury, the Cavalier Parliament acted strongly : Charles was forced to cancel his Declaration of Indulgence. Londoners rejoiced; it was, perhaps, the most significant royal capitulation of the century. Three weeks later Parliament passed the Test Act, which denied offices and places of trust under the Crown to anyone refusing to take the Oaths of Allegiance and Supremacy, together with the sacrament according to the Church of England. Clifford, the Lord Treasurer, declined, and after being replaced by Thomas Osborne, a firmly Protestant cavalier, went home to Devonshire and committed suicide. Norfolk, the Earl Marshal, also refused.

And, confirming all the national dread, York too. His appointment as Lord High Admiral was put into commission, and Rupert was given command of the fleet. Having lost his first Duchess – Protestant Clarendon's daughter, who died a Catholic to please York – the heir to the throne cast about for a Catholic princess to replace her. York would never change, people were saying. Had he been king he would have plunged England into civil war again by now. His only surviving children were both girls, the Ladies Anne and Mary. So why not persuade the King to admit his marriage to Mrs Barlow, and declare Monmouth Prince of Wales? Buckingham and Shrewsbury[5] had already suggested it; now it became Shaftesbury's much cherished hope.

Returning in April 1673 from a spell of military business on the Continent, to take the Test at St Martin's-in-the-Fields ('coming up all decently to the rails before the communion table', as Dr Lamplugh put it),[6] did Monmouth see it as a day of destiny, a day that hinted the unfolding of Pregnani's horoscope? 'I declare that I believe that there is not any Transubstantiation in the sacrament of the Lord's Supper, or in the elements of Bread and

Wine at or after the consecration thereof by any person whatsoever.'
York recoiled from the words in disgust, while James, in spite of his
early Catholic upbringing, probably spoke them and signed his name
below them with an inward shrug. As he strode down the steps of
St Martin's-in-the-Fields, the shouts of the admiring crowds rang
in his ears: 'A-Monmouth, A-Monmouth, God Bless him!' From
now on, in the Nation's eyes, York was 'the Catholic Duke,' James
'the Protestant Duke'.

Despite the rebelliousness simmering in London, Charles took no
steps to end the Anglo-French alliance, and James, ever since he
returned from the Continent the previous August, had been busy
recruiting. With an additional draft of Guardsmen,[7] he reorganised
the Royal English and also persuaded his father to help him raise
more Irishmen to fill the ranks.[8]

The Emperor and Frederick William of Brandenburg now joined
France against Holland, so Louis sent Turenne's corps to the lower
Rhine to prevent the Dutch linking forces with their new allies,
while Condé was dispatched to Alsace. In September, James tried to
join Turenne as a volunteer for the invasion of Brandenburg, but
that scheme fell through.[9] On 17 December 1672, however, he was
on his way back to France,[10] to take up a new command, and,
according to *The Heroick Life*, 'as soon as he came on shore [at
Calais] he was received by the Governor, who waited at the
landing-place with several persons of quality, and a numerous
company of coaches, in which his Grace and the gentlemen who
waited on him thither, were conducted to their lodgings, which were
the richest and noblest in the whole City . . . And, to manifest the
honour and veneration they had for his Grace, the Governor
commanded the Guards to be drawn up, and . . . all the great guns
firing for joy at the same time'. On January 29, 1673, Louis
appointed him Lieutenant-General and supreme commander 'de
tous les sujets du Roi d'Angleterre, qui estoient ou qui viendroient
en France'.[11]

Early in February he led his contingent to Lille, where he and
his senior commanders made a thorough study of Vauban's greatest
fortress. With his experience of siege warfare on the Ijssel in 1672,
James understood the implications of Lille's defensives. Riding in
towards the main gate, he must first have taken note of the pro-
portions of the outer bank, the palisade protecting the covered way;
the counterscarp behind it, the outer wall of the great ditch, behind
which rose the ring of demi-lunes, or ravelins, the detached triangular
works with close all-round defence. Next in depth, and a little higher,
were the hornworks, with their twin salients in musket range of
their neighbours, and tactically linked with the demi-lunes and with

the musketeers in the covered way. And behind those, and higher still, the ramparts, the main walls, with a wedge-shaped bastion at each corner. Having inspected the internal lay-out, the arsenals, powder-magazines and barracks, he climbed the walls for a bird's-eye view of the whole defence system, and noticed how the 12- and 16-pounders in the ramparts' embrasures were mutually supporting throughout the fortress, affording all-round fields of fire.

He observed, too, how all the defences were interconnected, affording easy access and egress, and therefore how resolute attackers, supported by really effective gunners, musketeers and grenadiers, having stormed the outer palisade and gained a lodgement on the counterscarp, could, from that base, proceed to clear a demi-lune, and find the way on to the connecting hornworks or flanking demi-lunes; and from there attempt the gates and the ramparts. None the less, they were the most formidable defences in the world. Monmouth would have enjoyed the thought of repulsing an invader from those walls.

It was not, however, as a potential defender that he rode into Lille that day, but as a commander of siege troops. Although, during the previous winter, Louis's army had marched over the frozen floodwater close to Amsterdam, a thaw forced them to withdraw, so that, on the Dutch land front, the stalemate continued. The Allied plan for the 1673 campaigning season was consequently twofold: to scatter De Ruyter's fleet – Rupert was in command, with d'Estrées leading the French squadron – and invade the Zeeland coast with the English force now encamped at Blackheath. And, concurrently, to reduce the mighty fortress of Maastricht in the Dutch enclave of the Netherlands, which Louis had cordoned in the 1672 campaign. The importance of this stronghold lay not so much in its powerful garrison of 8,400 (twice the strength of all six of those Cleves fortresses, won in 1672), as in its position on the Meuse, which commanded important lines of communication between Holland and her Imperial ally. Turenne's corps was left with a holding role against the Austrians on the Rhine, while Condé looked for fresh opportunities to go on the offensive towards Amsterdam. Maastricht was reserved for Louis's prestige.

James was learning the latest tactics of siege offensive. The old method of attack was simply to dig a single trench directly towards a comparatively weak point in the defences and, having prepared a forming-up place for the assault troops, to attack that point under cover of intensive cannonade. This method inevitably incurred heavy casualties, and probably many attempts before a lodgement was effected. On such a narrow front, only a comparatively small assaulting force could be employed, and this was often overwhelmed in its trenches with a quick sortie by the defenders.

Vauban's tactics had much more impact. His first trench, dug parallel with the ramparts and entirely surrounding them, but out of range of the fortress artillery, acted as a covered road and strong position, from which the advancing trenches could be supported and defenders' sorties repelled. From this first trench-cum-road Vauban had a number of approach trenches worked directly towards the objective, but zigzagging to give protection from both enfilade and defilade fire. Depending upon the ground and the defences, at least two further parallels (transverse support trenches) would probably be dug, the third quite close to the covered way. From this third parallel 'attacks' or 'saps' – fashioned, tactically, by specialist engineers ('sappers') – would be dug to bring numbers of marksmen into range, and, possibly, also to plant mines. All this time advanced artillery positions were established, while those entrenched in rear of the working parties gave covering fire. Finally, in a night of quietly bustling activity, the trenches were 'opened'; infantrymen crept forward to the 'attacks' and 'saps', deploying left and right along the intended course of the assault parallels, so that, at daybreak, the enemy would find themselves closely surrounded by a well protected siege force.

Maastricht was composed of four concentric walls with, at each corner, a wedge-shaped bastion. Its ramparts were surrounded first by a line of hornworks, and, beyond them, demi-lunes, which looked over the counterscarp of the moat to the outer line of infantry defence, the covered way. The governor of this citadel was called Fariaux, an experienced French officer in the Dutch service.

Louis's besieging force consisted of 19,000 cavalry, 26,000 infantry and 58 cannon. To deceive the Governor of the Spanish Netherlands he led this army on a meandering course, pretending first that Ghent, then that Brussels, were to be his objectives, and on 5 June he moved his army swiftly east to Landerhamme.

'His Grace of Monmouth marched that day at the head of the infantry,' *The Heroick Life* gushes, 'which he did with such indefatigable industry, and managed his command with such soldier-like gallantry, that the King took especial notice of it, admiring and highly commending the Duke's bravery, to those who were about his person.' And one can imagine the energetic James, cantering up and down the line, exhorting tired soldiers, rebuking careless ones, posting flank patrols, seeing rations distributed at the halts and ensuring distances were correctly kept on the march. On 7 June Louis went ahead with 5,000 infantry and an artillery detachment to trace the lines of circumvallation – the precaution against relief attempts and other outside interference – and to allot

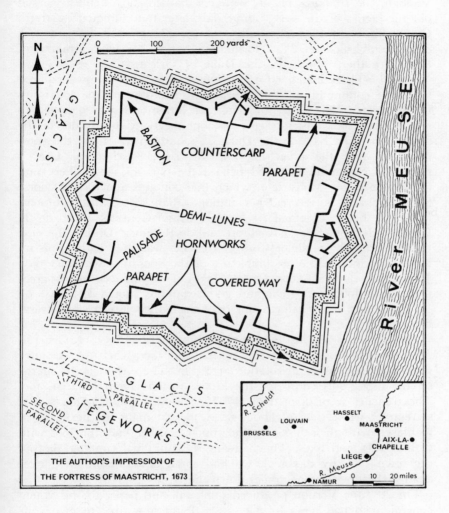

N

0   100   200 yards

GLACIS

River MEUSE

BASTION

COUNTERSCARP

PARAPET

DEMI-LUNES

PALISADE

HORNWORKS

PARAPET

COVERED WAY

GLACIS

SIEGEWORKS

THIRD PARALLEL

SECOND PARALLEL

THE AUTHOR'S IMPRESSION OF
THE FORTRESS OF MAASTRICHT, 1673

R. Scheldt

BRUSSELS

LOUVAIN

HASSELT

MAASTRICHT

AIX-LA-
CHAPELLE

LIÈGE

R. Meuse

NAMUR

0   10   20 miles

ground to the cavalry and areas for the reserve infantry, while Vauban, the *tranchée major*, with his mathematical genius, worked out the tactics of the siege. Three days later the mainguard arrived. On 11 June a bridge was built over the Meuse, and, beyond it, a camp established for the formation under titular command of Louis's brother, Monsieur, the Duke of Orleans.

Will Lockhart explained to Arlington how James now acquired his large command on the west front, in front of the garrison's Brussels gate: 'His Grace the Duke of Monmouth was designed to serve as one of Monsieur's generals, but the King, partly out of the great respect he has for the Duke . . . hath given [him] the command of half the great line on this side, so that his Grace's particular command marched behind the park of the artillery and the bridge below Maastricht, which line contains above 8,000 horse and foot, and is a greater command than any hath, Monsieur [Orleans] being excepted.'[12] James's Major-Generals were de la Fieuliad, de Lorge, de la Rochfort and de Rohanez. During the next thirteen days the main network of trenches was dug, with Louis up at three o'clock in the morning, to tour the lines at dawn every day. James was just as keen. 'The Duke of Monmouth takes great pleasure to follow so great and good example,' noted Lockhart on 15 June, 'and daily gaineth not only the King's esteem, but everybody else's.'[13]

He shared, with his four major-generals, the duty of General-officer-in-command-of-the-trenches for the day, each of the five relieving one another in rotation at 6 p.m. The one to be in charge on the day Louis chose for the attack would command that, too. The trenches were opened on 17 June, and Vernon, James's new secretary,* wrote that 'at about six o'clock at night the horse began to march with their fascines, and, upon another line, the foot with their spades and axes. They advanced within half musket shot of the town . . . by daybreak we had three batteries mounted over against the town as one comes down the river . . .'

On 20 June Vernon produced quill, ink and paper for his young general, who had news for Charles: 'I am now able to give your Majesty some account of the siege, which is very ill for them,' James wrote, 'for I never saw people that had so great a reputation for defending themselves do it worse. The trench was opened by Monsieur de la Fieuliad a Saturday night . . . The next night, which was Monsieur de la Rochfort's they fired a little more . . . I believe on Tuesday night, which is my night, I shall make a lodgement upon the counterscarp . . . I believe they depend . . . upon their

---

*Thomas Ross, remaining in London, was still Monmouth's Comptroller.

mines and, when they are once played, we shall be quickly masters of the town. . . . Monsieur de Schomberg is coming away, and, though he is not yet certain how your Majesty will have him command, he hopes you will have no one command him but the Duke [York] and that he may command immediately after'. Then there was some outstanding business concerning the Life Guards. 'Sir Philp Howard [Captain of the 2nd, Queen's, Troop] wrote word that your Majesty would have me write to my Lord of Rockingham to persuade him to buy the cornet's place in Sir Philip Howard's troop for his son [Edward Watson] that is here with me, so that when Mr [Capt. Francis] Watson [cousin of Edward] has taken the lieutenant's place of my lord Marshall as your Majesty has promised him, then my Lord Rockingham's son may buy the cornet's place of Mr Watson. I do assure you, Sir, Mr Watson has had a great care of my family [as aide-de-camp, Francis Watson was in charge of Monmouth's personal staff] . . . and has put it in much better order than ever it was . . .

'I stopped the express on purpose to give your Majesty an account of my night's trench', ran the postscript. 'They have fired extremely, but I have got within 30 paces of the counterscarp and could have made a lodgement upon it, but the King would not for fear of the mines, and therefore I fear we shall not attack in these two days yet, because we shall begin to sap . . .'[14]

The same day he wrote in his zestful style to the Secretary of State, Lord Arlington:

> . . . Pray tell the King that he [de Lorge] has advanced extremely considering the weather, for he has run the trench 200 paces forward, therefore I do not doubt at all but that I shall make a lodgement upon the counterscarp, which the engineers did all they could to keep for Monsieur de la Fieuliad, which is to come on tomorrow night, but I believe I shall have that honour . . . 'Tis such rainy weather that in the trench we are up to the knees in water, which is not very comfortable, especially when we are to stay 24 hours in the trench before we are relieved.'[15]

It was de la Fieuliad who completed the sap network and, reported Lockhart, 'joined the heads of our 2 attacks by a line of communication, by which the points of our trenches are secured from outfalls'.

A band of volunteer officers, who had accompanied James from England, now pinned their hopes with his on it being his day of duty and on his sector of the siege that Louis would order the attack. They were Lord Rockingham's sons, Lewis and Edward

Watson, their cousin and Monmouth's aide, Captain Francis Watson, the Marquis of Huntly, Charles O'Brien (the Life Guardsman who was wounded by Coventry on the night of the Haymarket ambush), Lord Alington, Sir Thomas Armstrong (late of Lord Oxford's regiment, now of the Life Guards, military mentor of Monmouth's and one day to be a political mentor, too), Capt John Churchill, the future Marlborough (then of the Duke of York's regiment), Captain Slingsby, Capt Charles Godfrey, Captain Villiers of the Life Guards (Lord Grandison's son), and one or two others.* Writing on 22 June, Alington notes his young general's thoughtfulness and attention to detail: 'His Grace took great great care that the trenches should be dry before the Duke de Rohanez relieved us, so that his men yesterday in the evening passed safe and dry to their several posts.'[16]

To draw and disperse the enemy, Louis planned three feint attacks, one across the Meuse, towards the eastern ramparts; one from the west, by General Montal; and a third on James's side, the south-west. At the same time James was to attempt the counterscarp facing him, and the demi-lune behind it, protecting the Brussels gate. It was to be an evening attack with three hours of daylight left to make the lodgement. James's main force was the French King's Own Regiment of Foot, commanded by the Marquis de Montbrun (the same whose daughter James, in 1669, 'swore was not painted') and the Royal Company of Musketeers under Capitaine d'Artagnan. These appear to be the only units directly allotted for the attack. If he required reinforcements, James was to apply to Louis. This daunting duty was rendered no easier by the fact that, as James said in his letter to Arlington, 'there had fallen so much rain as that part of the trenches were full of water, in some places to a man's waist'.

He organised an assault force from Montbrun's unit in three groups: one to make straight for the covered way, to grapple with the stakes on the palisade; a grenadier party to back them up, lobbing their missiles into the covered way; and a third, of musketeers, working their way forward by fire and movement on the flanks. D'Artagnan's men were in reserve.

Watching the artillery duel from an observation post, Louis now gave James the signal for attack, and, in a flash, his soldiers were through their sally-ports and across the glacis, grenadiers, musketeers and pikemen co-operating to occupy the covered way, which they soon cleared. James then sent his liaison officer 'to give him an

*Lewis Duras, one day, as Earl of Feversham, to be Monmouth's opponent (at Sedgemoor) was in reserve at the siege of Maastricht, with his troop of 150 Life Guardsmen.

account of how matters were'.[17] When he was told that the escarpment was difficult to hold, but that, on the demi-lune, the enemy were faltering, he went forward, amid the smoke and crackle of musketry, to issue orders for an attack on the second objective; and seeing it won, returned to his command post, all the time under continuous fire. During the night he satisfied himself as to the completion of the communications trenches to both objectives; and Alington reported that 'about two in the morning we went out with the Duke to see what was done'.

While the men were digging in on their objectives, a Dutch soldier who had hidden by the demi-lune, was about to explode a mine, when, just in time, one of James's orderlies spotted and pistolled him, and James had the fuse and powder removed. But a little before daybreak, by underground means, the enemy did manage to spring one of these mines on which the Dutch defence so much depended, and two officers and fifty soldiers were near enough to be killed by it. However, it took the Dutch several hours to organise a counter-attack party to take advantage of the confusion. James had already sent Villiers to Louis for reinforcements. Alington recalled that 'Between 12 and one o'clock, news was brought the Duke that the Dutch were preparing to make a sally, which they did with great order and bravery, the hand grenades falling very thick among our men.'

Sending back to inquire again about the reinforcements, James ordered d'Artagnan, whose musketeers were now the only reserve, to 'go and make good that post'. Two of his sub-units attempted it, but '. . . the enemy had already made themselves masters of the half-moon and were not to be easily dislodged . . .' The only immediately available reserve now was the balance of d'Artagnan's musketeers, the Duke's personal staff and the group of English volunteer officers, the total strength of which would have been about 70 men.[18] Anyhow, unless some decisive action was taken quickly, all that James and his men had striven for since the previous day might be irrevocably lost; and although it was not usual, even in the seventeenth century, for lieutenant-generals to lead spontaneous counter-attacks in person, James decided this was a moment to break with convention. ('At a glance', as Marlborough's biographer, General Lord Wolseley was to put it, 'Monmouth took in the critical state of affairs'.)[19] Nor would he waste time filtering his party through the sally port. 'After the Duke had put on his arms', Alington remembered, 'he went not out at the groyne, the ordering-place, but leapt over the bank of the trench.' One can imagine Monmouth, sword in hand, his elegant clothes spattered with mud, his hat set rakishly at the habitual 'Monmouth cock', leading that band of English officers and French musketeers over the wet, ball-ripped grass with his athletic stride. During the advance he shouted 'in a firm and reproachful voice' to several of Montbrun's men who were retreating towards him : 'Faut-il, camarades, que je vous montre deux fois le chemin moi-même pour aller aux ennemis?'[20] At which they turned and followed him back through the battle-smoke and onto the counterscarp.

Alington returned with Monmouth to the demi-lune. 'Thus we marched with our swords in our hands to a barricade of the enemy's, where only one man could pass at a time. There was M. d'Artagnan and his musketeers, who did very bravely. He would have persuaded the Duke not to have passed that place, but that being not to be done, this gentleman would go along with him; but in passing that narrow place, was killed with a shot through his head, upon which the Duke and we passed (where Mr O'Brien had a shot through the leg) . . . The soldiers at this took heart, the Duke twice leading them on with great courage.'

After half-an-hour's very hot hand-to-hand fighting, James exhorting all the time by word and example, the Dutch were at last driven off the demi-lune. But the position could not remain tenable for long. Where were the reinforcements? He sent Villiers back along the communications trenches to inquire, and : '. . . when those men came,' Alington said, 'our enemy left us without any further disturbance, masters of what we had gained the night before. So that, to the Duke's great honour, we not only took more than was expected, but maintained it after we had been in possession of it, but with the loss of a great many men and many brave officers.' Monmouth's formation suffered over 1,900 casualties. Sir Henry Jones and d'Artagnan were dead, Alington and Churchill wounded; and three weeks later Perwych was to record : 'just now we hear that Charles O'Brien is dead after his leg was cut off'.

'Some old commanders say this was the bravest and briskest . action they had seen in their lives,' Alington went on, 'and our Duke did the part of a much older and more experienced general . . .'[21] A French officer told Perwych that Monmouth displayed a remarkable tactical grasp throughout the operation, 'et une conduite d'un général qui auroit commandé 30 ans des tranchées'.[22]

There were no respite. De Lorge, whose division was on duty on the 28th, lost 200 men when he advanced to take a hornwork behind the demi-lune captured by James's men. After de Lorge's success, James and his contingent 'had nothing to do', as Alington said, 'but to secure ourselves in what he had taken, and carry our trench to the walls of the town, there to make our mine, which is so forward that this night the Duke de Rohanez will begin it under the walls'.

Four days later Maastricht surrendered, and the garrison was permitted to march out 'with bag and baggage, drums beating, Colours flying, matches lighted, bullet in the mouth, etc. with pieces of cannon and two mortar pieces'.[23] James's secretary, Vernon, witnessed the parade: 'M. Fariaux, their commander, saluted my duke as he passed along and did him that justice as to give him the honour of taking the town, telling him that it was that sally of his for the defence of the demi-lune that discouraged all his men, whom it was impossible to stop from running, though he [Fariaux] were himself at the palisades . . .'[24] One of the enemy regimental commanders, the Marquis de Morbecque, had been, says Vernon, 'well known to his Grace as he passed through Flanders. In paying his rsepects to his Grace he told him that they knew him when he sallied, and they imagined that he was to have been followed by some great force; and thereupon called to those in the demi-lune to have a care of being cut off . . . Had they been assured he was no better attended, they would have ventured from their works to have endeavoured to make him their prisoner.'[25]

Quoting Frenchmen returning to Paris from the campaign, Perwych recorded that 'much of the honour of the siege is attributed to his Grace of Monmouth'. Lord Sunderland, budding politician and eyewitness at Maastricht, told Alington that 'nothing is talked of here but the Duke of Monmouth's bravery, and that never any man had so gained so great a reputation'.[26] Lockhart thought 'It be a question whether his conduct or his courage deserves the greater share in the honour of those actions.'[27]

James's slight diffidence as well as his modest embarrassment at being honoured, without warning, by Louis with the colonelcy of the regiment of horse of the fallen Sir Harry Jones is reflected in this note to Arlington: 'I must make you now an excuse for not writing to you by the last express, but I fear I was so very weary . . . Sir Harry Jones was killed and the King has given me his regiment without my asking for it. Pray let me know if I did well to accept it.'[28] On being publicly thanked by Louis ('I am delighted to see you after all you have done for us') James is recorded as replying, 'We were not under particularly heavy fire', which Louis countered with, 'It is very modest of you to say so, but *we* saw for ourselves.'[29]

That modesty, whether genuine or contrived, is often there in James's rather slow and little-worded speech. According to Lediard his comment upon being congratulated by Charles was to the effect that his friend, John Churchill, at one moment saved his life and that Churchill's conduct was excellent.[30] It was on the strength of this report that Charles gave Churchill his first lieutenant-colonelcy (that of Sir Charles Littleton's Regiment), and that York appointed him his Gentleman of the Bedchamber and Master of the Robes. Churchill's ambition ran much deeper and was more calculated than Monmouth's, and he had to advance himself entirely on his own merit. To Churchill, James was more than a brave friend, fellow courtier and leader of the young nobility; he was the King's favourite son, with further military power obviously in store for him. The future Duke of Marlborough depended a good deal on the present Duke of Monmouth. But history does not record whether, in 1673, Churchill discerned that under the heroic image lay a character that could be easily influenced by devious men; that for all his physical courage he could easily be a moral coward; for all his apparent modesty he really loved to play to the gallery; and that, not having been brought up in a world of reality, he could not always distinguish between gold and tinsel.

8

PROTESTANT DUKE IN ASCENDANCY

'The people do nothing but confer honours upon him,' Vernon wrote to Williamson on Monmouth's return from the 1673 campaign; 'they will have him to be Master of the Horse in the Duke of Buckingham's place,[1] Commander of Scotland in my Lord Lauderdale's and General of the Land Forces.'[2] Henry Ball told Williamson that James '. . . wants no caresses to bid his welcome and to help it forward; the people will have him made Viceroy or Commissioner of Scotland, lieutenant-general, or whatever else can be imagined.'[3] And Robert Yard told him that he '. . . seems to have a very great interest as well at Court as in the city and people stick not to say great things are designed for him'.[4] So, if his ennoblement and elevation to fourth gentleman of the three Kingdoms, in 1662, was the first crucial turning-point in Monmouth's life, Maastricht, eleven years later, was the second. For England was somewhat disenchanted with her veteran leaders in the 1670s; she needed a fresh hero, and now she had one, a glamorous prince, at once brave and humane, artless and con-scientious, a hero who was not only of royal blood but one with whom the people could identify, because he was 'easy with all men'. More and more adherents were seen to honour him by tipping up their hats in the 'Monmouth cock', more shouted 'God bless the Protestant Duke' as he alighted from his carriage.

And events conspired to hoist him further up the ladder. Strategically, the capture of Maastricht was still to be complemented by landings on the Zeeland coast. Christopher Hatton, writing on 8 July from the camp of the expeditionary force at Blackheath, heard that 'the Duke of Monmouth is coming for to command us . . .'[5] while the agent Ball told the Secretary of State, Williamson:

'The Duke of Buckingham is resolved not to go under the Comte (Schomberg), nor he under him; the Duke of Monmouth's coming home, who will be here on Saturday next, will end all . . .'.[6] This was all wishful thinking, for the Zeeland expeditionary force had good cause for wanting Monmouth at their head. Schomberg, who had the command, quarrelled, not only with Buckingham and his senior officers, but also with Prince Rupert who was commanding the fleet.[7] By the time his army reached Yarmouth it was in a state of mutiny. Then Rupert, in a fierce battle off the Texel against De Ruyter and Tromp, was badly let down by the French squadron, commander, d'Estrées,[8] and the outcome, a bloody, drawn battle, meant that the invasion plan was postponed. At first it was decided to replace Rupert with Monmouth, 'assisted by Sir John Harman, who is to be with him in his ship'.[9] But that plan, too, was shelved, the fleet remained in port, the Zeeland operation was cancelled, Rupert kept his appointment as Admiral of the Fleet, and Monmouth, on York's recommendation, was, in Lord Mulgrave's words, 'put at the head of our military affairs'.[10]

Charles was very proud of the fact that his son had acquired such strong personal influence in the officer corps and had won the love of the army. Nor would the King have his armed forces, or the public, lose sight of the romance and gallantry of Maastricht, the greatest feat of British arms on land in his reign. The siege was re-lived as a tactical demonstration at Windsor that August. Evelyn was in the audience :

In one of the meadows at the foot of the long terrace below the Castle . . . bastions, bulwarks, ramparts, palisadoes, graffs, hornworks, counterscarps, and etc. were constructed. It was attacked by the Duke of Monmouth (newly come from the real siege) and the Duke of York, with a little army, to show their skill in tactics. On Saturday night they made their approaches, opened trenches, raised batteries, took the counterscarp and ravelin after a stout defence; great guns fired on both sides, grenadoes hot, mines sprung, parties sent out, attempts of raising the seige, prisoners taken, parleys, and in short all the circumstances of a formal siege . . . and what is most strange, all without disorder or ill accident, to the great satisfaction of a thousand spectators. Being night it made a formidable show. The siege being over, I went with Mr Pepys back to London, where we arrived about 3 in the morning'.[11]

The respect and affection which York had for his nephew at this time is given further proof in a note of Robert Yard's the following month :

His Royal Highness dined at the Duke of Monmouth's, who were together most of the afternoon, it being observed by those that are near HRH that he has a particular kindness and affection for his Grace, upon whom all the world looks as a rising sun. Many will have him to be Master of the Horse in the room of the Duke of Buckingham who, in the general opinion, is now declining in his interest at Court.[12]

It was in the following April, when Buckingham was in disgrace with the King, and Parliament, too, that James attained the coveted Court appointment of Master of the Horse,[13] (just at the time that he was 'in great affliction for the loss of his only son, the Earl of Doncaster').[14] In May 1675 he was appointed Privy Councillor for Scotland and, in July, installed as Chancellor of Cambridge University; in August he was made High Steward of Kingston-upon-Hull and, in October, Commissioner of the Admiralty. Lauderdale was out of favour now, and James who, as Duke of Buccleuch, was already Scotland's Lord High Chamberlain for life, was looked upon as the only man of sufficient stature to go as Scotland's Viceroy in his place. But – for all his public spirit and sense of duty (so often combined with an over-blind willingness) – James declined this offer, and with diplomatic sense. 'Last week the King proffered My Lord Duke to make him Commissioner of Scotland in place of my Lord Lauderdale,' said Vernon to Williamson on 17 November; 'but his Grace modestly refused it, telling his Majesty that he desired to appear in action while the war continued, and in a time of peace he feared that employment would draw upon him the envy of the Duke [of York]. The King commended him for his prudence, told him he was of the same opinion, and therefore, if he had not that, he should not long want some considerable charge in the kingdom.'[15] Within days of this he was recommended to succeed Essex as Viceroy of Ireland.

By the end of 1674, York was already jealous of Monmouth's advancement, and the first rupture between uncle and nephew had already occurred. In late summer there was 'a great feud between York and Monmouth; the whole Court backs Monmouth . . .'.

Anna, with whom James exchanged respect if not love, set the sights very high for her husband and constantly fed his aspirations. Lord Mulgrave, then only a regimental commander, who was much more ambitious, and intensely envious of James in his golden years, remembering 1674–5 at the end of his life, wrote: '. . . all things concurred with the Duke of Monmouth's ambition as soon as Prince Rupert was out of favour and the Duke of York out of capacity by reason of the late Test against Papists'.[16] Mulgrave recalled how

Anna used her close friendship with York to 'make her husband considerable', and how Monmouth, who now regarded York as a rival, 'had forbidden his wife to receive any more visits from him'.

Monmouth, owner of an ample heart and victim of a loveless marriage, was reputed to have a roving eye; Anthony Hamilton (de Grammont), ever exaggerating, went so far as to say that he was 'the universal terror of husbands and lovers'. York was no better; Arabella Churchill and Catherine Sedley were two of his better known mistresses. Burnet remarked that York 'was perpetually in one amour or other, without being very nice in his choice, upon which the King once said he believed his brother "had his mistresses given him by his priests for penance" '.[17]

At this time Monmouth, York and Mulgrave were all courting the same mistress, who managed for some weeks to hide the fact from each of them; this was the artful Moll Kirke,* Maid of Honour to York's Duchess. When Monmouth came to know of Mulgrave's rivalry, to keep him out of the way one night he ordered the Life Guards to detain him on some official, but unnecessary pretext. 'The Duke of Monmouth, being jealous of my Lord Mulgrave's courting his newest mistress, Moll Kirke, Lady Chaworth gossiped to Lord Roos, 'watched his coming thence late four or five nights ago, and made the Guards keep him up amongst them all night.'[18] Mulgrave's story was that 'the Duke of Monmouth, ever engaged in some amour, falls into great anger against me for an unlucky discovery that made too much noise in the Court at that time . . . [But] *he had always great temper*† and therefore offered no affront on the place . . .'[19]

This episode was soon public property, and York, at first believing it was only Mulgrave who had stolen an advantage on him, and still, despite the Test, holding considerable influence in the army, according to the Earl,[20] forestalled his appointment to command the First Foot Guards in place of the ageing Russell. But the Earl had his revenge by telling York that he 'had a more successful rival in his own nephew'. And, when York knew the truth of this, he could not forgive Monmouth.

If Anna was too cold, too strait-laced, too seriously intellectual to hold James's interest, Moll Kirke was no more than a passing infatuation. He soon took the lovely Eleanor Needham[21] – daughter of Sir Robert and sister of Mrs Middleton, perhaps the most celebrated of all the Court beauties[22] – as his mistress, and she bore

---

*Sister of Charles Kirke, one of Monmouth's Life Guards officers, and of Percy, then of Lord Oxford's Horse, and later notorious as Colonel of 'Kirke's Lambs'.

†Author's italics.

him four children, in less than four years. They assumed the name of Crofts.

But it was the army that held the greater measure of Monmouth's heart and allegiance. As his uncle's affection cooled, his father's love and respect waxed, and, towards the end of 1673, the King bolstered his authority by ordering that 'all military documents be brought forward for the Duke's approval'.[23] That September he crossed the Channel to consult the French command and reorganise the British units in their service.[24] On 26 January 1674 Vernon wrote that 'the King ordered him [Monmouth] to have an inspection into all things relating to the forces now on foot, so that all orders are brought to him, and he examines them and then presents them to the King to be signed . . . it is an initiating him into the business, and he is not like to be denied anything he shall be found capable to manage'.[25] The Earl of Craven (commanding the Coldstream Guards) was 'to command in chief during the King's absence at or near Windsor, all troops left behind for the security of London and Westminster . . . wherein he is to observe such orders as our dearest and most entirely beloved son, James, Duke of Monmouth, shall give from time to time'.[26]

The greater the responsibility the happier Monmouth was. Besides the care and control of the regular home-based units – two regiments of cavalry and four of foot, and thirty non-regimented garrison companies – he held a watching brief on the Tangier garrison, the forces in Scotland and Ireland, and the militia. He was also directly responsible for the welfare and replenishment of the contingent in the French service; for, although the Anglo-Dutch treaty was concluded in February 1674, none of the British units were withdrawn from Turenne's army. Under Monmouth's direction, assisted by the new Principal Secretary of State, Sir Joseph Williamson, nearly 5,000 reinforcements were dispatched there during the winter 1674–5,[27] and since there was no British formation, or co-ordinating commander overseas, it was to him, in London, that the active service regiments looked as their administrative chief. On James's shoulders also lay the executive responsibility for England's internal security. August 1675 saw the weavers – furious at French competition and the introduction of a loom by which one man could do the work previously done by twenty – out on the streets in riot, but Williamson reported to Coventry that 'the Duke of Monmouth being here I hope things will be a little better ordered than hitherto.[28]

On 27 May that year, 'a sad and dreadful fire broke out in Southwark, which burned with much violence all that day and part of the next, in which extremity his Grace [Monmouth] was pleased to take abundance of care and pains, in ordering and directing, and exposed his person to very great hazards, in assisting those who laboured to extinguish the fire, by blowing up of houses, and like discovering a great sense he had of the common calamity, very much sympathising with them in their suffering'.[29]

Everyone relied on Monmouth, and the qualities issuing from his office in the Cockpit are kindness, considerateness and compassion, coupled with a steady insistence on standards.[30] As Captain-Commandant of the Life Guards, James bore the day-to-day responsibility for the Guard at Whitehall, which then consisted of 100 'private gentlemen',* and in those days the King's Life Guard had the very real responsibility of safeguarding both the royal family and the central offices of government. His duties as Captain-Commandant and Master of the Horse frequently coincided. He was a very familiar figure at the Horse Guards, with its balconies and steps then leading from the brick façade of the first storey. With his charm, bustling style and capacity for organisation and getting the best out of people, one can readily imagine him on parade there, issuing orders and seeing them carried out – the distribution of equipment, positioning of men and horses, security, turn-out, timings and the staging of rehearsals.[31]

Master of the Horse, veteran cavalryman, champion race-rider and leader of the hunt, James was also regarded as the principal figure in the equine world; he supervised the breeding of the army remounts, and it was to him that foreign emissaries were sent when English horses were in demand.[32] There is evidence, too, that his finger was firmly on the pulse of his Chancellorship of Cambridge University,[33] his Chief Justiceship in Eyre of the Forests South of the Trent,[34] and his posts of Scottish Lord High Chamberlain and Lord-Lieutenant of Staffordshire. So his influence already extended broadly into civilian affairs.

But what of his feud with York? 'Protestant Duke' and 'Catholic Duke' were no light nicknames for the two aspiring princes. They were given with sinister and devious intent. Politics had long lain in ambush for James, Duke of Monmouth, and was now ready to spring its trap. So, fatefully for him, it was not only soldiers, sailors, dons, magistrates, deputy-lieutenants, sheriffs, wardens, foresters, grooms, postilions, trainers and jockeys who looked up to him in the 1670s as their figurehead and leader, but also the liberal sympathisers. These were largely the Dissenters and City merchants, the supporters of the Old Cause, the Commonwealth men and their sons, who were intent upon reducing the power of the Monarch and

*Two squadrons (in the seventeenth century, a squadron was a sub-unit of a troop).

English soldiers at the time of Monmouth's Royal service, by Colonel Clifford Walton: (a) Grenadiers, *c.* 1678; (b) a Private Gentleman of the 1st (King's) Troop of the Life Guards at about the time Monmouth assumed command of that corps (1668); (c) a General Officer, *c.* 1678

a

b

c

The Horse Guards, Whitehall, at the time of Monmouth's Lord-Generalcy

The Battle of Bothwell Bridge, 1679, artist unknown

transferring a great measure of it to Parliament, and upon shaping a more democratic constitution, founded on religious toleration and broad-based government. Catholicism, 'the religion of autocrats', was anathema for these men, and not only Catholics but anyone who opposed their own liberal-protestant philosophy was labelled by them as 'Papist'.

The figure emerging as the leader of the Country, or liberal, Party, was that rich, courageous and physically frail member of the Cabal, the Chancellor, Anthony Ashley Cooper, Earl of Shaftesbury. Shaftesbury had behind him a brilliant and extraordinary career. In 1643, at nineteen, he had, at his own expense, raised a regiment of foot and a troop of cavalry for Charles I. A year later he was a Roundhead, commanding a brigade in the West Country. In 1654 Cromwell elected him President of the Council. But Ashley Cooper was a Monck man and as such was one of those who in 1660 went to Holland with 'Parliament's humble request to His Majesty to return to his loving people'. Quickly finding a place in the Restoration Government, the following year saw him as Baron Ashley and Chancellor of the Exchequer. As a result of Clarendon's fall he became a member of the Cabal, and, in 1673, Earl of Shaftesbury and Lord High Chancellor. But then his career took another road. He had urged on Charles the toleration of Dissenters, excepting Catholics, and his attitude towards 'popery' was soon seen by the Court to be atavistic. Loudly he warned of the danger of Catholics in high places and was at loggerheads with the King, who disliked and mocked him. In 1674 he was dismissed from the Council, and the following summer was ordered to leave London.

Two months later, during a visit to a Dorsetshire neighbour, an incident occurred which vividly reflected the Court Party's suspicions of, and strong feelings against Shaftesbury. He was set upon by Bristol's son, Lord Digby, who drew his sword, shouting, 'You are against the King, and for seditions and factions, and for a Commonwealth, and I will prove it – and by God we will have your head at next Parliament!' Shaftesbury brought an action of slander against the young man, who was ordered to pay £1,000 damages. Shaftesbury's opposition to the King was now public knowledge.

He had it on very good authority that the King was a secret Roman Catholic; and he was horrified when York, in defiance of the nation, had taken a Catholic bride as his second wife. York *must* not, the Earl decided, *would* not, succeed. In his place a Protestant heir must be found, a prince who would be prepared to preside, to 'reign', not to govern arbitrarily as Charles II endeavoured to govern. Shaftesbury worked out the possibilities as follows. The Queen was now unlikely to have a child, and, since Charles would not divorce her, there seemed to be three alternatives. First there was Prince Rupert, who was Protestant, half-Stuart and anti-French. But he had to be discounted as being unmarried, foreign, too old, and too much engrossed with his scientific experiments. Second, there was William of Orange, who was Protestant, half-Stuart, young, and likely before long to marry an eligible Protestant princess, but who, in Shaftesbury's view, was ineligible because he was foreign, unattractive, and known to dislike the English and to be an advocate of absolute monarchy.

And third there was the King's eldest son, James, Duke of Monmouth. Not only was this prince Protestant and young, he was also practically treated as Prince of Wales; a peer had been appointed as his governor during his childhood; he was married to a great Scottish peeress and heiress; he wore his hat in the presence of the royal family and carried the royal arms on his coach; salutes were fired at his comings and goings; his father, over whom he exerted great influence, loved him dearly; he was virtually Commander-in-Chief of the army, very rich and, since the Test, the most highly honoured man in the three Kingdoms. Widely popular as 'the Protestant Duke', having the looks of an Adonis, charm and a fairy-tale charisma, an apparent love of liberty, a strong sympathy with the common man, a velvet-glove authority and constant willingness to serve those who needed him, he was largely endowed with the qualities required of the Country Party's 'heir'. Shaftesbury, sharing a place with James in the House of Lords, got on well with him, and found the Protestant Duke's political views, such as they were, very much in common with his own. Monmouth, for his part, was easily beguiled by 'Little Sincerity'.

There was only one snag: the technicality of James's birth. But the King's life-style during the years of exile was obscure, reasoned Shaftesbury, and there were plenty of rumours that he had been secretly married to Lucy Barlow. She and others had told Monmouth the truth of it. Either the King must be persuaded to admit the fact, and acknowledge his son, he decided, or witnesses must be found to the marriage, or 'some written evidence'. And, if that legitimacy could not be proved? Well, if there was to be a 'stadtholder, a republican prince, thought Shaftesbury, perhaps it would be more suitable after all (and more acceptable to the people) if the candidate was *not* in the line of lawful succession?

In 1675 a private Whig society was formed, with Shaftesbury as president, and with rooms at the King's Head in Chancery Lane as their headquarters. On special days their votaries wore ribbons in their hats, of 'Leveller green';* they called themselves the Green Ribbon Club. Monmouth, their patron, was a regular visitor; he wore the green, and they honoured him by tilting their hats and brims in the 'Monmouth cock' and toasting him as 'Prince of Wales'. Next in rank below him at the King's Head were the Duke of Buckingham and the former Irish Viceroy, the Earl of Essex; Lords Salisbury and Wharton; Ford, Lord Grey of Werke (a man with a good brain and a hot head, who proved to be very adept at looking after his own skin); Lord Russell, son of the Earl of Bedford, and West Country Member of Parliament; Thomas Thynne, of Longleat, Monmouth's good friend, 'the Protestant Squire'; and Sir Thomas Armstrong, Knight, the old soldier of fortune and Life Guardsman, who had been appointed by the King to James's staff for the campaigns of 1672 and 1673, and who, in spite of the difference in age, was always James's close friend.

Then there were the middle-class members, notably Robert Ferguson, native of Aberdeenshire, Shaftesbury's chaplain and secretary, the Whigs' chief pamphleteer, a fanatic preacher, who had served a prison sentence for treason, a tall, thin, wild-looking creature, described by Bishop Burnet as 'a hot, bold man, whose spirit was naturally turned to plotting';[35] Major Wildman, another revolutionary politician who had served a term of imprisonment; his brother-in-law, William Disney, an attorney; and young Nathaniel Wade, a law student, who, like so many of the militant Whigs, came from the rebellious West Country, the great wool region that produced such a high proportion of England's wealth.

It was not long before Monmouth found himself fully committed, insofar as his military and other duties allowed, to the Old Cause; for not only, apparently, did he share their philosophy, but their ambitions dovetailed very well with his own. So Charles, having trapped him in the false position of 'Monmouth without the Prince of Wales', unwittingly made a present of him to his own bitterest enemies, and James, for all his ability, was a little too straightforward, too imperceptive, to see how he might thus prove false to himself as well as to his father.

If he had been a superficial person he would have counted his blessings, self-indulgently basked in the glory of his Court and military career. But he was not superficial. His personal situation worried him deeply; he treasured the memory of his mother, hazy

---

*The distinguishing colour was adopted by Londoners demonstrating after the murder, by Royalists, in November 1648, of the most popular of Leveller leaders, Thomas Rainborough, who had been a famous sailor. They wore sea-green ribbons in their hats.

as it was; he desperately wanted it believed that his father and mother were married; not in order to be declared heir, but for his own psychological security. In the 1670s the evidence of that marriage still existed and was strong, and he knew it. And here, as he saw it, were these sincere, clever politicians, who actually wished for him the very thing he wished for himself: recognition of his legitimacy. And all the evidence shows that he, like them, was a genuine liberal. How could he refuse to be their figurehead? 'God bless the Protestant Duke!' Those words rang well in his ears. 'Long live the Prince of Wales!' That was even sweeter. He never ceased, in the 1670s, to hear his praises sung:

> Young Jemmy is a lad
> That's Royally descended,
> With every virtue clad
> By every tongue commended;
> A true and faithful English heart
> Great Britain's joy and hope . . .

9

LORD-GENERAL OF THE LAND FORCES

The 'papist threat' was not sufficiently visible to panic the English population into pronounced 'liberal' attitudes yet, and since commerce and the national economy were comparatively healthy, a climate rarely helpful to revolutionaries, James's political activities were still no great embarrassment to his father in the mid-1670s. Although Charles was almost permanently at loggerheads with the Commons, having abandoned Catholicism, but not absolutism, he succeeded in holding the political ring, while his First Minister, Danby, successfully consolidated the Tories, the nationalist party based on the old-school Cavaliers and Anglicans, as a counter-force against Shaftesbury's radical clique.

It was after a long period of prorogation that the King opened Parliament in February 1677, and for some weeks the Country Party, with the wily guidance of Shaftesbury, had been flooding the nation with pamphlets stating that, under an old act of Edward III's, a parliament that had not sat for over a year was *ipso facto* dissolved. When Buckingham, Shaftesbury, Wharton and Salisbury now argued this point vehemently in the Lords, their fellow peers ordered them to go on their knees before his Majesty to implore his pardon for their insolence, and, when they refused, had them hustled into the Tower. And so, for a while, the Green Ribbon Club was deprived of its president and three of its other peers.

As for the club's patron, its 'Protestant Duke', he was much too absorbed at this time in his soldiering and the business of his numerous offices to grieve over political setbacks. James's eyes were on foreign fields again, for Louis of France, like Charles of England, was as determined as ever to bring men who resisted him to their knees. The Anglo-French alliance had been dead three years now, but James still had an English brigade deployed under the French, who were involved in a skilful defensive campaign in Lorraine, thwarting the efforts of Charles V to recover his duchy, while the Duke of Luxembourg advanced in the Netherlands. Yet the King of England, with his double diplomacy, saw little wrong in sending a contingent of volunteers under old Ormonde's son, the Earl of Ossory (including James's half-brother, Plymouth), to fight for Orange, and at the same time extracting more money from Louis and allowing his Commander-in-Chief, Monmouth, accompanied by Feversham and Mulgrave, to take a command under Luxembourg.[1]

When Valenciennes, Cambrai and St Omer fell in swift succession to the French, the old fear ran among the English people : how soon will the papist Louis invade our shores to impose his *Catholicité* on us? But there is no mention that they expressed concern at the news of their hero, 'handsome Jemmy', riding at the head of a French wing again. There is just one nonchalant official note from the campaign mentioning that, in the smoke and confusion of pursuit, 'the Duke of Monmouth happened to take Lord Ossory's cloak with the Star, when the Prince of Orange removed from Charleroi, Luxembourg possessing the place'.[2] Following up this picture, one wonders what Monmouth's comment would have been if and when he found himself in possession of two Garter-pinned cloaks, that of his 'enemy' as well as his own; or, if he had lost his own, at having it so fortuitously replaced. Less than a month later, the three young officers, Monmouth, Mulgrave (who was so jealous of him) and Feversham, were in Paris celebrating the French successes.[3]

It was at this time, apparently, that James, the friend of old soldiers, pushed forward his plan to have an army pensioners' hospital built in or near London on the lines of the Hôtel des Invalides, in Paris. After he returned from the 1677 campaign he wrote a letter to Louvois that would set the course for the building of Wren's Royal Hospital at Chelsea : 'Vous voulez bien que je vous prie encore de me faire avoire le plan de l'hostel des Invalides tiré sure le modèle avec toutes les faces, car le Roi sera bien aise de le voir . . .'[4]

At Brussels he had found time to pen a note to Lord Melville, his Scottish agent : 'I shall come to London time enough before you go away, to thank you for all the trouble and pains you have taken in my business . . . Pray let me know if my wife begins to look after her business at home, and if there be any hopes of her being a good housewife . . .'[5] While Anna, who was neither affectionate nor domesticated, grew farther from him, Charles grew closer, and the trust he imposed in his son increased. But the King had not the least intention of admitting his marriage to Lucy Barlow, or of supporting the liberal movement against the accession of York, and declaring James Prince of Wales. This was where he always showed unswerving support for the brother he so much disliked. 'As well as I love the Duke of Monmouth', he promised, 'I would rather see him hanged at Tyburn than own him as my legitimate heir'.[6] All the same it suited his book rather well having his brother as figurehead of one faction, the so-called 'papists', and his son, the other contender for his crown, as counter-weight with the other, the Whigs. In this way, he was arguing in 1677, the scales of English political power might be balanced quite well.

But Danby went one better than his master. Since the Country Party insist upon *their* Protestant heir, he whispered to the Court Party, let us disarm them by creating *our* Protestant heir. Let us swing the moderates to our side. Have we not insisted upon the Duke of York's daughters' being educated as Protestants? Let us marry the elder, he suggested to Charles, to William of Orange; for the Prince has already hinted that he would not be an unwilling partner in that union. That would put a check on 'the gang in the City' and 'the Green Ribbonites'. When the offer was officially proposed, Orange, now more alarmed than ever by the French military advance, and wanting nothing more than an alliance that would bring over an English army permanently in defence of Holland, sent his faithful aide, William Bentinck, over with an unequivocal 'yes'.

The one to be most outraged at this proposal was not Louis, or Shaftesbury, but the girl's father, William's uncle. The fact that William of Orange was ugly, unhealthy, humourless, at heart anti-English and almost misogynist, mattered neither here nor there to York; nor in itself was it a factor of vital importance that he had always intended Catholic princes for his daughters, whereas Orange was that 'worst sort of Protestant, a Calvinist'. To York, the unpalatable truth was that William, like Monmouth, seemed to have emerged as a rival and an enemy. York's stubbornness in resisting the marriage exasperated Charles, who was now determined on it. 'God's fish', he let out, 'he must consent!'

At the end of September 1677, the King and Monmouth took a coach to Newmarket to enjoy their customary autumn hunting. On 9 October Monmouth sent a detachment of his Life Guards from there to Harwich to collect William, and escort him to the hunting-lodge; and on returning to London, on the 21st, Charles duly announced the engagement of his nephew of Orange and his niece of York. Protestant England, so long haunted by the dread of a Catholic succession, rejoiced. But the leaders of the Country Party, who saw in William another potential dictator for England's throne, were not so pleased. Nor was fifteen-year-old Princess Mary, who loathed the prospect of life in alien Holland with the cold and unattractive William. It was widely rumoured she was in love with Monmouth. She had fits of hysterics lasting several days. Charles was not in the least put out by that; he bade the bride make haste, lest her Catholic stepmother should bear a son before her. And he gave the same message to William.

It was the night of 4 November, the wedding was over and there stood James's father, by the curtains of the marriage bed, his square-jawed, pale face stark against the jet black of his long periwig, the corners of his broad cynical mouth and pencil-line moustache caught down at the corners by the grooves and folds of his maturity, giving a hearty shout as he flung the traditional stocking : 'Now nephew, to your work, hey ! St George for England !' And somewhere in the background, a first cousin to both the bride and the groom, and painfully aware of his own arranged marriage, was Monmouth. Three days later the new Duchess of York gave birth to a son, Charles, Duke of Cambridge. But (to Protestant relief and joy) the child died. To those who were supporters of neither York nor Monmouth the field now seemed to be open for William and Mary to produce England's heir.

The first positive result of their marriage was that, on New Year's Eve, England signed a joint treaty with Holland, aimed in general at the peace of Europe and, in particular, at security against French aggression in the Netherlands. James was therefore faced with the delicate task of reducing his forces under Louis and building them upon the Dutch side.

He had worked hard in the post of commander-in-chief for four years now. But, as it was only an acting appointment, he decided, in the spring of 1678, that it was time the King granted him the substantive commission. And so, more forcefully, did the Country Party. Trustingly Monmouth sought the advice of York. Predictably, the jealous uncle gave his opinion that the army did not need a general in peacetime, particularly since it was generally accepted that his nephew already enjoyed the authority of the supreme command and that his commission as Captain-Commandant of the Life Guards 'empowered him to command any forces that should be drawn out to quell an insurrection as much as he would had he the commission of general'.[7]

Shaftesbury and the Green Ribbonites were not to be fobbed off with that. James was urged to solicit the father who had never refused him. To York's disgust, Charles readily agreed that a more clearly defined authority was needed, and that his son, having held down the post so successfully and for so long, should hold the rank. So a commission was prepared for James as 'Lord General of all his Majesty's Land Forces'.

Shaftesbury and the others pressed their protégé to try to ensure that on the document the word 'natural' should be omitted before 'son'. But York, who knew all about his nephew's involvement with the Country Party and what the Country Party had in mind for Monmouth, would not let his brother's decision go unqualified. He had recently seen one or two lesser papers with reference to Monmouth, omitting that all-important word 'natural'. He therefore warned the Attorney-General, Sir William Jones, to pay careful attention to the wording of this document. He also passed a note to Sir Joseph Williamson, Principal Secretary of State and a friend of Monmouth's, desiring that 'if my nephew's Commission be not yet signed that you speak with me before you present it to his Majesty'.[8]

At the end of the next meeting of the Privy Council, Sir Joseph duly submitted this controversial document, together with a number of others, for the King's signature. When Charles, always bored by routine work, had laid down his quill, and sauntered into the Privy Garden, York scanned quickly through it and 'found the word "natural" scraped out in all places where it had been writ'.[9] Bitter, tight-lipped, furious, York strode smartly through the doors to the Privy garden, flourishing the offending commission before his brother. Charles replied with a silent smile, half-indulgent, half-cynical, and – 'to appease the Duke of York's anger' – by taking a pair of scissors from his pocket, cutting the document in two and having another prepared to contain the word 'natural'.[10] When York unbraided Williamson for letting James's tampered commission go before the King, the Secretary of State made 'a shuffling, insignificant excuse like one that had nothing to say for himself', so it was clear that Williamson had connived with Monmouth and his secretary, Vernon, and so, indirectly, with Shaftesbury, to have the words cut out.

But, throughout 1678, the new Lord-General's positive side was in far greater evidence than his negative. In Scotland, in the spring, when the Covenanters were in open rebellion, he was busy posting troops across the Border to underpin Lauderdale's garrisons and outposts. But James's heart was secretly with the rebels. When, in March, a delegation of the Scottish nobility gained an interview with the King to complain against the severity of Lauderdale's government, Monmouth was the one at Charles's side to take their part.[11] In particular, as a Scottish landowner, he saw no merit in 'the Bond', whereby all landlords were to bind themselves, their families, servants and tenants not to attend Conventicles or in any way associate with the Covenanters. There was worse trouble brewing for James in that quarter, and, a little over a year later, he was to find himslf more directly involved in the double role of King's general and sympathiser of Lowland rebels.

Now the new Lord-General's primary task was to build up an army to face his old friends, the French. For the Anglo-Dutch treaty of New Year's Eve was followed in March 1678 by a more concrete alliance, the Treaty of Mutual Defence, by which both countries undertook to enforce a peace on France, whereby Louis was to surrender seven fortress towns in the Netherlands, while retaining Franche Comté, Cambrai, Aire and St Omer. Charles had no intention of fighting his 'banker', Louis, if he could possibly avoid it; on the other hand, seeing no gesture from the French King to withdraw Luxembourg's army, he knew as well as Orange that the settlement must be dictated by armed force.

Monmouth had already regrouped the battalions that were serving under the French in a new Anglo-Dutch brigade under Ossory's command, and this formation was now attached to William's army near Brussels. In addition, Charles promised an expeditionary force of 11,000 foot and 1,000 horse, and the spring months saw James, with Williamson, busy levying thirteen new regiments of infantry, three of dragoons and four of cavalry. He was given the use of three Polderland towns as main bases, Ostend, Bruges and Nieuport (which were all very unhealthy and highly vulnerable to attack by the French). During the first few months of the year he was back and forth across the Channel seeing personally to the administrative arrangement,[12] and Henry Coventry wrote that 'the King has left entirely to the Duke of Monmouth's discretion what is best to be done'.[13]

James was appointed commander-in-chief of the expeditionary force, with the competent, if slow and uninspiring, Feversham as his second-in-command; Edward Villiers, Lord Alington and Thomas Dongan as his major-generals; Colonel Legge commanding his artillery; Sir Thomas Armstrong as personal assistant; James Vernon as military secretary; and George Gosfritt* as Paymaster. Late June saw him mustering his army at Hounslow, an army with a new tactical innovation, for James, much impressed by the French Grenadiers, had introduced sections of these soldiers into his own battalions at company level. On 29 June Evelyn had his first glimpse of them: 'a new sort of soldiers called Grenadiers, who were dextrous in flinging hand grenados, every one having a pouch full; they had furr'd caps with coped crownes, like Janizaries, which

---

*The relation of Lucy Barlow, who had known Monmouth during his infancy at Rotterdam.

made them look very fierce, and some had long hoods hanging down behind, as we picture fools'.[14]

Mons was under siege from Luxembourg's army, and Orange was marching south to engage the French and attempt to relieve it. James's tasks were to lift a force of eight battalions into the Allied reserve at Brussels, provide for the defence of the Polderland bases – elements of Luxembourg's army being less than thirty miles away – then to get himself forward to the main allied force, of which he would be lieutenant-general under William for the initial engagement. James had little trouble in selecting his route. Besides the fact that the road to Brussels would make a tiring three-day march, it was unprotected. So he decided to convey his force by the Scheldt, and duly placed an order for a fleet of bilanders, large flat-bottomed wherries, each with the approximate load capacity of an infantry company.

He appears to have run into few difficulties with transport; his chief problems concerned rations, medical facilities, maintaining company strengths and securing the co-operation of local authorities. In the seventeenth century no direct provision was made for rationing troops; they bought their own food, and shelter, too, from their pay, which included subsistence money. For the campaign of 1678 this was carried around in chests by Paymaster Gosfritt and his team. 'Mr Gosfritt is particularly ordered to furnish what money may be thought necessary for providing fresh straw for the soldiers, as often as you shall judge it fit,' Monmouth wrote to Littleton; 'I think it very reasonable what you propose that the poundage be paid by the twopences stopped towards the clothing, that the subsistence be not lessened on that score, nor the officers charged with paying the poundage on their companies . . . For providing shoes and other necessaries for the soldiers, the Paymaster has orders to advance to each corporal such a moderate sum as you shall agree on, which is to be stopped out of the twopences . . .'[15]

As regards rations, although the money reached the soldiers, the bread promised by the authorities in the Spanish Netherlands was not always available. As for first aid and nursing, other than the regimental 'chirurgeons' and their primitive 'medicaments chests' and the rough kindness of a few orderlies, there were no effective medical services, and, particularly in the unhygienic polderland barracks, very little could be done to prevent the spread of typhoid, dysentery and respiratory diseases.

On 28 July the Lord-General left Whitehall steps in the King's barge. On 29 July he boarded the *Cleveland*, sailing to Ostend to take command, and on 30 July 'his Grace upon his arrival took account of the strength of the companies, what stores they had and what treasure (imprest money) there was . . . The companies were many of them weak, the twelve companies there could not make above nine hundred men.'[16] That evening he rode straight on to Nieuport, where he found Colonel Henry Sidney* down with 'the country distemper . . . and several men fallen sick of agues and fevers, which', said Vernon, 'they attribute as much to the cold and damp lodging of the men in barracks as to the moist ill air'. Having personally organised the distribution of the rations, James hurried back to make similar arrangements at Ostend, and there wrote further instructions to Villa Hermosa, Governor of the Spanish Netherlands, and to Herr Lalec, Governor of Sluys, describing exactly how he wanted the bilanders to be divided. In a letter to his father, (addressed, simply, to 'King') he expressed some of his feelings about the value and tactical hazards of the bases, the low premium placed upon them by the Spaniards, and his impression of the Spanish troops:

> . . . I am come to Ostend with my Lord Howard's five companies, four of the Duke's [York's] and a hundred of the Guards, and I believe I shall have the rest of the troops tomorrow night. The Governor . . . makes no great difficulty of receiving any of our men; but the town has those privileges that it is impossible to quarter above 500 men, for the Governor cannot quarter any soldiers upon the burghers, so that I shall be forced to camp the rest . . . The Spaniards that are here . . . are the miserablest creatures that ever I saw, and there is but 400 of them, and that is all the garrison that is in Ostend, except those that I brought . . . I find, Sir, that the Spaniards do not care what becomes of Ostend, or any of the other towns, if Bruges and Nieuport be taken. For Bruges I do believe it is impossible to save it . . . but I am confident if Nieuport should be lost, it would put them into so great a despair that, in spite of anything that I could do, I believe they would open the gates to the King of France. But whatsoever you think of doing for Nieuport, Your Majesty must be pleased to send me more men for Ostend, for I cannot rely upon the men that belong to the garrison; and, besides, I do not think that 2 thousand men is enough to defend this place against so great a force as the King of France has. Whatsoever you do, be pleased to do it quick, for one day lost is a great matter here.
>
> I am your dutiful
> Monmouth.[17]

At dawn next morning he rode to the third base, Bruges, and called a commanders' conference. The deployment of units to

*Regional Commander and Governor of Nieuport Garrison.

embarkation points was no straightforward task, but Monmouth, with his experience six years previously of supervising the Royal English on their Rhine journey, took it in his brisk stride. After dinner with Littleton, he proceeded to Sluys to organise the provision of food for the battalions earmarked for the Allied main army. 'At his coming thither', the report continues, 'his Grace gave orders immediately for the baking of 1400 loaves of a shilling each and provided 32 tunns of beer for the two battalions that were to arrive the next day, which his Grace made them a present of, because they were immediately to embark'.

That night he stayed at the Castle as the guest of Herr Lalec, next morning again satisfied himself on every arrangement, and 'went to see the bilanders and was on board them and marked them out, and ordered beer to be put on board in a readiness'. When the other units arrived he found himself badly let down over rations : 'they arrived about 4 in the afternoon, the Coldstreamers coming first . . . When the King's battalion should have received theirs [bread] there was no more left than 76 loaves, either through the Town Major's neglect or scarcity of corn as he pretended, but it was promised it should be ready next day . . .' Having seen to every logistical detail, given orders for the defence of the bases, and handed over to Sir Samuel Clarke, 'his Grace thought fit he should go before to Brussels to take care for their coming'.

'Quickest is best' appears to have been Monmouth's travelling slogan. With the old warrior Tom Armstrong, who always was closest to him now, James Vernon and two servants, he took coaches across the Isle of Cadsand, then the ferry from Breskens to Flushing, where he boarded an open boat, sailing upstream until the wind and tide failed. He took first a wagon, then another boat on to Antwerp, where, in the middle of the night, he changed to a 'sculler' which got him to Willingbrooke at 2 a.m. and Brussels between 7 and 8. Here a letter awaited him from Orange, explaining what billets were allocated, and telling him that a guard of 400 horse and 100 dragoons, under Count Schalland, were standing by to escort him to the front. Still with no sleep, James spent the day inspecting and marking out quarters for the eight battalions. Then, at first light next morning, 4 August, he was on the Mons road, with his Dutch escort, and 'gained the rear of the army about 10 in the morning'. As the escort approached William's positions, and the soldiers recognised the tall dark figure with the easy, elegant seat, riding next to Schalland's guidon, they are said to have 'welcomed him with a great shout that was observed to strike terror into the enemy'.[18]

Luxembourg was apparently ignorant of the fact that the Peace

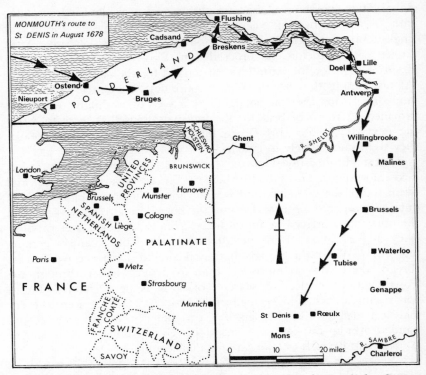

MONMOUTH's route to
St DENIS in August 1678

of Nijmegen had just been signed by Louis, Charles and the States-General. So was Monmouth. Orange, however, had the message in his pocket;[19] but, seeing the relief of Mons as a great opportunity to reclaim some of the military prestige he had lost in recent years, he chose to pretend ignorance, and to attack there and then. Luxembourg's army lay straight opposite him at St Denis 'in a plain between two thick woods . . . the wood on this side of the camp was near two great precipices, and a valley between them'. Luxembourg at his headquarters in the Abbey of St Denis was 'without suspicion', said a Dutch report, 'and . . . mocking when he was told . . . that our battalions were formed to fall upon him'.[20]

Monmouth rode across the front, making his ground appreciation and cantering back to advise Orange, who then ordered simultaneous attacks from both his wings, the Dutch and Spanish under Count Waldeck on the left, and Ossory's Anglo-Dutch brigade on the right. As lieutenant-general, James's next concern was with the artillery, and an eyewitness says he 'directed the planting of three batteries, each of which did great execution on the enemy'. He then joined Waldeck's assault and was 'in person where any action or danger was'. Tom Armstrong, always near him, was wounded three times

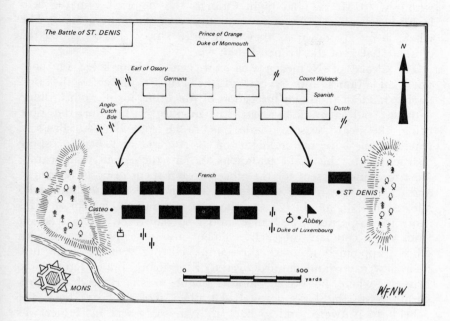

by ricochets, but James went through the hand-to-hand fighting unscathed. Having seen Waldeck's men on to their first objectives, he spurred his charger across to the right flank, where Colonel Douglas, commanding Ossory's vanguard, having just topped the steep-sided valley, 'pushed the enemy through the woods with the loss of 80 men and himself taken prisoner'.

James, following through at the head of the next line, forced the French off their position and occupied it.[21] Based on this newly won feature, the Dutch Foot Guards then went on to take Casteo and its churchyard, which were held by Luxembourg's German contingent. A French counter-attack was stopped by Ossory, but not without 'the loss of the greatest part of his men'. Another eyewitness recounted that, when Monmouth saw a Spanish squadron under Ossory's command fail to pursue a detachment of the broken French counter-attack force, he galloped over with two or three of his staff to give them a lead, but still they faltered. 'The Spaniards for their excuse say they knew not who it was who came to give them orders, and by that means his Grace was near being taken, had he not been advertised of his danger by Capt. Barker . . .'

The battle continued until 11 p.m., by which time Waldeck, on the left, had taken the Abbey, and the French, with both flanks lost, withdrew to Mons. That night Orange, the victor, 'lay in the field in his coach. The Duke of Monmouth lay by it on the ground. The whole army lay down as they were drawn up . . .' So ended the ultimate battle of the Franco-Dutch war.

The Peace of Nijmegen was now general knowledge on both sides, and James and 'several of the Prince's officers with him', having made a thorough inspection of the Mons fortifications, dined with his old comrade-in-arms, Luxembourg.[22] But, for the time being, the peace was a fragile one, so he rode back to Brussels, reaching the city at midnight on 8 August, and began issuing instructions for his eight battalions to join the Allied main camp. Next morning 'he sent for the officers to bid them to be in readiness, and . . . he sent to the Counsel for wagons for the battalions, who allowed him in all thirty'. On the 11th, at Tubise, he paraded his army for inspection by Orange, and next day 'drew out a sergeant from every company of each regiment and sent them before with officers appointed to mark the camp'. Having seen his corps into their new camp and handed over to Feversham, James returned to Brussels, where he stayed another night to superintend the preparations at the base hospital. He then took a boat down the Scheldt to Antwerp, and so back to Windsor where his father was waiting to greet him.

On the day Orange was inspecting the English regiments York was penning him a letter: 'I am glad my nephew the Duke of Monmouth, had the good fortune to be with you. He has done justice to your troops and gives the highest commendation to your Foot Guards and dragoons that can be, and which they deserve.'[23] As for James, his leadership was proclaimed by the English soldiery in a new marching song, beginning:

> . . . The Duke of Monmouth most valiantly
> Rode foremost of our whole army
> And he brought us again where the French did lye
> Fa la, fa la, fa la.
>
> Saying cheer up my hearts of gold
> For in England it ne'er shall be told
> That ever our English boys did fly
> Fa la, fa la, fa la . . .

10

COUNTER-INSURGENCY COMMANDER

The Country Party and the Green Ribbonites were especially delighted to have the Protestant Duke safely home in mid-August, with fresh laurels, but no scratches, on his handsome head, for England now seethed with a melodrama calling strongly for James's presence and leadership.

On the day after James's messenger reached the King from the battlefield of St Denis, Charles was accosted in St James's Park by a young man, who had recently worked in the Royal Chemistry Laboratory, called Christopher Kirkby. As the King strode well ahead of his entourage, Kirkby slipped a note into his hand. 'What is the meaning of this?' the King asked. 'Sire, keep within the company', Kirkby told him 'or you may be shot this moment. A certain Dr Israel Tonge, has disclosed a plot, a Jesuit plot, to take your Majesty's life.' The King ordered Kirkby to fetch Dr Tonge and report with him to his trusted servant, Chiffinch, at Whitehall that evening. Having interviewed the two men, Charles decided the 'plot' was a hoax (probably fabricated by Shaftesbury), and so, ordering Danby to investigate it at his leisure, he proceeded to Windsor where, a few days later, he greeted James home from the war.

But returning to London in September, on his way through to Newmarket with James, he heard that the Puritan Tonge was making more convincing 'Popish discoveries' and had him brought before the Council. It turned out that the original informer was the 27-year-old son of an Anabaptist minister, one Titus Oates, a renegade Catholic, who had gathered – stolen and eavesdropped mostly – his information at the Jesuit colleges of Valladolid, in

Spain, and St Omer, in the Netherlands. Oates was a gross, neckless figure with an immense chin and a low brow, midway between which his flat cold lips now formulated the information of his 'hellish plot' with an ugly, affected drawl. 'The Jesuits have offered to hire me and my friends', he told the Council, 'to ambush and kill the King and the Duke of Monmouth as they drive to Newmarket, so that the Duke of York may ascend the throne, and England be romanised by the Jesuits. The Irish Catholics are to be raised in arms for a French-backed invasion, and the City – for the second time by Catholic torches – will be fired from end to end. By the Pope's orders, sirs', Oates drawled on, 'the Jesuits have entered into negotiations with the Queen's physician and a priest of her household . . .'

The news spread through England with the speed and fury of wildfire. Ever since the reign of Bloody Mary, English men and women had been haunted by the fear of red cardinals and black priests, of totalitarian Catholic rule, and the stakes, racks and thumbscrews that had gone with it. Ever since the Gunpowder Plot they had walked in fear of sudden death and the overthrow of the Parliamentary system. Indeed, they had been warned since childhood to be on their guard against all the things Oates now told them had arrived.

James doubled the escort on his father's coach for their drive north, and, every day they were absent at Newmarket, Oates was pointing his accusing finger at 'papists' – including, for a change, one real Catholic agitator, Edward Coleman, erstwhile secretary to the Duke of York, and now to the Duchess. When Coleman's rooms were searched, and a box found hidden behind the chimney, containing treasonable correspondence (with the Papal Nuncio and the French King's confessor, Père la Chaise), Danby, Louis's implacable enemy, had the Duchess's secretary arrested.

Shaftesbury was delighted to see him locked up for more general and quite different reasons. In a violent speech, made early in 1674, the Earl had claimed that there were 16,000 papists in London ready to take the city by the sword.[1] Coleman's 'treason' seemed to him the strongest indictment of the Duke of York since his conversion to Catholicism. The way would soon be open, thought Shaftesbury, for the exclusion of York from the succession, and the promotion of young Monmouth. Could it be done without blood?

The first blood was spilled in October, the blood of a London magistrate, Sir Edmund Berry Godfrey. It was general knowledge that early in September Oates and his friends had gained an interview with the staunchly Protestant Godfrey and had made their 'papist' depositions to him on oath. On 17 October Godfrey's body was found in a ditch on Primrose Hill, run through with his own sword, with marks of strangulation on his neck and without a speck of dirt on his shoes. The verdict was that he had been throttled to death in Somerset House and his body then conveyed by coach, or on horseback, to Primrose Hill.

Having lain in State until 31 October, the body of the much-loved Godfrey was accompanied by a long, wailing procession to St Martin's-in-the-Fields, where it was buried. A commemorative medal was struck for him; inflammatory sermons and pamphlets poured forth, and a reward of £500 was offered for information about the murderers. It seemed to the authorities that his death was vitally connected with the Popish Plot. The City was deeply shocked; everywhere Protestants went in terror of their lives; a massacre was universally expected; Lady Shaftesbury, on her husband's instructions, carried a pistol in her muff and other women followed her lead; nearly every man who boasted himself a 'Whig', carried a 'Protestant flail', with which to defend himself, a weapon that could be easily hidden in the capacious cross-pockets of the frock coat, while the Protestant mob[2] turned out *en masse* to watch poor Edward Coleman suffer the traitor's death of being hanged, drawn and quartered.

Miles Prance, the Roman Catholic silversmith who was first

accused of the murder, was told he might save his own life by
implicating others. He confessed and named three servants of the
Queen's. A committee of inquiry was immediately convened with
Monmouth as chairman and Clarendon, Ossory and the Clerk of the
Council, Sir Robert Southwell, as members. Having made a tour
of the alleged scenes of the crime and interviewed all the witnesses
personally, 'and taken abundance of pains . . . his Grace returned
to Whitehall, and made a report thereof to his Majesty and the
Council, who were abundantly satisfied therewith'.[3]

But Monmouth's findings were, in fact, almost certainly false.[4]
Prance was blackmailed and turned King's evidence, and it was
widely believed that the Queen's servants were mere scapegoats.
It also transpired that Godfrey had warned Edward Coleman of
Oates's depositions, and when Coleman failed to destroy his letters,
as he had been advised, and was arrested, Godfrey had feared the
worst: 'I believe I shall be the first martyr,' he told one friend.
'I lie under ill circumstances,' he confessed to another; 'some great
men blame me for not having done my duty, and I am threatened
by others, and very great ones, too, for having done too much.'[5]
There was strong circumstantial evidence to support the Tory theory

that he had committed suicide and that Oates's henchmen had drawn a cord round his neck to give the impression of murder – followed by simulated suicide from the victim's sword – and then blamed the 'papists'.[6] However, some of the witnesses had been threatened, and rehearsed for their parts, in such way as to seem convincing enough to James and his court of inquiry.

If Titus Oates was the 'saviour from papism', James, Duke of Monmouth, counter-insurgency chief and commander of the nation's internal security, was the national hero. Having unwittingly gratified the people by finding Catholic perpetrators of Godfrey's death, he issued instructions for the expulsion of all Catholics from the army. Allotting special tasks to the Guards, the train-hands and the city militia, with his usual energy and practical efficiency, he tightened the security of every vulnerable point in London against the threat of Jesuit-trained insurgents; and as Captain-Commandant of the Life Guards, he persuaded his father to let him or one of the other captains 'attend on the King's person on foot, wheresoever he walks, from his rising to his going to bed, immediately next to the King's own person before all others, carrying in his hand an ebony staff or truncheon with a gold head, engraved with his Majesty's cipher and crown . . . near him also attends another principal commissioned officer, with an ebony staff and silver head, who is ready to relieve the captain on all occasions'.[7]

In November, Parliament, while crying for 'papist blood', presented the King with a Bill for placing the militia under their control, only to be told by Charles, using his power of veto, that he 'would not let that command pass out of my hands even for half an hour'. But, on the 25th, when he appealed to the Houses for money to maintain his troops in Flanders, Parliament's answer was that England could not afford them, they must be disbanded. And it was Monmouth, during the last weeks of 1678 and the first of 1679, who took charge of their run-down and discharge.

The young Captain-General was also involved at this time in the concerted effort to remove Charles's anti-French Chief Secretary of State, Danby, the architect of the Anglo-Dutch alliance. For the Country Party (as well as York and Louise de Keroualle, Duchess of Portsmouth, the King's French mistress) was against Danby, while Barillon, the French Ambassador, was instructed to do all in his power to see him toppled. But the man who contrived the downfall was Ralph Montagu, formerly English Ambassador to France, who produced before the Commons a letter written by Danby while Montagu was in Paris, applying to Louis for a pension of £300,000 a year for Charles, who endorsed it. The Commons saw at once that the King was as deeply as ever in league with a papist France.

But Charles could not be guilty; the Chief Minister must take the blame. A Bill of Attainder was duly brought against Danby, and Sunderland succeeded him as Chief Secretary. Montagu was endeavouring, at the same time, to see James advanced. 'Montagu hath proposed France should aid Monmouth in getting him declared Prince of Wales,' Barillon wrote to Louis on 30 January; '. . . the arguments that Montagu used were that a disputed succession in England would be of advantage to France; and that the severities against Roman Catholics in England would cease . . .'[8]

The end of the Cavalier Parliament meant a general election, and the Whigs, many of them James's friends, swept the Kingdom, coming to power for the first time, and claiming to represent the English people more convincingly than 'any other Parliament in our history'. After Danby's setback, York and Monmouth himself were also to suffer. Since the Popish Plot and Coleman's conviction, the King's brother was the most unpopular man in England. The Parliamentary campaign to exclude him from the Succession now began in earnest. Had a free vote been allowed in the Commons at that time, a majority would probably have gone in favour of Monmouth, and one outspoken M.P., Colonel Birch, proposed 'for the happiness of the Kingdom, that the Duke of Monmouth be elected heir there and then'.[9] Colonel Bennet, another who was in Shaftesbury's confidence, put it in a more veiled way: 'There being no time to seek for means in the future, which must be uncertain and distant, and that it would be much surer and more advantageous if the King of England had already a son capable of succeeding him.'[10]

'The Duchess of Monmouth', thought Evelyn, 'is the wisest and craftiest of her sex.' 'She is very assuming and witty,' was Henry Sidney's verdict; 'she governed the Duke [of York], and made him do several things for her husband which he repents of.'[11] York, who blamed James's cold, clever Duchess Anna, for 'putting high pretensions in her husband's head', must have begun to rue his own close friendship with her, for Monmouth was now openly against him. In November the Commons sent up to the Lords a bill for the exclusion of Catholics from Parliament, and the special clause for York's exception was carried in the Upper House by only two, Monmouth abstaining. Embarrassed by this outcome, Charles sent his brother into temporary exile, to Holland, and Protestant England rejoiced.

Before he set sail, the Catholic Duke, now seriously alarmed that he might be debarred from the succession in favour of his nephew, took the precaution of persuading Charles to make a public

announcement that he had never been married to anyone but
Queen Catherine,[12] and on 25 February Sir Thomas Thynne* was
telling Ormonde to 'take care no patent [in respect of Monmouth]
pass now or hereafter, without the word "Natural"; his Royal
Highness is most concerned on the point'.[13]

If the worst card in the Court Party's hand was York, the best
in the Country Party's was Monmouth, who never failed to play
the hero. In January, again with Feversham as deputy, he and his
soldiers saved many lives in fighting the fire that destroyed the
Middle Temple – 'notwithstanding all endeavours by blowing and
engines to quench it'[14] – a fire inevitably attributed to 'papist
incendiaries'. All through the spring he was seen to be very active
with his 'anti-papist' patrols and arms-searching parties. James and
his redcoats were indeed a welcome sight in a city as fearful as
London was then, in a city where an eclipse was melodramatically
associated with 'ghostly victims of the plot' and impending disaster.[15]

The Whigs, jubilant over the exile of the Catholic Duke, pushed
their Protestant Duke ever more confidently to the forefront, while
York, from Brussels, fulminated in letters to 'My Sonne, the Prince
of Orange', like these :

> I cannot now but look on the Monarchy as in great danger, as
> well as his Majesty's person, and that not from Papists, but from
> the Commonwealth party, and some of those that were lately
> brought into the Council that govern the Duke of Monmouth,
> and who make a property of him to ruin our family . . .

> May 29. In all my misfortunes, there is one thing that gives
> me a great deal of ease; it is that his Majesty appears very
> resolute for me and is very unsatisfied with the Duke of
> Monmouth.[16]

Nor did Charles like the new Council. 'Does your father imagine
I left him out because I did not love him?' he asked Lord Bruce;
'he was left out because I do love him . . . God's fish they have
put such a set about me, but they shall know nothing; and this
keep to yourself !'[17] Shaftesbury was the Council's President. James,
who was its senior member, managed to get Halifax elected – and
told Burnet that 'he had as great difficulty in overcoming that as
ever in anything that he studied to bring the King to'.[18] But Reresby
was right when he described Monmouth, in 1679, as 'the man then
in power'. That summer the King gave his son a military command
that brought him to the pinnacle of his authority, while York, to
quote Shaftesbury, 'could dream of nothing but his brother's
crown'.[19]

*Not to be confused with Monmouth's friend, 'Tom o' Ten Thousand'.

11

1679

TO SCOTLAND WITH A VELVET FIST

As Duke of Buccleuch and husband of Anna, James had been a Scottish landowner from the age of fourteen; he was Scotland's Lord High Chamberlain and a member of its Privy Council and, up to the time of his involvement with the Country Party, he had been regarded by ministers of all political persuasions as the most suitable successor to the bombastic Lauderdale. He was kept regularly informed by his Scottish tenants and retainers, as well as by his fellow landowners, about the Viceroy's oppressive administration.

Basically, the Scots wanted total liberty of worship, but a parliament ruled by the Kirk. To Lauderdale this aspiration was tantamount to a bid for freedom from central law and government. Scotland's hatred of Catholicism went at least as deep as England's; ever since the Reformation her habit had been to fight it with Covenants, drawn up and signed by all those who pledged themselves to maintain the Presbyterian doctrines. The Solemn League and Covenant sought independence from the English church, too, for the Covenanters would not accept the English liturgy, and deeply resented the fact that the senior Scottish clergy were appointed from London.

Until now the Convenanters had done little more than simmer and sulk beneath Lauderdale's hammer but, with Monmouth as 'the man in power', and Shaftesbury as Lord President, both holding sway against the conservatives, they took new heart and went into open rebellion. Top members of the Country Party and the Green Ribbon Club were soon in close and clandestine touch with their Scottish counterparts, while Shaftesbury increased the pressure to have Lauderdale removed and Monmouth sent to replace him.

Bishop Burnet recalled how, with York and Danby, who were Lauderdale's 'chief supports', temporarily neutralised and 'the Duke of Hamilton and many others coming up to accuse him . . . the King resolved to let him fall gently and bring all Scotch affairs into the Duke of Monmouth's hands'.[1]

On 8 May, a motion was carried by a large majority in the Commons for Lauderdale's dismissal. Next day, James, sitting among his fellow peers at Westminster, heard his father announce to the House the news of the murder of the vindictive turncoat, James Sharp, who, many years before, had gone to London as Minister of the Crail, and returned, his Presbyterian mask removed, as Archbishop of St Andrews. On 3 May a gang of Covenanters held up his coach on the lonely Fifeshire tract of Magus Muir, a few miles from St Andrews, and, dragging him from the protecting arms of a gallant daughter, hacked him to death with their claymores.

And so, as May went by, James, an anxious Lord-General, heard of a reign of terror building up in the Lowlands, known as 'killing time' and spiralling into widespread revolution. He heard that a field-conventicle, 600-strong, at Drumcrog, near Glasgow, had scattered, in headlong flight, a troop of horse under the command of Captain John Graham, of Claverhouse – the future 'Bonnie Dundee' – an officer who had served as a volunteer under James in the Netherlands.[2] Lord Linlithgow led an expedition of 2,500 to break up the rebel force but, when his reconnaissance parties informed him that their strength had multiplied to 7,000, he retreated to Stirling. So the Covenanters, reckoning they had Scotland to themselves, drew up a manifesto of demands. 'When the news of this came to Court', Burnet remembered, 'duke Lauderdale said it was the effect of the encouragement they had from the King's hearkening to their complaints, whereas all indifferent men thought it was rather to be imputed to his insolence and tyranny.'[3]

On 9 June Charles announced in Council that, as Linlithgow had been warned, 8,000 Covenanters were in open and armed revolt. He wanted no recriminations, only prompt amends. When James's close friend and fellow Green Ribbon Club member, Lord Russell, rose dramatically to his feet, to lay the blame squarely on the hated Lauderdale, the King faced him quickly with the words, 'No, no, sit down, my Lord, this is no place for addresses!' But that did not prevent the liberal Duke of Hamilton insisting that peace could be restored immediately and without bloodshed 'if the government was changed'.

When it was first proposed that a punitive expedition be dispatched, Shaftesbury, hoping to see the Scottish revolution succeed, objected that it was illegal, under the constitution, for

English troops to invade Scotland. But, the moment James was voted to command the expeditionary force, 'Little Sincerity' saw the situation in a quite different light. For might not Monmouth treat with the rebels? And, perhaps, with them, even take Scotland for the Whigs? Then 'all might go forward for the Earl's ambitions'.[4]

At no period in his reign did the King give a subject greater authority than he now gave James, nominating him 'Captain-General of all his Majesty's Forces, already raised as well standing as Militia, with . . . absolute power of bringing together and exercising the said forces, to resist all Invasions, to suppress all Rebellions'.[5] In Brussels, York wrote another sour note 'to my sonne the Prince of Orange . . . I think what may follow upon the Duke of Monmouth's going down thither may be of ill consequence.'[6]

Lauderdale, now in London, had misgivings, too. At the next meeting of the Council, while Charles read out and signed this commission, Monmouth saw the Scottish Viceroy looking across at him, glum and agitated. When the meeting dispersed, Lauderdale, respecter of no man, followed Charles into his bedchamber and gave a caveat:

'Sire, you should rescind that part of the commission which might be used to encourage rebellion in Scotland, and raise another in England . . . if you do not change your orders, and send them positive to fight, and not to treat, the mischief that befell your father, in like case will overtake you.'

'Why did you not argue this in Council?' Charles demanded.

'But Sire,' returned the Viceroy, 'were your enemies not in the room?'[7]

When on 15 May the Commons voted to exclude Lauderdale's patron, York, from the succession, Monmouth's stock went soaring again, while York wrote bitterly to his brother: 'Now is the time to break in upon [your enemies] before they are formed, or have a man to head them, and the only person capable, I think, of that employment (pardon me for naming him) is the Duke of Monmouth . . . I beg your Majesty will have a watchful eye upon his actions . . .'[8]

Monmouth's task was to raise a British field force to complement Linlithgow's army, take command of Scotland's internal security as a whole, seek out and break the rebel force, and restore law and order. Having been obliged, during the previous winter, to disband all troops, with the exception of the Guards, he spent the next hectic days re-mustering his own line regiments, one of horse and one of foot, Albemarle's two line regiments and Feversham's dragoons, and attempting to raise three more for command by Country Party noblemen: Gerard, Grey of Werke, Cavendish, and Russell.[9] Having ordered the Earl of Oxford's Regiment to Berwick, and the Border counties militia to mobilise, and having issued instructions to his deputy, Feversham, James set off from Whitehall at 3 a.m. on 15 June 'not sleeping otherwise than in his coach until he came to Edinburgh, where he arrived on June 18th . . . his presence affording infinite satisfaction'.[10]

That was not to be wondered at, given James's reputation in contrast to Lauderdale's. They thought 'gentle Monmouth' had come to set them free. But there was one snag : Charles, 'making as the Lord Commissioner advised'[11] in the Royal Bedchamber, to the great disappointment of the Covenanters and the Country Party, had sent peremptory orders after the Commander-in-Chief telling him 'not to treat with the rebels, but to fall on them at once'. Thus Shaftesbury saw himself tricked, while James's friends of the Whig nobility, Gerard, Cavendish, Russell, Grey of Werke and Thomas Thynne of Longleat, resigned their commissions,[12] in protest, as they said, because it was illegal for English troops to 'invade' Scotland.

But this did little to tarnish the Lord-General's prestige. With ears echoing to the adulation 'of all the common people of Edinburgh', he was deferentially received at the head of the Council table, but, while his grandiloquent commission was read out, a jealous General Dalyell withdrew as Commander-in-Chief in Scotland, apparently 'refusing to serve under him, and remaining in his lodgings in Edinburgh until his Grace should be superseded'.[13] Meanwhile, Lauderdale, according to one Covenanter source, set a spy on James, to remain near him throughout his time in Scotland 'to see if he could find him trip in any piece of his management'.[14]

With the English force well below strength and several of the Scottish regiments committed to internal security duties in the towns, the Anglo-Scottish army was composed of a high proportion of the Shire Levies, and it amounted to less than 3,000 men.[15] The rebels were encamped near Hamilton, and James had sent orders from London for his army, which he was to join en route, to begin their march in that direction without delay. But, owing to 'the great rains, and that some things for the ammunition and artillery'[16] were not ready in time, its departure was delayed until 17 June. Having, on the 18th, the day of his arrival and reception in Council, assessed the Covenanters' strengths, support and dispositions in the kingdom generally, taken stock of the security arrangements for the major towns, ports and other vital points, and examined what other intelligence was available, James dashed next morning to the camp at Blackburn, where he called a conference and infused the somewhat dispirited and not entirely co-operative Scottish regimental commanders with his zest and optimism.

When he asked for a report on supplies, he found, just as he had found the previous summer in the Netherlands, that rations had been skimped, so next morning the Council received a curt message in the Lord-General's hand: 'The bread is come up, but so much short it will not serve us one day . . . and, therefore, with some sharpness, I urge you to send what you promised, and give orders that your stores be daily sent up to us . . . You may not infinitely prejudge his Majesty's service.'[17] The Council promptly dispatched nineteen cart-loads.

The enemy, who had been reinforced from Galloway with 'near 1,000 horse and foot'[18] and were now 'well over 7,000 strong', had 'posted themselves not unskilfully behind the River Clyde',[19] with defensive positions on the slopes west of Bothwell bridge, a narrow crossing about nine miles east of Glasgow, and a mile or two north-west of Hamilton. Under command of the able, if irresolute, young Robert Hamilton,[20] the rebels had been drilling regularly and diligently, and training with the small arms they had stolen from the Glasgow arsenals.[21] As hill farmers, hunters and cattle robbers, they had no difficulty in filling the ranks of their mounted units, and 'they displayed all the insignia of war, and yielded implicit faith to their preachers, who affirmed that God had at length heard their prayers, and delivered their enemies into their hands'.[22] They were in their clans and did not lack spirited leaders at any level of command.

'I intend to be within a mile of the enemy tomorrow,' James informed the Council from his new leaguer at Muirhead, by Kirk o' Shotts, on 20 June.[23] He had put Major Theophilus Oglethorp* in command of an advance guard with orders to obtain a detailed situation report and to eliminate any subsidiary bridgeheads. In the early hours of the 21st, this detachment pushed the only such bridgehead, a ford near Hamilton, to the west bank of the Clyde, killing its commander, James Cleland, in the process.[24] With muskets primed and matches ready, James's army looked like a procession of pilgrim monks as they topped the ridge east of the Clyde. 'A little before day we saw the enemy kindling their matches a great way off,' wrote James Ure of Shargarton, one of the rebel lairds, recounting his first experience that Sunday.

James's army was less than half the size of his opponents', so he extended his units widely to right and left to make a greater show of strength. He set his spyglass on Bothwell bridge. It was

---

*His substantive commission was as Major to Feversham in the Second (Duke of York's) Troop of the Life Guards.

heavily barricaded with timber and boulders, and guarded by two companies of infantry and a troop of horse. Linlithgow and Mar, the Scottish generals, advised him to cross the Clyde by fords. But the fords were not easy, and James was determined to get his guns over safe and dry. Having often seen the salutary effect of cannon-shot on French and Dutch veterans, he had a shrewd idea that weakly disciplined rebels would not wait for second salvoes, so he rated his superiority in artillery as a cardinal factor in this contest. He was informed that his enemy had only one field-piece. He would silence that soon enough; then his whole army could defile over the narrow stone span in perfect safety. 'The Duke was obstinate', said Creighton (then one of Claverhouse's subalterns), 'and would pass no other way than that of the bridge.'[25] But another report said that 'there was no coming to them [the enemy] but over that bridge.'[26]

James's first moves were to order his advance guard to entrench – 'to cast a little ditch'[27] – on the reverse slope of an eminence lying within musket range of the bridge and to move forward his four field guns into hidden sites under the dragoons' protection. Some shots were then exchanged, resulting in one or two casualties on both sides.

Meanwhile, avoiding Lauderdale's spy, James had secretly sent a messenger '. . . to the rebels' army, to Mr John Welch and Mr David Hume . . . to tell them from him that they might send a petition, and that they might expect good conditions'.[28] So, as he was trotting forward to make his personal reconnaissance and check his artillery's fields of fire, a rebel messenger duly crossed the bridge under a truce flag, asking for 'his Highness the Lord-General'. Would his Grace meet the Covenanter representatives, William Fergusson, laird of Caitloch, and the Presbyterian minister, David Hume, who had a 'supplication' to read? Nodding his assent, James had his drummer beat the parley, and – probably accompanied by Linlithgow, Melville, Vernon, Armstrong and a bodyguard from his own very depleted regiment of horse, under Major Mayn – he rode on down the slope, 'visited the dragoons' post', took careful note of how the bridge was defended, then went to meet Fergusson and Hume, who read their supplication. It ended 'We know you are a patient man, who takes no joy in bloodshed.'[29]

'This is proof enough of my patience,' James returned, 'that I can wait here while you speak this treason against the King. I cannot agree to a single item of your declaration. But I have a better proposal: lay down your arms and accept the King's mercy.'

Hume, the rebel spokesman, looked bitter: 'That would be but to lay our heads upon the block,' he replied.

'Will you own the Rutherglen testimony?' James demanded.

'God forbid. We own the Hamilton testimony. We would have the Kirk established in the same manner as it stood at the King's Restoration, and that every subject be obliged to take the Solemn League and Covenant.'

James waved his arm towards the uniformed ranks of cavalry, musketeers and pikemen, ranged against the heather behind him. 'Take a look at them and change your mind,' he warned.

Hume was not impressed. Thinking numerical superiority in muskets and sabres, coupled with ardent Covenanter faith, meant greater military strength, he gave James a haughty answer : 'See *our* force' – he tossed his head to the side – 'every man of which is prepared to die where he stands for the Covenant.'

'A few minutes'll prove the truth of *that*, if they refuse my offer', promised James; 'you may tell it your leader.'

While Fergusson and Hume rode back to confer with Hamilton, James sent his battery up the rise into fire positions, allotted Oglethorp an extra company (from the Scottish Foot Guards) and ordered him to prepare to assault the bridge. Then he issued a detailed order of march to follow up the assault crossing of the river and a redeployment on the west bank.

Ure of Shargarton remembered that when Robert Hamilton was told of the Duke's surrender offer he gave a caustic laugh, with the dismissive comment 'and hang next'. Yet an hour passed before the delegates returned. James sent Mayn to receive their answer. No, they could accept nothing but the Declaration. 'Well inform them that since they trifle', James replied, 'they shall hear from me in a different way.'

The bulk of the rebel horse was placed on the left of their main army : a few rounds of ball among them, Monmouth, the artillerist, reckoned, and they would turn tail and, with luck, so would the Foot on their heels. He therefore pointed out a second phase position for David Lesley, his Scottish chief gunner. But first there was the bridge to clear. James gave the signal to fire.[30] By chance, as the cannonade began, the rebels' field-piece found its target first, with a direct hit on Lesley's battery. The Royalist gunners were scattered. But, exhorted by Lesley's taunt of 'Would you fleg [fly] from country fellows?'[31] they soon had their weapons in action again, and, putting a few shots among the Covenanter horse, drove them, as James had guessed, out of control and up the hill.

Oglethorp's dragoons and the Scottish Foot Guards won the small-arms duel, too, 'upon which his Grace ordered the said Major to take possession of the bridge'.[32] Too impulsive in their pursuit, the Royalist Scots, under Linlithgow's son, Lord Livingston,[33] were

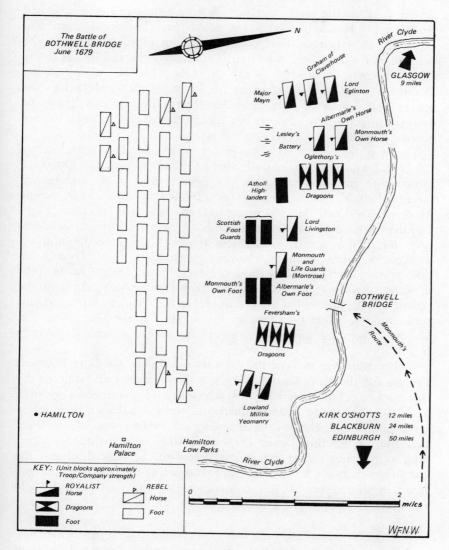

6. The author's impression of the main deployment for the Battle of Bothwell
Bridge, June 1679

driven back to the river; but the enemy's whole bridge guard had
retired on their main body, not to return. Their only gun was
captured, and their muskets pushed well out of range. Led by the
balance of the Scottish Foot Guards, and accompanied by his newly
raised Fourth (Scottish) Troop of Life Guards, under young
Montrose (grandson of the great Montrose), James rode across the
bridge and began to reorganise his little army in two lines, the
infantry in the centre, the cavalry on the flanks and Lesley's battery
on that slope above the river on the right.

The gun teams hauled their pieces, four men to a rope, across
the bridge and 500 yards north along the valley, with the dragoons'
escort, stiff and heavy in their pot helmets and back- and breast-
pieces. Behind them, ready to exploit an advantage, came
Monmouth's Own Horse, under Mayn, and the Scottish Light
Cavalry with pistols primed and scabbards, suspended from shoulder-
belts, flapping against their chargers' flanks. Then came the infantry,
musketeers and pikemen, changing formation from column to
line as they debouched beyond the west bank, their officers, pike
in hand, directing the dressing and pointing the way. And, at the
centre of all, James, hat over one eye in the 'Monmouth cock', his
commander's gorget twinkling at his throat and the Garter Star on
his tunic, sending aides-de-camp in this direction and messengers
in that.

This manoeuvre marked the critical point in the Battle of Bothwell
Bridge, for the Covenanters were not only numerically superior by
three to one but they had the advantage of dominating ground,
and had they made a determined and unified advance they might
have caught the reorganising Royalists off balance and driven them
into the Clyde. But James knew that they lacked that resolution
and, as a senior officer eyewitness described, he now displayed the
battlefield flair, eye for ground, and presence of mind which rendered
him, in the eyes of his contemporaries, an outstanding field
commander :

His Grace, observing that they strengthened their left wing with
design to take advantage of a hollow ground . . . ordered the right
to be strengthened, and . . . 100 Highlanders of the Marquis of
Atholl's regiment to post themselves in that hollow, and the 5
troops of English dragoons were to second them; this was no
sooner done but they advanced upon us at the same time that
his Grace was forming the second line . . . Our Highlanders and
their foot began to fight in the hollow ground . . . At the same
time the cannon fired upon their left, where their strength lay,
and had not fired twice round when the horse began to run;

James, Duke of York, by Sir Godfrey Kneller

ncess Mary of Orange, later Mary II of
gland, after Wissing

Prince William of Orange, later William III,
after Lely.

Opposition leaders: (a) George Villiers, Duke of Buckingham, by Sir Peter Lely;

(b) William Lord Russell, artist unknown

(c) Anthony Ashley Cooper, Earl of Shaftesbury, after J. Greenhill;

(d) Colonel Algernon Sidney, by J. van Egmont

whereupon his Grace ordered Major Oglethorp with the dragoons, Major Mayn and Captain Claverhouse with their troops of horse and the Earl of Eglinton with his troop of volunteers to pursue . . .[34]

The right wing of the Covenanter force withdrew 500 yards to Hamilton Heath, where they made a brief stand. But, as Ralph observed : 'The Duke's cannon, which seem to have been of singular service to him on this day's adventure, again got the better of the [rebels'] bravery'. 'The heat of the business', Newcomb reckoned, 'was over by one o'clock.' Thus, in the space of a little over six days, James had made the jolting coach journey of 400 miles from London to Edinburgh; presided at Lauderdale's divided Council; made many arrangements for the additional security of the Kingdom; assumed command of the field force, twenty miles away, for the last forty-eight hours of its forced march to the Clyde; firmly supervised the supply problems; and then, by deft handling and interplay of the various arms, won a smart victory, driving an army, albeit irregulars, three times the size of his own, from the field in less than twenty minutes encounter battle, and with 'only three or four common soldiers killed'.[35]

Having ordered the cavalry to take up the pursuit, he led his infantry into Hamilton Park, where he found a pair of gallows, 'with a cartful of new ropes at the foot',[36] apparently all ready to string up himself and his commanders. Many of the enemy sought hiding places in the corners of Hamilton Park, and the Convenanter Duchess of Hamilton sent a message 'imploring his Grace not to search in the Park for fear of disturbing the game', a request with which James happily complied.[37] 'The Lord General hath behaved himself with exceeding great conduct and magnanimity,' said the official report,[38] which was endorsed, however grudgingly, by the Duke of Lauderdale. The rebels thought so too :

> The hardy peasant, by oppression driven
> To battle, deemed his cause the cause of Heaven;
> Unskilled in arms, with useless courage stood,
> While gentle Monmouth grieved to shed his blood.[39]

Of the Covenanters' 7,000, 700–800 were killed, and, entirely owing to James's firm insistence that the cavalry avoid bloodshed, as many as 1,200 taken prisoner. He ordered these to be marched to Greyfriars, in Edinburgh, and sent his own surgeons to dress their wounds.[40] Lauderdale, in spite of his suspicions about the Lord-General, received him politely : 'I am very sensible of your extraordinary care, diligence and conduct,' he said,[41] to which James replied, 'I hope it may prove happy for the King both here and in England.'[42]

While the Lowland Yeomanry, hell-bent on revenge, were still in pursuit of Archbishop Sharp's murderers,[43] Edinburgh granted James its Freedom. The city was not slow to appreciate, as Dundee's biographer, Mark Napier said, that 'the Battle of Bothwell Bridge settled the attempt of the Solemn League and Covenant to supersede Magna Carta'. It was no mean achievement, they reckoned, for a man who was just turned thirty. As Bishop Burnet remembered, James was determined to do all in his power to reduce the tension and bitterness in Scotland. 'The Duke of Monmouth sent home the militia, and put the troops under discipline,' he said; 'so that all that country was sensible that he had preserved them from ruin, the very fanatical party confessed that he treated them as gently as possible, considering their madness.'[44] But Burnet was partisan, and Monmouth, gentle, merciful and generous as he was, had, as Lauderdale knew, used the campaign to win hearts for his candidacy. His father was waiting at Windsor to confront him with that charge.[45]

12

ZENITH AND ECLIPSE

Driving southwards across the Border with Tom Armstrong, did James's memory return to stories told at his father's knee, stories of 1651, when Charles, submitting to every humiliating term dictated by Argyle and the Covenanters, had led the Scottish invaders to ignominious defeat at Worcester, before he took flight to repeated exile? James's imagination must often have conjured pictures of those anecdotes. And how often had he heard it said at the Green Ribbon Club's premises, in the King's Head tavern that the Lowlands would make the best base for armed revolt through the three kingdoms? How many of its more hot-headed members were suggesting that, if James had played his cards properly, he would now be marching south at the head of a Scottish army, to overturn his father, to create universal democracy?[1] But, at present, James had not the least intention of heading a revolution; he wished only to lend his name to the 'popular party', get himself officially legitimised and, if possible, declared heir to the throne.

He enjoyed a close bond with Tom Armstrong, and doubtless the younger man would have listened with respect as the veteran prattled on about soldiering and what a triumph the Scottish expedition had been; and speculated as to how James would set about disbanding and posting the regiments; how Shaftesbury was progressing with the Exclusion Bill, and how the King would receive James, considering the lies which had been spread by 'Lauderdale and his creatures'. On 9 July 1679 they were crossing Yorkshire by the old Roman way when Sir John Reresby heard they were coming and offered to be their host at Doncaster. James was so late that Reresby, giving up hope of seeing him, took the room which he had reserved for his celebrated guest. Eventually James woke him up about midnight, and Reresby moved to a less exalted room. 'The Duke came in with Sir Thomas Armstrong,' Reresby recalled, '. . .

and would not have the sheets changed but went into the same bed
. . . Sir Thomas told me that the King had heard some falsehoods
concerning the Duke, and had, in all haste, sent for him out of
Scotland.' Next morning, James, wishing to speed up his journey,
dispensed with his slow vehicle and borrowed the hospitable
Reresby's coach and six.[2]

Clattering at sunset along the grimy track that was the Great
North Road, between the pastures of Edgware and on to the cobbles
of the City, they were met with the smoke of bonfires and the
flash of fireworks, and a great jostling crowd to greet 'the merciful
conqueror'. 'Long live our Protestant prince! God bless your
Highness and the devil take the Pope! A-Monmouth, A-Monmouth,
A-Monmouth!' For, as Sir William Temple said, 'on returning from
Scotland the Duke of Monmouth was greater than ever'.[3] The
voice of the people always rang sweetly in James's ear. But what
of the voices of Council, Court and Parliament, the voices that
decided England's fate? He learned their tenor as soon as he reached
the Cockpit. On 3 July his father, afraid of the Whigs' new-found
strength and their obvious determination to push through the
Exclusion Bill, announced his intention to dissolve Parliament, and
not to call a new one until October. It was the old story, no
Parliament, no vote of money; so Charles was prepared, at a political
price, to be the pensioner of Louis again. The Whigs, knowing the
King's son to be the only man capable of preventing it, prayed he
would return from Scotland before the decision was made. But
they prayed unavailingly.

James made his report at a meeting of the Council at Hampton
Court,[4] then drove on to Windsor. As proud as ever of his able son,
Charles received him with warm congratulations, but the part of
him that was soured by York and Lauderdale could not forbear a
taunt: 'There'd have been no prisoners if I'd been there!'

'I could not kill men in cold blood,' Monmouth recoiled; 'that is
work only for butchers.'[5]

While Charles made a sea voyage, viewing the coastal defences
from Woolwich to Portsmouth, James busied himself posting or
disbanding the regiments. Then, soon after he took his turn as
Gold Stick-in-Waiting to the King, again at Windsor, there came
a dramatic and astonishing turn of events. On 21 August, Charles,
following a programme of tennis, hot rubbing and a walk by the
Thames in the evening chill, went down with a heavy fever. On
the 25th James wrote to the Lord Mayor, that 'it is the opinion of
his physicians that his distemper will turn into a Tertian ague,
but . . . I do not doubt but you will take effectual care for quieting
men's minds'.[6]

The King's condition deteriorated, but he was not too ill to comply with his son's request (doubtless prompted by Shaftesbury) to forbid, 'in express terms', the return of the Duke of York.[7] An apprehensive England read the news-sheets, and waited. What if the King died? 'Good God! What a change would such an accident make,' wrote Henry Savile from Paris; 'the very thought of it frightens me out of my wits'.[8] Shaftesbury, determined to keep York at bay at all costs, was ready for a coup, ready to see James assume his father's mantle, if not his crown, to become 'Protector' if not King; to declare a republic, if not a constitutional monarchy. Was Monmouth ready for it? Of course he was, avowed the Green Ribbonites. Had he not the political support of the Whig leader and Lord President of the Council? Was he not also supreme commander of the armies of both England and Scotland?* Did he not hold the lieutenancies of the East Riding and Staffordshire and governorship of Hull? Were not the Scottish moderates – and also the Covenanters, whom he had crushed – ready to rise in his name against the menace of the 'Catholic Duke'? Would not the English populace shout their willingness to follow Monmouth to the grave, from the moment of his father's last breath?

But there was a powerful middle-of-the-road party, backing neither York nor Monmouth. They were men who, fearful of the prospect of civil war if Charles died, would have preferred to see Mary of Orange acting as regent for her father. And they were quite willing to get York home as prelude to that regency. Their leaders, known as 'the Triumvirate', Essex,† Halifax and Sunderland – in concert with Feversham, who, as Captain of York's troop of the Life Guards, shared, with Monmouth, the duties of Gold Stick[9] – sent a secret request to the King's brother to come home. Needing little persuasion, York arrived at Windsor at 7 a.m. on 2 September.[10] Monmouth, who had been out hunting, could not disguise his annoyance to find his uncle at the Castle, and York remarked that he noticed 'a sort of disorder and disturb'd carriage in him'.[11]

But Monmouth was not the only one who was worried about York's return; others feared that anti-papist rioters and demonstrators would seize control of London. This was Sir William Temple's reaction:

I went to Windsor, and the first man I met was Lord Halifax coming down from Court on foot, and with a face of trouble . . . as soon as he saw me, with hands lifted up two or three times; upon which I stopped, and, alighting, asked what was the matter:

*His command in Scotland was to last until October.
†Essex was also a member of the Green Ribbon Club.

he told me I knew as well as he; that the Duke [York] was come; that everybody was amazed; but where we were, or what would be next, nobody knew . . .[12]

Fortunately for York, he came home at a time relatively free of tension. On 18 July, Wakeman, the Queen's physician, who had been accused of conspiring to murder the King in the Jesuit cause, had been acquitted; Oates's voice grew quieter and, with it, murmurings of the Popish Plot. Ironically, so-called 'Jesuit powder' (the modern quinine) had restored the King to the point of 'eating mutton and partridges', and on 9 September York wrote to Orange: '. . . his Majesty is, God be praised, very well, and has quite recovered his strength.'[13] With the King better, there was no excuse for the Catholic Duke to tarry. But York did not consider it fair, he told Charles, that he should be sent away again, unless the impertinent Monmouth be banished too, *and* deprived of his Lord-Generalship. He would not go, he insisted, unless Monmouth went, too. Sunderland backed York: 'Your Majesty must demonstrate to the Country Party your determination to defend the legal succession.' The King knew that if the Catholic Duke stayed he would be impeached, and that that might rock the Monarchy to the point of capsize.

There was little choice left open to him, and the blow fell swiftly. On the 13th, Charles Hatton told his brother that 'the Duke of Monmouth is turned out of all command and banished the three kingdoms. This day he is gone to Windsor to surrender his patents . . . This news yesterday morning, like gunpowder set on fire, did in an instant run over the whole city to the general amazement of all people.'[14] York could not withhold his pompous satisfaction from William of Orange:

> Though it may make the Duke of Monmouth . . . more popular amongst the ill men, and seditious people, [it] will quite dash his foolish hopes that he so vainly pursued. This his Majesty resolved in, upon it being represented to him that it was not reasonable to leave the Duke of Monmouth here, and send me back again into Flanders . . . As for the Generalship, nobody will have it more. One of the Secretaries, which will be the Earl of Sunderland, is to manage that affair, as M. de Louvois does in France.[15]

But York wrote to his aide, Colóney Legge that 'there is one thing troubles me and puts odd thoughts into my head; it is that all this while his Majesty has never said a word, nor gone about to make a good understanding between me and the Duke of Monmouth, for though it is a thing I shall never seek, yet methinks it is what his Majesty might please'.[16]

The King followed up his action by depriving Shaftesbury of the office of Lord President of the Council, Lord Robartes being later promoted Earl of Radnor to take his place. Tom Armstrong, who loved James like a son, and had long been in the King's bad books, was ostracised. There was more for Charles to hate about that roguish old cavalier, whom he had knighted, than his speaking so loudly for the Exclusion Bill. For not only had Tom partially usurped Charles's paternal role, but he was one of those who had, briefly, shared the royal exile, and knew much more about the true nature of the King's liaison with Lucy Barlow than was good for the throne. Having married a niece of Clarendon's, he was related to York, who also loathed him, and now snubbed him. 'Most of the nobility about town have been at Windsor to congratulate his Royal Highness's return and kiss his hand,' John Verney reported; 'and, amongst the gentlemen, Sir Thomas Armstrong coming to do it, was refused, and the Duke turned off from him'.[17]

Monmouth despondent and unwilling to be an exile, conferred with Shaftesbury and his Green Ribbon friends. They assured him it would not be for long and that the punishment would make a martyr of him, and might help their cause. Given a fortnight to leave, he handed over his command with his usual thoroughness, and instructed deputies to carry on the work of all his other offices. The last letter in *The Book of Entries of the Duke of Monmouth's, when General of the Army*,[18] which can be seen in the Public Record Office, is signed 'Monmo', and, reading it now, one can imagine him sitting at his desk in the Cockpit, overlooking Horse Guards Parade, his soldiering, even in this crisis, utterly absorbing him, his pen hovering over the half-written signature, as Vernon, his devoted secretary through the six years since Maastricht, accosts him from the doorway: 'Your Grace's carriage is ready, and we are late!' When he came to take leave of his father he found him in Arlington Garden, next to St James's Park, and Charles wrote the final order for his departure 'with such pen and ink and paper as the carpenter there at work could furnish him with.'[19]

At five that evening James boarded the royal barge at Whitehall steps and sailed to Greenwich, where he slept on the yacht that would carry him next morning to Holland, the land of his birth and childhood. Thus, within two weeks, James, Duke of Monmouth, K.G., sometime Lord-General of all his Majesty's Land Forces, fell from his zenith into eclipse. Protestant and nonconformist England was staggered and outraged. How long must it be, they asked, *how long*? Nationwide the ballad-singers echoed the remorse in naive verses, addressed to Charles:

> Is *Monmouth* banish't? Must he not stay here?
> Can he, Eclips'd, so quickly disappear?
> Methinks we sink, and our disjoynted State
> Rowles headlong down the precipice of Fate . . .
> *Monmouth*, so truly Loyal to the Throne,
> Wou'd *Atlas*-like, with his strong shoulders bear
> The weight of our declining Hemisphere . . .
> He whom the Scots next to their God and Thee
> Fear'd, and Ador'd, like a new Deity . . .
> Sure, Poysonous Envy did their Breasts invade,
> Who did your Majesty to this persuade;
> You were abused when you banisht thus,
> Him, the delight of your Self and us.

13

RECALCITRANT SON

Monmouth, accompanied by Colonel Roger Langley, the commanding officer of his foot regiment, now made his way to the Hague – to
the house of his father's ambassador, Henry Sidney,* an Exclusionist,
but a favourite of the King's to whom he had been Master of the
Robes. Sidney has left a number of vignettes of James's activity that
autumn; and so has Comte D'Avaux, his French counterpart. Both
diplomats were watching a group of squares on the chessboard of
Europe with growing apprehension. Would the Bill to exclude the
Duke of York from the Succession go through the English Houses
of Parliament, and, if so, in favour of which alternative candidate,
Prince William of Orange, coupled with York's daughter, or their
first cousin, the King's eldest son?

D'Avaux, whose master's only motive in the issue was, through
bribery, to separate the English King from his Parliament, and so
allow him freedom to pursue an independent (or pro-French) policy,
wrote, in his memoirs for 1679, that he 'could not forbear mentioning the connections which the Prince of Orange formed with the
English Members of Parliament, and the views he entertained from
this time of making himself King of England, in prejudice of the
Duke of York'. He went on to describe the suspect liaison between
Orange and Monmouth, and how in his opinion this was 'the
foundation of the revolutions, which afterwards happened in
England . . . Monmouth went to the house of Mr Sidney, which
much displeased the Prince of Orange'.[1]

It displeased William, not because his old comrade-in-arms,
Monmouth, had made himself the enemy of Princess Mary's father,
but because he appeared to be a rival for the English throne, and

---

*Son of the Earl of Leicester, younger brother of the republican Algernon
Sidney and of the Dowager Countess of Sunderland.

Sidney had not made entirely clear in which of the 'Exclusion camps' his interest lay. D'Avaux says that William received James 'very coldly', and that Mary 'contrived to be at play when he entered, and scarce condescended to rise, when he kissed her hand'.

But William could not wait to know where his cousin stood and, when James announced he would leave next day, William 'asked him if he would not dine with him before his departure, and the Duke made answer he intended to do himself that honour'. Then they '. . . went down to Bantheink garden, and having disengaged themselves of Mr Sidney [as James told D'Avaux] he [Monmouth] showed the Prince a letter he had just received from the King of England, in which he assured him always of his friendship and that his exile should not be of long continuance'. When William asked about the nature of his mother's marriage to the King, James gave a guarded reply, with words to the effect that 'it was not thought to be suitable foundation upon which he could claim to be the true heir'.

William went on to say that 'as long as [Monmouth] should maintain such pretensions as were given out, he could not be his friend'. James is thought to have said that what he wanted to see for England was a new commonwealth. William, having satisfied himself on this point, 'they entered into mutual engagements to assist each other with all their interest, and thence was formed that union betwixt these two princes, which gave rise to so many disorders'.[2] Endorsing D'Avaux, Sidney confided that William 'told me a good deal of his conversation; and one particular : that if he thought of the Crown, he could not be his friend in that, but in everything else he would'.[3]

James, whose days had been filled with high responsibility and duty these last ten years, immediately felt his deprivation. He was offered a senior command in the Polish army, then at war with the Turks, and would have liked to accept; but he was now too deeply enmeshed in the English power game. He had to be at Shaftesbury's beck. Sidney remarks that he was 'melancholy' and resentful of the cynical attitude of his father, who, James said, 'told my Lord Oxford, that if he could be well as long as he lived, he cared little what happened afterwards. Since that', he shrugged, 'I had no hopes of him.'[4] Meanwhile, as a temporary compromise, Charles had arranged for York to be superimposed on Lauderdale as Viceroy in Edinburgh and, when James heard that his uncle was coming to the Hague to fetch his Duchess and younger daughter, he withdrew to Utrecht. York, taking leave of William on 9 October, told him that he suspected Sidney 'was too much the Duke of Monmouth's friend'.

On the 29th, the English Ambassador left on a visit to London, and that evening Sunderland told him that if the King had died Monmouth would 'have made great troubles, either setting up for himself, or for a Commonwealth'. On 14 November Sidney had an audience with the King at Hampton Court, where 'Mr Hyde and my Lord of Essex . . . bid me tell the Prince that they are endeavouring to get witnesses to swear the King was married to the Duke of Monmouth's mother'.[5] Tom Armstrong and Robert Ferguson, the Whig pamphleteer, were then in Amsterdam, engrossed with James, on that very project.

They were probably searching for, among other clues, those vital papers, which Charles attempted to seize from Lucy in the mid-1650s. Had somebody kept them all those years in Amsterdam? Ferguson, on Shaftesbury's instructions, was also writing the first of his famous pamphlets, designed to convince the nation that, once the Exclusion Bill was finalised, Monmouth, after his father, would be the best candidate to lead England. Entitled *An Appeal from the Country to the City for the Preservation of his Majesty's person, liberty, property, and the Protestant religion*, it begins with an outline of the Country Party's case, the dangers generally posed by 'papism', and the sinister significance of Charles's deal with the King of France. It then warns of the danger, if the King suddenly died, of what 'will proceed from a confusion and want of some eminent and interested person, whom you may trust to lead you up against the French and Popish army . . . For which purpose no person is fitter than his Grace the Duke of Monmouth, as well for quality, courage and conduct, as for that his life depends upon the same bottom with yours. He will stand by you, and therefore you ought to stand by him. And remember the old rule is *He who hath the worst Title ever makes the best King* . . . Instead of "God and my right", his motto may be "God and my People".'[6]

Shaftesbury was working harder than ever to whip up support for the Exclusion Bill, and to keep the country's abhorrence of 'papism' aflame. On 17 November, ostensibly celebrating the birthday of Queen Elizabeth, 'the Protestant Queen', he organised what was probably the most bizarre political pageant the capital had ever known. At about twilight Londoners were attracted by the tolling of a bell, accompanied by an eerie, brazen voice, calling 'Remember Justice Godfrey! Remember Justice Godfrey!' from the direction of Chancery Lane. There they found a massive crowd, silent and agog at what it saw. Following the herald was a single horse, carrying a stiff and dreadful figure, splashed all over with blood, a replica of the martyr of the Popish Plot – Sir Edmund Berry Godfrey. It was held up by a fiendish-faced, black-cowled priest, and flanked by wind musicians, playing whining dirges.

Next came popish bishops, bloated under luxurious purple, silk and velvet, Jesuits with daggers dripping blood, and behind them a blood-curdling model of the Pope, his devilish face sculptured to make pits of darkness, his eye-sockets staring ahead, his rigid figure swaying with the movements of his open coach. 'Remember Justice Godfrey! Remember Justice Godfrey!' And, standing on the balconies of the Kings Head tavern were Shaftesbury, the Master of Ceremonies, smiling his cat-smile, flanked by Russell, Wharton, Howard of Escrick, Thynne, Wildman and other leading Green Ribbonites. Shaftesbury's message to London was in this vein : 'You are all in imminent danger of bloody papism; if the Duke of York succeeds "Old Rowley", popery and slavery are in store for you; neither freedom of religion nor speech shall be yours, no dissent, no redress of wrongs; but higher taxes and lower wages, dragoons to watch you at every street corner and the Frenchman on your doorstep. Therefore support our candidate, support the Duke of Monmouth with all your hearts and souls.' Well satisfied that this signal had reached London's heart, the Whig leaders stepped down to the street and watched the sinister ritual of pope-burning, the flames' reflections giving their faces a glow to share with the common people.

Shaftesbury's timing was always carefully calculated, and this ceremony of 17 November was the harbinger for a greater sensation. On the 27th James returned to London without leave. He stayed a night with his friend, Captain Godfrey (who had been with him at Maastricht), then went to Hedge Lane. His arrival put London in an uproar. Charles Hatton related :

> Bells in all churches rung all morning incessantly and bonfires presently kindled in several places, and great acclamations in all streets : joyful news to England, the Duke of Monmouth returned ! . . . It is very difficult to express fully the prodigious acclamations of the people, nor can anyone credit them who was not an eye or ear witness . . . Last night there was more bonfires, I am confident, than ever was on any occasion since those for the restoration of his Majesty. I seriously protest I am most confident that there was above 60 betwixt Temple Bar and Charing Cross. The rabble being very numerous stopped all coaches, even my Lord Chancellor's, and would not let him pass till he cried : God bless the Duke of Monmouth ! . . . But, though his Grace was thus triumphantly received by the people, he was not so at Court . . .[7]

James tried to secure an interview with his father through Nell

Gwyn. 'An event has just occurred which would have appeared most extraordinary in any other country,' wrote Barillon to Louis; 'the return of the Duke of Monmouth, who every night sups with Nelly, the courtesan, who has borne the King two children.'[8] Proud to assert her role as 'Protestant whore', Nell 'begged of his Majesty to see him, telling him he was grown wan, pale, lean and long visaged, merely because he was in disfavour, but the King bid her be quiet, for he would not see him'.[9]

Since he must have realised, beyond question, that he would be *persona non grata* at Court, why did James return? His message to Charles was that he wished to clear himself of the 'Protestant Plot', of the charges brought against him by Dangerfield. But that was nothing but a screen. The answer was that James was the central and vital piece in the Country Party's strategy. Shaftesbury knew that Charles would never restore James's command to him while he was committed to the Whigs and their ambitions for him. Monmouth could not play two roles at once, Captain-General *and* rebel chief. At this crucial stage of the Exclusion Bill, the Party might as well have him home in his true colours.

Clearly Dutch William, too, had taken a hand in this political move. Although he was no friend of Shaftesbury, and remained aloof from the Dutch Republicians, *les Messieurs d'Amsterdam*, William sought a position of influence among their counterparts in the Country Party. D'Avaux wrote to Louis that Monmouth 'had brought Sidney into the Prince of Orange's interest . . . this Minister was entirely opposite to the Duke of York . . . I was apprehensive that a protestant league would be formed during Monmouth's residence at the Hague. And upon . . . Monmouth's sudden departure for England . . . I wrote . . . that I strongly suspected this step was concerted with the Prince of Orange.'[10] On the other hand Sidney himself claims that when William heard of James's departure for England he exclaimed, 'It is not fair play considering we were acting together!'[11]

On 29 November Sir Charles Littleton was confiding in Lord Hatton: 'The King sent my Lord Macclesfield to [Monmouth] in the afternoon, to tell him out of great tenderness he gave him till night to be gone; but he stayed, and the bonfires were kindled again all over this part of the town.' Although James was no longer Lord-General, technically he remained the army's senior officer, but Charles now divested him of all authority, Littleton telling in the same letter how the King 'at night sent for Colonel Russell and all the chief officers of the Guards, horse and foot, to command them to receive no orders from the Duke of Monmouth, which as senior colonel before they ought to have done'.

Charles had only one message for his son: to go back whence he came. James refused. The Court Tories were outraged. Treacherous ungrateful bastard! Could any of them sympathise? Not unless they understood the problems of his life. Anna knew those problems, because when her marriage was arranged Charles had assured her mother that James was legitimate. Anna could rationalise, could remind and reassure herself that, although her husband must wear the outward and visible signs of bastardy for expediency's sake, because Lucy Barlow had been 'unsuitable', only he, of all the royal children, was in fact legitimate. That is why she helped to 'put pretensions' in his head. But she was wiser than her husband: too wise to pin her hopes on Shaftesbury and the Country Party.

Until the autumn of 1679 we see only caricatures of Monmouth: his uncle's caricature, which is all vanity, ostentatiousness, insubordination, gullibility and wicked ambition. And the people's caricature of the brave, handsome, skilful general with the laughing eyes and common touch, as busy as the day was long.

But why was he always so busy, why the 'most skittish, leaping gallant' that Pepys ever saw? It astonished Court and country when, on his own initiative, the 'pampered bastard' threw himself feverishly into his military and other duties. But did anyone sense that the ceaseless activity was partly an escape from the truth, an attempt to erase the past, to forget that he had been made to feel ashamed of his mother; and partly to reach the top of the world's ladder, so that being denied the title of Prince of Wales would not hurt so much? What does being a bastard matter, Charles would have argued, considering *he* took such pride in this golden son, who was more handsome and elegant, charming and gallant than any other young man in the three Kingdoms?

That was why, until the autumn of 1679, Monmouth set such great store by his superficial qualities, why he was vain, and given sometimes, to dissolute behaviour, why he was a womaniser. Yet the yearning of his life, always there, was to be recognised as his father's heir. The one passionate statement recorded from his childhood – 'I will kill any man who says my mother was not married to the King!' – rose again in his man's throat, to be stifled, and rechannelled into plotting against his father and uncle; that was why he was so easily enmeshed in the coils of men who dangled before his eyes the prospect of 'legitimacy'.

'The Duke of Monmouth's . . . life depends upon the same bottom with yours,' Ferguson had written in his *Appeal*. There was more truth in that than 'the Plotter' probably saw. Although James had a measure of conceit, although he was addicted to the acclamation of the people, a more important factor was involved. From his innate sense of being 'underprivileged' sprang his liberal sentiments, his championing of the common man. His preoccupation with the lot of officers, soldiers, servants and others that were destitute, wronged, unpaid or maimed, as evinced in his *Book of Entryes*, is readily explained, for he could identify with the needy. How often and how easily must he have seen his autocratic father and uncle through the eyes of Covenanter clergymen, dissenting peasants, republican yeomen, Quaker shopkeepers, mechanics with Leveller green in their hats (or men like Benjamin Harris, the printer, who would soon be locked in the pillory for printing Ferguson's *Appeal*, while the common hangman burned a copy of it at his face, and 'Harris's party holloaed and whooped, and would permit nothing to be thrown at him'). James shared their simplicity, and he was their champion, because he had been placed, like them, beyond the pale: he was at heart a nonconformist and a democrat, the role in which he was now cast.

It was the end of 'Royal' Monmouth. Old Monck's son, the Duke of Albermarle, became Captain-Commandant of the Life Guards, Mulgrave was given the Governorship of Hull and the lieutenancies of the East Riding and Staffordshire, while the Wardenship of the forests went to Chesterfield. All James kept was his Mastership of the Horse, and Chancellorship of Cambridge.

Charles made one last plea, through Sir Stephen Fox, for his son 'to pass beyond the sea'. But James replied with a caustic laugh, that 'it was very strange he should now [thus] be commanded after the loss of all his employments. But if his Majesty pleased to send over the Duchess of Portsmouth, Duke of Lauderdale and Lord Sunderland, which would be as useful to him, he would go in the same yacht, tho' he liked none of their companys.'[12]

Shaftesbury and his friends pinned much faith on the qualities James had displayed as a military commander: courage, energy, humour, buoyancy, a flair for organisation, loyalty, a great capacity to inspire the men he led and the constant will to win. But how many of them wondered if he possessed the necessary moral strength, ruthlessness and personal judgement to fight the Establishment, to make a revolutionary?

On 7 December Mun Verney wrote 'My Lord George, the duke of Monmouth's son being sick, the King give him leave to go to see him, and since his death, the duke has leave to be with the duchess at the Cockpit, so many hope he will come in favour again . . .'[13]

They hoped in vain. Some of the Tory Establishment could only jeer; but others were very sad to see the King's successful soldier-son enticed into the opposition camp. Reflecting their sentiment, John Dryden, the Court poet and Poet Laureate, was soon to write his masterpiece of a Biblical analogy, *Absalom and Achitophel*, in which Monmouth and Shaftesbury have the title roles and Charles is David:

> . . . several Mothers bore
> To Godlike David, several Sons before.
> But since like slaves his bed they did ascend,
> No True Succession could their seed attend.
> Of all this Numerous Progeny was none
> So Beautifull, so brave as Absolon . . .
> Early in Foreign fields he won Renown,
> With Kings and States allied to Israel's Crown:
> In Peace the thoughts of War he could remove
> And seem'd as he were only born for love
> What e'er he did was done with so much ease,
> In him alone, was Natural to please.
> His motions all accompanied with grace;
> And Paradise was opened in his face.
> With secret Joy, indulgent David view'd
> His Youthful image in his son renew'd
> To all his wishes Nothing he deny'd
> And made the Charming *Annabel* his Bride.
> What faults he had (for who from faults is free?)
> His father could not, or he would not see.
> Some warm excesses which the Law forebore
> Were constru'd Youth that purged by boyling o'r . . .

Dryden goes on to describe the setting for the turn in Monmouth's career: the emergence of Shaftesbury (Achitophel) as Whig leader, the rise of Oates and the misery of the Popish plot. And how Shaftesbury sets Monmouth up as the Whig figurehead:

> *Achitophel* still wants a Chief, and none
> Was found so fit as Warlike *Absolon* . . .

Shaftesbury tries to persuade Monmouth that a constitutional monarch's 'limited command, given by the Love of all your Native Land', is a far worthier aspiration than hereditary and arbitrary kinghood:

> If you as Champion of the publique Good,
> Add to their Arms a Chief of Royal Blood;
> What may not *Israel* hope, and what Applause
> Might such a General gain by such a Cause?
> Not barren Praise alone, that Gaudy Flower,

Fair only to the sight, but solid Power :
And nobler is a limited Command,
Given by the Love of all your Native Land,
Than a successive Title, Long and Dark,
Drawn from the Mouldy Rolls of Noah's Ark . . .

Monmouth answers :

. . . what pretence have I
To take up Arms for Publick Liberty?
My father governs with unquestioned Right;
The Faith's Defender, and Mankind's Delight . . .
Why then should I, Encouraging the Bad,
Turn Rebell, and run Popularly mad? . . .
. . . Yet oh that Fate Propitiously Enclin'd
Had raised my Birth, or had debas'd my Mind . . .
. . . I find, I find my mounting Spirits Bold,
And David's Part disdains my Mother's Mold.
Why am I Scanted by a Niggard Birth? . . .

Another voice tells Monmouth he would have gained most power
by siding with his father, and how much happier he might have
been had destiny 'higher placed his birth, or not so high' :

Secure his Person to secure your Cause
They who possess the Prince, possess the Laws.
He said, and this advice above the rest,
With *Absolam's* Mild nature suited best;
Unblam'd of Life (Ambition set aside)
Not stained with Cruelty, nor puft with Pride;
How happy had he been, if Destiny
Had higher plac'd his Birth, or not so high!
His Kingly Vertues might have claim'd a Throne,
And blest all other Countries but his own :
But charming Greatness, since so few refuse;
'Tis juster to lament him, than Accuse . . .

Aptly described by Dryden, Monmouth now sets out to achieve
his revolution by winning the hearts and minds of ordinary people :

Surrounded thus with friends of every sort,
Deluded Absolam forsakes the Court :
Impatient of high hopes, urg'd with renown,
And fir'd with near possession of a Crown :
Th'admiring Croud are dazled with surprise,
And on his goodly person feed their eyes :

His joy conceal'd, he sets himself to show,
On each side bowing popularly low :
His looks, his gestures, and his words he frames,
And with familiar ease repeats their Names.
Thus, formed by Nature, furnish'd out with Arts,
He glides unfelt into their secret hearts :
Then with a kind, compassionating look,
And sighs, bespeaking pity ere he spoak.
Few words he said; but easy those and fit :
More slow than Hybla drops, and far more sweet . . .

Book II

REBEL CHIEF

. . . the first part of [Monmouth's] life was all Sunshine, though the rest was clouded. He was Brave, Generous, Affable and extremely Handsome: Constant in his Friendships, just to his Word, and an utter Enemy to all sort of Cruelty. He was easy in his Nature, and fond of popular Applause, which led him insensibly into all his misfortunes: But whatever might be the hidden Designs of some *working Heads* he embark'd with, his own were noble and chiefly aim'd at the Good of his Country, though he was mistaken in the means to attain it.

JAMES WELWOOD, MD,
Stuart Chronicler,
acquaintance of Monmouth
and afterwards physician
to William III

14

THE CAMPAIGN TO WIN HEARTS

'You must needs hear of the abominable disorders amongst us,' wrote the Dowager Countess of Sunderland to her brother, Robert Sidney, in the Netherlands, on 6 January 1680, 'calling all the women whores and the men rogues in the playhouses, throwing candles and links, calling my Lord Sunderland traitor, but in good company; the Duke, rascal; and all ended in "God bless his Highness the Duke of Monmouth. We will be for him against all the world." '[1]

To the Duke of York, seeing in the dawn of the New Year in Edinburgh, the news from London sounded very bad. As he saw it, the unfortunate King was beset on every side by those clamouring for a Parliament. There were not only the rascal Petitioners, but King Louis, through the Duchess of Portsmouth and Ambassador Barillon, was treating with Shaftesbury, and bribing other Whig malcontents to keep up their troublemaking, so that Charles should be on bad terms with his Parliament and thus continue to be dependent upon France. Lord Danby still languished in the Tower, while Sunderland and Godolphin, whom York had thought to be loyal, had joined the Exclusionists. York himself was now reviled as the popish devil incarnate, while Monmouth was rapturously received exerywhere, and more and more people believed, or wanted to believe, in his legitimacy.

Charles needed his brother at his side, York decided, so he applied for leave to abandon Edinburgh and come to London, and this was granted. The first thing that must be scotched was the veracity given to the marriage ceremony with Lucy Barlow. After all, thought York, clinging to his Catholicism as thought it were his very skin, it could not have been a *valid* union.

He had long been aware of the rumour of a certain 'black box', which was said to contain the marriage certificate, and kept by Dr John Cosin, afterwards Bishop of Durham, and, so many believed, left by him to his son-in-law, Sir Gilbert Gerard, an active member of the Country Party.[2] 'They talk of another successor in a black box,' exclaimed the Yorkist Lord Dartmouth, 'but if that Pandora's box is opened, I hope it will be in my time, and not in that of my children, that I may have the honour of drawing my sword in support of the rightful heir!'[3]

York happened to know that this 'black box' was a myth, and reasoned that if it could be shown up as such Charles's first marriage could be exploded as myth too. So he pressed the King to have the 'black box' investigated. In April Sir Gilbert was duly examined before the Council. He knew 'nothing of any such box, nor had any such box been entrusted to him at any time whatever, nor paper relating to any such matter'.[4] The announcement of Gerard's denial was followed up by cross-examination of various people who had spoken of the marriage,[5] and, when Charles ('the King whose word no man relied on') put out another official statement that he had never been married to anyone except Queen Catherine, York said smugly that 'the Duke of Monmouth can never go about any more to pretend to be Prince of Wales'.[6]

But the Country Party were well aware that the Black Box was simply a hare started by York himself, and that the reason Charles denied the marriage now was that, having swept it under the carpet in the 1650s in order to gain his throne, he felt he must deny it still. He rationalised, too, that his union with Lucy Barlow was not tantamount to a King's marriage. Naturally enough he was very apprehensive about the inquiry. 'The King is, by observation of all about him, extreme uneasy,' wrote Bishop Burnet in a letter of 12 June 1680; 'and has complained, to one or two, of the Duke's [York] being so busy and giving him no rest.'[7]

But York had the tables turned on him by one whom the government spies and constables knew as 'a tall lean man, dark brown hair, a great *Roman* nose, thin jawed, heat in his face, speaks in the Scotch tone, a sharp piercing eye, stoops a little in the shoulders . . . hath a shuffling gait that differs from all, wears a periwig down almost over his eyes'[8] – that is Shaftesbury's chaplain and scribe, Robert Ferguson. 'The Plotter' spent long hours 'in an ale-house in Chancery Lane' penning the Country Party's replies: *A Letter to a Person of Honour Concerning the Black Box* and *A Letter to a Person of Honour Concerning the King's disavowing his having been married to the Duke of Monmouth's Mother*. The purpose of the 'Black Box inquiry', Ferguson argued, had been to ridicule the whole question of the marriage. There was no justice in that. A genuine inquiry of this nature would have been held before Parliament, with witnesses who had some knowledge of the King's life during his exile. Monmouth's mentor, Sir Thomas Armstrong, the old soldier recently deposed from his command in the Life Guards, was one who had been there, and heard that the King's marriage to Lucy had taken place at Liège. He it was who was sitting next to Ferguson in the ale-house parlour as he wrote, and who had the wicks lit as the spring evenings drew in.

There was enough circumstantial evidence to show that the marriage *did* take place, although, of course, in an autocracy such as England's, the King having denied it, witnesses did not think it safe to come forward. Margaret Sambourne, *née* Protheroe, Lucy's aunt, for example, who had possession of some letters written by Charles to Lucy, was still alive, but reticent.[9] There was also the young Walter who was employed at Court at the Restoration, and who 'spoke very broad of his sister having been married to the King'. There was the royal document which Cromwell's agents confiscated from Lucy when she took James to London; and there was the current news that 'Dr Fuller [Bishop of Lincoln] married the King to the Duke of Monmouth's mother . . . and the bed is still shown at Liège where they were first received . . . and Lord Chancellor Hyde being taxed about the marriage of the Queen, as if he designed his own family to the crown, excused himself in the House of Lords, for [Hyde said] the Duke of Monmouth is legitimate'.[10]

The exiles knew the identity of the document which Charles Stuart took such pains to steal from Lucy Barlow: it was the marriage certificate. Most were aware that York exercised a strong hold over his brother. York knew that the King was a secret Catholic. If that secret leaked Charles would be likely to lose his throne. If he compromised York by admitting his marriage to Lucy Barlow, York knew how to avenge himself by blackmail. Robert Ferguson did not specify such details as these; he wrote as though it were common knowledge that Monmouth was legitimate, and went on to inform his *Person of Honour* why it was denied:

It is no surprise seeing the Duke of York hath gotten the ascendant of the King, he should hector him into, or at least extort from him, the aforesaid declaration. For can any imagine that he, who for some time renounced his own wife, and had provided persons to swear a familiarity with her, which made her unworthy of being Duchess of York, should scruple to importune the King to do as much by Mrs Walters, though it were never so demonstrable that he was married to her . . . There are few had better opportunities of being acquainted with this whole affair than my late Lord Chancellor Hyde . . . That very lord, being in danger of an impeachment in parliament, for advising and persuading the King to a marriage with Queen Catherine, excused himself from all sinistrous ends in that affair by affirming that his Majesty had a lawful son of his own by a former marriage, specifying by name the Duke of Monmouth, to succeed to his crown and dignity . . .[11]

Ferguson's letters were soon printed and being passed from hand to hand through every major town in England. 'One of them', said his friend, Zachary Bourn, 'got thrown on his Majesty's hat as he walked on the Tarras Walk at Windsor, and another laid under his pillow.' But it was not the Country Party's policy to prove the marriage now; nor did they expect the King to be pushed into owning James as his legitimate son; the aim was to get the Exclusion Bill passed, *then* prove James's legitimacy and prepare him as heir in the role of constitutional monarch.

Charles's health did not improve. If he died, it would be assumed by the Country Party, of course, that he had been murdered either by York or by the Jesuits. And Shaftesbury claimed to have agents spread throughout London who could raise a rebel army – 'my brisk boys of Wapping,' he called them – within an hour of a sudden succession crisis.

The next move, the Whig leader decided (nursing the possibility of armed insurrection), must be to boost young Monmouth's following in the provinces, and count the rebel heads there. So James began a series of tours, ostensibly sporting and social, actually political and revolutionary. The cover looked fairly authentic, for his outstanding ability as an athlete and horseman had been famous since childhood. It was generally accepted that no one in the whole nation could run faster, jump higher or longer, or ride a race-horse with such skill as the King's eldest son. A decade earlier he had won the jockey's laurels from Tom Thynne. He carried off the international plate at St Germain in 1675, and, in the following year, when 'Lord Montagu sent to the King word that if his Majesty would give his leave, he would, at Newmarket, run every horse in his stable with his Majesty's',[12] it was James who was dispatched to do the riding and prove the Royal flyers triumphant. It would be natural, thought Shaftesbury, to display his prowess to the people.

Monmouth began at the flagrantly anti-papist Sussex town of Chichester, whose citizens spat at the sound of York's name.[13] Based on Up Park, the home of Shaftesbury's young friend, Ford, Lord Grey of Werke, the most turbulent and unstable of the aristocratic revolutionaries of the 1680s, James hunted from nearby Charlton, a famous establishment of venery whose kennels were first established by the Earls of Arundel in Queen Elizabeth's day. Grey's pack was claimed to be the first ever to be entered to fox only and Charlton was one day to be described as 'the Melton Mowbray of its day'.[14] James, who had enjoyed his first Charlton hunting with York in 1674, now founded a foxhound pack of his own there, with Squire Roper, a Whig sympathiser, as huntsman. 'When I am King,' James is said to have announced, in his jocular, self-mocking way, after a particularly good run that ended in a kill, 'I will come and keep my court at Charlton!' His portrait, in the hunt uniform, by Kneller – not, by comparison, a good one – now hangs at Goodwood House.

Chichester's enthusiasm showed James and Shaftesbury what might be done in the prosperous though industrially troublesome, West Country – Somerset, Dorset and Devon – the proud provincial stronghold of the Whig opposition, 'Little Sincerity's' native land, with its mines and woollen trade and its lusty, mostly Nonconformist, people, who were mercilessly and conscientiously punished with fine and whip and prison bars for their dissent, and as consistently protected and encouraged by the Whig gentry and Nonconformist clergy. In the last week of July, James, still a very rich young man (he was busy having a new house built for himself in Soho Square) packed up and loaded his coaches in Hedge Lane. And, 'attended with several of the gentry and nobility', he set off for Bath, where '200 citizens on horseback'[15] waited on the approach road to escort him to their city centre, to the accompaniment of pealing bells and bonfire flames. The father who loved him, however, did not share their joy. 'His Majesty has commanded me to assure you', wrote Jenkins to the Bishop of Bath and Wells, 'that he utterly dislikes the proceedings of the Duke of Monmouth; that he desires his friends not to show him any respect nor to have any commerce with him in this ramble.'[16]

That crisp injunction did nothing to dampen James's receptions. From Bath his coaches and the smart gallants who trotted behind them turned south towards Longleat, near Warminster, the seat of one of his closest friends, Thomas Thynne, Tom o' Ten Thousand, 'the Protestant Squire', Dryden's *Wise Issachar* in *Absolam and Achitophel*:

> The Croud (that still believe their Kings oppress)
> With lifted hands their young *Messiah* bless:

Who now begins his Progress to ordain;
With chariots, horsemen, and a numerous train :
From East to West his Glories he displaies :
And, like the Sun, the promis'd land surveys . . .
Each house receives him as a Guardian God;
And consecrates the Place of his aboad :
But hospitable treats did most Commend
Wise *Issachar*, his wealthy western friend . . .

About the time that Anna was travelling towards Paris with their three surviving children, 'for the recovery of her health',[17] James drove on to White Lackington, near Ilchester, the home of another Whig champion, George Speke. '2,000 persons on horseback' escorted him to the Manor, where there were 'another 20,000 to receive him', and where Speke's railings were broken down 'to enlarge their passage to the house, where his Grace and all this numerous company were entertained in an extraordinary manner'.[18]

James took off his boots to run in heats with the local gladiators; he wrestled with them, vaulted on to their horses to 'make eight furlongs' through the lush August meadows and the poppy- and cornflower-bordered heaths; and, to deafening cheers, he won nearly every time. They taught him the country dances, he showed them some Court steps; he picnicked with them, drinking their cider and their elderberry wine, and chatted and joked with them under the park trees.

They had never seen a member of the royal family before and, although their attitude to Charles and York was ambivalent, they conceived royalty to be the most glorious and awe-inspiring thing in the world. James, Duke of Monmouth, was always for them the apogée of royal glamour, and here with them now *was* this charming hero, the late gallant Lord-General of the Army; here was Monmouth, the King's glamorous son, who slept in palaces with a train of eighty servants; here was the fairy-tale prince stepped down into their world — their craftsmen's, peasants' and tradesmen's world of tiny shacks and half-timbered cottages, whose earthern floors were shared with the livestock — to take their humble fare and wine, to pass the time of day as ordinary folk did, to run barefoot with them between the honeysuckle clumps :

Young Jemmy was a lad
Of Royal birth and breeding,
With every beauty clad,
And every swain exceeding,
A shape and form so wondrous fair,
So charming every part
That every lass upon the green
For Jemmy had a heart.[19]

If those country folk little knew that James's visits were designed as a harbinger of revolution, the great Whig squires with whom he stayed knew it: Tom Thynne and George Speke; Sir John Sydenham, of Brympton D'Eversy, Yeovil; Sir William Strode, of Barrington Court, Ilminster; Edmund Prideaux, of Ford Abbey, Chard; Sir Walter Yonge, of Colyton Great House, Axminster, and, of course, the Earl of Shaftesbury.[20] From the Yonges – with 'God bless the Protestant Duke!' ringing from every thatch and wattle-and-daub village – his cavalcade sauntered on to Exeter, where, says his contemporary biographer, 'he was met by the citizens, and the people of all the adjacent parts to the number of about 20,000 persons. But that which was more remarkable was the appearance of a brave company of brisk stout young men, all clothed in linen waistcoats and drawers. White and harmless, having not so much as a stick in their hands, they were in number about 900 or 1,000.'

Sporting, singing, joking, learning the West Country customs and being adopted so spontaneously as their hero must have given James a strong sense that their ideals were the same as his, that his future was linked with theirs. A thousand men in uniform; that,

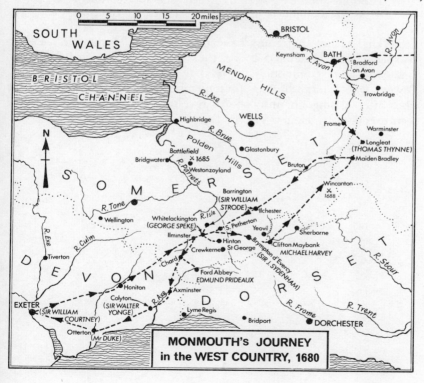

MONMOUTH's JOURNEY
in the WEST COUNTRY, 1680

he might have thought, was two regiments. How many men of the West would follow him if he came to them with a drawn sword? thirty thousand? forty thousand?

There was a particular incident concerning their hero which the people of the West would never forget: while James was George Speke's guest, a girl called Elizabeth Parcet, a victim of scrofula, 'the King's Evil', came forward and touched his hand. Her case had long been regarded as incurable, but within forty-eight hours she was completely recovered.[21] This young prince, they all said, is indeed the heir to England's throne!

'Vain, pretentious bastard!' muttered the London establishment. 'Prince Perkin . . .' On his way back, he took part in the Oxford races, where, following the heady wine of his West Country acclamations, he was sobered by an ignominious finish, prompting this sarcasm from a Court versifier:

> Another man wonne
> Tho' his Grace himself run,
> For he ended too slow, and too fast he begun,
> So his horse over stran'd, turned jade and fell downe,
> As 'tis thought he may do in his course at ye crowne.[22]

'Perkin!' How that must have rankled with Monmouth! Perkin Warbeck, who pretended to be the younger of Edward IV's two sons, who were commonly supposed to have been murdered in the Tower. Did James shudder to remember the fate of the impostor who, after raising an unsuccessful revolt in the West Country, had been executed by Henry VII?

15

THE OXFORD PARLIAMENT

While James had been away Shaftesbury and fourteen other members of the Opposition had the temerity to indict York as a popish recusant and the Duchess of Portsmouth as a 'public nuisance'; and, although Chief Justice Scroggs found an excuse to discharge the jury investigating the bill, Charles, anxious for his brother's safety, after a lapse of two or three months hurried him back to Scotland. James then moved about London openly again, and took his place regularly in the Lords. The London scene was set for the duel between Shaftesbury and Halifax, author of *The Trimmer*. Monmouth was ready for the kill, and, as though to advertise the fact, his coach door wore a new crest: a heart wounded with two arrows, below the three feathers of the Prince of Wales, with angels holding up a scarf on either side (the baton sinister was missing).

James's stock was high. Henry Sidney, home from the Hague, seeing him at the Lord Mayor's Show on 29 October, noted that 'he had great respect shown him', and two days later Ambassador Barillon, wrote to Louis:

> I don't see a person who is not persuaded that the Duke of Monmouth will soon be replaced in all his employments. Mr Montagu* says the Duke of Monmouth at present shows no other design but that of procuring the good and advantage of all the nation by the Duke of York's exclusion. . . . He alleges that once he is re-established at Court, he will advance his affairs, and succeed more easily by the means of parliament, and by keeping himself always united with those who have the greatest credit among the people.[1]

*Ralph Montagu, formerly British ambassador in Paris.

'Let us quickly push through the Exclusion Bill' was Shaftesbury's scheme; 'get popular young Monmouth declared heir, and when the King dies, which must surely be soon, I will govern England for Monmouth.' But Halifax, the pragmatist middle-of-the-road conservative, reasoned with more rational subtlety than that. 'If the Exclusion Bill be passed', was his thinking, 'we shall be faced with the threat of imminent civil war, with the upper classes split, the Catholics and the old-school Cavaliers for York, the yeomen and the City largely divided between the Monmouthites, the Orange faction and the republicans, and the artisan and peasant classes (for what they are worth) for Monmouth. A repetition of the 1640s has to be avoided at all costs. Therefore, since York is so widely regarded as unacceptable, let us substitute the Bill for strict limitations of power on a Catholic monarch, limitations which York could never accept; then, when the King dies, which may be quite soon, we will invite William and Mary in as regents, until her father's death, when Mary can be Queen.'

On 11 November the Exclusion Bill passed its third reading in the Commons with a very clear majority. Four mornings later Shaftesbury, though weaker than ever from illness and old injury, climbed into his coach at Thanet House, Aldersgate, and with his team of link-boys running either side, trundled away to the Lords' debate, his face shrouded by his massive auburn periwig, his hands clutching the rolled parchment that was his speech.

That speech was long and it was petulant; it cried for the King's divorce, and for the rest was all about 'papism's' threat to democracy and the liberty of the people. His fellow peers did not like it. The Whigs wondered if he was still one of them, or whether he had joined the mechanics and merchant-class agitators, or set himself up as a peasant leader. They preferred the no less forceful, but more rational, persuasion of Halifax. Barillon told his master that Monmouth made a good speech, but that when he stressed the current dangers to his father's life Charles, who was listening intently, hissed 'the kiss of Judas!'[2] After ten hours' debate the Lords threw the Bill out by 63 votes to 30. They did more : they condemned 'Little Sincerity's' speech as treasonable and had it burned by the common hangman. 'Lord Halifax', said Reresby, 'was then beheld as the rising man and premier favourite.'[3]

On that momentous night of 15 November the Lords knew, and the Commons, too, that Monmouth and his party could never win their campaign by constitutional means; now it could only be by agitation, coercion and open rebellion. Charles remained deeply afraid of the Exclusionist party. On 29 November, its clamouring drove him to sign the death warrant of the aged Catholic Thomas

Howard, Viscount Stafford, who was accused of attempting to assassinate him in the 'papist' cause. Charles was afraid, too, of the London rabble-rousers, as his father had been in the days of Pym and Hampden. He would have no new Parliament in Whiggist Westminster. He dissolved this Parliament and, to the fury of the Opposition, called a new one for 21 March 1681, to sit at the Court stronghold of Oxford.

Shaftesbury had considered starting a revolt in London during Parliament's absence, but changed his plan at the last minute, telling his friends that an overwhelming show of Whig strength at Oxford would be more profitable. On the 21st James rode in over Magdalen bridge, flanked by Grey of Werke and Tom Armstrong, and hundreds of their faction riding or running behind, many of them with Whig-blue ribbons in their hats, daubed with the slogan 'no slavery, no popery!' Most were well armed, some with the 'Protestant flail', the invention of Stephen College, hater of Charles and York, and beloved leader of London's lower middle class. James, with the Earl of Bedford, his son (James's friend, William, Lord Russell), the Earl of Essex and Lord Lovelace 'and many other lords, kept a public table', Grey – who was sharing quarters with his friend Shaftesbury – remembered, 'to which we every day invited several of the house of commons, and by that means had often opportunities of discoursing with them, without great observation'.[4]

But, although James was now firmly committed to the rebel cause, it was typical of him to find no reason why he should lose his valued Court friends. Writing in the 1730s the old Earl of Ailesbury recalled March 1681, when he was young Lord Bruce, an equerry to the King. Taking a morning off for a ride out of Oxford, he 'met the Duke of Monmouth, with thousands after him, on horseback and on foot, with great cries of joy; my Lord Grey of Wark, since Earl of Tankerville, on his right, and Sir Thomas Armstrong on his left . . . That duke came towards me, and saluted me tenderly, to the great astonishment of those next to him, and I was so to him to almost his very last . . .'[5]

On 24 March, Shaftesbury came, wracked with pain, before the Lords at Oxford. He had a paper, he said which he would show the King. The Marquess of Worcester, Lord-in-Waiting, asked if he might read it. 'The King must see it first,' replied 'Little Sincerity'; 'it is an expedient that will satisfy the people.' Judging from Shaftesbury's smug smile, Worcester thought this was a jest, but carried the paper to Charles, repeating '. . . an expedient that will satisfy the people'. The King read it. Its advice was that Monmouth should be declared successor now.

'Ay, marry!' exclaimed the astonished Charles, 'here's an expedient indeed, if one would trample over all laws of God and men.'

The exchange was loud, and the Lords listened with rapt attention. The man whom Charles had made an earl and nicknamed 'Little Sincerity' came close, with as deep a bow as his aches and illness would allow: 'Sire, will you give me leave to make it as lawful as we can?'

Charles looked back sternly: 'Whoever goes about such things can be no better than knaves. By the grace of God I'll stick to that that is law!'

'The law, Sire, will be on our side,' replied Shaftesbury; 'we will make laws to give legality to a thing so necessary to the quiet of the nation.'

But the King would not be intimidated: 'I'll never yield, my lord,' he promised.[6]

Barillon, who noticed James half listening to the dialogue, wrote to Louis four days later:

The Duke of Monmouth was near enough to hear it, and he was talking in a low tone as if in ridicule of the letter presented by Lord Shaftesbury . . . The friends of the Duke of Monmouth seek to derive advantage from this incident and represent it as a great thing for him that this proposal has been brought before the King of England and publicly advocated by a man so highly thought of [*aussi accrédité*] as Lord Shaftesbury. They say one must not regard as final the answer of his Britannic Majesty, which could not be other than it was . . .'[7]

The Oxford Parliament ended on 28 March with dissolution by the King, who 'went with such haste to Windsor', said Bishop Burnet, 'that it looked as if he was afraid of the crowds that this meeting had brought to Oxford'.[8] Two days later he concluded a new treaty with Louis, securing £400,000, to be spread over the next three years, and further subsidised his capital by expanding the customs revenue. He thus dispensed with Parliaments for good and all. Nor did his rupture with the House of Commons obstruct his attack on intriguers of all colours. He had 'papist' Edward Fitzharris beheaded 'for endeavouring to raise an insurrection', and Lord Howard of Escrick,* one of Shaftesbury's fellow plotters (a man who was to prove treacherous to Monmouth's clique as well as to the Court) locked in the Tower on a charge of high treason. And, on the pretext that Shaftesbury had attempted to suborn

*William, 3rd Baron, who had inherited from his brother Thomas, one of Monmouth's commanders in the 1678 campaign, who died in Flanders that year.

The bas-relief memorial, commemorating his murder in 1682, to Thomas
Thynne, in Westminster Abbey

Robert Spencer, Earl of Sunderland,
after the portrait by Johannes Mytems

The Marquess of Halifax, *c.* 1675, attributed to
Mary Beale

King's Men: (a) Louis Duras, Marquis of Blanque-fort, afterwards Earl of Feversham, by J. Riley;

(b) Judge Jeffreys, attributed to W. Claret

(c) 1st Duke of Lauderdale, by J. Huysmans;

(d) Christopher Monk, Duke of Albemarle, artist unknown

some Irish witnesses in the Popish Plot, he ordered the Earl's rooms at Thanet House to be searched early one morning when he was still asleep, and there found a number of seditious Party papers.[9]

Having seen 'Little Sincerity' into the Tower, the King turned his attention to the mob. He knew who their strong man was: the clever, fearless 'Protestant Joiner', Stephen College, who, when told by a fellow plotter that the nation's troubles would soon be over once the Exclusion Bill was passed, replied 'No, no, now you are mistaken, for Rowley is as great a papist as the Duke of York is, and every way as dangerous to the Protestant interest.' The man College so disrespectfully referred to as 'Rowley' now arrested him on a charge of writing treasonable ballads and of conspiring to overthrow the Parliament at Oxford. When the Whig jury, in London, quilled 'ignoramus' on the indictment, Charles, on the pretext that College should be tried where his principal 'crime' was committed, had him rowed up river to Kingston, put under guard of a troop of cavalry, and hustled to Oxford. Here the implacable Judge Jeffreys was waiting for him – to condemn him on the hearsay evidence of an obscure Irishman and ex-Catholic priest. 'This is a horrid conspiracy', cried College, 'not only against my life but against all the Protestants of England!'

'The Protestant Joiner's' last words were repeated with tears and horror through the nation. 'Where is my dear son that I may kiss him?' Then, 'Dear people, dear Protestants, dear countrymen . . . the occasion of my coming to Oxford, I do say, was voluntary . . . the Duke of Monmouth called me to him, and told me he had heard a good report of me, and that I was an honest man, and one that was to be trusted, and . . . with several Lords and Commons, did desire me to use my utmost skill in searching all places suspected [by the Country Party], which I did perform, and from thence I had, as I think, the popular name of the Protestant Joiner, because they had entrusted me before any man to do that office . . . My friends, I am innocent of treason!'

Then College was pushed away in the shimmering August heat to be hanged, drawn and quartered.[10] When Charles gave permission for College's quarters to be buried, not hung on the London railings, he slighted the favour, saying, 'I care not whether I am eaten up by flies or worms.'[11] That same month Titus Oates was forbidden to come to Court and his weekly allowance was stopped. So far as Charles was concerned the Popish Plot was over. Soon, he reckoned, the rebel son, whom he so badly wanted back at Court, would have no springboard for rebellion.

Court and Tories followed up their cruel triumph over 'the Protestant Joiner' by bringing 'the Protestant Lord' to the Old

Bailey. But London's Sheriffs procured a picked jury for Shaftesbury, 'ignoramus' (the Whigs' favourite word for Tory charges) being emphatically penned across the indictment. Bail was granted, and to the King's great annoyance Monmouth stood surety. Shaftesbury was unanimously hated in Court circles. The Earl of Ailesbury was said by his son, Lord Bruce, to have been approached repeatedly by 'Little Sincerity' and his friends with a view to securing his support for the Exclusion Bill and the Country Party, but Ailesbury 'had nothing to say to them on a subject so odious to him, and he . . . was quit of them all, save the Duke of Monmouth, who was ever to us both a noble and good friend'.[12]

16

1681–1682

UNDER ARREST

While College suffered under Jeffrey's stinging tongue before the intestines were drawn from his still living body at Oxford; while York imposed his inflexible discipline with the dreadful 'boot' and thumbscrew at Edinburgh; while 'Little Sincerity' played endless games of piquet with his Countess in the Tower, William of Orange was on a visit to Windsor, trying to persuade his uncle Charles to call a new Parliament, which, he knew, would in its turn shout again for the disinheritance of York. And Monmouth, who had returned from racing his horses in the south Midlands, pursued his role of winning hearts, this time accompanied by Tom Armstrong, Ralph Montagu and Lords Grey and Herbert, in 'the Garden of England'. He centred himself on Tunbridge Wells, 'the rallying-point', as Anthony Hamilton called it, 'when the time comes to take the waters, of all that is fairest and most gallant in both sexes'.[1]

It was a place very much after James's heart, and so was his reception. 'An incredible number of people', gushes the *Heroick Life*, 'came from all the adjacent places, and rudely crowded after their rustic manner, to see the eldest son of their King and Sovereign, everyone extolling him to the skies, crying one to another, Oh what a brave man he is!' After a month of meeting as many country folk as he could, under the guise of hunting, taking the waters, playing bowls and generally disporting himself, he journeyed home, via Riverhead, where his friends 'drank his Grace's health, commending him to the protection of Heaven'.[2]

He needed that protection. Secretary Jenkins's spies, who had dogged his steps in Kent, soon reported him in and out of London, down to Chichester and back again by 17 November, to London – for the festivities centred on the burning of the Pope's Effigy 'where the rabble all the while drank healths to the King and the Duke of Monmouth conjunctively'.[3]

Two days before those festivities, James's West Country host, Tom Thynne, of Longleat, 'the Protestant Squire' was married to a beautiful and very rich widow, Elizabeth, Countess of Ogle, a daughter of the Earl of Northumberland. But because the girl was as unfaithful as she was unstable, the marriage was to be short-lived. Lady Elizabeth Thynne eloped with an unscrupulous young Swedish adventurer called Count Königsmark. And, on account of this scandal and the violence that followed it, James was to lose one of the firmest friends and most influential supporters he had. He and Tom Thynne (who had been removed from his command of the Wiltshire Militia for his Country Party sympathies) used to spend hours in political discussion.

Perhaps the chief problem they spoke of as they drove round Hyde Park in Thynne's coach on the evening of 12 February 1682 was Thynne's marital tragedy. As it was getting dark Thynne dropped Monmouth off in Hedge Lane (where Trafalgar Square now is), and continued his journey with a round of City visits. An hour later, when he was half-way up St James's Street – just short of what is now Piccadilly, then known as the Road to Reading – three horsemen trotted from the shadows, held up the coach and shot point-blank at Thynne, 'mortally wounding him with five shots from blunderbusses'.

James, who was first to be told of the murder, and first at his friend's bedside, immediately sent his coach and page to fetch Sir John Reresby, the Yorkshire squire who had entertained him on his return from the Scottish campaign in 1679, and who was now the most efficient man with powers of arrest he could think of. James's and Reresby's forthright inquiries led them to a Swede, who, in Reresby's words, 'being brought before me, confessed himself servant to a German captain, who told him he had a quarrel with Mr Thynne'.[4] The German was duly arrested in bed (his sword being 'some distance from him on the table'). During the investigation Reresby was summoned by a messenger from the King, who examined the prisoners himself. It transpired that the man behind it all was young Count Königsmark, then a student of Monsieur Foubert's academy in London. A servant of Monmouth's arrested him as he was making his escape, at Gravesend, and escorted him to London, where he appeared before King and Council. Reresby, who was in attendance, observed that Königsmark 'appeared before the King with all the assurance imaginable. He was a fine person of a man, and I think his hair was the longest I ever saw . . . Being at the King's couchee on the 21st, I perceived that he was willing the Count should get off . . .'

While Königsmark, the instigator of the murder, went free, 'the

captain and the other two were, pursuant to their sentence, hanged
in the street where they perpetrated their crime', as Reresby and
James witnessed on 10 March. Thynne's widow soon married again,
not Königsmark but the 'proud' Duke of Somerset – and twenty
years later, was to be famous as the successor to Marlborough's
duchess Sarah, in the role of Mistress of the Robes to Queen Anne.
As for Monmouth, he would mourn the loss of the 'Protestant
Squire', for practical as well as personal reasons, to his dying day.

March 1682 was indeed a grim month for James. By the time
he attended Thynne's funeral at Westminster Abbey he had been
humiliated by an open message from his father to 'keep a respectful
distance from the Court', and had witnessed the return from
Scotland of the uncle who had engineered his fall and disgrace.
Through York, James had already, in 1681, lost his Mastership of
the Horse to the Duke of Richmond, And now one of the first
actions the Catholic Duke took on reaching London was to persuade
the King to deprive his son of the Chancellorship of Cambridge and
bestow it on Albemarle.

On 21 April, when the Artillery Company invited York, as their
honorary Captain-General, to a dinner, the Whigs planned a rival
celebration for the Protestant Duke, but 'this sociable meeting being
misrepresented to his Majesty, he was pleased to forbid the same'.[5]
The harsh wedge between his father and himself was hammered in
again when James, at his most tactless, approached Lord Halifax
in the entrance to St-Martin's-in-the-Fields : 'My lord, I have heard
you moved the King in Council for a proclamation to forbid all
persons keeping me company?'

'Pray, who told your Grace I had done so?' asked the 'Trimmer',
indignantly.

'I cannot say that, my lord.'

'Then since your Grace is upon those terms I do not think fit to
tell your Grace whether I made such a notion or no . . .' The two
men were on the verge of a duel before Halifax turned on his
heel and strode away.

The King was so angry when he heard that his son had
impudently, and in such place, questioned Halifax, on a point
arising in the sacrosanct Privy Council, that he issued the
order that 'no person whatsoever having relation to my service
shall henceforth have any communion with the Duke of Monmouth'.[6]

York 'having left his Duchess in Scotland big with child, returned
thither again in May'. His frigate struck a sandbank, several of the
crew being drowned in the wreck. But the Yorks reached London
safely, and when Shaftesbury noticed how friendly the Duchess was

with Anna he feared a reconciliation between the two Dukes, which he took steps to prevent.

His recently drafted manifesto, *An Agreement with the People*, was, according to the rebel Robert West, designed to 're-cast the nation's political life'. The enfranchised classes, which were to be broadly extended, would virtually govern the country; the electorate would go annually to the polls to choose their M.P.s; Parliament would never, except by their own consent, be prorogued, or dissolved; the House of Lords would contain a fair proportion of life peers elevated from the Commons; Parliament would have the nomination, if not the election, of all judges, sheriffs and Justices of the Peace; Acts, passed by the Houses, would become law without the monarch's consent; and the Privy Council would be composed partly of Lords elected by M.P.s and partly of M.P.s elected by the Lords. The 'stranglehold of Crown and Church on the Country' would be removed.[7] Reigning over this system – if it was not acceptable to Charles – would be James, Duke of Monmouth, as 'James II', England's first constitutional monarch, 'at heart a true democrat', it was claimed, 'a peoples' prince'.

But the King had hardened his line so severely that all this would now be possible, only as the Whigs acknowledged, through armed insurrection. Steering his course of absolutism, James's father set about to destroy their hold on local government, and, with his bullying tactics, resolved to remove their popular control of the boroughs through quo warrantos. By various manipulations he had a Tory Lord Mayor and sheriffs appointed for a London that was predominantly Whig. Supported by his royal master, the new Mayor, Sir John Moore, issued a write of quo warranto calling on the citizens to show by what right they held their liberties and franchises, and then proceeded to confiscate them; new regulations were issued giving the Monarch a veto over their choices. Quo warrantos were then extended throughout the nation, and so the Court and the Tories gained absolute rule. Religious dissent implied political dissent. James's father tightened the curbs on Nonconformists: 'Laws are to be put in execution against Dissenters,' ran the typical message of a newsletter; 'Sir George Jeffreys has ordered that next Sunday the constables are to fall on meeting-places with all severity.'[8]

The Whigs and Nonconformists groaned, saying that the new Recorder of London, the odious Tory Jeffreys, was an instrument of popery and slavery! Bloody Jeffreys, murderer of good Stephen College! For all Charles II's pledges at the Restoration, they reckoned, his appetite for totalitarian government is at least as greedy as Charles I's. And his heir? York was an avowed papist who would trample the people more cruelly still. Who would save them? James of Monmouth, a body of them insisted – 'the Protestant Duke', a kind and liberal prince, and a proven commander, too; he would save them.

But could Monmouth lead them through the testing endeavour of revolution? the Whig militants asked. In his love-hate relation-ship with his father, which passion held greater sway? What portion of his heart remained at Court? Might he not be prevailed upon by Lord Halifax and others to be reconciled with his father again? Might he not soon appreciate that his role as commander-in-chief and principal courtier in 1679 carried far greater prestige than the applause of all the crowds in the world? Knowing how urgently his father wanted him back again, they wondered, might he not go to him with bended knee and lowered head and the words 'Father, I have sinned against Heaven and before thee, forgive me and take me back to thy house'?

On the other hand Monmouth had never been known to let down his friends. He was sincere, brave, quick-witted, stimulating, of splendid presence. But they knew how weak he was over many things; he was too gullible, too easily influenced by flatterers . . . and he was very vain. How he glowed, they remembered, on his tours of Sussex, Kent, and the West Country. The people's adulation was for him as nectar is to the Gods. And they would not forget for a moment that he was the King's son. After all, it might have been expedient *to kill the King* as well as York. . . .

And there were others – republicans – who wanted no princes at all. But the Monmouthites soothed them. Rest assured, they said, because, before he sits on the throne, we shall pinion him more closely than the Doge of Venice.

'The King's son is coming! The King's son is coming! A-Monmouth, A-Monmouth!'

In September 1682, Monmouth, his hat tilted rakishly, was in the Whiggish north-west Midlands now. As he approached each town he quitted his coach and rode in, his friends riding ahead of him and, 'at a distance behind him, the servants and tenants . . . He gave orders for 200 covers to be prepared wherever he dined.'⁹ People went down on their knees to salute him with 'God bless our Protestant Prince!' as he led his cavalcade into their towns. They lit their bonfires and broke the church doors to get at the bells; they crowded into their upper windows and on to their rooftops and balconies for a glimpse of him. And they went to watch him dine, when 'two doors were thrown open, that the populace might see him enter at the one, walking round the table to see their favourite, and giving place to those who followed them, by going out at the other'.

But he did not have it quite his own way this time. At Lichfield some Court party supporters had hired a room next to his own and were shouting him down and drinking York's health 'to the accompaniment of fiddles and horns', while a large band of influential Tories gathered in Delamere Forest, in case of any 'ill attempts'. Yet the loudest cry was still 'A-Monmouth, A-Monmouth!' At Liverpool he touched for the King's Evil and was made a Freeman of the City; at Wallasey people gathered in their roaring thousands to watch him spur his fastest racehorse first past the winning-post – 'to the inexpressible grief of his enemies', says the *Heroick Life* – and win £60 and the 12-stone silver-gilt Plate, '. . . which he was pleased to bestow on the Mayor of Chester's daughter, for whom he had stood godfather, and to whom he had given the name of his illustrious grandmother, Henrietta'.

He ran foot-races, too, as he had done in the south-west, and 'as he was of wonderful agility . . . when he had outstripped the swiftest of the racers, he ran again in his boots, and beat them, though running in their shoes'.[10] At Chester, where he stayed at the 'Feathers', 'nothing was heard in the streets but "A-Monmouth, A-Monmouth" '.[11] At Nantwich an old peasant woman kissed his knee, with 'god in Heaven bless you; you're so like your father, I'm sure, you're no bastard!' And, at Gawsworth Hall, young Lord Brandon held his stirrup-iron, subserviently, as he mounted his horse, looked up and swore, 'By God you shall be King!'[12] Lords Rivers, Delamere and Macclesfield,* and the ancestor of the Dukes of Sutherland, William Leveson-Gower, all had him to stay, while the Whig squirearchy as a whole pledged their support.

This was what James had come for: to see whether Cheshire and Staffordshire were prepared to rise for him. 'Tell Cheshire to stand up to take up arms,' impatient Shaftesbury had urged him; 'then fly to the West Country, to Taunton, and raise your standard there. And once you are there in arms I shall be at the head of my Wapping brisk boys!'

But James, even if he was one day to lose it, now kept his *sens du practicable*.[13] First he had to know if the north-western Whigs were ready. So, while the corn-sheaves were drying and the apples ripening on their Cheshire estates, Rivers and Macclesfield, Brandon and Delamere, Leveson-Gower and a score of other west Midland squires were sitting round banqueting-hall tables listening to James's situation report and his stream of questions: The rebels in London

---

*Formerly Lord Gerard of Brandon, whom Monmouth succeeded as Captain-Commandant of the Life Guards in 1668.

and the West were nearly ready, the Scots were well ahead with their preparations, his own following in Kent and Sussex was assured. How many would follow them? What arms and ammunition could they provide? What were their plans to seize the arsenals and the strong-points? Who were the most dangerous Tories and what were their plans for arresting them? What areas could they be certain of holding? How large would be their mobile column to link up with our army in London? . . . And pondering on their answers, he decided that Britain was *not* ready for the *coup*.

At Whitehall Jenkins read the news-sheets, then listened, with grave concern, to his spies' accounts of Monmouth's public receptions. The King, about to leave for the autumn racing at Newmarket, saw the shaming broadsheets, heard Jenkins's collated report and shook his head with sorrow and anger: his son's tour was nothing less than incitement to national rebellion. It must be stopped.

On 20 September James was walking the streets of Stafford when Ramsey, one of the Sergeants-at-Arms, came to arrest him. James spoke quickly to Tom Armstrong: He ordered him to ride to London for a habeas corpus, and to meet him with it as he was escorted south.

17

1682

A COUP D'ÉTAT
IS PLANNED

'The Duke of Monmouth is bailed,' one high Tory told another[1] on 26 September. But 'the King, by the vice-Chamberlain's letter, has forbid him coming into the Park, or any part of Whitehall, as well as when his Majesty is out of town as in it. The King is very angry with him, and resolved to take every way to undeceive the world that think he is not . . .'

James was *persona non grata*, too, with Shaftesbury, whose opinion it was that, instead of allowing himself to be arrested at Stafford, the Protestant Duke should then and there 'have set up his standard and declared for a free parliament'.[2] As soon as he heard of the arrest, Shaftesbury buttonholed his young friend, Lord Grey. 'The Duke of Monmouth is an unfortunate man,' he told him, 'for God has thrice put it into his power to save England, and make himself the greatest man in Europe, but he has neglected the use of all those opportunities; one was in Scotland, when he was general, the other in the West, and now in Cheshire.'[3]

On the contrary, it was demonstrably clear that James would have been most ill-advised had he attempted a revolt in any of those situations. Only the extremists supported Shaftesbury on that score. As regards Cheshire, Robert West, a barrister of the Middle Temple, conceded that 'his Grace followed the wiser dictates of his own prudence [when he] surrendered himself into the hands of justice'.[4]

Afraid of another stint in the Tower, Shaftesbury, wrapped up to his eyes in a cloak, crept out of Thanet House, Aldersgate, in September, and went into hiding in Wapping, close to his rank-and-file henchmen. Riddled with gout, and growing still more ill, he must have known he had little time to live. Bitter at the frustrating of his revolutionary aspirations, he now made the task of sinking the royal brothers and 'saving England' a matter of the direst urgency. 'The turbulent lord worked night and day to put the nation in a flame, and to raise a rebellion,' as Lord Bruce recalled. '. . . I know the Duke of Monmouth reproached him, saying his hot head and airy notions would be the ruin of them all.'⁵ By a subterfuge the Earl tried to steer James back to Cheshire, there to begin the national revolt. He accosted Grey of Werke again. 'My Lord Grey, if you wish well to the Duke of Monmouth, to the Protestant interest, to yourself and all of us that are concerned, you must cheat [him] this time, and tell him it is the advice of my Lord Russell, myself and all his friends in the City, that he go back into Cheshire; nothing but that can save England . . .'

Misjudging, in his derangement, the conditions necessary for a successful *coup d'état*, 'Little Sincerity' thought it only required a few men with great names, such as Monmouth, Essex, Russell and himself, to go out into the streets, lift their swords, and shout 'In the name of liberty – *now* !' for stout companies of 'brisk boys', who were discontented men, to rise all over the country to topple King and government. As Bishop Burnet wrote : '. . . the Earl of Shaftesbury . . . believed the first appearance of the least disorder would have prevailed on the King to yield everything. But the Duke of Monmouth, who understood what a rabble was and what troops were, looked on this as a mad exposing of themselves and their friends.'⁶

The result of all this was a fatal division, Shaftesbury throwing in his lot largely with the republican element. '. . . Any other design but a Commonwealth would not go down with my people now,' was his opinion. Among the lower-rank rebels were Lieutenant-Colonel Thomas Walcot, a loud-mouthed and ruthless Irishman, who had helped to guard James's grandfather at the scaffold; Colonel John Rumsey, another Cromwellian officer, who was now a tax-collector at Bristol; Nathaniel Wade, also a Bristol man, a lawyer and Whig politician; Wade's friend, James Holloway; Robert West, the Middle Temple barrister, an atheist and a close student of Machiavelli; Richard Nelthorp, another barrister; and Richard Goodenough, 'one of the late popular under-sheriffs of London'.

Then there was Major John Wildman, 'one of Cromwell's majors, a bold and desperate fellow'; William Hone, a joiner; John Rouse, a servant of Whig Sir Thomas Player; Thomas Sheppard, a rich merchant, unswerving Nonconformist and disciple of Robert Ferguson's; John Ayloffe, a lawyer (who had distinguished himself by planting a French wooden shoe on the Speaker's Chair of the

House of Commons); Aaron Smith, a solicitor, who had helped prepare Stephen College's defence; Francis Charlton, a teacher with forceful libertarian views; Josiah Keeling, an Anabaptist, a dyer by trade, but a declared bankrupt; Richard Rumbold, a one-eyed maltster, whose wife had recently inherited a significant property near Hoddesdon, in Hertfordshire, called the Rye House. And, of course, the most devious, conceited and brilliant of them all, Robert Ferguson himself, whom the constables had registered as 'tall, stooping, heat in the face, speaks in the Scotch tone . . .'.

Ferguson 'the Plotter' favoured a simpler and quicker means of revolution, and so did Shaftesbury and many of his new coterie: to assassinate the King and York. How? They might ambush him as he stepped from his coach at the Guildhall or, on his return from there, in St Paul's Churchyard, or under Ludgate. Or pistol him at dinner in the Guildhall; or ram and overturn his barge on the Thames.[7] Or, in West's words, by planting assassins in the playhouse, '. . . in the pit under the King's box, and some at the back of it, armed with pocket pistols, hand blunderbusses, or muskatoons and swords, who, between some of the Acts, should fire into the box'.[8] William Hone, 'another Godly joiner',[9] proposed to 'have them shot from Bow steeple, as they passed, with cross-bows'. Some of the other conspirators thought that a surer way would be to ambush the brothers as they drove home from Newmarket, using, as a base, Rumbold's Rye House, which conveniently overlooked a short cut on the royal route.

This assassination plan, known as 'the Lopping Point' to distinguish it from the national uprising, 'the General Point', was the favourite subject of the bourgeois plotters on those autumn evenings, as they huddled round City tavern tables, drinking their sack and ale and sucking their clays, each passionately whispering his argument for this method or that for disposing of 'Old Rowley' and the loathed York, (and complaining between whiles of the 'Great Men's lack of action').

But, at every meeting, the 'Lopping Point' foundered on the question 'Where does the Duke of Monmouth stand in all this?' The true answer was that, since he was the people's choice, in whatever capacity – be it as King, stadtholder or Lord Protector – when the revolution was over he would be the national figurehead, if not precisely head of state. But the great majority in England would not accept either him or the perpetrators of the deed, if he were to step in over his father's dead body. There was another point: 'Is there any guarantee', one of them asked, 'that his Grace will not execute the assassins to acquit himself from the suspicion of being a party?'[10]

Nathaniel Wade agreed: 'The Duke of Monmouth, could not, if he should be King, refuse the execution of justice upon us for the murder of his father and uncle.'

'Then, whatever the Great Men say, he must be served in the same manner,' one of the others (Rumsey or Walcot, probably) answered, grimly.[11]

'Plotter' Ferguson smiled back at them: 'What if I get it under his hand', he asked, 'that the actors in it shall *not* be prosecuted?'

But when, a day or two later, Ferguson 'mentioned something concerning the King to the Duke of Monmouth, but not assassinating him', James replied – 'somewhat sternly' – 'You must look upon me in the capacity of a son.' 'Which answer', said West, 'for some time dampt the design and always clogg'd it.'[12]

All the 'Great Men', James's clique, were firmly against the 'Lopping Point'. What was their approach and their philosophy? The first of them, William, Lord Russell, the Earl of Bedford's son and heir, aged forty-three, was an upright, deeply religious man, a libertarian, who was appalled at the way the citizens' rights were vanishing under Charles. 'Arbitrary government cannot be set up in England', he promised, 'without wading through my blood.' He was a close personal friend of James, whom he held in high esteem and wanted as King. With his influence in Devon, where he had been an M.P., Russell held supervisory responsibility for the revolutionary preparations in the West Country.

Colonel Algernon Sidney, son of the late Earl of Leicester and brother of Charles's Ambassador at the Hague, was a tough, plain-spoken man of sixty years, with no frills, an unalloyed republican, who had commanded a regiment for Cromwell and been a commissioner for the trial of Charles I. He had been the Commonwealth's envoy in Denmark, and penned the blueprint for William Penn's democratic American colony. He also wrote his political ideas in a pamphlet, which was soon to be held to be treasonable. In it he stated that 'power is originally in the people of England, and delegated to the Parliament; and that the King is subject to the law of God, as he is a man, and to the people that make him, as he is a King'.[13] Although, on principle, Sidney 'hated princes' and had only known James briefly, he was another strong admirer, and thought that because of 'the flaw in his title' the Protestant Duke could not do otherwise than govern democratically.

Next was Arthur Capel, Earl of Essex, fifty-one, son of the Royalist Lord Capel of Hadham, who was executed by Cromwell. Essex, former Viceroy of Ireland and head of the Treasury not long before, 'threw every honour of government behind him', in Dalrymple's words, 'because he preferred the people to the King'.[14]

He had a strong respect for James and saw him as the most appropriate future head of state. John Hampden, twenty-nine, grandson of the hero of the Long Parliament, formerly Whig M.P. for Buckinghamshire, and described by Bishop Burnet as 'a young man of great parts – one of the learnedest young gentlemen I ever knew',[15] was in much the same position as Sidney and Essex.

On the fringe of this cabal were two men whom the others should never have trusted : the first was Lord Howard of Escrick who was said to have a 'subtle, personal fascination', but to be 'zealous for no government save that under which he could get most'. And the second was Shaftesbury's young friend, Lord Grey of Werke, the Cold Caleb of Dryden's *Absalom and Achitophel*, a man of considerable resourcefulness and wit, who had shown ability in Parliament, but who was a man of meagre integrity.

Shaftesbury and Ferguson were trying to push the other 'Great Men' into action. Ferguson – 'out of my sincere regard to the public cause and the unfeign'd love I bear to the person and interest of the Duke of Monmouth' – went to James warning him of the 'Lopping Point'. James was naïvely appalled that any of them could harbour such a criminal idea. Indeed it was probably his unrelenting emphasis on the need, generally, to minimise bloodshed that put the hardest brake on the rebellion's impetus. Lord Russell was the same.

Shaftesbury told Grey that 'my Lord Russell is too wary and timorous a man for such an undertaking as ours'.[16] And when, at one of their meetings, Russell and James cautioned him for his impatience, 'my Lord Shaftesbury, in the greatest passion I ever saw,' said Grey, 'replied that patience would be our destruction'. Shaftesbury added that 'since I see myself forsaken by you, I am resolved to stand upon my legs, act by myself, and have the honour of saving the kingdom'.

'My Lord's acting will be running away,' James whispered in Grey's ear. Then – aloud to Shaftesbury, who was always boasting of his '10,000 brisk boys' – 'Where, my Lord, are your 10,000 men quartered?'

'I shall tell no man that,' rejoined Shaftesbury; 'but you will see them at Whitehall gates before you are many days older.'[17]

James knew perfectly well where the 'brisk boys' lay and who their gang leaders were, and that they were not nearly in such strength as Shaftesbury claimed. The Protestant Duke could make a much more realistic appreciation of the King's forces, too. Only three years ago, he had personally controlled the deployment of the regular units,[18] and had approved, if not drafted, the standing orders for all the London garrisons.[19] And, having sanctioned the security arrangements for the Tower, the Exchange and the Horse Guards, he knew more or less how they would react in the event of an alarm, and what reserves were available to support them.

James reckoned that the City's vital points, however readily they might be seized, could not be held for long, unless some diversion was staged to draw a substantial element of his father's army away from the capital.[20] On his tour of 1680 he had seen how the turbulent, Non-conformist West Country, whose revolutionaries were potentially well led and had plenty of arms and ammunition hidden, was the only area that could be immediately relied upon to stage an effective rising. So he instructed John Trenchard, (Taunton's Whig M.P., and son-in-law of George Speke, who had entertained Monmouth in Somerset), to establish close touch with the Western leaders and warn them that the moment for action was near. Trenchard undertook to raise 1,000 foot and 200–300 horse.[21] James anticipated that once the risings in London and Wessex were successful Cheshire and Scotland would follow, and with them all Britain.

Shaftesbury and Ferguson had figured largely in the preliminary negotiations with the Scottish rebels, whose chief was the Earl of Argyle. Son of the 8th Earl and 1st Marquis, who crowned Charles at Scone in 1651 and was executed at the Restoration for his complicity with Cromwell, this Argyle, having refused York's Scottish Test, was imprisoned in 1681 on a high treason charge. But, cleverly disguised, he escaped,[22] and made his way to London, where he was soon in close touch with James, discussing the now imperative subject of a rising in the Lowlands.[23] Pointing out that the Scottish lairds were poor men, he asked for £20,000 for arms and ammunition, later bringing it down to '£8,000, and 1,000 horse to be sent to Scotland'. (Argyle was always a tough bargainer). When London got too dangerous for him, he decamped to Holland.

At first, it was decided that 17 November – the anniversary of the start of the reign of Elizabeth, the 'Protestant Queen', a suitable day to rise, and one, as Burnet said, 'to cover their running together till they met in a body' – would be the best date to launch the revolt. But when that inspiration was weighed in the balance against the army's being on patrol in general, and on the watch in particular for pope-burning riots, Sunday the 19th was chosen instead – '. . . for this reason', Grey tells us, 'that on that night, all shops are shut, and the streets fuller than any other night, many people returning late home from visiting their friends and other diversions'.[24] James said 'it would be absolutely necessary to have some common bank of £25–30,000 to answer the occasions of such an undertaking',[25] and began to supervise its collection.

His plan for London[26] was that, as soon as the West Country was in arms, the City 'brisk boys', organised chiefly by the ex-under-Sheriff Richard Goodenough, would rendezvous at a number of houses, earmarked as bases for this operation: his own house in Hedge Lane, Northumberland House (which would be his head-quarters), and Bedford House (between them these would hold 500) and 'four or five meeting-houses in the City'. The initial manoeuvre, to be made an hour or so before midnight, was to be an attack on the train-bands at the Exchange, followed by the seizure of Newgate, Ludgate and Aldersgate. He determined 'to receive the first attack of the King's Guards' at Fleet Bridge and on the dominating ground of Snow Hill, both of which he would have occupied in defensive depth. At Snow Hill he 'intended to make a barricade, and plant three or four cannon upon ship-carriages'. At Fleet bridge he would use his cannon 'upon land-carriages and . . . make a breast-work for [the] musketeers on each side of the bridge next us; and to fill the houses on that side the ditch with men who should fire from the windows, but the bridge to be clear'.

At the same time, said Grey, 'we intended to possess ourselves of London Bridge, to cut off the correspondence between Whitehall

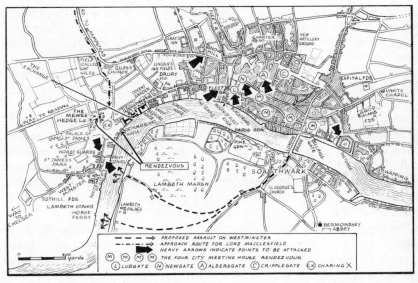

8. The author's impression of the plan for the seizure of London, 1682–3

and the Tower. These three posts we thought we could keep with two thousand men, till the rest were got together and in order . . .'

James instructed Lord Macclesfield to make a detour to attack the royal forces from the north-west, while another party, 'as many more men as we could spare', as a back-up operation, was to cross London Bridge, march east to west through Southwark, then row over, from Lambeth to Westminster, in lighters, to make an assault on Whitehall Palace. But 'we hoped there would be no great use of this last detachment'. For, by then, it was reckoned 'that the King in this conjuncture would be advised to go for Portsmouth . . . which we thought would so dishearten his forces that in a few hours we should be masters of London'. That October Monmouth, accompanied by Sir Thomas Armstrong, made detailed reconnaissances of the Tower and all the other strong points, and in doing so, according to Grey, frequently foiled the sentries.[27]

Sanguine as the rebel plan for London may have sounded, it is clear that James – who, except when he forgot his qualms in the heat of battle against a properly defined enemy, had always shunned killing and maiming – fancifully envisaged a quick capitulation, a more or less bloodless *coup d'état*. 'I could not kill men in cold blood – that is work only for butchers.' Those were his words on being upbraided by his father for failing to cut down the fugitives after his victory of Bothwell Bridge. Russell, talking with him one day, remembered 'asking, if the thing succeeded, what must be done next but mastering the guards, and killing them in cold blood? which I looked upon as a detestable thing, and so like a Popish practice that I could not but abhor it. And at the same time the Duke of Monmouth took me by the hand and told me very kindly "My Lord, I see you and I are of the same temper – did you ever hear so horrid a thing?" And I must needs do him justice that I ever observed in him an abhorrence of all base things.'[28]

Shaftesbury, still lying low in Wapping, refused to discuss the situation with James, and when Russell asked whether he, Monmouth, was willing to speak with the Earl, the reply was 'with all my heart – there is nothing so much I desire'.[29] But, as it could not be arranged, the main responsibility was now the Protestant Duke's. In the second week of November, all were eagerly expecting the uprisings to begin on the appointed day. But, when James inquired about the situation in the West, Trenchard proved a weak reed, making stammering excuses for 'the forces he had promised there not being ready'. Reminded of 'the different account he had first given of the situation at Taunton', he was silent, and James, after cross-questioning him, remarked that 'Mr Trenchard turned so pale I thought he would have fainted'. He immediately called a meeting at Sheppard's wine shop, and, after outlining the general situation and his 'viewing of the guards and the careless posture he found them in', he went on to say that the whole plan must be postponed as the West Country was not ready : 'the rising is impossible, I cannot get the gentlemen of the West to stir yet'. Which, Grey admitted, 'put a great daunt upon all of us'.[30]

James did his best to maintain their enthusiasm and morale. 'Though we are now put off,' he encouraged them, 'we must not be idle; for it will be impossible to hold off any longer. I have been at Wapping all night and never saw brisker and bolder fellows in my life. I have been round the Tower and seen the avenues of it, and I do not think it will be hard in a little time to possess ourselves of it . . . we are engaged to be ready in a fortnight and therefore now we must apply ourselves to it as well as we can.'[31] And 'he ordered Mr Ferguson to get four more field-carriages made against that time'.[32]

A few days later, however, something happened which prompted James to postpone the whole scheme indefinitely. Howard of Escrick, who had been siding with the regicides, dropped hints of the'Lopping Point,' saying it might be a good deal more than a last-resort expedient.

'God so ! Kill the King !' – James 'struck his breast with a great emotion of spirit', turning on his informant in horror – 'I'll *never* suffer that !'[33]

He looked upon himself as his father's saviour, not his destroyer. As he saw it, Charles, egged on by the implacable York to crush the libertarian Whigs, and rule through a Tory autonomy, had allowed himself to become an insufferable tyrant. The revolution was inevitable. For James, the problem was not so much how to spark it off as to how to prevent a blood-bath and, above all, save his father's life. He dashed off in search of Tom Armstrong, found him at the playhouse, clutched him by the shoulder and ordered him 'up and down the City' to pass word round that *all* preparations were to be suspended until the 'Lopping Point' was quashed.[34]

Then, on 19 November, the day for which the risings had been planned, there was a fire in the City and another dramatic turn in events to disconcert him. Shaftesbury, hearing a rumour that troops were on their way to arrest him, disguised himself as a Presbyterian minister and fled. 'That very day and hour in which it was designed to set the nation aflame, became the signal for a great fire in Wapping (a place whence a great part of their force was expected), by the light of which', Robert West remembered, 'the Earl of Shaftesbury ran away down the river to Gravesend . . .

and sailed to Holland with Walcot and Ferguson attending him.'[35] As he fled, he shouted across his shoulder to his friends : 'Our design cannot long be concealed, there being so many acquainted with it.'[36] The three of them got clean away, but only two months of life were left to Shaftesbury, who had once been Lord High Chamberlain of England, and who had enticed James, Duke of Monmouth from the straight bright road of Captain-General and senior courtier on to the murky crooked track of rebel leader. On 21 January, with Ferguson and Walcot at his side, the 'Protestant Lord', aged sixty-one, breathed his last.

'We shall see who will take his place!' wrote York to the Prince of Orange. But Charles had no need to wait. He knew his son was the rebel generalissimo and Whig leader now, and he feared for them both, because his devotion to Monmouth was much too deep-rooted to be extinguished by the fact that he led the enemy.

18

1683

THE PLOT THAT FAILED

Although only Russell and Grey of Werke, of 'the Great Men', envisaged a monarchy in England's democratic future – Sidney, Essex and Hampden still placed their faith firmly in an aristocratically led republic – there was no question in any of their minds as to who was the fittest person to command them now that Shaftesbury was gone. Monmouth, the experienced military chief and natural leader of the people, was their man. 'I know but of one general we can have', Colonel Sidney, the civil war veteran, insisted, 'and that is the Duke of Monmouth, whose conduct and integrity I do not doubt.'[1]

As soon as James heard of 'Little Sincerity's' death he formed a committee, consisting of Sidney, Russell, Essex, Hampden and Howard of Escrick.* Although Sidney said afterwards that Howard 'was trusted by none of us', it was he who voted him into this committee, and it was Essex who kept giving assurances of his trustworthiness.[2] Lord Grey would probably have been included had he not been in public disgrace.[3] (Having been found guilty of abducting his young sister-in-law, Lady Henrietta Berkeley, and being ordered to hand her over to her father, the Earl of Berkeley, he refused to do so.[4] 'I married her eldest sister, and expected a maiden's-head,' he told the court, 'but not finding it, I resolved to find one in the family if any be left.'[5])

Algernon Sidney took on the Scottish responsibility, corresponding with Argyle in Holland, and sending Aaron Smith to the Lowlands to keep abreast with their leaders' progress. Sidney thought the main chance would be in in Scotland, and his advice was that James should take command there. But James argued that the plan for

---

*The Earl of Salisbury was also invited to join the Council but declined on grounds of ill health. He died that May.

the seizure of London depended largely on a successful rising in the West Country, and it was now perfectly clear, as Sir William Courteney, who had been acting with Trenchard, confirmed, that 'the West would not engage to rise but upon the promise of the Duke of Monmouth's being with them'. That was the measure of the people's extraordinary devotion for, and faith in, him. According to Grey, the rebellion would be 'before the harvest', when the greatest number of country folk was still available. Argyle was to be lent £10,000 to set the Scottish rising on the move 'before the end of June'. A messenger was to carry the news of this rising to Monmouth, who would be in hiding in Grey's house, near Chichester. Monmouth would then gallop to Taunton to be met by Trenchard and his men. Macclesfield would be waiting in Cheshire in a similar role.[6]

Cavalry would be at a premium. It was hoped that a large body of horse could be raised from the area of Chichester, to escort James to Somerset. So he drove to that city with Grey on 7 February to see what the local dissident leaders could muster. A party of 800 horsemen were to have met them outside the walls, but the Sheriff had received orders from Charles to prevent the assembly; therefore, when James and Grey wheeled up, they were met not by their own supporters but the sheriff's troop. However, they were not refused entry. Jenkin's informers reported that 1,000 people gathered to cheer James in the town centre. 'The rabble behaved very tumultuously and insolently wishing [him] welcome with loud acclamations . . . and withal swore they would set the crown on the Duke of Monmouth's head in spite of all the Tory soldiers . . .'[7] James was duly confident of his support there,[8] and seeing his Chichester accomplice, Richard Holmes, a little later, in London, he bade him 'remember me to all my friends, for I will come and hunt there again'.

Although he never would return to his beloved Sussex, there was time, notwithstanding his cloak-and-dagger preoccupation, for one more very important sporting engagement. In mid-February he sailed his 'running horses' to France, for the great royal international meeting.

The background to this was that, as horse-racing had proved such a success in England, Louis determined to make it a national pastime in France, too. In order to foster public interest in the turf, he offered a plate valued at 10,000 pistoles to be run at Achères, near St Germain. Soon many entries were registered, not only from France and England, but from all over Europe. A short time before the date of the race it transpired that a little-known gelding entered for the big race by a 'Green Ribbonite', Thomas Wharton, had been privately and very heavily backed by a large number of the English aristocracy.

Reports of this were at first received incredulously. When it suddenly came out that Monmouth the 'English champion', was to ride the 'dark horse' the owners of the foreign favourites became seriously alarmed. And they had good cause : to the admiration of the King and Queen and a host of high-ranking Europeans James spurred Wharton's gelding first past the winning-post with considerable ease and against a number of horses with much better track records.[9]

James was also given the almost unprecedented honour of being allowed to drive his coach immediately behind Louis's into the courtyard of the Louvre,[10] an honour normally reserved only for the French royal family. Knowing Monmouth to be in disgrace, people in Paris must have gleefully assumed this to be a deliberate affront on Louis's part to William of Orange, and a snub, too, perhaps for his cousin, Charles of England, whom the 'Sun King' liked to keep in a state of perpetual, if mild, embarrassment.

But straight ahead a violent storm lay in wait for James and his revolutionaries. In February, Grey of Werke was in the dock again, this time with Richard Goodenough and others, for causing a riot during the previous midsummer elections, and for assaulting Sir John Moore, the new Tory Lord Mayor of London. On 8 May, Grey was arrested and tried, on a spy's information, that eighty firelocks were concealed in his house. Typically he had a good excuse for the court that tried him. 'They were bought long before, and very publicly,' he pleaded, 'and lay so in my house to the view of all my servants, for near two years, and were not bought with any other intent, but to furnish my three houses in Essex, Sussex and Northumberland'. Nevertheless, he admitted, 'I was obliged to enter with my sureties into a recognisance of £20,000 for the keeping of the peace. After that . . . I went down into Sussex, where I thought there was no great danger of forfeiting my recognisance before the time of our rising.'

In the next passage of the confession he made to York two years later, when York was King and he York's captive, Grey endorses Russell's statement about James's ingenuous faith in the prospect of a non-violent rebellion. And he shows how horrified James was, not only at the idea of his father being threatened with assassination, but at York's being so threatened, too. Deep in an all-night discussion with Grey, in Soho Square, James gave the opinion that, as soon as Charles saw how strong the revolt was, 'there would be little blood shed, for all would end in an accommodation between King and a parliament'. James then recounted how Macclesfield had proposed murdering York 'to frighten the King into compliance', and his own reaction to that proposal, 'which was one of the greatest abhorrence . . . that can be imagined, and the Duke of Monmouth said he would not consent to the murdering the meanest creature (tho' the worst enemy he had in the world) for all the advantages under heaven, and should never have any esteem for my Lord Macclesfield while he lived'.[11]

Too many untrustworthy men had heard the assassination plot discussed. One of them, Josiah Keeling, the bankrupt dyer, desperately in need of cash, turned Judas. On 12 June he sneaked into the offices of York's aide, Lord Dartmouth. He reported that the previous April a plan had been afoot to murder the King and York as they returned from Newmarket to London. They would have been ambushed at a property called the Rye House, belonging to Captain Rumbold, one of the Whig plotters. This house over-looked a side-road, a short cut near Hoddesdon, which the King normally took on his return journey.

Two assassins, disguised as labourers, were to have pulled a cart across the road in front of the royal coach; then a party of musketeers would have fired at the royal postilions from a garden wall, while a party of horsemen – forty or fifty men with blunderbusses were to do the job – closed on the coach and escort, killing the King, the Duke of York, and the Guards. This mission successful, three or four horsemen would have galloped to London to give the signal for a general rising . . . It was only because of the fire at New-market in the previous week, and their decision to leave the place early, that the King and the Duke of York were still alive.

Dartmouth packed Keeling off to Secretary Jenkins, who extracted an even more dramatic version of the story. Jenkins demanded the names of those involved. Keeling's list included the Committee of Six, as well as all the lesser plotters. As the news spread through the Tory establishment, satisfaction mingled with alarm. For this was just what the Tories suspected of the militant Whigs, that they really intended to raise the old green Leveller flag, destroy the monarchy, extinguish the Cavalier class and elect a government representative of the merchants, yeomen and wage-earning classes. This was what York wanted to believe of Monmouth, that his nephew's heart was set upon becoming a constitutional king over Charles's dead body and his own.

By broadsheet and handbill, from the pulpit and street corner, word was quickly given out that the King and the Duke had, by God's miracle, narrowly escaped 'the assassins' vicious hand' and that 'there is [still] a body of men ready to rise, and to take immediate possession of the City and Tower, and consequently of the whole nation . . . and the Duke of Monmouth is ready to head the insurrection'.[12] In fact Charles and York had been nowhere near 'the assassin's vicious hand'. The object of the exercise was much more nearly confined to Nathaniel Wade's definition: a non-violent revolution 'for redressing of grievances; the bottom of it was the Bill of Exclusion, and to declare the Duke of Monmouth Prince of Wales'.[13]

When, a week later, rumours reached the conspirators that Keeling had split, few thought even remotely of the Rye House scheme. After all it had only been mooted and considered, but never properly planned, let alone rehearsed. They imagined, besides, that it was the 'General Point', not the 'Lopping Point' that was given away. Some – notably West, Rumsey and Sheppard – terrified for their necks, followed Keeling and turned informer. Others whispered frightened questions at each other in the murky Whig taverns. What should they do? Lie low? Give themselves up? Flee? Disguised as working men, Ferguson, who had returned to London soon after Shaftesbury's death, and Armstrong took passages to Holland. 'Gentlemen, you're strangers to this kind of exercise', 'the Plotter' laughed at his awestruck confederates, as he prepared to leave: 'I've been used to fly. I'll never leave off as long as I live, and I hope to see some of you at Dunbar before Michaelmas!' There was £500 on each of their heads.

On James's and Grey's too. A news-sheet, headed 'The Hue and Cry after J—— Duke of M——, Lord G——y and etc.,' suggested that 'as there's no great hope of finding him [Grey] with his lady, he probably is to be found with a near relation of her ladyship's' (meaning her sister). It was on a visit to London that Grey was arrested. But, always very ingenious at saving his skin, he slipped away. It was late at night and, finding the Tower gates locked, his escort took him to the Rummer Tavern for the night. Grey got him dead drunk, then dashed to the Thames and hired a boat.* A young soldier from the Tower overtook him, but the wily peer bribed the guardsman to desert. The two of them commandeered hackney-horses and raced to Up Park, where they picked up the truant Lady Henrietta Berkeley and two servants.[15] One of Jenkins's Sussex spies saw, 'at an arm of the sea called Cockbush, five men in disguise and a woman, and, by all circumstances, it is the Duke of Monmouth, Lord Grey and others of their gang, for they walked in a wood four hours for the tide'.[16] The party was soon at Flushing, and on to Cleves, where they joined Armstrong and Ferguson. But James was not with them.

Howard of Escrick, taken at his Knightsbridge house, 'in a

---

*The escort, a sergeant-at-arms called Henry Dereham, was formerly gentleman of horse to the Lord Chamberlain and quartermaster to Sir Charles Littleton. After Grey's escape the King had him sacked 'from all his places' and put in a Tower dungeon.[14]

cunning hole behind a hanging',[17] had no hesitation in giving his friends away. 'So soon as he came to the King he fell a-crying bitterly,' Sir Charles Littleton wrote on 10 July, 'and desired pen and paper that he might recollect and discover what he knew; so has been writing his narrative ever since.'[18] Russell, Essex and Hampden, secure in the belief that nothing incriminating could be proved against them, remained with their families, imagining, when the soldiers came for them, that they would probably only be required to give evidence. They were astonished to find themselves marched to the Tower on high treason charges.[19]

And James? As soon as he heard that Russell was taken, he got a note through to him: 'I'll come in, and we'll run fortunes together!' To which Russell replied: 'It will be no advantage for my friends to die with me.'[20] So, for the time being, he hid in London. The soldiers tried Anna's house first; then, among others, the Drury Lane home of Monmouth's friend, the Earl of Anglesey; then Eleanor Needham's lodgings; then twice – a detailed search, the second time, probably, with the floor-boards up – Whig Councillor Thompson's house in Essex Street.[21] Welch, James's coachman, was next to be questioned. In May Welch had been attacked in a hatter's shop by a party of Life Guardsmen – for 'wearing a Whig's livery, the son of a whore's livery' – and cut about the cheeks with a pair of the hatter's shears.[22] Now the brave coachman, when faced by one of Jenkins's sergeants, 'fell into a passion, saying "the evidences against my master are a company of perjured rogues not fit to be believed!"'

'If his Grace be clear,' asked the sergeant, 'why does he not render himself to the King and Council and justify himself?'

''Tis not fit for my master to appear before his enemy', Welch returned, 'without his sword in his hand.'[23]

But James was in none of those places. He was too wary and quick, too animal-like, to be snatched by the redcoats who had once looked up to him as their Captain-General. He had hidden where few would expect to find a rebel, in the dwelling of a friend he had made at the House of Lords, a doorkeeper. Eventually, the Guards, picking up clues, cordoned the house off and entered it at night. Alert and supremely agile, James leaped from his bed, jumped across the roof-tops, found a horse and made his way north, via Hampstead, Hendon and Edgware. The route he took that June night led to a great manor-house called Toddington, in Bedford-shire, a place in which he was to hide for five months. It was the home of a woman with whom his fortunes would be linked from now on, whom he would cherish as his 'wife' to his dying day. She was Henrietta, Baroness Wentworth of Nettlestead.

19

TODDINGTON

Even if James had not been deeply and irrevocably attached to Henrietta Wentworth, he might well have chosen Toddington as a refuge for its own sake. Set upon a rise in the forests of Bedfordshire, this great Elizabethan manor-house was built around a quadrangle, with a tower at each corner. Behind its chapel, library and ballroom, its lofty hall and other reception rooms, its banqueting hall and minstrels' gallery, its multitude of guest-rooms, including the Queen's Chamber and Leicester Chamber – reminders of Elizabeth's visit a century before – Toddington was a rambling warren of cellars and secret passages, priests' holes, hidden vaults and gigantic fireplaces, concealing trapdoors, while its numerous windows afforded a man in hiding fine fields of view across fish-ponds, herb gardens, parterres and terraces, to a circuit of radial avenues, reaching into rides, carved from the woodland beyond. As for Toddington's servants, all were implicitly loyal to their young baroness.

Coming of age in August 1682, Henrietta, or Harriot, as James called her, an only child, had been mistress of this palace for less than a year. Even now she was mistress only in name, for her mother, Philadelphia, Lady Wentworth, a widow since 1666, had ruled Toddington too long and too absolutely to release her grip at once. Henrietta's father, the 5th Baron Wentworth, was a spendthrift, as her grandfather, the 1st Earl of Cleveland, had been. And it was due only to Philadelphia's deft management of the estate, with what little money was left, that the Toddington Estate was in a thriving condition by the time Henrietta reached twenty-one – that and the support the widow had from the tiresome opinionated little Sir William Smyth, a Civil War turncoat, who had been Henrietta's guardian since her assumption of the title, Baroness Wentworth of

Nettlestead, at the age of five. Henrietta was a wilful, independent child. She had resented Smyth's intrusion from the start, so she found great release in her coming of age, and, in theory anyway, being free to do as she pleased.

If she was free to have her lover at Toddington it had not always been so. Until now, fearing her tempestuous mother, she could only receive James by deceit, through secret messages. It was on account of James's attentions that, in 1680, Philadelphia had removed her daughter from Court, where she was Maid of Honour to the Duchess of York. The mention of the lovers together was in 1674, when Henrietta acted with him in John Crowne's *Calisto, or The Chaste Nymph.*[1] James, the romantic military hero, Whitehall's brightest star, was dressed in sheepskins then, carrying a shepherd's crook, while Henrietta, a very susceptible fourteen-year-old, playing Jupiter, cried 'Love, what pleasure dost thou here prepare . . .?' They must have known each other before that, too, because Henrietta was a cousin of James's guardian, Lord Crofts, and she stayed frequently at Crofts's home, Saxham Hall,* in Suffolk.

A comparison of her background with his soon shows how the dashing general, who was also the King's son, would naturally prove her *beau ideal.* The Wentworths had served their monarchs as soldiers and courtiers since the Conquest. Henrietta's grandfather, Cleveland, a tall, splendid-looking warrior, had a brilliant record as a Royalist regimental commander in the Civil War. Her father fought alongside him then, and both were with their new young King in the disaster that ended at Worcester, Cleveland being captured by Cromwell. Afterwards, Wentworth, although a rather wild young man, was given the honour, during the royal exile, of raising Charles's First Foot Guards (the Grenadiers). Old Cleveland died in 1667, Wentworth predeceasing him by two years.

Had she been better endowed materially, their heiress might have been the most sought-after young woman on the English marriage market. At least four names had been linked with Henrietta's: her neighbour, the Earl of Ailesbury's son and Charles's equerry, Lord Bruce, who was also a close friend of James's; the Earls of Thanet and Shrewsbury;[2] and James's former major-general, Louis Duras, Earl of Feversham, a man whom he would one day face on the battlefield. ('I hear Lord Feversham shall have Wentworth,' Dr Denton told Sir Ralph Verney a month before James reached Toddington, 'and that she shall be groom of the stool to the

*The house was not far from the original Wentworth home, Nettlestead, which was sold to pay family debts. Toddington came to them through marriage into the Cheney family, two generations before.

Queen.'[3]) Bruce admitted that 'I greatly esteemed and loved her, but her fortune not being clear and proportionable to what my father expected, out of duty to so good a father, I laid aside all thoughts, but my esteem I could not blot out so soon'. He added that 'had she been brought up by a discreet and good mother, she would have made a perfect good wife'.[4]

Bruce – Tory courtier and son of Bedfordshire's Lord Lieutenant, devotedly faithful to the King and knowing how deeply the King loved his son – did James more than one kindness during the Toddington months. Jenkins's spies and an anonymous writer (addressing Lawrence Hyde, Earl of Rochester) had reported precisely where the Protestant Duke was hiding,[5] but Charles, with his easy dissembling, made it clear he did not want him caught. Bruce recalls how, when he was on duty at a levée, he 'found the King in the privy garden, setting his watch at the sundial'; and how Charles took him on one side, and ordered him to assume the temporary 'government of Bedfordshire', and to go straight to Toddington and put James in custody. Bruce, knowing 'the passion the King had for that Lord', objected that 'the house was surrounded with vast ponds, and that there were many vaults underground by which he might escape, and if I raised a militia troop he would hear of it'. The King's face lit up at this excuse 'and he never spoke to me more on this subject'. Bruce adds that Charles consented to James's 'being put into the proclamation, with such ill company, against his natural inclination'.

A little later Bruce and his father were out hunting when the stag 'swam the ponds at Toddington, which never happened before'. There, says Bruce, 'I saw a tall man in a country habit opening a gate for me. I took no notice, but casting my eye, perceived it was the Duke of Monmouth, who was so indiscreetly mingled with the crowd at the death of the stag very soon after'. Whereupon Bruce kept up such a loud monologue to distract Ailesbury's attention that the old man thought he was drunk.

Unmistakably, as the same witness relates, James was seen again. Philadelphia invited Ailesbury and Bruce to dinner ('which she had never done before') twice while James was in hiding at Toddington, 'in all appearances for a blind', Bruce reckoned; 'but she never permitted us to see the apartments above'. Nevertheless, he remembered that, not long after the deer-hunt, a mutual friend of his family's and the Wentworths' went to dinner there, following evening chapel, and Philadelphia carelessly let her wander among the upstairs rooms. Reaching Henrietta's open door the guest chanced to see her dressing, with a tall and handsome young gentleman 'sitting in a great chair by the fireside, watching her'.

(That room and the connecting one were known ever after as 'the Duke's and my lady's parlours'.)

Taking after her fanciful father, and perhaps, to escape her domineering mother, Henrietta lived much in her world of escapist romance. Bruce called her a 'visionary', and this was a shared characteristic which drew the lovers together, swirling them in the treacherous current of their life's tragi-romantic course. When James was taken prisoner, two years later, his escort found numerous trinket charms in his pockets, together with a little pocket-book.* This contains many omens and superstitious remedies, charms 'against enemies' and 'for deliverance from pain', methods of 'foreknowing sundry circumstances as a result of sickness or a previous fidelity', and astrological wheels, at the foot of one of which he wrote, in French, that, in 1681, 'life would be happier shared with another' ('avec plus de plasir dans le 2 que dans le 1').

Living together for five months at Toddington the lovers found an infinite spectrum of instinct and interest to share. She, who had been reared on the concept of the pre-eminence of military valour, would have spoken glowingly of her grandfather sacrificing all in the cause of the Martyr King; of her father, the founder of the English Foot Guards, and of both of them at Worcester. She would have laughed at James's imitation of his father's repetitive stories of that battle, and of the ensuing escape, and he would have regaled her with incidents, dramatic or bizarre, from the battles of Lowestoft and the Rhine Castles, of Maastricht and Charleroi, and of Mons and Bothwell Bridge; of great hunts and races in Sussex and Holland, at Newmarket and Windsor, and on the plains beyond Paris.

She must have revelled in his sense of fun, the humour reflected in most of his portraits; the impish instinct that prompted him to leap on the stage, to hang that heavy sword from the French actor's waist in 1670; the bubbling laughter that delighted the Merry Monarch throughout the buoyant, golden years; the gleefully impertinent side of his character that suggested to his father in 1679 that if he cared to exile Lauderdale, Sunderland and Louise Portsmouth, too, 'he would go in the same yacht, though he liked none of their companys'; the charming sense of the ridiculous with

---

*Now residing in the British Museum under the reference Egerton MS 1527. At the time of the French Revolution, the President of the English College in Paris suggested that James II's manuscript books, one of which was this pocket-book, should be sent to England for safety. But the parcel containing them got delayed. For fear of the new authorities it was buried, but later dug up and most of its contents burned. But Monmouth's pocket-book, its incriminating Royal Arms having been cut out, was saved. It was picked up on a Paris bookstall, in 1827, by an Irish Divinity student, and was eventually sold to the British Museum.

which he could mock himself, the ex-Commander-in-Chief, spying
on the royal sentries last autumn, with the long faces of Grey and
Armstrong looking anxiously through the railings.

How Henrietta loved that mesmeric voice, immortalised by
Dryden – 'Few words he spoke, but easy those and fit,/more
slow than hybla drops and far more sweet' – which helped draw
her lover to the hearts of the English masses. She would have basked
in the knowledge that she held the devotion – as no woman had
ever done before – of the most adored figure in the three Kingdoms,
and, at the same time, have chided him for his vanity, accusing him
teasingly of following her only because she had made sheep's eyes
at him at Court. And James, conceding it, perhaps, would have
convinced her with all sincerity that he loved her for herself now,
and it would always be so. As for his vanity (he would have claimed
with his ready laugh), that had mostly dried up with the rigours
and problems he had had to face, out of office and in disgrace,
these last three years. And then they must have reminisced about all
their old friends at Court, Bruce and Moll Kirke, Churchill and
Sarah Jennings, Ossory and Mary Blague, Princess Mary of Orange,
Princess Anne, old Buckingham and Castlemaine's brood. And Anna.

Anna? James would have soothed Henrietta, reminding her that
Anna was a person of quite dissimilar temperament, who had been
arbitrarily imposed upon him as a child. 'You and I commit no sin,'
he might have said to Henrietta, as he would one day insist to
four senior clerics; 'that which passes between us is very honest and
innocent in the sight of God.'

'O how blest and how innocent and happy is a country life,'
Monmouth versified in his pocket-book; 'free from tumult and
discontent/here is no flatteries nor strife . . . hence gentle peace and
love doth flow.' Toddington provided myriad avenues of escape
from the tangled, vicious world he left behind :

> We'll to our bowers
> And there spend our hours
> Happy there we will be
> We no strifes there can see
> No quarrelling for crowns
> Nor fear the great ones frowns . . .
> We'll sit and bless our stars
> That did this glorious place give
> . . . Did us Toddington give,
> That thus we happy live.

As happened to nearly all the Stuarts, his hair began to turn grey
early, and James did not like it. 'To make the hair grow black,

though of any colour,' he notes on another page, 'take a little aqua fortis. Put therein a groat or sixpence as to the quantity of the aforesaid water, then let both dissolve before the fire, then dip a small sponge in the water and wet your beard or hair therewith, but touch not the skin.' But, in spite of all his worldly vanity, he was a man of strong Christian belief, as the humble and heartfelt prayers in his notebook show, and the superstitiousness (noticeable to others, even in that superstitious age) that played such a prominent part in his and Henrietta's lives, was offset by a sincere shared faith. They would pray together, morning and evening, and, in between, they would read the books in Toddington's library, collect baskets of fruit, ride in the woods, fish in the garden ponds, explore the crannies of the great house, pluck herbs, carve their names on an oak (which was to become famous as 'The Toddington Oak') and study the mysteries and messages of their trinket charms and symbols.

How realistically did the Protestant Duke now take stock of himself? Did he regret having rebelled against his father? Could he still convince himself that, just because he was gifted with an immense capacity for exciting affection, and because – backed by the might of government – he had commanded conventional armies with quick-thinking skill and courage, it followed that he had the steel to lead a revolution? Whatever doubt or assurance he gave himself on this point, however much he blamed himself for the failure of the Protestant Plot, however much he longed for his place at Court and his old prestige, in order not to let down his confederates, he resolved to do and say nothing that might prejudice their safety.

But how should he now act? How soon must the dream end? Should he attempt an escape to the Netherlands and take up that open offer of a general's command in the Spanish army?[6] With £500 on his head and the ports closely watched, what chance of success could he hope for? Surely he would be caught, locked in the Tower and tried as a traitor? As Lord Argyle had written, from Holland, in code, to a London friend on 19 June, 'if the Duke of Monmouth be made prisoner he is lost to all intents and purposes'.[7] He meant: 'and his cause, too'. For James's torch was the Protestant hope. If, on the other hand, he gave himself up, would he not be brought before the Council and forced to make confessions that might speed his followers to the scaffold?

20

1683

RECONCILIATION

So James waited, listening for snatches of news that Henrietta and her mother brought him, not much of it good news, not even the announcement of the engagement of his cousin, the Princess Anne, to Prince George, who, as brother to the King of the Danes, was aligned with the French camp. He would have heard how Hone and Rouse suffered the traitor's end, and – perhaps in the gory detail that Evelyn recorded – of the death of Lord Essex from a slit throat in his Tower cell privy: 'it was wonder'd by some how it was possible he should do it in the manner he was found, for the wound was so deep and wide, that being cut thro' the gullet, wind-pipe and both jugulars, it reach'd to the very vertebrae of the neck . . . There were odd reflections upon it.'[1] There were indeed. The Whigs swore it was murder;* the Establishment, of course, registered it as suicide.

Word would also have travelled soon enough from London to Toddington of the fate of poor Lord Russell (whose family, at Woburn Abbey, were only a walk across the fields. from Henrietta's house). The morning Essex died, Russell was escorted into the Old Bailey, to face the Lord Chief Justice, Pemberton, assisted by Jeffreys, for the last day of his trial. At one moment, while Howard of Escrick, the chief witness for the prosecution, was giving evidence, his cheeks suddenly went white, and his voice quiet and hoarse, as, behind him, two clerks began whispering in horrified tones of the bloody melodrama in the Tower. All faces in the courtroom, including the anguished beauty of Lady Russell, who was taking notes for her husband, turned and strained to catch his words:

*When, ten years later, Holland, a servant of Lord Sunderland's, was charged with the murder of Lord Essex, 'he seemed much dejected, but could not deny it, and [for it] the said Lord Sunderland has many times supplied the said Holland with money'. (Somers Tracts, x, 127.)

heer w'ill euer bee
w'ill sit and bles our stors
that from the Noises of wars
... did this Glorious place giue
... that Thus wee happy liue.

Song

O how blest and how innocent
and happy is a country life
free from tumult and discontent
heer is no flattery nor strife
for t'was the first and happiest life
when first man did injoie himsalfe

This is a better fate then Kings
hence jentle peace and loue doth ...
for fancy is the rate of things
I'm pleased because I think it so
for a hart that is nobly true
all the worlds art can n'er subdue

si il est dans la mo: le ma:
mou:

25.
15

(1680)

Il sera v:t en l'anné 1681.
Il Demeurera 21 m: 5. sa ma:
Il viura auec plus de plaisir
dans le 2. que dans le 1. Il se
ma:a une P:s v:t

onmouth's Pocket Book: (a) a page of verses;

(b) Monmouth's horoscope

Monmouth, an engraving after Lely

A photographic restoration of the monument in Toddington Church, Bedfordshire, to Henrietta, Baroness Wentworth of Nettleside

The 9th Earl of Argyle, artist unknown

'We cannot hear you, my lord!' One of the jury complained to Howard.

'Pray, my lord, raise your voice,' requested Pemberton, 'or your evidence will pass for nothing.'

'There is an unhappy accident that has sunk my voice,' Howard explained; 'I was but just now acquainted with the fate of my Lord of Essex.'[2] According to Burnet, he added: 'I cannot go on till I have given vent to my grief in some tears.'

Howard, the only member of the committee of six who had condoned the 'Lopping Point', had his acquittal, for the price of dishonour, while James's friend was condemned to death. In vain, Russell's desolate wife and father, the Earl of Bedford, pleaded with the King for him.[3] Jack Ketch, taking three blows to sever his head, would one day be taken to task for his bungling by Monmouth.

However much the King favoured arbitrary rule, he liked neither his brother's heavily repressive brand of it nor the alienation of his son as part of the price of it. The Whigs' real hope was a reconciliation of the King and the Protestant Duke. And, as Doctor Welwood observed: 'King Charles lov'd Monmouth tenderly; and all the Disgraces and Hardships that had, of late years been put upon him, were rather the effects of Fear and Policy, than Inclination or Choice.'[4]

Charles yearned for a return to the old balance, in which York was played off against Monmouth, in which Monmouth was the sunbeam breaking through and breaking up York's grim clouds. More than anything else in the world, the King wanted his son back at Court, to organise the Life Guards and run the Court schedules; to supervise the garrisons and the royal sports with his old good-humoured efficiency; and, above all, to refresh his jaded father with his bubbling company. Now that Shaftesbury was gone, and the other leading militants were either dead, broken or scattered abroad, that move at last seemed feasible. And Monmouth, like a fly trapped on the royal web, would have little choice but to return on his father's terms. Of course York must be mollified: James must plead for his uncle's forgiveness with bended knee and lowered head. Then, thought Charles, there would be a public pardon. York, to gratify his self-importance, would be dispatched on some useful mission – perhaps as Viceroy of Scotland again – and, one by one, young James would have his posts restored.

The man who helped the King in this endeavour was that master-diplomat the Marquess of Halifax, the Lord Privy Seal, the man who owed his election to the Council in 1678 to Monmouth. 'Trimmer' Halifax had almost as much to gain from the manoeuvre as the King. He, too, looked back regretfully to the late 1670s when the scales of power were weighed more or less evenly between authoritarian York and libertarian Monmouth. Halifax, who was well aware of the source of York's hold over his brother – the King's surreptitious Catholicism, the treasonable Secret Treaty and the bond with the King of France – was determined to see the Catholic Duke's power reduced, and with it the influence of three people who threatened his own position and career, as well as England's interest.

These were the King's French mistress, the Duchess of Portsmouth; York's brother-in-law, Lawrence Hyde, Earl of Rochester; and the opportunist Earl of Sunderland. A nephew of Henry and Algernon Sidney, Sunderland had once been pro-Orange and Exclusionist. Then, sensing the inevitability of York's succeeding, he made friends with Barillon, the French Ambassador, and through him Ports-mouth's, and so joined the Catholic Duke's faction. Since holding the Northern Secretaryship of State, Sunderland had been 'the Trimmer's' most dangerous rival.

'Impressed by the urgency of the crisis and by a sense of his own political impotence,' writes Halifax's biographer, 'he saw no hope of transfoming the situation save by the introduction of some personal element which might neutralise the pernicious influence of the Duke of York.'[5] That personal element was Monmouth.

The secret negotiations for his return to Court can be followed through James's diary, which, together with his pocket-book, was taken from him in 1685. Dr Welwood, a man who strongly appreciated Monmouth's qualities, recorded parts of this diary in his *Memorials of the Most Material Transactions.*[6] James gave all the characters concerned code letters, or numbers : Halifax, for example is thought to be 'L'; the King, '29'; and York '39'. On 13 October he summarised the result of a surreptitious visit to London :

L came to me at eleven at Night from 29, told me 29 could never be brought to believe I knew any thing of that part of the Plot that concerned *Rye House*; but as things went, he must behave himself as if he did believe it, for some reasons that might be for my advantage. L desir'd me to write to 29, which I refus'd; but afterwards told me 29 expected it : And I promised to write tomorrow, if he would call for the Letter; at which S.L. shew'd a great Concern for me, and I believe him sincere, though 3 is of another Mind.

Here, at last, was a bright ray of hope for James. Thinking optimistically, if warily, ahead, he imagined himself a power a

Court again, not only playing his old conventional roles, but –
elevated from City taverns and coffee-houses to Whitehall's seat of
power – as a lofty Prince of Protestants, Whigs and People. But first
the pill of ignominy, however bitter, had to be swallowed. So the
message of his letter to his father, written next day, was full of
humble denial of being involved in the Rye House plot and of
promises to serve him. 'The whole study of my life shall be to show
you how truly penitent I am . . .'

To bolster his promises, James sent a second letter by Anna, over
which she penned her own note : '. . . I beg your Majesty will not be
displeas'd with me, since I doubt not but his letter is of consequence, because he press'd me to deliver it with all speed to your
Majesty.'[7] On the 20th James recorded : 'L came to me at S with
a line or two from 29 very kind, assuring me he believ'd every
word in my Letter to be true; and advised me to keep hid, till he
had an Opportunity to express his Belief of it some other way. L
told me that he was to go out of Town next Day; and that 29 would
send 80 [Jenkins?] to me in a Day or two, whom he assur'd me I
might trust.' 'The Duke of Monmouth negotiated his peace so well',
as Lord Bruce admitted,[8] that after the King's return from Newmarket on 20 October a meeting was arranged at the Whitehall
apartments of Mrs Crofts, a former governess of James's.* 'L came
for me to——, where 29 was with 80. He received me pretty well
and said 30 and 50 [Armstrong and Grey?] were the Causes of my
Misfortunes, and would ruin me. After some hot words against
them, and against S [Shaftesbury?], [he] went away in a good
humour.'

So this entente, this royal bond, so significant for the temper of
the nation, which was broken in 1679, was reforged in 1683. And
thus the balmy days of Toddington, where the trees had turned
autumn gold and Henrietta nursed the memories of her magic
summer, were left behind, never to return.

*Probably the sister of his former guardian, Lord Crofts.

21

1683–1684

THWARTED BY
THE DUKE OF YORK

When James left Mrs Crofts's Whitehall apartments, after enjoying the first friendly encounter with his father for over four years, he was wrapped up to the face in his cloak, with a broad-brimmed hat pulled well down over his eyes. But Colonel Edward Griffin, the Life Guardsman who had served from Cornet to Lieutenant-Colonel[1] under James, recognised him, and dashed breathless to the King, who had by then reached his own rooms : 'Sire, Sire ! I have seen the Duke of Monmouth !'

Charles returned Griffin's alarm with a look and voice of utter scorn : 'Odds fish, you *are* a fool; James is at Brussels !' Bruce adds that the King had never held Griffin 'in his graces', but now, for the crime of so insensitively threatening to disrupt the priceless reconcilation he could, 'after that officiousness . . . never bear the sight of him'.[2]

The following day James, as he related, was nearly caught by more of his old Life Guardsmen. 'I went to E——, and was in danger of being discover'd by some of Oglethorp's Men, that met me accidently at the Backdoor of the Garden.' On 2 November he resumes the narrative of this delicate game which the King and he were hiding from officialdom :

A Letter from 29, to be tomorrow at seven at Night at S, and nobody to know it but 80 [Jenkins?]. [November] 3. He came not, there being an extraordinary Council. But 80 brought me a copy of 50's [Grey's? Argyle's?] intercepted Letter, which made rather for me than against me. Bid me come tomorrow at the same Hour, and to say nothing of the Letter, except 29 spoke of it first. [November] 4. I came and found 29 and L there. He was very kind and gave me Directions how to manage my Business, and what Words I should say to 39 [York]. He appointed 80 to come to me every Night till my Business was ripe, and promis'd to send with him Directions from time to time.

[November] 9. L came from 29, and told me my Business should be done to my Mind next Week, and the Q[ueen] was my Friend and had spoke to 39 and D[uchess] in my Behalf; which he said 29 took very kindly, and had express'd so to her. At parting *he told me there should be nothing required of me, but what was both safe and honourable.* But said there must be something done to blind 39. [November] 15. L came to me with the Copy of a Letter I was to sign to please 39. I desir'd to know in whose Hands it was to be deposited; for I would have it in no Hands but 29. He told me it should be so; but if 39 asked a Copy, it could not well be refus'd . . .

The entire purpose of this more important letter from James to the King, drafted by Halifax, was to dupe and soften York ('blind 39'), who is given to understand that the whole negotiation began with his nephew's *submission.* Monmouth's key sentences were 'neither do I imagine to receive your pardon any otherwise than by the intercession of the Duke, *whom I acknowledge to have offended,* and am prepared to submit myself in the humblest manner'.

With York sufficiently, if grudgingly, appeased, by this grovelling address (which had all the appearance of being his nephew's personal initiative), Charles took the next trump from his hand and cast it on the table. He had Jenkins send James an official declaration: 'If the Duke of Monmouth desire to render himself capable of my mercy, he must render himself to the Secretary, and resolve to tell me all he knows, resigning himself entirely to my pleasure.'[3]

'L came to me from 29 and order'd me to render my self tomorrow,' wrote James on 24 November. 'Caution'd me to play my part, to avoid Questions as much as possible, and to seem absolutely converted to 39's Interest. Bad me bear with some Words that might seem harsh. [November] 25. I render'd my self . . .'

What a jolt it must have been, after four years of revolt and five months of Toddington, the bolt-hole from what he called 'the Great Ones' frowns', to confront that authoritarian circle in Jenkins's office. There, 'upon the solemn promise it should not be used against his associates', he made his public confession: he told the assembly all he knew of the plans for the *coup d'état.* Then, having knelt before the King and been led by his Majesty to kiss the Queen's hand, he submitted to the same humiliation with York and his Duchess.[4] York, giving his grudging acceptance of the apology, could bring himself to make no more severe or retaliatory request for the moment than that his nephew should be sobered with a stint in the Tower.[5] But Charles merely ordered that James be confined to his lodgings under the eye of a sergeant-at-arms, until the pardon was signed and announced. He also, apparently, gave him a present of £6,000.[6]

'At Night 29 could not dissemble his Satisfaction, press'd my Hand; whch I remember not he did before, except when I return'd from the *French* Service,' wrote James. '29 acted his Part well, and I too. 39 and D[uchess] seem'd not ill pleas'd.' Welwood put it less modestly: . . . the Night [Monmouth] appear'd first at Court upon his Reconciliation, King *Charles* was so little Master of himself, that he could not dissemble a mighty Joy in his Countenance, and in everything he did or said: insomuch that it was the publick Talk about Town.'[7] '39' was 'blinded'; Charles was happy; his joy spread through the kingdom, and James heard his name echoing in the London streets again: 'The Protestant Duke is home! A-Monmouth! A-Monmouth!'

It sounded as good as a return to the 'Duking Days', when Shaftesbury was a power to be reckoned with, and the Green Ribbonites, led by their Great Men, swaggered across the cobblestones, hats at the 'Monmouth cock', below Whitehall; when the City was all saucy gossip of 'Jemmy' travelling in the West, 'dancing on the green' and 'carrying off the Plate'; and toasts were drunk, 'God bless his Majesty and confound the Duke of York', with little fear of the pillory or Newgate. Particularly in the West Country, the Dissenters were reported as 'strangely impudent' when they had news of Monmouth's being back in favour.[8] There was a sense, germinating in England, that, because the Protestant Duke, 'the harbinger of freedom', was reunited with the King, the old political balance might soon be restored, and, with it, the City Charters and Protestant liberty, in perpetuity.

But no member of Monmouth's committee of six would live much longer, if York could help it. When James remonstrated with his father as to 'how cruelly that noble lord [Russell] was dealt with', Charles, showing again how far he had slid under his brother's thumb, replied, in the words of James's diary, 'that he inclin'd to have sav'd him, but was forc'd to it, otherwise he must have broke with 39'.[9] And, while James's pardon was going through, the treason case of York's other *bête noire*, Algernon Sidney, the cleverest and toughest of the insurgents, was heard at the Court of the King's Bench.

To clinch it, Sir George Jeffreys had been appointed to succeed the relatively impartial Pemberton as Lord Chief Justice. Sidney defended himself courageously and skilfully. And, because Howard of Escrick produced the only valid evidence* – that of Sidney's sending Aaron Smith to Scotland and attending the Council of Six meetings – Jeffreys decided, quite unlawfully, that the accused's revolutionary, if unpublished, *Treatise on Government*,[11] would do in place of a second witness. When the jury returned their verdict of guilty, Sidney pleaded with the new Chief Justice for a fresh trial : 'My lord, there is one person I did not know where to find then, but every body knows where to find him now, that is the Duke of Monmouth . . . If he will support the evidence, I will acknowledge whatever you please.'

'That is over,' Jeffreys replied, tight-lipped; 'you were tried for this fact; we must not send for the Duke of Monmouth.'[12]

Then he pronounced poor Sidney's sentence : 'that you be carried hence to the place from whence you came, and from thence you shall be drawn upon an hurdle to the place of execution, where you shall be hanged by the neck, and, being alive, cut down, your privy-members shall be cut off, and burned before your face, your head severed from your body, and your body divided into four quarters, and they be disposed of at the pleasure of the King. And the God of infinite mercy have mercy upon your soul.'

'Then O God! O God!' cried Sidney, 'I beseech thee to sanctify these sufferings unto me, and impute not my blood to the country, nor the city through which I am to be borne. Let no inquisition be made for it, but if any, and the shedding of blood, that is innocent, must be revenged, let the weight of it fall only upon those that maliciously persecute me for righteousness' sake.'

At which Jeffreys rounded on him : 'I pray God work in you a temper fit to go unto the other world, for I see you are not fit for this.'

Sidney held out his hand for all the court to see : 'My lord, feel my pulse, and see if I am disordered; I bless God I never was in a better temper than I am now.'[13]

But Algernon was brother to the Earl of Leicester, to Sunderland's mother and to the diplomat, Henry Sidney, so, 'for the sake of his family', his sentence was commuted to beheading only. It was enough to satisfy York.

'As for news here,' he wrote to Orange on December 4, 'Algernon Sidney is to be beheaded on Friday next on Tower Hill, which besides the doing justice on so ill a man, will give the lie to the

---

*The King himself said of Howard, 'he is so ill a man, I would not hang my worst dog upon his evidence'.[10]

Whigs, who reported he was not to suffer. The Duke of Monmouth also, I am told, will somehow or other give them the lie, by owning in a more public way, than he has done yet, his knowledge of the conspiracy.'[14]

York's vindictive suspiciousness, and Monmouth's fears that the *rappochement* might turn sour, were hinted in the diary as early as 26 November : 'Coming home, L told me he fear'd 39 began to smell out 29's Carriage. That——said to 39 that Morning that all was done was but a Sham. 27. Several told me of the Storm that was brewing. *Rumsey* was with 39, and was seen to come out crying that he must accuse a Man he lov'd.'[15] By going about Court boasting that 'James has confirmed all that Howard has sworn',[16] Charles abrogated the promise that his son's confession would be treated in strict confidence. York did it with still more deadly effect: two days after the submission he had his nephew placarded in the Court Gazette as having practically turned King's evidence.

Furious at being thus cheated in the pledge that had been his only condition for the bargain, James felt quite justified in spreading the word among his friends that the gazette report was a lie,[17] that he had never endorsed the evidence of Howard of Escrick, and, furthermore, he believed Howard to be 'a liar and a rogue'. This statement, said Burnet, 'was set round the Town by his creatures, who run with it from coffee-house to coffee-house,' while at Whitehall James denied and ridiculed his father's loud claim of his 'confession' as energetically as he knew how.

So Halifax, who had been congratulating himself on the success of the *rapprochement*, and now seeing it in grave jeopardy, went hot-foot to the Protestant Duke, urging him to put his own version of the confession in writing. Reminding Halifax that he had been required to do 'nothing but what was safe and honourable', James wrote a statement of which nobody on his own side could complain. When York's people read it, they protested that it looked 'more like a justification of the plot (and to make them guilty who had assisted in all the prosecution'), than a confession. The Council rejected it out of hand.

Halifax said that York 'was perhaps more troubled at it [Monmouth's return] than at anything that ever happened to him in his life'.[18] For, in his heart, the Catholic Duke realised there was no longer room for both his nephew and himself at Court. He knew how to get rid of him, too : by urging the King to have him sign a paper that would hazard his friends' prospects. York was no genius, but, by thus placarding his nephew, he effectually checkmated the ablest man of his day, since to Halifax the move was as embarrassing as to the young Duke himself.

Charles, desperately anxious for the safety of the reconciliation, tried to steer his son before the Council again, to say his piece afresh. James objected: 'I said enough on Tuesday!'

'Yes, you were there with much ado forced to say something,' retorted his father with rising impatience, 'and did like a blockhead!'

'You have merely brought me back to do a job!'

'And why not? A better man than you – Gaston, Duke of Orleans, brother to Louis XIII – could not otherwise make his peace, and was forced to hang his comrades. You, if rightly served, should be forced to do the same!'[19]

James stood his ground. The King had another confession drawn up and demanded a holograph of it from his son, who objected to various sentences. 'It must be that or nothing!' snapped Charles, implying that the pardon would be withdrawn.

The trial of John Hampden, now on bail, the last surviving member of the Committee, was the next most important item on Jeffreys's schedule, and James was by no means sure that the unscrupulous York would not do his utmost to have anything he had written used as evidence for the prosecution. So he took the original copy of the King's concocted 'confession' to show to Hampden's father, who was that evening dining with Trenchard. Neither of them liked it. Afterwards, when young Hampden himself had a glimpse of it, he was aghast: 'I look upon it', he exclaimed, 'as my death warrant!'

James must have experienced a strong feeling that day of the goodness of men like Russell, Sidney and the Hampdens, father and son, and of their honour and courage. And, at the same time, have sensed something of the prostitution of his relationship with his own father, who, however infatuated he was with him as a son, seemed to despise him as a bastard, upon whose honour he placed little value. Contrasting himself, perhaps, with Hampden, who had the total support of *his* father, and whose life now balanced so precariously in the scales, James returned to Whitehall with a resolute refusal: 'I will not sign – it will hang young Hampden!'

'It will not,' Charles replied; 'nor will it ever be used for such a purpose.'

'I want the holograph back!' the Protestant Duke requested. Charles said he could have it on condition he first returned the original. James lied that he had burned it, but Halifax reasoned with him to give it up, which he did. James then put out his hand for the holograph, but Charles clutched the document tightly: 'Look you, if you do not yield in this you will ruin me!' he shouted.

James turned on his heel, Halifax followed and pleaded with him not to spoil it all. But James was obdurate. Halifax returned to find Charles shaking with fury. He thrust the paper at his Lord Privy Seal with a simple, final message : 'Tell him he can go to —— !'[20]

A few hours later the King sent his Vice-Chamberlain to forbid James the Court and 'to dislodge him from his lodgings at the Cockpit'.[21] James retired, first to his Holborn house, then to Moor Park – where he heard of Sidney's end and his last words before he rested his head on the block for Ketch – 'Now am I to suffer for the righteous cause'[22] – while on the same day, 7 December, York wrote a further bulletin to his son-in-law :

> '. . . Now 'tis visible to all the world that [Monmouth] only design'd by his coming in to get his pardon, and to keep his credit with his party still, both which he has now done . . . I hope this good will come of it, that his Majesty will now never believe any thing he says again, and then he can do but little harm. Algernon Sidney was beheaded this day, died very resolutely, and like a true rebel and republican.[23]

To complete his triumph, it only remained for York to see his nephew out of the kingdom. This he effected, in January, by arranging with Jeffreys – again in breach of the condition for James's submission – to have him subpoena'd to appear as 'first witness for the Crown' at Hampden's trial. Monmouth, as soon as he was warned of it, saw only one possible course : to retire to the Continent. So he bade goodbye to Anna and the surviving children he loved so deeply – James, the nine-year-old Earl of Dalkeith, Lady Anne, aged eight, and Lord Henry, aged seven. And with Roe and Williams, his servants, he took coach and horses across the icy roads – it was one of the bitterest winters of the century, with the Thames frozen over so hard that a coach and four could cross it with ease – and made his way to Greenwich, where he hired a fishing boat for the Netherlands.

Hampden got away with a crippling fine. And, as Burnet said, Monmouth 'was, upon this, more valued and trusted by his own party than ever'.[24] Nor, in spite of everything, had his father's love diminished : 'King *Charles's* Kindness ended not here,' Welwood observed, 'but attended him to Holland . . . He found secret means to furnish him with Money, and sent him messages from time to time, and sometimes writ to him in his own Hand. He could not bear any hard thing to be said of him in his Absence; and some officious Courtiers found to their Cost, that it was not the way to make their Fortune, to aggravate *Monmouth's* Crimes : Nor did the King take any thing more kindly than the noble Reception

Monmouth receiv'd from a Prince of his Blood in a foreign Country, when he was forc'd to abandon his own.'[25]

That prince was William of Orange, in whose politics James was now to become deeply embroiled.

22

1684–1685

'THE KING IS DEAD, GOD SAVE THE KING'

The Marquis of Grana, Governor of the Spanish Netherlands, anti-York and anti-French, received James warmly, awarding him the precedence of 'Royal Highness' and an annuity of £6,000. 'De Grana knew from whence the King's displeasure came,' said Ambassador Bulstrode; 'that it was the Duke of York that was the great enemy of the Duke of Monmouth, whom the King loved as his own eyes.' De Grana also gave him the colonelcy of a Spanish regiment, though there is no record as to whether the appointment was in an honorary or an active capacity. Whatever it was, having never thrived on in-activity James had no intention of being inactive now. He was absorbed in his soldiering studies; in his pockets were always a note-book or two, filling up with memoranda on fortifications and weapons and regimental organisations.[1] 'The Duke of Monmouth . . . has since his arrival been to view diverse places and especially such as are of strength,' wrote an English witness, 'observing the works, and curiously taking notice of such parts and places as are defective, showing himself therein not only a soldier, but an expert engineer . . .'[2]

He read a lot, too : 'He used to complain of the little care that had been taken of his Education,' Welwood remembered, 'and in his Disgrace endeavour'd to make up that Want, by applying himself to Study, in which he made, in a short time, no inconsiderable Progress. He took the occasion of his Afflictions to inform his Mind, and recollect and amend the Errors of Youth, which it was not strange he should be tainted with, being bred up in all the Pleasures of a Luxurious Court.'[3]

Henrietta Wentworth was soon firmly established in Flanders, as his 'wife'. 'Desperately in love with him', as Burnet said, 'accompanied by her mother, she followed him to Brussels', where they lived in a large house with a substantial retinue of servants.[4] Since James's favourite diversions were racing and hunting, and at Moor Park and Newmarket he stabled a most envied string of horses, many of which he had bred and schooled himself, it is not surprising he should want them with him in exile. Nor did Secretary Jenkins fail to keep himself informed of the Duke's way of life. On 13 March 1684 the Secretary's agent, John Elton, took note of the pattern of three-masters at the port of Harwich, lying still upon the water as upon a millpond, and of a shipment of valuable horse-flesh* going from the dockyard lines to the quayside:

I saw one of the Duke of Monmouth's servants in a disguise, so I pretended not to be well Saturday night, and did not go by the mail. Here are 13 horses of the Duke of Monmouth . . . with their grooms going for Ostend, on pretence of going for Zuricksee to a merchant, and a pilot is sent hither by the Marquis of Grana to conduct them thither . . . The horses are shipped to-day, but I think the wind will not carry them away . . .[5]

Although James contrived to surround himself with his worldly requirements, his enemies still found thorns for him. York sent orders, under the King's seal, to Bulstrode, to the effect that his nephew was not to be saluted, or honoured in any other way, by the officers of the English garrison. On 1 July, Chaloner Chute wrote from 'the camp at Lessenes' to the Countess of Rutland: 'The gracious prince [Monmouth] is our neighbour here at Brussels and, as it is said here, the Lady Harriot W—— with him . . . He had an affront put upon him the other day by the English officers in that service, all of them refusing to salute him at a review that there was there.'[6] A former army subordinate of James's and a relation of Henrietta's, Bevil Skelton (who was described by Burnet as 'the haughtiest, but withal the weakest man'), now an envoy in Germany, replying to a letter from Bulstrode that summer, said he was 'very much troubled to understand . . . that the Lady Hen Wentworth is so dangerously sick, but am much more concerned that the D. of Monmouth takes such care of her, and think it were better she should die than bring a scandal upon her self . . . I must confess I approved not of her conduct and much less of her mother's, who humours her in it . . .' When Bulstrode opened de Grana's eyes to

*This included his racehorse, Tankard, for which a very high price was soon to be given.

the lovers' true relationship, they were asked to leave the country.[7]

But James knew of another sanctuary. During his sojourn in Flanders he had been shown 'the utmost marks of friendship' by his first cousin, William of Orange, who (in the words of Louis's devious Ambassador, Count D'Avaux) 'commanded all the troops of the States to pay the same honours to the Duke of Monmouth, as they did to Count Waldeck, their general'; and when the English officers, complying with York's order from London, declined to salute him, William 'sent to the principal persons amongst them, informing them that he would break the first man who should fail to treat the Duke of Monmouth as he commanded'.[8] It was a deliberate affront to his father-in-law.

But, fond as he was of his handsome cousin, Orange valued him primarily for the same purpose that he prized his Stuart princess, as a mounting-block from which to climb into the English saddle, ultimately the only position, as he saw it, from which he could defend his country from the imperialist ambitions of Louis XIV. It seemed to William that, unless he could treble his strength, a French hegemony of all Europe, perhaps even a Catholic hegemony, with Holland the next to be engulfed, would be inevitable.

England, he told himself, was the only hope – not in some half-hearted alliance, but in full coalition with Holland, with William at the helm of both countries. And he recognised, in Monmouth, a vitally important piece in the power struggle, for he knew the King of England 'loved his son as his own eyes', that Charles was determined to banish York, and have Monmouth home at Court. William realised, too, that by befriending Monmouth now, by taking him into his confidence and forming a political bond with him, he might easily persuade him, as soon as Whitehall's revolution was accomplished, to invite him on to the Privy Council, and then – with his impossible Catholic father-in-law safely in Scotland and the Exclusionists powerful again – they, William and Mary, would be proclaimed heirs, while he himself might be hailed as the Protestant saviour of Europe.

And Monmouth? He had told William he had no ambition to be King of England. Besides, William was quite aware that the strongest element of the Exclusionist group wanted him and Mary, not Monmouth, to rule next. So William, having a high opinion of his cousin as a military commander, saw him returning to his old appointment as Captain-General and as commander of the Anglo-Dutch defence force. D'Avaux, still writing reports, which would catch Barillon's eye, reports intended to alienate the Dutch from the English, gives his version of the reception lavished upon 'England's outcast':

The Duke of Monmouth has been for some days . . . at Dieren; the Prince of Orange not only entertained him there in the grandest manner, but . . . took care he should be received in his journey to Nimejgen with extraordinary honours . . . The Prince and the Duke continue to hunt together at Dieren . . . The Princess of Orange has shown extraordinary marks of honour to a young lady of quality from England [Lady Wentworth], who passes for the Duke of Monmouth's mistress . . . The Duke of York writes twice a week to the Prince [who] generally shuts himself up for two hours with the Duke of Monmouth, when he receives these letters . . .[9]

Of course York was furious to hear that his son-in-law received the outrageous nephew at all, and receiving no response to his indignation from William, he tried Mary: '. . . it scandalises all loyal and monarchical people here', he told her, 'to know how well the Prince lives with, and how civil he is, to the Duke of Monmouth . . . let the Prince flatter himself as he pleases, the Duke of Monmouth will do his part to have a push with him for the crown, if he, the Duke of Monmouth, outlive the King and me . . . It will become you very well to speak to him of it'.[10]

William was right. Charles, more weary than ever of York's arrogance, bigotry and domineering ways, was looking earnestly for an opportunity to send his brother away and have Monmouth back at Court. And Halifax was quite ready to help him, for 'the Trimmer's' opinion had not changed since his speech in 1681 threw out the Exclusion Bill: William and Mary were the best candidates to follow King Charles. Meanwhile Monmouth's potential and essential roles remained the same: to keep the balance of power in London right, to overshadow Catholic York, to regain the correct place in English politics for the Popular Party, and thus to pave the way first for the recall of Parliament, then for a Stuart–Orange dynasty.

When Charles objected, for his brother's sake, to the warm hospitality shown to James at Dieren, William knew he was bluffing. Because once, when the Prince visited England, Charles, the arch-dissembler, showed him one of his seals, and told him that whatever he might write of a controversial nature, if the letter was not sealed with that seal, the Prince could disregard it, or 'look on it as only drawn from him by importunity'.[11]

This compact with William placed Monmouth in a very difficult position apropos the other members of his party, some of whom had been hiding in Holland for over a year. For while he had his pardon they were outlaws, wanted for treason, and if word went back to his father that he was consorting with them, it would certainly jeopardise his chances of being recalled to London. So he left them severely alone, and, as Lord Grey of Werke says in his account of those days, he in particular, strongly resented it.[12]

Charles, for his part, was determined to destroy the chief revolutionaries, so that when the time came for a full and lasting reconciliation with his son the old evil influences would be eliminated. The one he wanted most urgently removed was Sir Thomas Armstrong, who had been hiding under the name 'Bowman' and was now 'Henry Lawrence', the man who, Burnet says, 'was trusted by the Duke of Monmouth in everything', the old warrior who had partially usurped Charles's position as father. So Chudleigh, the English envoy at the Hague, was told to be on a sharp look-out for Armstrong, for whose capture there was a reward of 5,000 guilders (which, the chronicler Eachard said, was 'equal to the greatest'[13]).

One day Chudleigh's scouts, spotting Sir Thomas and Grey boarding a boat at Leyden, crept aboard and pounced on them. Grey, ever the slippery eel, wrenched himself free and dashed ashore; but Armstrong, sixty now, weakened by the rigours of penniless exile, and terrified of facing judgement in England, tried first to stab himself, then to throw himself overboard. However, Chudleigh's men got him in chains, unscathed, and took him to London. Jeffreys, knowing how badly the King wanted him sent to a traitor's death, but finding no witnesses against him (except Titus Oates, who had nothing relevant to say, but was only trying to make himself popular at Court again), argued that, being stigmatised an outlawed traitor, the captive was not entitled to a trial.

Armstrong reasoned from the dock of the King's Court Bench that, having been abroad, he had not heard he was a wanted man, and that, besides, having come into custody within a year, as he now did, the outlawry was annulled. Jeffreys replied that, since he had failed to surrender himself, that clause did not apply: 'We think it quite to the contrary, Sir Thomas!'

'I ought to have the benefit of the law,' Tom cried across the courtroom, 'and I ask no more!'

'That you shall have by the grace of God. We have nothing to do upon this record before us but to authorise execution.' Jeffreys turned to the Keeper of Newgate. 'Capt Richardson, what are your days of execution?'

'Wednesdays and Fridays, my lord.'

'Then see that the execution is done on Friday next, *according to the law*.'

Standing beside him, Tom's daughter, Mrs Matthews, who had

already forcefully petitioned that her father 'might have a writ of error allowed him to reverse the outlawry', shouted from her box at Jeffreys: 'My lord, I hope you will not murder my father?'

'Who is this woman? . . .' asked the Lord Chief Justice. 'Must you take upon you to tax the courts of justice when we grant the execution according to the law? God Almighty's judgement will light upon those who are guilty of high treason . . . Take her away!'

'This is murdering a man!' shrieked Mrs Matthews, assaulting Jeffreys's sang-froid again. 'God Almighty's judgement light upon *you*!' she yelled.

'I thank God I am clamour proof,' said Jeffreys, quietly, as he watched Tom's daughter dragged away to prison.

'My blood be upon your head!' Armstrong hissed.

'Let it, let it, I am clamour proof . . .'

Being married to a niece of Clarendon's, a cousin of Rochester's and of the first Duchess of York's, besides having held senior rank in the Household Cavalry, Armstrong might have expected, like Russell and Sidney, the privilege of Ketch's axe. But the King denied him even this. Surrounded by a huge party of guardsmen, some of whom had served under his command, the old warrior, who had survived so many campaign adventures with the Protestant Duke he loved, was hanged, drawn and quartered. By the evening one of his forequarters was on its way for public display in Stafford, for which town he had once sat as a Member of Parliament, while his head was impaled on a spike between the hideous blackened skulls of Cromwell and the regicide, Bradshaw.[14]

William, sympathising strongly with James's shock and despair over his friend's fate, was very angry that Armstrong had been captured and removed from Holland. D'Avaux, 'King Louis's prying eyes at the Hague', gave his master an account of William's interview with certain deputies shortly afterwards; of how 'the Prince of Orange . . . came to them, and, without allowing them to speak, told the bailiff of Leyden that he was extremely impudent to dare to come into his presence after the infamous action he had been guilty of, in delivering up Armstrong to the King of England; and asked him if he knew the danger he was in at Dieren, for the Duke of Monmouth was there, and would perhaps take vengeance on him for the shameful action he had committed'.[15]

Starting out from William's palace, that November of 1684, James paid a visit to London. His pocket-book recalls his surreptitious route: 'The way that I took from Dieren when I went for England Nov the 10.84. From Dieren to Arnhem, 3 leagues. From Arnhem to Nijmegen, 3 leagues. From Nijmegen I turned back again and went to Wychen, 2 leagues from Nijmegen to the right hand . . .' Two weeks later he had a secret interview with his father. There is only one account of the mission : it comes from the pen of the Presbyterian minister and scholar, the Rev. William Veitch (who last reported on James's fortunes after the Battle of Bothwell Bridge, in 1679). A faithful and well informed, if heavily biassed, witness of the political scene in London at the time, Veitch states that James made his journey with the greatest anxiety, after receiving very positive reports of 'the Duke of York and his jesuitical cabal's plotting how to take the King off the stage'.

Reaching London, says the priest, James '. . . sent for Lord Alington,* then governor of the Tower of London, being his great friend and favourite, telling him that he must needs go to the King and acquaint him that he is in town, and has a business of great importance to impart to him'. When James gave his warning, the King showed great surprise, 'not so much from his not being apprehensive of the thing, as it should have come the length of [Monmouth's] ears abroad, as that he should have showed so much kindness as to make such a dangerous adventure to inform him. So that after they had discoursed to the full, ere they parted, the King gave him as many jewels out of his cabinet as were valued at £10,000 sterling, as it is said : so he returned incognito again to Holland.'[16]

When Charles asked Alington – 'he being a wise man and one of his greatest confidants at that time' – what he should do, the old soldier, who had fought under James at Maastricht, and whom James had always held in great respect, merely confirmed all that the King knew in his heart to be true : 'Sir, you have brought it upon yourself, by turning the Duke of Monmouth out of all his places, especially his command over the Guards about your person, and suffering such to be put in who are the Duke of York's creatures.'

'But what shall I do now?' asked the King.

'Sir, I neither can, nor dare, advise you in that matter,' answered Alington – knowing, as Governor of the Tower, the jealousy of the York faction – 'for if it be heard, as likely it will, it may hasten both our ruins !'

When Alington was given satisfaction that any counsel he offered would be treated in the strictest confidence, he is said to have spoken his mind as follows : 'Now Sir, my advice is this, that seeing, within a few weeks, the appointed time will be that the Duke of York is

---

*William, 2nd Baron Alington, of Killard, in Ireland, in 1682, he was also created Baron Alington of Wymley in Hertfordshire. He was Constable of the Tower at the time of Essex's death. He married Lady Diana Russell, sister of William, Lord Russell. He was a principle chronicler of the siege of Maastricht.

obliged to go to Scotland, to hold the next session of his parliament, take care to give him his commission, and send him timeously away; and, when he is there, send for the Duke of Monmouth, restore him to all his places, and remove from the Court all persons that are suspected to favour the Duke of York's interest.'[17]

'King Charles, Welwood remembered, 'tir'd out at last with the uncontroul'd hardships that were every day put upon him by the Duke's [York's] Creatures, and ashamed to see his own Lustre obscur'd, and his Power lessen'd by a Party that had rais'd themselves upon Monmouth's Ruin, he resolv'd to shift the Scene; and, in order to make himself easy for the rest of his Life, as he expres'd it, he determin'd to send away the Duke of York and recall the Duke of Monmouth.'[18] At the end of the month, states Veitch, York was duly warned by his brother that he would be required to preside over the Scottish session the following February.[19] York, finding himself in a corner, jibbed, saying 'I have a great trade at Calais and other foreign places, and many years' accounts to clear with these foreign factors, wherein I and other great merchants in the City are concerned. Being now upon our journey, I must needs stay to clear with them, and, therefore, I desire earnestly to be excused.'

'Either you must go', Charles told him, 'or I must go.'

York, who knew that Scotland meant banishment, irrevocable replacement by Monmouth, and, perhaps, ruin, was then openly rebellious : 'I will *not* go !'[20]

Eventually, Charles made his wishes clear, in York's presence, before the Council : 'In February His Royal Highness shall go to Edinburgh, to open, and to preside over the Parliament.' So everything seemed to be settled for Monmouth, who had left London on 10 December. On the 19th he wrote in his diary at Dieren : 'A letter from 29 [Charles], bidding me stay till I heard farther from him.' And early in the New Year : 'I receiv'd a letter from L [Halifax], mark'd by 29 in the Margin, to trust intirely to 10 [William?]; and that in *February* I should certainly have leave to return. That Matters were concerted towards it; and that 39 [York] had no Suspicion, not withstanding of my Reception here . . .'

If we are to believe D'Avaux, the more certain Orange became of his cousin Monmouth's restoration the more indulgent he was towards him. The Ambassador tells how William invited James to the Hague and how Mary at first refused to receive him, 'it being the eve before sacrament-day there was not a lady of the Hague with her'. How William forced her to play hostess to James, and how, 'though [the Prince] is asthmatic and fond of no recreation, much less of dancing', he not only 'continued to heap carresses upon the Duke of Monmouth' but joined in the dancing every evening. How he and Mary and James 'went on a sledge on the ice . . . to a seat of the Prince three leagues from Hague; and, when they danced, the Princess of Orange was the Duke of Monmouth's partner. He went every day regularly to the Princess, at her dinner-time though she dined alone and in private . . .' And D'Avaux wondered how William, 'who is by nature the most jealous of all men living, could suffer all those airs of gallantry, which were so public to the world, between his Princess and the Duke . . .'[21] But, as James was to prove, this was simply D'Avaux's troublemaking: his heart was only for Henrietta Wentworth.

On 3 February he caught up with his diary: 'A letter from L that my Business was almost as well done; but must be so sudden as not to leave room for 39's party to counterplot. That it is probable he [York] would chuse Scotland, rather than *Flanders* or this Country.' Welwood recorded that 'April was the time agreed on to put this Resolution into practise; but there is little left us by which we can judge whether Monmouth was to be recall'd to Court by a formal invitation of the King's, or whether King Charles's usual Thread of Dissimulation was to be spun out to that length that Monmouth was to land with an armed force . . .'[22] Whatever the scheme James was exultant: very soon, he supposed, after the torment of five and a half years' banishment, he would be home, in London, in favour again, and his enemies struck low. It would be a victory greater than Maastricht or Mons or Bothwell Bridge; it would, in a way, be the greatest triumph of his life.

But a brief note in the pocket diary for 16 February tells of the dreadful reverse James now suffered. 'The sad news of his death by L. O *cruel* fate.' His hopes were dashed at a single stroke.

Lord Alington had died of poison two days before the King. The Rev. William Veitch says this was done 'by bribing his cook and master-household'. If so, who made the bribe? Could it have been York? Or Lord Sunderland, who had recently been appointed Secretary of State for the South, and, closely committed in York's intrigues, would have had as much to lose as anyone if Charles had followed Alington's advice? There is a good case against Sunderland for the murder of Essex. If the King 'should have succumbed to any accident', Alington would have been a dangerous witness.

In Veitch's version, York was informed by his spy the moment Alington's 'breath went out', so that he 'should be the first that should carry the news to the King, lamenting such a heavy loss to blind the matter'. Veitch states that the Catholic Duke ran to Charles 'in great haste, with one of his shoes down in the heel, and one of his stockings untied'. The King's comment in reply to his brother's simulated remorse ('a very sad stroke to the Court', said York) was, according to Veitch, 'aye, and his servant thinks he was poisoned : I wish you have not a hand in it, of which, if I were sure, you should presently go to the Tower, for I am like to be next'. York, 'entreating his Majesty to have no such thoughts, and acknowledging his fault in refusing to go to Scotland', Veitch continues, 'said he was now resolv'd to comply with his Majesty's commands, and take journey next week for Scotland, come of his business what would; and therefore desir'd his Majesty to expede his commission next week, that he might not be hinder'd'.[23]

Veitch then sets out a detailed account of the King's death, naming the physicians who vouch he was deliberately poisoned. Separately, Bishop Burnet gives a similar opinion,[24] and so do the Bishop of Salisbury, the Duchess of Portsmouth and the Earl of Mulgrave. 'From what [the Bishop of Salisbury] says of that death,' wrote Oldmixon, 'there is no room left to doubt that he was poison'd . . . To prevent that King's intention to recall the Duke of Monmouth the Papists would doubtless have sacrificed . . . whomsoever lay in their way.'[25] Doubtless, too, there were, in the Whig ranks, plenty of witnesses who would have been prepared to speak, had they not valued their personal safety more than they wished the 'truth' to be broadcast. Or was the whole thing a fabrication, stemming only from Whig malice? Whatever we are to believe, in the analysis of Monmouth's career, it is not especially important whether his father was poisoned, or whether he died of 'gout' or an 'apoplectic fit', as was given out. What mattered was the substance of the reports that reached the ears of England's disaffected faction, of Monmouth himself and of the exiles and outlaws in Holland. Their intelligence was unequivocal : it was that Charles, as well as Essex and Alington, were 'murdered by the Duke of York and his creatures'. As far as many of them were concerned, York had also usurped the throne, for Monmouth was the rightful heir.

How was the news received at the Hague? D'Avaux reported to King Louis that, when James first heard it, he retired 'to the Prince of Orange's apartment till ten at night, and they two remained shut up by themselves till midnight', and that 'the Duke of Monmouth has been ever since like a man raving mad. He has been heard, in the little house where he lodges, making bitter cries and lamentations.'[26]

The moment Charles was taken ill, York had all the ports closed and the coastal garrisons put on the alert, and his first move as King was to send an express to William demanding that his nephew be arrested and sent prisoner to England.[27] In reply William protested that he 'only took the Duke of Monmouth into his protection for the sake of maintaining the Protestant religion in England'.[28] But people who were close to William, and other interested parties who had their ears close to the ground, observed that, although the Prince must now exile the 'Protestant Duke', he remained in political league with him almost to the end.

James, however, was not immediately in the mood for intrigue. Having lost the father who had been the anchor of his life, his only desire for the moment was to have the solace and comfort of Henrietta. Indeed his life seemed to be repeating the pattern of his early childhood – the pattern of being harassed in the Netherlands, in the company of a woman who adored him. Would he find a permanent refuge there in her arms? Or would he be tempted by the astrologer who told him he could 'be a great man again'? Or was he so crucial a piece on the chessboard that his future could no longer be determined by his own will? Was he rather a man of destiny whose part must be played remorselessly through for the sake of England's political evolution? From the day the news of Charles's death reached the Netherlands the Monmouthite exiles, previously toasting their figurehead as 'Prince of Wales', now lifted their glass to 'King James'.

Exiled from Holland at such short notice there was only one way James and Henrietta could turn, and that was to the Spanish Netherlands.[29] De Grana, fond of them both, despite his ethical reservations, would have kept quiet about their arrival there, and allowed them to stay, but the King of Spain, eager to comply with the wishes of his Catholic cousin of England, ordered their arrest. De Grana gave James a day in which to make good his escape, and Henrietta three days. For the moment the lovers parted ways.

An anglophile officer, called Don Valera, captivated by Henrietta, gave a farewell ball in her honour at Antwerp. But, having no other desire but to be with James, she thought the dance a great bore, and sighed with relief to receive, just as the music was striking up, a furtive messenger who had mingled with the guests, to hand her a note from James telling her where he was hiding in the town, that the coast was clear and to come quick. So, informing her host she would return in a few minutes, Henrietta lifted her skirts above her toes, and, creeping down the backstairs, as poor Don Valera afterwards told Lord Bruce, 'left him the jest of the company'.[30]

James decided they must return to Holland, where, although they would be branded as outlaws, it was unlikely they would be in any danger from William's men. The hazard was English agents. When they stopped at an inn, on the way back to Rotterdam, a servant of James's went down to fetch their supper, and heard two Englishmen speaking in a shouted whisper. 'That fellow who went upstairs looked very like the Duke of Monmouth!' one of them said, thinking no doubt of the fat reward that was out for James. The servant hurried to his master, who quickly packed and led the party out by the back entrance, and on to Gouda, twelve miles north-east of Rotterdam. There James's 'friend and factor', James Washington, had found them a home.[31]

One imagines a bourgeois house of red brick and white stone, with fancifully stepped gables and a heavy front door, lit by an oil lamp, giving out on to a scrubbed pavement, and inwards on to a lofty *voorhuis*; a floor of great chequered flagstones, and walls lined with Gouda tiles, with the smell of peat coming from a hearth, backed by a tarred wall. Behind that, a spotless kitchen, full of shining pots and plates and scrubbed boards; above the heavy staircase, two or three bedrooms with four-poster beds, intricately carved, with, in place of sheets and blankets, heavy, feather mattresses. And mullioned windows, thrown open, with this clear spring of 1685, to show a flat, open landscape of vivid pastures, placid dykes, poplars and watermills. Had James not seen himself labelled as an outlaw for ever, it is doubtful that he would have even envisaged the drastic step he was about to take, but would have remained forever in this Dutch – or some other – Toddington. 'In all human probability', thought the contemporary historian, Ralph, 'if the new King had not follow'd him with persecutions and branded him in his letters with High Treason, the Duke of Monmouth had never been over-persuaded to incur the guilt of it'.[32] 'It' was the armed invasion of his uncle's Kingdom.

23

March–May 1685

PLOT OF INVASION

The Earl of Argyle, Chief of the Campbells, small, dark and intense, had, since his dramatic and ingenious escape from Edinburgh Castle in 1682 and his flight from London to Holland in the year of the Rye House Plot, been living on his estates in Friesland. And, for over a year now, he had been planning to invade the West Highlands, home of his Covenanter clansmen, to lead a revolutionary army against Edinburgh and to overthrow the English Viceroy. Raising money from his Dutch estate and being made a present of £10,000 by 'one Madam Smith, with whom he lived in Utrecht' (as Nathaniel Wade alleged[1]), Argyle was the richest of the exiles, and for the past ten months had been sending shipments of arms for distribution among his Highland confederates.[2]

The man the Covenanter Earl hated, perhaps most in the world, was the Prince who had proved such a vindictive Scottish Viceroy, who had unjustly imprisoned him and was prepared to see him executed, the Prince who had recently succeeded to England's crown as the first Catholic monarch since 'Bloody' Mary. Immediately on receiving the news of Charles's death, Argyle sped to Amsterdam to finalise his invasion plans, for he was determined to raise the clans before the new King's coronation, or at least before the assembly of Parliament, which, to the surprise of many, the King had promised for April (although he had no intention, in principle, of ruling through the Houses[3]). But the accession of James II also complicated Argyle's plan, for – since Monmouth had been in correspendence with his father in the full expectation of reconciliation, an end to his outlawry and return to favour – most of the English exiles, yearning for action, had offered their services to the Scots Earl; and, but for the death of Charles, would have found themselves on a Caledonian adventure. Now, however, they looked with fresh hope towards their own natural leader, the Protestant Duke. What they proposed was a joint command.

But a man like Argyle, who would not debate his plans, or divulge his operational secrets, or delegate any but the most elementary tasks, to his (perfectly competent) lieutenants,* but took all the decision making, without consultation, on himself, was not likely to enter a partnership with the merciful victor of Bothwell Bridge, of whose stature and popularity in Scotland he was jealous. In March, however, another Scot came to Amsterdam with the express purpose of bringing Monmouth and Argyle together. This was the very influential Sir Patrick Hume, who not long before had been released after four years' imprisonment in Stirling Castle. Hume, a former M.P. for Berwick (and one day to be celebrated as the Earl of Marchmont and Lord Chancellor of Scotland), found Argyle extremely difficult – 'high, peremptory and passionate' he called him – very touchy where Monmouth was concerned and given to quite unwarranted optimism about his prospective support in Scotland.[4] It was therefore with rather a heavy heart that the practical and rational Hume set off in search of Monmouth.

Monmouth's prestige as military commander was not easily forgotten on the Continent, and, as soon as his father died and it was known that his name headed his uncle's list of traitors, there were others, besides Hume, clamouring for his services: the Emperor of Austria had again, through Orange, offered him a generalcy in the campaign against the Turks;[5] the Elector of Brandenberg had a command waiting for him if he would take it;[6] and the French Protestants, who were at this time planning an armed revolt against Louis, had, with the approval of their unofficial allies – Brunswick, Brandenberg and Orange – invited him to come in and lead them.[7] But, in Monmouth's head, their appeals were drowned by the persistent pleas of his confederates.

The psychological upheavals of the last few years – the moral conflict of his liaison with Henrietta, and the responsibility owed, but scarcely paid, to his Duchess and children, the violent deaths of so many close friends, the ignominy of his exile, the hope and sudden disappointment of the previous February, and the mourning for his father – had deepened James's personality, rendered him a more serious man, one for whom revenge on his uncle and the setting free of the English people from the Tory régime and the threat of 'papism' had become an abiding purpose. How many times during his exile, pricked by a genuine devotion to his fellow countrymen,

*Lord Melville, Sir John and Sir George Cochrane of Ochiltree, and Argyle's kinsmen, Sir Hugh and Sir George Campbell, of Cessnock.

did he hear the phantom echoes of 'A-Monmouth! A-Monmouth and the Protestant Religion'? Or see, in his mind's eye, that vivid scene of a thousand young West Countrymen marching out to meet him four and a half years earlier, 'brave companies of stout young men, all cloth'd in linen waistcoats and drawers'? And how often did he see them in the vain eye of his mind with 'pott, breast and back, musket in the hand, sword on the waist'? And yet, as he was to tell everyone to whom he spoke on that subject, he knew the time was not ripe for invasion. The trouble was that the firebrands he was dealing with knew him to be a man who could easily be swayed against his judgement.

The fact that his fellow exiles were down-at-heel and out-at-elbow – without a change of stockings or cravat, and never quite sure where the next meal was coming from, and certainly unable to raise so much as 50 guilders to buy a campaign-worthy musket – did little to restrain their eagerness to spill their blood in a cause for which they had sacrificed everything else during the past seven years. Soon 'Plotter' Ferguson conferred with Grey of Werke, 'in that lord's garret in Amsterdam', telling him that 'if the Duke of Monmouth did not act speedily for the redemption of his country, there were those that would without him'.[8] Feelers were extended on both sides. Captain Edward Matthews, the son-in-law of Tom Armstrong, who was now Monmouth's aide-de-camp, was sent to 'enquire if my Lord Argyle's party would communicate',[9] while one of the Englishmen in the Covenanter Earl's camp – Heywood Dare, probably, the old Taunton goldsmith whom Monmouth liked and trusted most – wrote asking if the Protestant Duke was prepared to take the lead again. James's reply, written from Gouda and recorded by Welwood, was cautious, rational and apparently honest:

. . . You may well believe I have had time enough to reflect sufficiently upon our present State, especially since I came hither. But whatever way I turn my Thoughts, I find insuperable Difficulties. Pray do not think it an Effect of Melancholy, for that was never my greatest Fault, when I tell you, That in these three Weeks Retirement in this Place, I have not only look'd back, but forward; and the more I consider our present Circumstances, I think them still the more desperate, unless some unforeseen Accident fall out, which I cannot divine nor hope for . . . Judge then what we are to expect, in case we should venture upon any such Attempt at this time. It's to me a vain argument that our Enemies are scarce yet well settled, when you consider that Fear in some and Ambition in others have brought them to comply; and that the Parliament being made up for the most part of Members that formerly ran our Enemies down, they will be ready to make their Peace as soon as they can, rather than hazard themselves upon an uncertain Bottom. I give you but Hints of what, if I had time, I would write you at more length: But that I may not seem obstinate in my own Judgement, or neglect the Advice of my Friends, I will meet you at the Time and Place appointed. But for God's sake think in the mean time of the Improbabilities that lie naturally in our way; and let us not, by struggling with our Chains, make them straiter and heavier. For my part I'll run the hazard of being thought any thing, rather than a rash inconsiderate Man. And to tell you my Thoughts without disguise, I am now so much in love with a retir'd Life that I am never like to be fond of *making a Bustle in the World again.* I have much more to say, but the Post cannot stay; and I refer the rest till meeting, being entirely Yours,

Monmouth.[10]

Had the sixteen lines of cipher, contained in the middle of that letter, been translated for posterity, we might have been shown that he was already more deeply involved in the plans than he pretended. In any case, it was a willing enough Monmouth that Lord Melville and Sir Patrick Hume met a little later in Amsterdam.[11]

'In what character would your Grace go with us?' (Hume gave a stilted recording of the interview in a letter to his sister[12]).

'As a Protestant and an Englishman, for the liberties of the Nations, and against the Duke of York . . .' replied James.

'Do you consider yourself the lawful son of King Charles?'

'I do.'

'Are you able to prove your mother's marriage to King Charles?'

'If certain people are not dead, I shall be able to prove it,' James told him. (Margaret Gosfritt would have been one to whom he referred.)

'Does your Grace intend to claim the Crown?'

'Not unless I am so advised. I would lay no such claim, nor use any such title, but to the advantage of the common cause. If victory is given me I will lay it down in the hands of the people or their representatives, for the establishment of their religion and good model of government. I shall cheerfully accept what station in the Government they shall bestow on me.'

James added that he would be willing, at a propitious time, to go to Scotland in joint command with Argyle. But, when Hume passed this on, 'the Erle started exceedingly . . . and expressed great dislike of the Duke going to Scotland, saying he could signify nothing where he had so little acquaintance'. And that, while he was perfectly aware of Monmouth's great name as a commander of regular troops, 'he knew him not very fit for making the best of a few parties, which would be our first work'.[13]

What was certain was that when James – with his affability, tact and long-tried facility for reconciling differences – took command of the English exiles, most of the bitterness and disharmony existing between them disappeared. As Ralph said: 'Like all projectors not being as yet dispos'd to submit to a Master, each had a scheme of his own and insisted on the pursuing that or none. When therefore his Grace came among them his first business was to make up their quarrels.'[14] Burnet said much the same: 'The Duke . . . came secretly to them and made up all their quarrels.'[15]

Argyle and Monmouth met on 6 April at Heywood Dare's house in Amsterdam, where they agreed upon concerted invasions of England and Scotland. What was not so easily agreed was the timing. While the Earl was adamant in his opinion that they should converge to land before the coronation, or as soon as possible after it, James did his best to persuade him to postpone the expedition. He stressed that the English party, whatever funds might be available, would need several months in which to collect all the arms and stores necessary for such an expedition, to train and to shake down into a disciplined hierarchy and credible skeleton order of battle, and to gather and disseminate intelligence.[16] James pressed another argument on the Scot: 'The Duke of York has remedied the most crying need of the last reign' – all the exiles continued to refer to the new King by his former title – 'by calling a Parliament in both kingdoms. Do you not see, my lord, the time of sitting being at hand, the Parliaments will grant him all the assistance he demands, and their authority will be great.'[17]

The only voices in tune with James appear to have been those of Captain Matthews and of a thirty-year-old intellectual laird, Andrew Fletcher of Saltoun. Otherwise the Scots and the leading English rebels, too – Grey, Dare, Ferguson, Ayloffe, Rumbold and Wade – urged the earliest possible military operation. The people, they insisted, especially the Londoners, Midlanders and West Country-men, had never been in such a rebellious mood, and never longed more fiercely for 'the second coming of the Protestant Duke'. The Guards, who remembered and loved His Grace, they said, would desert; the Whig gentry would bring over the militia; the Prince of Orange was their sponsor, and above all 'the Duke's popularity would be a certain overmatch for the King's power'.[18] They urged immediate action, an invasion four months before harvest time. James paused. In 1682–3 it was he who had been the cautious one,

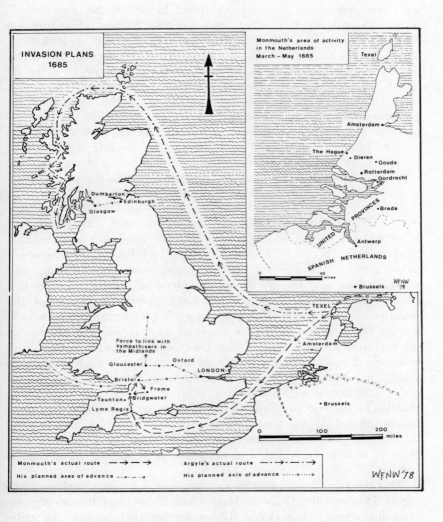

Invasion Plans, 1685; and Monmouth's area of activity
in the Netherlands, March–May 1685

he who had accused Shaftesbury of recklessness. And what had been the result? Many heads had rolled and the Tories were stronger than ever. If only he had acted promptly *then*!

It was a majority decision, and James, being the Duke of Monmouth, a man who in great issues rarely kept the courage of his own convictions, could only shrug his shoulders, promise nobly 'I will not fail my Lord Argyle', and proceed to work out the strategy of an operation he only half believed in. ('The Duke of Monmouth', said Ferguson, one of his three most ardent tempters, with crisp, indulgent hindsight, 'suffered himself to be overruled.'[19])

The Covenanter Earl made him promise to aim at sailing for England not later than six days after the Scottish embarkation. Their plan was intrinsically the same as that adopted for 1683: simultaneous risings in Scotland and the West Country, to draw off the King's forces from the capital, where an insurrection would begin under the City leaders. The forces of the West, led by Monmouth, would march north to seize Bristol and Gloucester, link up with the rebels of Cheshire and Staffordshire, then advance to occupy London. All agreed that the English landing should be at Lyme, in Dorset, as being the nearest convenient port to the rebel capital of Taunton. The next step was to galvanise the co-operation of the rebel leaders in London, Cheshire and the West.

Major William Disney, the exiles' agent in London, now sent over a courier to inquire 'how things stood with the Duke' and whether 'there is an understanding between his Grace and the Earl of Argyle'.[20] This man, Robert Cragg, alias John Smith, afterwards wrote down a full account[21] of the transactions for the King, and parts of these are also mentioned by Grey and Wade. On his first visit to Amsterdam Cragg gave a very favourable report of the situation at his end: 'There was never greater spirit [to revolt] among the common people of England . . . It was the opinion of all I conversed with that, if the Duke of Monmouth landed anywhere in England with a switch in his hand, he might march in safety to Whitehall, there was such a universal longing for him . . .'[22] Ferguson, Monmouth's 'political adviser', informed Cragg that his Grace was preparing what strength he could, that he aimed to set sail within fourteen days of Argyle's departure and to land 'at least before the Parliament sat down'. But the Duke was very short of money, he added, and needed at least £6,000 from English sources.

This intelligence was met in London with open-mouthed astonishment. This was the Duke of Monmouth at his most headstrong, his most ill-judging! The Green Ribbonites felt that because the exiles had been kicking their heels too long they were too restless, too eager for a fight. They must be totally out of touch with reality. The main spokesman was Major John Wildman, a man of sixty-two, who had spent his life in intrigue, a crafty man who had been released from the Tower, in 1684, on account of 'lack of evidence' of his part in the Rye House plot, a man with a very different character from Monmouth – mean, blunt, dictatorial and cautious. 'People here, in England, are cold' (Cragg recorded Wildman's reaction for the exiles); 'there is a great backwardness . . . his Grace has not said what manner of Government he intends . . . he should be persuaded to go rather to Scotland with my Lord of Argyle. First he should come over *incognito* and lie hid in London . . . There is no likelihood of raising any money here, especially in so short a time, for people are so cautious and fearful that they will not trust one another to discourse of any such matter.'[23]

After his next report to James and his Council in Amsterdam, Cragg wrote that 'the Duke was very much troubled to meet with so much backwardness and coldness in his friends'. He told how the usually mild Monmouth, instead of heeding the caution, let out a string of abuse against Wildman :

Major Wildman would govern everybody ! He is the cause of the others' backwardness. He likes nothing of anybody's business but his own . . . He was always the governor of Mr Hampden and the rest. But he shall not govern *me* in this affair ! . . . Ha ! Major Wildman thinks that, by keeping his own purse-strings fast and persuading others to do the same, to hinder me in this thing, but, *by God, he and they shall be mistaken* !

Young Wade spoke next : 'Considering the many protestations of Major Wildman's party to assist his Grace in case of the death of the late King,' he said furiously, 'no man almost could have doubted he would advance the money now . . . But then we *all* know the Major to be a great *husband* !'

'It may be he expects to be some chief Minister of State, as Lord Chancellor, to carry the Great Seal' – 'some person or other' (Dare, perhaps) jested with heavy sarcasm – 'I think it better to send him a Dutch butter-print for a seal !'

James, who was accustomed through lifelong habit to being obeyed, turned to Cragg with his orders now : 'You are to tell them I have promised the Scots to go for England and would not deceive them, but would hazard my life and all rather than be found false to them . . . I have already dispatched Mr Battiscombe* into the

---

*Dorset landowner, lawyer and ardent Monmouthite, described by Sir Leoline Jenkins as 'a young short gentleman, usually wearing a long black periwig'.[24]

West to prepare the gentlemen there, and Capt Matthews will also be leaving to sound certain people. If those in London send no money, I will go with what I have, but I desire that between £5,000–£6,000 be sent at once. I also desire Colonel Danvers[25] and Majors Wildman and Disney and the others to hold regular meetings. Mr Hampden is to be approached about raising money.† Sir Samuel Barnadiston is to be asked to raise £3,000. Major Wildman is to press my Lord Delamere and my Lord Macclesfield and the rest of the Cheshire gentlemen to make all the provision they can . . .' (James turned questioningly from Cragg to his own colleagues at this point) 'I fear the Lord Macclesfield will not be easily prevailed to immediate action, for he is old and his blood is cool.'

'Then his son, the Lord Gerard, must do the more,' said one of the others, 'and the Lord Stamford should be desired to join them.'

'. . . And Mr Charlton should be spoken to, to try the Lord Devonshire;‡ he is the fittest person to deal with him in it.'

James's next concern was security. 'The matter began to be talked as freely of in Amsterdam and Rotterdam amongst the Dutchmen as any other news,' said Wade, 'and we expected every day to hear of it in their public gazettes.'[26] He was also anxious about Argyle's strategy: 'The Duke pressed us make haste saying he would be ready before us,' wrote Hume to his sister. 'He told us that he found Argyle was fond of the Western isles of Scotland . . . and entreated us that we might hinder his stay, and get us quickly to the Lowlands; for, said he, if I did not know you were able to over-rule his inclination in this, and to effectuate it, I should not stir a foot.'[27]

It was a sad, head-shaking Disney that Cragg met next week at the Young Devil Tavern at Temple Bar in a London now festooned to crown its 'papist' King, a London also redolent of plotters' muttering in dim-lit taverns, and, with their hat brims down and their cloaks fetched around their chins, at bleak street corners. Cragg told how he was sent with 'one Chadwick to Mr Hampden, who was walking with a gentleman in the King's Bench Garden . . . I waited on the other side of the Garden', said Cragg, 'till Chadwick returned, who told me that Mr Hampden was busy, and besides I was a stranger to him and he did not care to speak to me'. Then he went to Lincoln's Inn Fields in search of another agent in 'a great long coat', who would answer to the codeword 'Diss'. Cragg

---

†Having received a crippling fine, in 1683, Hampden was doubtless still more concerned with raising money for himself.

‡Ardent Whig and Exclusionist, previously Lord Cavendish.

claimed not to have discovered who this was, but remembered the stranger's dark, muted message: 'Who are the Duke's counsellors in this thing? As I have heard it the way they take is to ruin himself and the nation. He has had better advice given to him if he would take it – to join with Argyle!'[28]

But Wildman, obviously beginning to believe the adventure might well succeed after all, now did a turnabout. This time he sent encouraging exhortations with Cragg: 'His Grace should certainly take the title of King – it will bring in the nobility . . . He should not concern himself about money for arms, because I know that all our fellows in the West are already well armed . . . Why, all is well omened, to be sure. Henry VII invaded England with only 140 men.[29] The people . . . are generally inclined to rise, and the properest time would be after my Lord Argyle's landing, for that will put fire in all . . . As to our friends in the City they are all ready, but very impatient . . . They will obey the commands I have given them from his Grace; they have prepared above 500 men, as well horsed and armed as the Guards in London and Westminster . . .'[30] Disney flung in a final plea: Would the Duke send over some instructions about safeguarding his children?

So Cragg braved the hazards of the Harwich security and the North Sea for a third mission to Amsterdam. He began his bulletin with an account of the Coronation, laughing to recount that – to the delight of the people – the crown had slipped over the King's narrow head and found his nose. 'Colonel Danvers and others of our friends in the City prevented some hot-headed men rising to oppose the Coronation,' he continued. 'They were dissuaded by being assured from good hands that the Duke of Monmouth would land very suddenly, and desired them to have patience till that time.'[31] If Cragg expected any of his other messages to strike gloom in Monmouth's Council he was mistaken. Grey, always buoyant and eager for adventure (except in the presence of physical danger), re-emphasised Wildman's remark about Henry VII.

'Aye, but he was sure of the nobility,' countered Fletcher of Saltoun, 'and *they* were little princes in those days.'

' It is a *good* cause,' chipped in Ferguson; 'God will not leave us unless we leave him!'[32]

Done with reasoning why, Monmouth, the soldier, saved his breath for more orders: 'Major Wildman must not dispute any longer: he must send £4,000 . . . See that a press stands ready to print bulletins of the revolution and the campaign . . .'

'I heard Major Disney say he was preparing of that before I came away,' answered Cragg; 'and that also there should be a person appointed to lie continually ready at Mr Lock's and another at Mr Black's in Covent Garden to receive such messages as your Grace should send.'

'That is good,' James went on; 'as soon as the forces are drawn out of London, Major Wildman and Colonel Danvers are to stir up and secure the City. I want as many officers in the West as can be spared from London; in particular you are to say that if Sir Richard Paton will meet me I shall be glad of him, for he is an experienced officer of foot and a great drill in that discipline. The services of Mr Mead of Essex will be required . . . How will those 500 horse reach me from London? . . . I want Major Wildman to arrange for my horses to be sent down to the West from Moor Park . . . The Cheshire gentlemen must unite their strength to divert the forces coming upon us at our first landing, and until I have formed my army and established a fortified base. I shall not fight for six weeks or two months if I can avoid it . . . My apologies are to be sent to the Cheshire gentlemen that my expedition is not in their country, but for the West Country, where leadership is most needed. I want a daily consult to be held in London . . . The Lords and gentlemen of my party are to repair immediately to my interest . . .'[33]

James then gave a summary of his manifesto before entrusting a copy of it to another agent, called John Jones, to be carried for duplication and distribution in London the moment the landing at Lyme was effected. 'For several years past', the document ran, 'our religion has been undermined by Popish counsels . . . the life of the present Usurper hath been but one continued conspiracy against the Reformed Religion and Rights of the Nation . . .' The 'Duke of York', it said, 'was the instigation of all the crimes of the last reign'. He had murdered Essex and his own brother, the late King. The document then proceeded to 'proclaim and publish what we aim at'. This was firstly a limited monarchy: 'we are not come into the field to introduce Anarchy and Confusion, or for laying aside any essential part of the old English government . . . but to reduce things to that temperament and Balance that future Rulers may remain able to do all the good that can be either desired or expected from them, and it may not be in their power to invade the rights and infringe the Liberties of the people'.

The second aim was liberty of conscience, equal rights for all Protestants, and the raising to civic power of the dissenting classes, with Roman Catholics to worship as they please.

Third, annual Parliaments, which cannot be prorogued or dissolved except by consent of Parliament. The House of Commons to be the seat and fountain of power. Fourth, the judges and officers of the law to be subjected to the approbation of Parliament. Fifth, all the old City and town charters to be restored. Sixth, no standing army except by the authority of Parliament. Seven, 'although the Duke of Monmouth can prove satisfactorily that he is the legitimate son of Charles II, he does not at present insist upon his title and leaves the determination thereof to the Wisdom, Justice and Authority of a Parliament legally chosen, and acting with freedom'.[34]

After the meeting James took Cragg on one side. He had heard that Anna had dismissed a manservant who was 'well beloved of the children'. Asking the agent to visit her and implore her to reinstate the man, he took from his pocket 'a gold seal set with diamonds, which was well known at the Court of Whitehall', to hand to her as a token of trust. But Cragg respectfully refused: 'The Earl of Argyle was shipped with all his men and ammunition and was gone towards the Texel,' he explained, 'and I therefore conceived that all passengers to England would be stopped and examined, and I told the Duke that if I should be searched and such a seal found about me it were sufficient reason I should be suspected . . . to have stole it, for such a seal as that did no way become one of my mean figure and quality'.[35]

Argyle's three ships, *Anna*, *David* and *Sophia*, were loaded up at the end of April with 500 barrels of powder, arms and ammunition for 8,000 men and an expeditionary force of a hundred, including 'a great many Scotch officers which had been drawn from the Prince of Orange,[36] and from several German princes'. As a pledge of mutual trust the two leaders made an exchange, James sending young John Ayloffe and Richard Rumbold, the one-eyed Cromwellian veteran of Rye House, with Argyle's expedition, and keeping the Scotsman, who had volunteered to run fortunes with him – Andrew Fletcher of Saltoun. While they loaded up and prepared to set sail, the Scottish party 'saw Skelton and others from the English Consulate with telescopes, watching them from a boat, which rowed round and round several times'.[37] With a fair wind and a calm sea, Argyle set his course parallel with England's east coast, on 2 May, while Cragg crossed to London for the last time.

He found Disney just as willing, but no more optimistic: 'Neither Major Wildman nor the Cheshire people will come to any resolution until the Duke is landed. Nobody has approached my Lord Devonshire,' Cragg was told; 'there is no more fondness among the nobility and gentry; Mr Mead remains in Essex, his friends will not let him come to town; the Parliament is about to meet and those who should be there will not be absent for fear of giving suspicion. But Hewling and some others have gone for the West. Colonel Danvers will not meet Sir Richard Paton, not trusting him . . .'

Cragg eventually met Paton at the Ross Tavern in Leadenhall Street. 'But when I told him what message the Duke had sent, he said he could do him but little service . . . and he did not care to have his brains beat out alone.'

At last, late in May, there was a positive report from Holland. Jones, the agent who was entrusted with London's copy of the declaration and a paper ('which he promised the Duke of Monmouth he would not open till he was at sea, wherein he named the place he would land at'[38]), returned to report that 'when I came through the Texel I saw the Duke with all his ships under sail for England, and was so near one or two of them that I waved my hat to some one I knew standing on the deck . . . Before he left, his Grace ordered that messengers should be sent to the Red Lion, at Taunton, for thither he intends immediately upon landing to send a messenger to signify what he would have done and how things were with him.' James did not embark until 24 May, and his ships lay tossing in the Texel, waiting for a favourable wind, for nearly a week more.

The delay was excusable. James was to have sailed in three small ships, but reports of increasing naval patrols in the Channel prompted him to replace one of them with a 32-gun fifth-rate. The one he hired, *Helderenberg*, cost him £5,500, and negotiating, through his agent, James Washington, with the merchant, M. le Blon,[39] it took him several days to find the money. Wade said that 'he was forced to pawn all he had in the world, even his biggest George'. At great expense he had bought four cannon, too, 1,460 helmets and suits of back-and-breast, 100 muskets and bandoliers, a number of carbines and pistols, 500 pikes and as many swords, 250 barrels of powder[40] and 'a good number of campaign coats, red faced with purple'.[41] Even if there was some truth in Wildman's 'all the country people are now well armed', James knew there would be many hundreds without. Raising money, as it was, had been like a nightmare. Anna had thwarted his attempt to sell their Manor of Spalding for £10,000. He commissioned Henry Ireton, son of the Parliamentary Commander, to try and raise £4,000 on a part of Moor Park, but Ireton was arrested before he could do so.[42] Not one penny was forthcoming from England. But £3,000 was given by Dutch and English sympathisers in Holland, and £4,000 raised on jewellery belonging to Henrietta and her mother.[43]

What was in Henrietta's mind when she relinquished everything for James's cause? And what in his own when he allowed her to do so? She, whom Bruce called a 'visionary', must have seen her lover as a man of magnificent destiny, and would have imagined him soon riding into London at the head of the 'people's army', to be declared their Prince and Protector. If it was a mission fraught with every sort of danger, it was also one decreed by God. Therefore every worldly valuable must be sacrificed in the cause. The astrologers had said he had nothing to fear if he 'outlived St Swithin's day'[44] and that was only eight weeks away. The horoscopes promised that what he was doing was right – and he had about his person many charms of good fortune. Of course she could never share his throne, nor provide his heir; these were for Anna. But Henrietta did have James's son.* Were all the verses, written so meticulously in his little pocket-book, her inspiration?

> All ye Gods that are above
> Why so cruel to such love?
> O how often have you seen
> When on our knees we have been
> To thee offering sacrifice
> Pure as virtue could devise
> Thus our hearts have ever been . . .[46]

And James? He saw himself as something very different from the saintly hero of the English peasantry's imagery. The pocket-book contains twenty-four pages of prayer, imploring God's forgiveness for his 'unfaithfulness, neglect and weakness'. He confessed he had 'lived many years by all sorts of debauchery', women had been only for gratification, '. . . until I had an affection for the Lady Harriot . . . I have prayed that if this is pleasing to God it might continue; otherwise that it might cease; and God heard my prayer. The affection did continue, therefore I doubt not that it is pleasing to God, and that not by lust, but by Judgement upon due consideration . . .'[47]

'I am now so much in love with a retired life', he had written a month earlier, 'that I am never like to be fond of making a bustle in the world again.' Yet it had not proved difficult to tempt him. As the wind and rain of early summer raged around the house at Gouda, Henrietta would have been often on her knees, seeing, in her mind's eye, the three little ships swaying and bobbing on the water, while she prayed, with tears of craving and anguish.

The churches of Amsterdam and Rotterdam were filled with other good Protestants, imploring God that Monmouth's invasion fleet would land safely in England, and there win victory against the terrible English Catholic oppressor, the friend and abettor of Louis of France. And the Prince of Orange may have offered up

---

*R. Wentworth Smyth Stuart, adopted after Lady Wentworth's death by a close friend of hers and Monmouth's, Colonel Smyth, who educated the boy in Paris and made him his heir.[45]

the same prayer while the ships thus marked time before their perilous mission. For, in spite of the promises he had made to his father-in-law, William, who obviously thought the invasion had a very fair prospect of success, had been in close league with his cousin of Monmouth throughout the planning stages. ('The Prince of Orange knew the Duke of Monmouth to be brave and enterprising and infinitely beloved by the Common People', Ralph wrote, 'who are the greatest weight in violent revolutions . . .'[48]) James told William his ambition went no further than to be 'Protector' of England, so, if the enterprise succeeded, William reckoned, nothing could be better designed to pave the way for an anti-French, Anglo-Dutch union under himself and Mary.

Monmouth, duly grateful to his cousin for turning a blind eye on his preparations and generally abetting him, took him more or less fully into his confidence.[49] His mission, immediately prior to making a last visit to Gouda and Henrietta and then embarking at Amsterdam, was to go to William and advise him of his final plans. William's thanks for this faithfulness was – the moment the fleet was clear of the Texel – to send his trusted Bentinck over to inform the King of England.[50]

24

May–June 1685

BEACH-HEAD AT LYME REGIS

The Ministers in Amsterdam were more helpful. Skelton, the King of England's heavy-handed envoy, who had been shown a list of James's cargo, demanded that all the passengers be arrested. But the authorities deliberately withheld the relevant orders from the harbour police until the last moment when, says D'Avaux, 'the yacht which they sent found that they had already weighed anchor; and that, going to board one of them, it had been repulsed by a discharge of cannon and muskets. The English captains, whom the Prince of Orange favoured so much, and whom the King of England cashiered, were on board those vessels . . .'[1] Had they seen the commander of the expedition it is unlikely they would have recognised him, for James was dressed 'in seaman's apparel, with great whiskers', said Captain Tellier (one of those who later claimed that he was given the choice of being put in irons or taking a commission under Monmouth[2]).

Now, on this 400-mile journey, which was to take eleven days, in *Helderenberg*'s 'great cabin' James issued his commissions for a command structure under which the anticipated thousands of young West Country working men would soon be divided, trained and armed: Samuel Venner, an Old Cromwellian officer was to command the Blue Regiment, with Nathaniel Wade as his major, and Richard Goodenough, the former Under-Sheriff of London, as his 'eldest captain'. Lieutenant-Colonel Fowke (one of the officers cashiered, at the King's request, from the English regiments in the Dutch service[3]) was to command the White, with Goodenough's brother as second-in-command. Edward Matthews, Monmouth's principal emissary in the West Country, would have the Red;

Major Fox the Yellow; and Lieutenant-Colonel Abraham Holmes, another old Ironside, the Green; while Fletcher of Saltoun would be Lieutenant-Colonel of the Cavalry, which was under the nominal leadership of Grey of Werke.

Heywood Dare was appointed military secretary and paymaster (with the special initial role of going on ahead to warn the Whig gentry that Monmouth had landed), and Ferguson was political adviser, chief of propaganda and chaplain to the army. A German soldier of fortune, Anthony Buyse, was in charge of the artillery, with a skilled Dutch gunner as second-in-command. James's total fighting strength at this time was between eighty and ninety. Every volunteer was posted to a regiment, and training had already begun. James then apportioned his arms and stores, went over the plans on his campaign map, rehearsed and practised battle drills and orders of march, set programmes of musketry and fieldcraft training, and gave strict contingency instructions to forbid looting, swearing and the use of private accommodation without permission.

It was first light on the last morning of the voyage, 11 June, and the three ships were off the Dorset coast, by Chideock Bay, when James, lying on his quilt on *Helderenberg*'s deck, felt a tap on his shoulder : 'Sire, are you awake?'

'Who is it?'

'Your humble servant and slave, Ferguson' ('the Plotter' himself records the dialogue). 'I want to ask your Majesty that you will not bestow any title or employment until, by the Grace of God, you shall set foot peaceably at Whitehall.' (From the beginning of the enterprise Ferguson had tried, unsuccessfully, to persuade Monmouth to take the title of King, while Grey of Werke threatened to desert the army unless he did so.)

'Why?'

'Well, your Majesty, all people are more or less filled with vanity and fancy themselves capable and worthy . . .' (Ferguson, as Grey often complained, was ever slow to come to the point – in this case that he sought a senior appointment in Monmouth's government.) 'Thirty persons might aspire to the same reward, and, if you granted to one, you send away the rest discontented.'

'Your reasons are good, but with an exception to one.'

'It is not for such a worm as I am to enter into your Majesty's secrets,' replied the sly Ferguson.

'Oh, but I can trust you. I have promised to be Prime Minister

---

*In relating the conversation to Lord Bruce, Ferguson ended : 'this is true before the living God'.[4]

and Secretary the same that holds that employment now.'* A man like Ferguson might have guessed that Sunderland, always running if he could, with both hare and hounds, would have made it his business to contact the Protestant Duke in exile – to be sure of his favour, in case the rebellion succeeded. Sunderland, the King's Chief Minister of State, had in fact written to Monmouth encouraging him to make the attempt.[5] (Yet Sunderland was not to prove Monmouth's friend, let alone his Prime Minister.)

James spoke to Heywood Dare next – a man he infinitely preferred to Ferguson – then saw him, with Samuel Venner and Hugh Chamberlain, on to a ten-oared long-boat to land on Chideock's shingle, and take horses as fast as they could to alarm the rebel squires, John Trenchard, George Speke, Sir Walter Yonge, William Strode and Edmund Prideaux. Venner returned with a little intelligence scoured from the village: the Duke of Albemarle (George Monck's son, the man who, to the dismay of the Household Cavalry, had relieved James in its command five and a half years earlier) had gone to Exeter to raise the Devon militia; and the Somersetshire were already on foot.

Soon after 9 a.m. the little fleet was off Lyme, and the town buzzed with speculation and rumour. Word was in from neighbouring Chideock that three strangers, who were landed there early from a foreign ship, offered the fishermen neat's tongue and canary wine, inquired what news there was – whether, in particular, 'any of rebellions' – then asked the way to Hawkchurch. And now here were these three ships, lying off the Cob. The Lyme sailors put up their spyglasses. The three-master was a man-o-war, the two-masters, a pink and a fisherman – a dogger. But whose? Dutchmen or Frenchmen, probably. It was a Thursday, and the Royal Mail duly arrived with the weekly newsletter from London. Three vessels, it told the people of Lyme, had recently left Holland, laden with arms, and with the Duke of Monmouth aboard.

As the wind turned away from the north, the ships began to move in shore to anchor. 'Let us fire a warning shot!' exclaimed old Gregory Alford, the Royalist Mayor, who was playing bowls on Church Cliffs with his friends.

'It cannot be done – there is no powder,' Samuel Dassell explained (rather shamefacedly, for he was the customs officer responsible for seeing the harbour guns were supplied). Someone from his office told him there was powder aboard a merchantman from Barbados, lying within the Cob. So, having sent Thomas Tye, the port surveyor, to challenge the stranger fleet, away he rowed to borrow the powder.[6] But Captain James Hayes, commanding the pink – the powder sloop – quickly arrested Tye and his crew and transferred them to *Helderenberg* where, says Wade, predictably, 'the Duke treated them very civilly'.⁷ Dassell saw the strangers in their seven long boats now, rowing for the shore. 'You should turn your guns on them,' he told the merchantman's captain.

'Nay, I cannot do so, for I know not whether they be friends or enemies.'

If Dassell did not know who were the enemies of the people of Lyme, it would soon be made abundantly plain for him. Their enemies were the Royalist squires and magistrates, the Tory mayors, the hard-line Anglicans, all members, official and unofficial, of the Stuart Establishment – in fact men such as himself. And their friends? Why, the 'Protestants' (that libertarian label which was so much more political than religious): 'We Protestants, we free-worshipping yeoman, we shopkeeping and wage-earning classes, agricultural labourers, weavers, miners and quarrymen, many of whom once followed Oliver (or our fathers did so); who hate the Catholic King and his taxes and the cruel penalties of his "Clarendon code". Yes, Protestants, honest, freedom-loving, working men and women, who are angry because we are exploited by the Tories, and their King; yes, we Dissenters, who want to think and worship according to our own consciences . . . It is the same all through our West Country; we Englishmen, who know that the Duke of Monmouth is the one man of quality in the kingdom that believes passionately in the rights of the Common Man; we would, under his leadership, give our lives that our children might be free . . .'

The Duke – no longer dressed in his common sailor's homespun, but in royal purple, the Garter star twinkling silver above his heart, sword on his thigh and dark brown periwig neatly combed – was welcomed as he stepped ashore, so it was said, by a Royalist, Lieutenant Bagster, a naval officer on leave. Recognising the legendary ex-Captain-General in the prow of the landing-boat, Bagster leaped into the shallows and, splashing a dozen paces through the surf, offering his knee as a stepping-stone.

'Brave young man, will you join me?' James tapped Bagster on the shoulder.

'No, Sir, I have sworn to be true to the King, and no consideration will move my fidelity.'⁸

But everyone in the throng on the beach, when they knew who it was, went wild with joy: 'The Protestant Duke is come! Blessed be God! King Charles's son, the lovely hero! A-Monmouth, A-Monmouth!' They watched him – followed closely by Grey of Werke, with a brace of pistols in his belt and a musket on his shoulder – hold up a hand to the others, then drop on one knee on the shingle, lower his head, and put his palms together before his face to thank God for their safe journey, with his eighty followers imitating. They saw him rise to order his standard to be unfurled, his banner of Leveller Green inscribed in letters of gold 'Fear nothing but God' – then draw his sword and wait while his army formed a column behind him.

'We marched very well armed and clothed to Lyme in a military manner,' said Nathaniel Wade proudly, 'the Duke at the head of us.' To avoid the guns of the fort, James took a back route into the town – up the cliffs that have since slipped into the sea – with the great admiring crowd, which followed on either side, thickening all the time, and some that were level with him dashing forward to kiss his hand as he led his little army into Lyme, where, Wade remembered, 'We were received by the shouts and acclamations of the people, the Mayor being fled.'

Did those who had seen James in 1680 notice a change now? The same hail-fellow-well-met affability, the gift for meeting ordinary folk on their terms, the 'common touch', was as prominent as ever. Yet the old self-assurance had been knocked and dented by hardship, personal loss and frustrated ambition. Beside a new humility there was a touch of melancholy, qualities which helped to make him exceptionally attractive to an even wider circle. 'By God, for this man I would die!' people were heard to say as they watched him. Now he stood on the Town Hall steps, facing the people. On his left was Joseph Tyler, a Bristol man, to read out Ferguson's long-winded *Declaration of James, Duke of Monmouth, and the noblemen, gentlemen, and others now in arms for the Defence and Vindication of the Protestant Religion, and the Laws, Rights, and Privileges of England, from the invasion made upon them; and for delivering the Kingdom from the usurpation and Tryanny of James, Duke of York* . . . After the last sentence Tyler paused. Then he enjoined them : 'Now let us play the men for our people and for the cities of our God, and the Lord do that which seemeth good to him.'

By sunset, James, given 'good assistance from mariners and townsmen', had his four cannon, small arms, ammunition and equipment concentrated in the Town Hall. All through the hours of darkness recruits were flocking in from Dorset, Devon and Somerset. By dawn there were 1,000. Late that evening he reconnoitred the approaches to the town and posted strong guards on each. By sunrise, his first recruits had reported to the officers commanding those guards, for lessons in musketry and fieldcraft. 'Thank God for such a happy entry into Lyme, thank God for the popular response !' That must have been the thought foremost in James's mind as he dressed in his room at Lyme's great coaching inn, the George,* in Coombe Street. But shadowy misgivings would have begun to form as well. The militia were too close; how had the Royalists anticipated his landing so accurately?

Few of these good fellows, who were walking in to join him by the hundreds, were armed. Perhaps when he was on the march volunteers would risk the Royalist patrols and bring their own muskets. Or had Wildman entirely misled him? Did the country people hide no weapons of their own? This did not bear thinking about. There was little money for bribes or payment. He had taken what public money there was in Lyme, but, as his personal servant, William Williams, said, he landed with no more than 90 guilders.[9] Another ominous sign: not a single member of the upper levels of Lyme's society had stayed to join him, let alone welcome him; all had buried their valuables and fled. When James knew that, how Cragg's voice, retailing Disney and Danvers, must have echoed in his ears: 'there is no fondness in the nobility, we discern a backwardness in the gentry'. But surely the Whig squires would come in when they knew where the populace stood?

It was about 4 a.m. on the 13th that James II – fifty-two years old and the occupant of England's throne for a little over three months – was roused from his bed at Whitehall to be told that Lord Churchill and his father, Sir Winston, sought an urgent interview. They brought news of a landing in Dorset by the Duke of Monmouth and some eighty armed followers. With his Lordship and Sir Winston were two of His Majesty's customs-house officers from the port of Lyme Regis, eyewitnesses of the event. Lyme's Mayor, Alford, the King was informed, had taken the news to Honiton and Exeter, while these two dutiful customs men, Dassell and Thorald, had exhorted the townsmen of Lyme to resist the invasion, and, being unsuccessful in that, had ridden to London at commendable speed. The grateful King (though not considered to be generous by nature) ordered £40 to be brought from his chest, and handed them £20 apiece.

This was not the first the King had heard of his nephew steering for British shores. Orange's minister, Bentinck, had arrived about a week before to say that the three-ship fleet had left the Texel 'with martial intent'; and, at about the same time, a letter from some London source was intercepted in Somerset, speaking of Argyle's 'great success', and insisting that 'all true Protestants must stick together' and be prepared for 'the appearance of a certain person among them'. When it looked as though 'that most factious

*Destroyed by fire in 1844.

region', the West Country, might give trouble, the King sent orders to the Duke of Somerset* to raise his militia, and dispatched Albemarle, Devon's Lord Lieutenant, with the same mission in his county and Cornwall. But other factors had pointed to the likelihood of Monmouth joining Argyle in the West Highlands. If that were so, King James had thought, so much the better, for already the whole of the Scottish militia, 22,000 strong, was in arms, while 4,000 from their regular army had been posted to that region. Such a force would be irresistible. Otherwise the King's opinion had been that Lancashire or Cheshire would be his nephew's choice, and he had written to Orange, saying so, only the day before.

Meanwhile the King did what could be done to resist the evil danger of insurrection. In London he put the train-bands on the alert with orders to apprehend anyone who uttered the least murmur of revolt, or of support for Monmouth. The Green Ribbon Club squires of the West, Sir Edmund Prideaux and Sir William Strode, were in town? They were probably in touch with the City; it was thought wise to place them under precautionary arrest. Trenchard was another with a bad record. (He was the one who, when buying firearms in Taunton, had boasted that 'such guns will serve to take off the fellows in scarlet', and who kept a rebels' club in that infamous town's Red Lion Inn.[11]) But the Guards said he had fled White Lackington. His father-in-law, Speke, was there but he could not do much damage – he was too old.

Copies of Monmouth's Declaration,† which were burned before the public by the hangman at the Royal Exchange, had been traced to one Major William Disney, (whom the Guards found in bed with his mistress, and were so impatient to have in prison that they would not let him put his breeches on[12]). Disney would die the traitor's death before the month was gone. Many others were safely behind bars; but Danvers and Wildman were still to be caught.

King James was gratified to have so many loyal assurances at this time, from the Whig nobility and gentry as well as the Tories. He was glad, too, to receive from Parliament a grant of £400,000, to suppress the two invasions. It had also enacted a bill of attainder (opposed in the Lords only by Anglesey and Delamere) against the nephew, who was to be known henceforth to loyal England as James Scott, *late* Duke of Monmouth, while £5,000 was offered to the man who could capture or assassinate him. A Bill was brought

*The 'Proud Duke', who married the widow of Monmouth's friend Thomas Thynne in 1682; Gentleman of the Bedchamber since 1683.
†'The most villainous and abominable in its language, as well as the most traitorous, that was ever put forth,' said Rochester.[11]

in, making it high treason 'for anyone to say or justify that the late King was married to the late Duke of Monmouth's mother', and the heralds were ordered to St George's, Windsor, to 'deface and obliterate the arms and trophies of his Garter'.[13]

The militia were called up, and, on 15 June, four troops of Lord Oxford's Regiment of Horse, two troops of the King's Own Royal Regiment of Dragoons and five companies of the Queen Dowager's Regiment of Foot – all under command of the peer who had brought the Lyme customs men to the King's apartments, John, Lord Churchill – were mobilised with marching orders for the West Country.* With the 'citts' subdued, only the 'bumpkins' remained to be disposed of! There could be little to oppose the King's forces: after all no leader in history had made an effective fighting force out of ordinary, common untrained men.

The City's common men and women, who had waited so long for the clarion call of just two or three brave men to give them a lead to rise against the Stuart and Tory tyranny, now listened in desperation to the reports that their leaders were either arrested or unwilling to act. And they watched all those countermeasures – the train-bands on street patrol day and night, the redcoats in column of march for the West and the great guns rolling down the pavements from the Tower – with eyes of silent despair. Their lips moved in fervent prayer for the Protestant Duke. For here in old London the light of freedom seemed to be extinguished; in Scotland it flickered and guttered, while in Cheshire the spark had failed to produce a flame. Only in the West where 'brave Jemmy', their champion and general, rode, did it shine forth as 'a beacon of hope for all Protestants'.

---

*Of the three regiments concerned, Lord Oxford's became the Royal Horse Guards (The Blues) and was elevated to become a part of the Household Cavalry in 1820. The Dragoons (previously the Tangier Horse and afterwards the First Royal Dragoons) were amalgamated in 1968 with The Blues to form a new regiment of Household Cavalry (The Blues and Royals). The Queen Dowager's became the Queen's West Surreys.

25

'OUR LAWFUL AND RIGHTFUL SOVEREIGN'

'All diligence possible', said Wade, 'was used to get horses.' And, on the morning that the first report of the landing reached the King, what a happy sight it must have been for Monmouth to see old Heywood Dare come trotting into Lyme at the head of forty riders – their mounts from Prideaux's stables at Forde Abbey – with Dare himself astride a quality animal, beautifully schooled. Not only was it a relief to know that the tough, avuncular Taunton goldsmith – upon whose knowledge of and prestige in the West, and all-round competence, he so much relied – was safe and well; but, to James, any additions of good horseflesh, and volunteers who could ride, were immensely welcome.

For no one knew better than he, the lifelong hunter, the champion race-rider of Europe, the ex-Master of the Horse, Colonel of the Life Guards and leader of cavalry in several campaigns, the value of equestrian mobility. No one was more aware that, without it, he could not adequately protect his flank and rear on the march from enemy cavalry, or have the means of seizing and holding key positions, or, by pursuit, exploit a successful attack or counter-attack, let alone take on the King's cavalry in pitched battle. So he sent out search parties on every side to scour the farms and stables for any animal, broken to the saddle, that could be found to fill the squadron ranks now being organised by Andrew Fletcher of Saltoun, his Lieutenant-Colonel of Horse. But, watching them come in, he must also have remembered with some anguish that, in the old days, he would never have counted a trooper as fit for service with less than six months' training, or a horse with less than a year's schooling.

And the hopes he had harboured of the Whig squires each raising a well-disciplined, well-horsed troop for the cause faded again with Dare's news : except for old Speke and his son, the Whig gentry either were arrested or flown or abstained from the revolution.

Nevertheless, James's officers – Grey, Fletcher, Holmes, Dare and his son, Thomas, Matthews (now returned from his clandestine mission), Venner, Fowke and Fox – having successfully invaded England, gathered 1,500 recruits into their units and defied the militia – were ready to celebrate. This they did by dining as gaily as they could at Lyme's George Inn that evening. Well wined, Dare took his leader into the June sunset, to the tavern's stable-yard to inspect the horses. But Fletcher, the jealous cavalry commander, having his eye on the beauty Dare had ridden in, strode ahead and jumped into the saddle, claiming it for himself.

Dare, rough and irascible at the best of times, lost his temper; he clutched the bridle and ordered the young laird to dismount, and when Fletcher refused he went at him with his whip. Perhaps there was some latent antagonism between the two men, the patrician Lowlander, whom James valued for his sharp intelligence and early experience with the East Lothian yeomanry, and the veteran self-made goldsmith, who was so influential among the people of Taunton Dene. As they struggled – Dare with one hand on the shying charger's bridle and the other lashing at the Scot with his whip – Fletcher, more drunk than he owned, drew a pistol from his belt and shot the Somerset man between the eyes. Thus, in a single moment, James lost the two most valuable officers he had. For he could not keep Fletcher now, not with young Thomas Dare demanding instant vengeance and the prospect of the people of Taunton wanting it, too. On the other hand he could hardly execute a man who had come to run fortunes with him. So he placed him under arrest, ordering him aboard *Helderenberg*. And he never saw him again.*

Wade said that as a result of these losses Monmouth assumed a melancholy which he never really shook off. His life had been dogged by personal loss : first his mother, when he was eight; then his adored young aunt, 'Minette', when he was twenty-one; then Thynne, Shaftesbury, Russell, Sidney and Armstrong; then his father at the moment of reconciliation; and now Fletcher and the father-figure, Helwood Dare on whom his fortunes in the West

*The pilot, Walters, was under orders from Monmouth to proceed to Carrickfergus, in Ireland, where he was to land an agent, who was to contact the dissident elements, inform them of the 'successful invasion of England' and urge them to stage a rising. But Fletcher forced the pilot to steer for Spain.[1]

Country largely rested. And the rebel officers were soon to find that the Duke of Monmouth, for all his buoyancy in times of triumph, was not a man who could weather a quick succession of personal disasters.

Eager as he was to push on to Taunton, James – recruiter, trainer, horse thief and tactician rolled into one – was not yet ready to begin the march. He wanted to build up his strength, not only of personnel and horses but of weapons and stores, and he wanted to strike some blow at the militia, to try and show the Royalists that it was dangerous to get too close to him. Hearing that the Somersetshires were guarding Bridport with about 3,000 men, but not very vigilantly, he decided on a dawn raid, 'to beat up their quarters', as Wade put it, 'by light of day'. James selected a composite strike force of 400, with a hard-nosed vanguard of 40 musketeers, and, taking up the rear, a party of horse under Grey who, owing to his social rank, was technically in overall command of the party, but 'ordered to take the advice of Colonel Venner'. Wade, Venner's deputy, describes how they came up to the town in a thick mist: 'the militia had no outguard', surprise was complete and the enemy was in confusion, with 'riderless horses up and down the street'.

Two militia officers, Edward Coker, who himself shot Venner in the waist and Wadham Strangways, were killed as they prepared to mount their horses,[2] and several other ranks went down in the street-fighting. Venner, then coming up against the well-defended bridge at the east end of the town, sent Wade back 'to desire my Lord Grey to advance with the horse'. But at 'a volley from the bridge', which killed two rebel cavalrymen, 'my Lord Grey, with the horse, ran and never turned face till they came to Lyme where they reported all the foot to be cut off'. The rebels lost forty men in this action; Venner's wound was more serious than he had thought, and it was Wade who conducted the withdrawal. James, who was at the head of a relief force, rode up to meet him: 'Is it true that my Lord Grey ran away?' Receiving an affirmative, he turned to Matthews: 'What would you do with my Lord Grey?'

Matthews knew exactly what he would do with Grey: 'You are the only general in Europe', he answered bitterly, 'who would ask that question.' James had never much affection for Grey of Werke, 'the legacy of Lord Shaftesbury', Dryden's 'Cold Caleb'; but he was the only other 'man of quality' the army had. Unless he was given a command equal to his social rank he would certainly have deserted, and this was a threat, the luxury of which James, who was fighting an unequal battle to 'bring in the gentry', could not afford. The tragedy was that, if Fletcher of Saltoun had still been there, Grey would not have been the man to whom the cavalry looked for their inspiration and guidance.

As news of the army's strength filtered through the villages of Dorset, Somerset and Devon, hundreds more men came into Lyme, said Wade, 'and offered their services to the Duke . . . some said they were in bed when they heard the news, but they immediately rose and came away'. The men who volunteered were nearly all tradesmen, mechanics and miners; the tenant farmers and agricultural workers did not dare join without a lead from their landlords. But as one volunteer, a Quaker, John Whiting, said, 'their hearts were towards him [the Duke] if they durst have showed it'. Riding through Wrington, Whiting himself was challenged by a militiaman; who thrust the spike of a halberd towards his chest, demanding to know : 'Whither are you riding?'

'I told him southward,' said the Quaker, adding in parenthesis – intimating that the militiaman was in sympathy – 'which was directly towards the Duke'.[3] Daniel Defoe, then aged twenty-five, was another who went 'to trail a musket with his Grace'.

While these adventurers filed into Lyme on the afternoon of the Bridport affair, James sent a fighting patrol of fifteen, 'mounted for the most part by officers and gentlemen who came over with the Duke', to raid another militia post, where they killed two. Just as this party returned to base others reported that the two county militias – the Devonshire under Albemarle from the west and the Somersetshires and Dorsetshires under Sir Edward Phelips, from the east – were converging in an obvious effort to hem James in at Lyme. So, although he would have preferred one more day of training and preparation, he gave marching orders for the early hours of the 15th. He led them to a high point, from which they could keep the militia under observation – 'a crossway, where we posted ourselves advantageously in the hedges and straits' – and there, under a starlit June sky, they lay down with their arms at their side, by rank and file, the cavalry clutching, as they slept, the bridles of those motley nags stolen from coach, plough, meadow, staging-post and livery stables.

Next morning, James, seeing the militia regiments marching towards each other – 'to a conjunction, we supposed, at Axminster' – send Wade's battalion hurrying on to occupy an advance post on the dominating ground to the west, at Shute, while he increased the mainguard's pace for Axminster, where he quickly deployed for defence.

Wade's narrative shows how promptly his leader had these soldiers, of only two or three days' standing, making tactical use of the enclosed country. 'The militia,' the rebel major remarked, 'discovering we had lined the hedges and strait ways very advantageously, withdrew within minutes of the first contact . . . the withdrawal of the Somersetshire forces being little better than a flight, and many of the soldiers' coats and arms being recovered and brought to us.' Wade, commanding at Shute, wanted to go in pursuit, but James stopped him, saying it was 'not their business at present to fight', but to speed on to Taunton. Meanwhile there was the triumph of having nearly half the Somersetshires come over to their side. One of them, John Coad, stole out of the camp, 'wading through a river to escape the watches, and . . . came to Axminster, and tendered myself and arms to the Duke, and was kindly accepted, where I found Mr Ferguson at prayer'.[4]

Next day Lord Fitzharding wrote to the 'proud' Duke of Somerset, who was at Wells: 'Your Grace will find by this the rebels will soon be master of this country. Where they will stop God only knows.'[5] At the same time the 23-year-old Somerset himself reported to Sunderland that '. . . I have here stopped ten idle lusty fellows we suspected to be going into Lyme that could give no account of themselves, and one of them confessed that he believed the Duke of Monmouth an honest man, and was sure that he was a friend of his, and upon this we have sent them all to the jail of this town. I find all the gentlemen very well inclined to do the King service, and the militia is in very good order for militia, but . . . the common sort of people, if they durst, would rise every minute . . .'[6]

On 17 June the rebels arrived at Chard, where young Speke came in 'with 40 ragged horse', and on the 18th — the sixth anniversary of James's triumphal entry into Edinburgh before the Bothwell Bridge campaign — at Taunton, 'the sink of all rebellion in the West', as Whitehall called it, the capital of the serge trade, whose Dissenters had promised 'we'll see bloody noses ere we desert conventicles.' The militia had fled on the night of the 16th, and a Royalist, the Rev Thomas Axe, recalled the circumstances:

At about four in the morning the rabble of the town, perceiving the soldiers were gone, began to gather together; about 5 they came down to the church in a tumult . . . With ladders they got in at the windows and up to the leads, and, breaking open some doors, got the arms that were there . . . I went out myself to try if my presence, or any thing I could say, might put a stop to the violence, but a sour, saucy fellow put a musket to his shoulder, with the rest about him, and told me in these words: 'By God, the towne is ours now, and you shall know it' . . . About four o'clock came into town a troop of horse, commanded by Hucker . . .[7]

Captain John Hucker, one of Taunton's rich serge manufacturers, rode on to prepare his house, near the Red Lion, for James to stay in, while the town went wild with delight. Nearly everyone wore a sprig of Leveller Green, and anyone who failed to look happy and shout 'A-Monmouth and the Protestant Religion!' was clutched by the lapel and asked why not. The 8–10-year-old students of Taunton's Academy for Young Ladies had been busy embroidering twenty-seven banners to be carried by the regiments, and, on the 19th, with a huge chattering crowd in attendance, they waited, under their headmistress, Miss Blake, opposite Hucker's front door, for Monmouth to appear. It was a charming occasion, uniquely Monmouth, for here, with that gentle, winning affability, devoid of affectation or assumption, he was at his stylish best, and the Tauntonites adored it. Miss Blake (a name well loved there since Cromwell's admiral became a hero of the West Country) was the first to step forward. In one hand she held a bible and in the other a drawn sword as presents for him.

Taking the bible, James raised his voice for all to hear: 'I come now into the field with a design to defend the truths contained in that book, and to seal them with my blood if there should be occasion for it.' Miss Blake's deputy, Miss Musgrave, then advanced, followed, in turn, by the twenty-seven girls each with her banner, and lastly by the senior, Mary Mead, whose own gorgeously fringed creation was embroidered – to show the wishes of the people of Taunton – with the initials JR and topped by a king's crown. Saluting each child with a kiss and cheerful word, James saw them into a crocodile, 'every one led by a man', to join the army, which waited behind, in column. Then, with himself and Grey mounted at their head, they marched round the town, and down to the camp.[8]

But not all were willing to sacrifice themselves and their kin in Monmouth's cause. Mrs Scott, who was the sister of Whiting's financée, Sarah Hurd, was 'exceeding sad and sorrowful when her husband took his horses . . . to the Duke'. The Quaker tells how, when escorting Mrs Scott into Taunton, they

. . . soon met with her husband, and reasoned with him about it; but he had appeared to the Duke, and involved himself so with his horses that we could not get him home with us. It happened that the Duke and the Lord Grey were then at dinner at Capt Hucker's over against the . . . inn; and she, with her sister, Roman, went over to speak with the Duke and desire him not to take it amiss if her husband went home, for it was contrary to our persuasion to appear in arms, because we could not fight;

and had a pretty deal of discourse with him (for she was a woman that could handle her tongue as well as most). The Duke seemed to take it well enough, and told her he did not desire that any should appear against their consciences, so they left him and came away . . .'[9]

Behind the euphoria, fear reigned. Albemarle was only six miles south-west, at Wellington, and Churchill was closing in from the south-east. Although the gentry were mostly in sympathy – and in the mood of Speke's daughter, Lady Jennings, who, according to Whiting, was 'all afloat about the Duke and thinking the day was their own' – few raised their swords for him. Over a week had gone by and still there was no word from London. That is why that morning Monmouth had sent his personal chaplain, Nathaniel Hook, post-haste to the City with the message 'Now is the time to rise, now!'[10] If only Shaftesbury were in the capital, James must have thought, with brave Stephen College as his rabble-rouser; if only Russell and Tom o' Ten Thousand were down here in the West to give the nobility a lead, if *only* there was good news from Scotland or Cheshire.

Planning the next march north he wondered how many more troops his uncle would allot to the West. What if the road to Bristol was defended by the regulars as well as Beaufort's militia? After all, the rebels' 6,000 was not such a strong force when 1,500 carried nothing more lethal than clubs, when the cavalry was unschooled and the greatest weight of artillery that could be deployed was four small Dutch cannon. And how soon might these stout West Country hearts grow faint as they marched away from their home ground? How long before the soles of their shoes wore through, and their breeches and their homespun turned to rags? Or before they dropped from exhaustion; and then, surrounded by the Royalists, were two weak even to defend themselves?

Two assassins, one at Lyme and the other here at Taunton, lured by the £5,000 reward offer, had fired their pistols at the 'Arch Rebel' and narrowly missed him. How long before the next bullet found its mark? Life was very precious to James, Duke of Monmouth. Whiting saw him with his affected Taunton smile – his public mask – down. He saw James and Grey of Werke take horses 'and two great guns were hauled down before them, to plant, as they said, at the town's end, it being reported that the Duke of Albemarle was coming against them . . . I thought the Duke of Monmouth looked very thoughtful and dejected in his countenance, and thinner than when I saw him four years before, as he passed through Ilchester in his progress . . . so that I hardly knew him again, and was sorry for him as I looked at him . . .'[11]

Grey, Ferguson and others urged him time and again to allow himself to be declared king. Surely the reason why the nobility had not come in was because they thought he stood for a republic? They carried the argument further: 'The only way to provide against the ruin of those that have already come in, in case you fail in the attempt,' they persuaded, 'is to declare yourself King that they may be sheltered by the Statute made in the reign of Henry VII in favour of those that should obey a King *de facto*.'[12]

James called a Council of War – 'the first that he held', noted Wade, 'doing all things before by his own judgement'.[13] He had said in his Declaration, and he had said it often enough before, that he did not 'insist on his title', but would take the crown if it was considered necessary he should do so, and once he was convinced there was an overwhelming lobby in favour of it. So he accepted it now and was duly proclaimed.

The townspeople were rapturous at the words they heard at the Market Cross:

> Whereas, upon the decease of our Sovereign Lord Charles the Second, late King of England, the right and succession of the Crown of England . . . did legally descend and devolve upon the most illustrious and high-born Prince JAMES DUKE OF MONMOUTH . . . but James Duke of York, (taking the advantage of the absence of the said James Duke of Monmouth beyond the seas) did first cause the said late King to be poisoned, and immediately thereupon did usurp and invade the Crown, and doth continue to do: We, therefore, the noblemen, gentlemen and commons . . . do proclaim the said high and mighty Prince James Duke of Monmouth, our lawful and rightful sovereign . . .'*

Meanwhile the new 'king' had written to 'our trusty and well-beloved Cousin and Councillor, Christopher, Lord Duke of Albemarle . . . Whereas we are credibly informed that there are some horse and foot in arms under your command for James Duke of York, which are purposely raised in opposition to us and our Royal authority, we thought fit to signify to you our resentment thereof . . . it is our Royal will and pleasure, and we do hereby strictly charge and command you . . . to cease all hostility . . . and that your Grace would immediately repair to our camp, where you shall not fail of a very kind reception by us . . . James R.' Returning

*Quoted in full at Appendix B

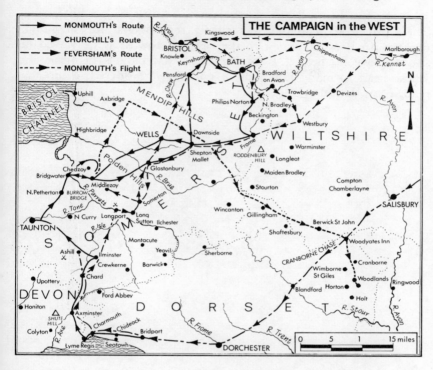

his answer to 'James Scott, late Duke of Monmouth', by the same trumpeter, Albemarle wrote:

> I received your letter, and do not doubt but you would use me kindly if you had me; and since you have given yourself the trouble of invitation, this is to let you know that I never was, nor never will be, a rebel to my lawful King, who is James the Second. If you think that I am in the wrong, and you in the right, whenever we meet I do not doubt but the justness of my cause shall sufficiently convince you that you had better have let this rebellion alone, and not have put the nation to so much trouble.'[14]

James had been in Taunton three days; it was time to march on to Bristol. Reinforced by a fifth regiment, composed of Tauntonites, under Colonel Basset – most of them ex-militiamen and some deserter professionals – the army, now amounting to about 7,000,[15] set off on the Bridgwater road early on the morning of 21 June. They were in buoyant spirits, born of a feeling of great adventure, independence, and love for their 'King Monmouth' (the soldiers refused to call him 'King James' – a title with a bitter ring). Their exit from Taunton was chiefly remembered for Ferguson's cry, repeated several times, to the ecstatic crowds, as he waved his sword above his head: 'I am Ferguson, that famous Ferguson, for whose head so many hundreds of pounds were offered; I am that man, I am that man!'[16]

26

THE RACE FOR BRISTOL

The morning Monmouth marched out of Taunton was a Sunday, and John, Lord Churchill, a fine looking soldier of thirty-five, with intelligent eyes and resolution drawn on his lips, attended matins at the fifteenth-century church at Chard. In the pews behind the Brigadier-General of his Majesty's expedition against the rebels in the West sat the bulk of his detachment, the scarlet-coated horsemen of the Royal Regiment of Dragoons, whose Colonel he had been since 1683, and the Queen Dowager's Regiment of Foot, interspersed with the dark-blue coats of Lord Oxford's Royal Regiment of Horse. If Lord Churchill did not care to listen, that sultry June morning, to the Rev. Mr Rich's monotonous and rather repetitive preaching on the text of 'they who resist shall receive to themselves damnation', what were his thoughts? Were they of James Scott, late Duke of Monmouth? . . . Poor Monmouth: to be that father's son, yet not his heir! To be told, and to believe, that the plum at the top of the tree was sweetest of all, but to find it always beyond reach.

But how easily his Grace could win affection! What a marvellous courtier and what a very pleasant companion he had been in the 1670s, when Churchill was a mere Captain of Grenadiers. What a debonair and stimulating commander, what an excellent officer he had proved, when backed by an experienced, level-headed staff; and how the army had loved him. (Most indeed still did love him.) But now? There was certainly not another Englishman alive who could have rallied 7,000 ordinary common fellows, all volunteers, behind him, and shaped them into a credible hierarchy, into a force that could give the militia a bloody nose and defy the might of England for a week. But what wrong-headed ambition was behind it! As Captain-General of the Land Forces Monmouth had the world at his feet; as 'Gaffer Scott', at the head of 7,000 'vagabonds', he was its ridicule! Besides, he lacked the necessary ruthlessness, the strategic judgement and tenacity of purpose for this role. Look how he dallied in Taunton, taking silk banners from schoolgirls!

Nor, thought Churchill, the High Church Tory, were there any solid grounds for this rebellion. Considering the King had called a Parliament, it was little wonder the nobility and gentry kept loyal. And Monmouth must be insane to think that by declaring himself king, he would bring them in, when, even in the hottest Exclusionist days, the Monmouthites were hardly supreme. He must be mad to rely on counsellors such as Grey and Ferguson. 'King Monmouth'! What a tragi-comedy it all was.

But the net was closing. Lord Feversham had left London the previous day with a troop of the Life Guards and sixty Horse Grenadiers. (And that stalwart of the Household Cavalry, Colonel Oglethorp, was doubtless with their van.) Tomorrow the main artillery train would leave the Tower, with an escort of Sir Francis Compton's troop of Lord Oxford's regiment – '16 large cannon with carriages, powder, ball, shovels, pickaxes and other warlike provisions'[1] – and eight more field-pieces were already on their way from Portsmouth to Sherborne under that excellent gunner, Mr Sheres,[2] with an escort commanded by Churchill's brother. Albemarle would have no trouble reoccupying Taunton. Pembroke was in good control of the Wiltshire towns and villages. Beaufort, that most energetic of the Lords Lieutenant, with the militias of three counties, had good care of Bristol, while Colonel Percy Kirke – so rough, but so efficient! – with his Tangier 'Lambs' and the rest of the dragoons, was already at Chard. Yes, the net was tightening. But Monmouth's army was in good morale, and in a fighting mood, too. The day before, Churchill had sent out a party of Lord Oxford's Horse under Lieutenant Monoux to see what damage could be done to the rebel outposts at Taunton, and, in a skirmish at Ashill, Monoux got a pistol shot through the head for his trouble.[3] There was much life in the trapped lion.

Standing at the door of the long, low church at Chard, he thanked the Rev. Mr Rich for his apt sermon and wished him a very good morning. Then he repaired to his quarters and took another look at his map. Clearly 'King Monmouth' would march for Bristol, which commanded the mouths of the Avon and the Severn and which lay on his probable axis to the West Midlands and where he could count on a host of sympathisers. It must be hoped that someone would have the sense to have the bridge over the Avon at Keynsham destroyed. But that was not Churchill's business, for he had been superseded in command by the Earl of Feversham.

On the same morning that Churchill attended matins at Chard

the Protestant Duke's column marched north, their thirty-five supply wagons, and their four guns strapped on to ploughs drawn by oxen and shire horses; and 7,000 men kicking up, with their labourers' shoes, the dust of three miles of road, a column punctuated all down the line by the twenty-seven banners presented by the maids of Taunton. Behind the vanguard, escorted by his forty hand-picked Life Guard of Horse, dressed in purple and Garter Star and dark brown periwig, topped by a black-plumed beaver, rode James himself. One regiment, Colonel Basset's, broke the procession with a solid ribbon of scarlet, and down the line were dots of red or yellow, belying a militia deserter or a lucky fellow who had snatched up a Royalist's coat. But for the rest the only uniform was workmen's jerkins and breeches and a bunch of twigs, oak, ash or elm, a 'Monmouth sprig', rammed in a buttonhole or hatband, if they had one.

Only about one in every three carried a musket or a pistol, the rest having clubs, or at best rusty swords. But it was an animated, happy army, and, if you were close enough, you would have heard them singing the songs of Taunton, Axminster and Lyme, or even perhaps of their own regiment, for they were already proud to belong to the Red, Yellow, Blue, White or Green. Somerset at its most lustrous: the trees in full vigour, the foxgloves and crane's-bills in flower, the hedges white with hawthorn, and the red dust of the Bridgwater road billowing behind, combined to give them a sense of strength rising from the very soil of their West Country and of their own youthful superiority. And they were as scornful of their noblemen and landed gentry not joining their 'king' as their officers were. 'We wonder the gentlemen come not in,' they said; 'well, we will do the work without them, and then we will have their estates, too.' Next Saturday they would be in London placing their king upon the throne.

The people of Bridgwater gave the 'king' a right royal reception, and the Dissenting Mayor was backed by an enthusiastic corporation when he read James's Proclamation at the Market Cross. Hundreds of fresh volunteers came in, and nearly half as many were turned away for lack of arms. James, with his old tactical imagination, had scythes converted into hand-weapons. He ordered out collecting parties to bring them in from the surrounding farm-steads (everyone around Bridgwater was hostile to the Royalist forces); he had the blacksmiths working day and night to fix blades on handy-sized poles; then he organised scythe companies, one per regiment, and gave them battle-drills and daily stints of training. He saw them, in particular, as of great potential value against charging horses.

He slept that night at Bridgwater Castle, but there was little to encourage sleep. The failure of the London and Cheshire people, coupled with the news that Feversham was on his way with a detachment of the Life Guards and Horse Grenadiers, kept him preoccupied with strategy, for with no open support coming from the north it might be neither possible nor expedient to march immediately for Gloucester. If he were to avoid the short (Axbridge) route to Bristol, and instead move east to Wells, he would be in a good position from which either to strike at the city, via the Keynsham bridge, or, if Feversham marched rapidly enough to join hands with Beaufort's militia in the defence of Bristol, he might give the Royalist commander the slip, and march on to a now scarcely protected London.

The weather broke next morning, 22 June, as the army came on to an extensive tract of level, peaty common land, called Sedgemoor. His men were soaked through, and, camping around Wells and among the ruins of Glastonbury Abbey, they built huge bonfires to dry out their clothes. Next night they were at Shepton Mallet, where James was given a bed by Edward Strode (brother to William Strode, of Barrington Court, a 'duking days' host). The latest intelligence of Feversham's progress showed James that he had a good chance of winning the race to Bristol, so next morning he switched northwards and put on top marching pace. Hearing, at Pensford, that his opponent had ordered the Avon crossing at Keynsham to be broken, and a body of Gloucestershire militia to prevent interference with it, he sent Captain Tyler's troop galloping forward to drive them off and repair the bridge. Then he sent patrols through it, sounding the enemy's strength.

'In a meadow near the South gate of the City of Bristol', a heavily-built, middle-aged Royalist, with a general's crimson sash athwart his scarlet coat and the three ostrich feathers of the Life Guards, two white and one red, in his beaver, received reports of the rebels' march to the Avon. At the King's behest, the Keynsham bridge was broken and its ruins well guarded. The Earl of Feversham, his Majesty's General commanding the West, barred this eastern highway to Bristol city with a good contingent of the Guards, backed by the best of Lord Pembroke's militia, totalling 3,000 men; while, behind him, in the city itself, was the Duke of Beaufort, who he knew would have no qualms in hanging the first man in Bristol – and burning down his house, too – who spoke a word, let alone raised a finger, against King James the Second. Patrols from Lord Churchill's and Colonel Kirke's were hot against the backs of those rebels, and very soon the thirty heavy guns from the Tower would be here. Under all these pressures a rabble must very soon break.

The Protestant Louis Duras, Marquis de Blanquefort and Earl of Feversham, a nephew of Marshal Turenne, came to England early in the last reign to escape King Louis's measures against the Huguenots. King Charles, feeling himself under heavy obligation to Turenne for various favours and kindnesses during the exile, gave the young Huguenot a commission, which soon put him on the path to command York's troop of the Horse Guards – an influential military appointment – and, later, his English earldom. The present King put the highest trust in him. Indeed, Feversham lacked neither courage nor sincerity, and serving under James, Duke of Monmouth, on active service in the 1670s, he won the commendation of his Captain-General three times over. But, after suffering a serious head injury when helping Monmouth organise the fight against the Middle Temple fire in 1679, the chirurgeons had trepanned his skull – perforated it with a cylindrical saw – and this had helped neither his brain nor his spirit.

Burnet called him an 'honest, brave and good-natured man, but weak to a degree not easy to be conceived', adding (which was less than fair) that, in this campaign, 'he conducted matters so ill that every step he made was likely to prove fatal to the King's service'.[4] His officers had little respect for him – 'too fond of eating and sleeping', they said – and, even if he had not been a Frenchman, the soldiers could never have liked him. Perhaps he had always been envious of the love that Monmouth inspired in his troops, just as he must have been jealous that Henrietta Wentworth showed little hesitation in giving her heart to the disgraced (and married) Duke, when she had the offer of Feversham's coveted hand. Not that he would have regarded that fanciful, flighty woman a great catch for anyone now, beautiful though she was.

An aide-de-camp cantered up and saluted. The late Duke of Monmouth, he told the general, has repulsed our bridge guard, repaired the bridge under cover of darkness, and marched over.

By ten o'clock in the morning the whole rebel army had crossed Keynsham bridge into Gloucestershire, to form up in a meadow called Sydenham Mead. One of the many villagers gathered round the army, in curiosity, afterwards described how Squire Creswicke walked across the bridge and handed some papers to Lord Grey, 'who passed them to a man with a star on his left breast'. The same witness related that a messenger came from Lady Hart's house to say that if Monmouth's column should pass her farm (which was called Filgrove) on the way to Gloucester, she would give him 'some hundreds of cheeses'.[5]

Later in the morning two parties of cavalry – one of Life Guards under Oglethorp and the other of Horse Grenadiers, led by Captain Parker – had converged on Keynsham, thinking it to be still in Royalist hands. There was a scuffle in which the cavaliers came off best, and James was convinced it was Feversham's vanguard on the attack. What other mixed intelligence he received indicated that the Huguenot was deployed in great strength, that Beaufort had tight control of the city, that all its leading Dissenters had been removed to prisons in Gloucester and that there was 'a considerable body of horse and dragoons in our rear'.[6] It seemed to James that he had lost the race for Bristol.

It is not difficult to imagine the nervous scene at Keynsham, as his command group – Grey, Holmes, Venner, Fowke, Matthews and Basset – each offered their views on what course should now be taken. Most were in favour of abandoning the northward advance. Two Bristolians however, Wade and John Roe, both with an inside knowledge of the subversive strength of the town (but neither of them in the Duke's confidence), urged him to be bold and march on, for 'all the citizens would rise for him', they said. If James was not already convinced that to attack Bristol in the changed circumstances would have been suicidal, his mind was soon made up for him when he heard of the Duke of Beaufort's incendiary plans. Last night the sky had been lit by a ship set on fire in the harbour. Obviously, he imagined, it was the property of someone who had made a move for him, so it looked as though Beaufort's 'giving notice that the moment the citizens took any disloyal step, he would fire the town about their ears',[7] was no mean threat. 'God forbid', said James, 'that I should bring such calamities as fire and sword on so noble a city.'[8]

Hearing that sentiment, did Wade and Roe exchange glances which said, 'Look at our rebel chief, now! He shies from the most important step in the campaign, for fear of seeing blood spilt and a single town set in flames'? But their voices were in the minority, and James – rejecting another suggestion that they should march straight to Gloucester, and thence to Cheshire, via the Severn's left bank – looked eastwards. After all, the capital had been drastically denuded of troops. Surely if Paton, Danvers, Wildman and the 'brisk boys' heard that the 'army of liberation' was coming, they would appear, armed, on the streets soon enough. And there was another lure: a Mr Adlam had ridden into Keynsham with the news that a regiment of '500 well-armed horse' was waiting to join the rebel army in west Wiltshire. So, under cover of darkness, James stole away along the south bank of the Avon and, next morning, Albemarle, reflecting a new Royalist panic, wrote to Sunderland:

"Spyes who came this day hither from Monmouth's army do inform me that it is the general discourse among the rebels that they will march directly for London if possible, and they are now in the direct road thither."[9]

27

25–30 June 1685

HIT AND RUN

On the Bath road, bad news awaited James. His cousin of
Orange was sending across the English regiments in the Dutch
service for the King's use and they were already on their way to
camp at Hounslow to assist in the defence of London. All the
leaders who had originally pledged their support had let him down
– the London and Cheshire faction and the Whig quality of the
West – and now here was downright treachery. Monmouth was
shattered. So! William had waited to see what support the Protestant
Duke would be given; and, once he was sure the nobility refused
to stir in his favour, he decided to throw in his lot with his father-
in-law. If the Prince of Orange thought by this he would see the
movement crushed, and step over the dead bodies of its heroes, to
claim the Crown in the name of his Stuart princess, so far as the
Duke of Monmouth was concerned he was mistaken.

Perhaps it was clear to him now where the Earl of Sunderland
stood in the matter; he was another who had insured himself not
to be on the losing side. If the King knew that, alas for Sunderland!
The plan to make for London was called off without further
question. 'We drew up before Bath', Wade remembered, 'and
sounded it only in bravado.' The messenger who rode forward,
demanding the town gates be opened, was shot dead in the saddle.

James headed south to occupy Philips Norton, where, said Wade,
'. . . he was very disconsolate and began to complain that all people
had deserted him, for there was no appearance of the Wiltshire
horse Mr Adlam had talked of, although we were near enough to
have joined them if they had had any stomach for it. Indeed the
Duke was so dejected we could hardly get orders from him . . .'[1]

But he shook off his despondency quickly enough on hearing
that Churchill had joined Feversham and that the combined forces

Ford, Baron Grey of Werke, *c.* 1675, by
Sir Peter Lely

th Earl of Salisbury (foreground)
the son of Monmouth's friend
upporter, the 3rd Earl, who was
d to join the rebel Cabal under
Protestant Duke's leadership in
Being taken ill at that time he
ned and retired from London to
eld House, where he died a
weeks later. When Monmouth
attainted in 1685, the 4th Earl,
ing himself to be in danger by
ying a portrait of his father's
d, had William Wissing super-
se his own portrait over that of
mouth. It was not until the 1870s
picture cleaners, in stripping off
rtion of the top painting, un-
ed the Duke's head.

were on his tail. He trotted out to Philips Norton's entrances, allotting defensive tasks to a company there and a troop here and ordering a thick barricade of wagons to be pushed across the Bath road and tipped up on their sides, to be manned, in the first line, by 'Captain Vincent and 50 musketeers'. He posted two of his cannons there and two on the higher ground forward and to the right, all strongly protected by detachments of horse and foot. The surrounding country was again tightly enclosed with hedges, ditches, banks and walls, and, just as he had done at Axminster, James used the features to the best advantage. Giving instructions for the bulk of the army to rest, he detailed the 'Duke's Own Regiment' to be prepared to make their way round the right flank, making full use of the enclosed and broken ground, to take the Royalists in enfilade. His men, still in good heart, sang a song for him which their descendants were to repeat until well into the nineteenth century. They roared the chorus as they went about their soldierly duties:

> The Duke of Monmouth's at Norton Town
> All a fighting for the Crown
> Ho – boys – ho ![2]

James placed himself in the tallest window in the village and turned his spyglass on the Bath road, down which files of scarlet soon appeared. It was his half-brother, Grafton,* with Feversham's advance guard. So, according to Wade, 'the Duke caused his own regiment of foot to creep round under cover of the hedgerows and a gentleman's court and attack them on the flank, which was done, and the regiment being much superior in number, we fell with a good part of them into their rear, so that they were surrounded on all sides . . .' He next ordered Holmes forward to take on a party of infantry, who had '. . . lined the hedge that flanked us, which he did, and, after about an hour's dispute . . . made them retire from hedge to hedge . . . The King's army was drawn up in a plowed field about 500 paces from the hedge. We, having gained the hedges next the field, drew up all our foot, ranging in one line all along the hedges, our horse behind them . . .'

Dummer, the artilleryist, giving the Royalist side of the picture, also reflects Monmouth's able defence of the town : '500 foot, with some troops of Horse Grenadiers and Dragoons, were detached, under command of the Duke of Grafton, to fall upon their rear, which was accordingly done, but with ill success. The rebels had posted themselves so advantageously that we lost about 50 men, the Duke [of Grafton] himself narrowly escaping . . .'[3]

*Henry Fitzroy, Duke of Grafton, son of the Duchess of Cleveland.

It was late afternoon and the rain was pouring hard. 'We could do nothing on either side but fire our cannon', said one Royalist, Lord Dunblane,[4] and another said that 'the ground being wet, and our arms, too, by the abundance of rain that fell that day . . . and having no tents, about 4 in the evening we drew off in order, without any interruption from the enemy, and marched that night for Bradford'.[5] James was eager to pursue, but having 'no manner of confidence in the horse', prepared to march on to Frome. All the same it was a rebel victory, the Royalists suffering over a hundred killed, and Monmouth's army only half a dozen. These included Colonel Holmes, with an arm ripped off, and his subaltern son, killed. And so the army plodded south 'in a miserable rainy night almost up to our knees in dirt, and almost to the destruction of our foot'.

John Coad, who was badly hurt at the barricade, recalled the journey: 'My wounds being judged mortal and wondering I was not dead, the chirurgeons refused to dress [them]; but the same evening, notwithstanding the great rain that fell, our camp moving southward, I was cast on a waggon with few clothes about me. The shaking of the waggon made my wounds bleed afresh, and . . . [later] one Mr Hardy, an apothecary in Lyme, cutting off my body clothes, ketched and stuck fast to my body, in searching found the bullet lodged in the loins of my back, cut it out . . .'

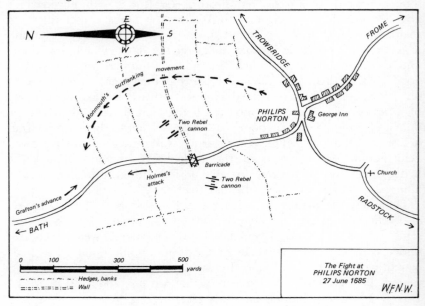

Clapping the town Royalists behind bars and listening rapturously to Monmouth's Proclamation, the people of Frome had raised a company for him, but this was quickly dispersed by Lord Pembroke with the Wiltshire militia. In their turn the militia fled before the oncoming rebel army, the head of whose column reached the little manufacturing town, soaked through, at 8 a.m.

Frome marked the nadir of James's misfortunes so far. Here Adlam's '500 well-armed horse' proved to be either a myth or an impossibility; here he received definite news of the arrival at Hounslow of the regiments sent over by Orange, and that they were poised to join Feversham; that the artillery train from the Tower, composed of thirty cannon, was within a day's march of the Royalists. And – more serious still – he learned of Argyle's defeat and capture : how the Scot, with 2,000 men (raised in a very different manner from the West Country army – 'vassals from 16 to 60, who were under pain of military execution if they refused to join him') marched towards Glasgow; how this force was gradually reduced to 200 from desertions; and how, when Argyle heard what strong forces were facing him, he took to the hills and was caught.

Not one of those friends in London, Wiltshire, Cheshire, Shropshire and Staffordshire, who, time and again, during the last three years, had pledged their active support if James gave a lead, lifted a finger to help; nor was there any news from Ireland. Nowhere in the whole of Britain, save here in Somerset, was there a spark of revolt, and the whole world, Protestant as well as Catholic, Whig as well as Tory, seemed to be against him. No additional arms or ammunition had been found and there was no more money to pay for billets and provisions. He knew his army lacked the capacity to make a bold march north or east, and yet, successful as they had so far been, it seemed futile to continue these evasive hit-and-run tactics in the faint hope there would be a rising elsewhere. James, the only real soldier among his 7,000, knew these tactics could only lead to rout and destruction. What *could* be done?

There seemed to be only one sensible way out. The King had just issued a proclamation undertaking to pardon all – except the eighty who had sailed from Holland – who would lay down their arms and give themselves up. James called a Council of War. Would the fairest course of action not be for the eighty who had come from Holland to make for Poole and 'save themselves by ship for a more favourable time, and leave all the army to take the benefit of the pardon offered'?[6] Venner and Parsons were strongly in favour of this, but a slight majority – including Grey, who always put on a gallant face out of battle – voted to soldier on. James immediately accepted the majority decision; he sent Venner and Parsons, whose hearts were obviously no longer in the enterprise, to Amsterdam, to try to raise money and arms, in the slim expectation of other risings or some diversion occurring. Young Speke resigned at this juncture.

James consulted his map for a new plan. The first one he considered was to strike east for Warminster, to give encouragement to his many sympathisers in Wiltshire, but he abandoned this on hearing that Feversham was moving south and would cross his proposed line of march. Besides, his soldiers needed rest, and the security of a large, friendly and well provided town in which to service their weapons and equipment and tend to their horses was needed, a base from which further operations might be staged. And the answer to that was Bridgwater.

Ever since his last stay in Bridgwater, he had been haunted by talk of a club-army, a band of men gathered together for mutual protection, and in this case one raised as a contingency against a rumoured second invasion on the Severn coast. A certain Quaker had ridden in to James at Glastonbury informing him that these club-army men were now willing to lend their strength in his cause. The Quaker described as 'a busy and cunning fellow', but one whose intelligence sounded plausible enough, next came to Frome to tell James that 'the country is rising for you' and that the club-army, grown to 10,000 and well armed, was concentrated at Axbridge. If the Duke of Monmouth would retire westward, this army would certainly join him. On 30 June, after two nights in Frome, the army moved to Shepton Mallet. 10,000 was probably a gross exaggeration, James must have thought; but even 5,000 would be an immense help, for word had got round his own camp about the pardon, and many were already deserting.

'The Duke of Monmouth . . . was very diligent in training and animating his men,' wrote Bishop Burnet; 'his own behaviour was so gentle and obliging, that he was master of all their hearts.' That evening, as was his habit, he walked from company to company and troop to troop in their bivouacs, discarding his dreadful despondency and talking cheerfully to his men and instilling fresh hope in them. But he knew, as they did not, that unless some miraculous initiative could be snatched, and that soon, the army must be doomed.

28

1–6 July 1685

THE PATH TO SEDGEMOOR

Hearing, at Shepton Mallet, that a supply train containing substantial quantities of arms, ammunition and provisions, had been
left in Wells by Colonel Kirke, James detailed three troops to
capture them, which they did,[1] but not without vandalism. ('The
Duke's soldiers, thinking some of the cathedral men at Wells a little
too impertinent, were somewhat free with their appurtenances,
which I think was all the damage done by them,' said the Bridgwater observer, John Oldmixon, with some understatement.) The
next night the army bivouaucked on Pedwell Plain, where James was
greeted with further bad news: the promised club-army, said to be
10,000, proved to be only 160 (and, as though adding insult to
injury, they carried a white apron for their banner).

Next came a deputation from Taunton, terrified that Feversham
would burn down their town and pleading with the Duke not to
return. 'They had done well', replied James bitterly, 'not to have
desired me to come from Lyme to them . . . I will do as I think
best.'[2] One of them brought along the King's Proclamation of
Pardon, and had it shown round the rebel camp, which resulted in
some 1,000 desertions. James immediately sent a party to arrest
this traitor, his punishment being conscription into the army. The
Bridgwater people, having painful memories of the burning of their
town in July 1645, made a plea in the same tone as Taunton's, at
which 'the Duke was much offended'. But, in spite of all these
affronts, with a typical Monmouth gesture, he marched into the
town the following morning, not leading his main army, but at the
head of the 160 club-men, 'as a mark of his particular kindness'.[3]
His total strength was down to about 4,000 now. But in the rest of
England it did not seem that his game was up by any means. Reflecting this feeling, Barillon wrote to Louis XIV:

'The Duke has advanced to Bridgwater, which he means to fortify; this is a position in which it is said he can subsist his army conveniently, having behind him an abundant country, and full of disaffected persons . . . It is certain that Monmouth supplies his army with ease, and that the people furnish him with provisions more willingly than they do the King's troops . . .'[4]

Did the spire of St Mary's Church, rising from the centre of Bridgwater like a symbol of God and human fate, remind James of the story his father told time and again when he was a boy, of the withdrawal into Worcester in 1651, the siege, the fight, the escape, the oak tree, the disguises and the furtive stealing across the Channel, to safety and Lucy Barlow's arms? If so, did he long, with a stronger love than ever before, for Henrietta, and wish more fervently still that he had never allowed himself to be persuaded into an enterprise which was as ill advised as Charles's had been thirty-four years ago? Did it toughten his resolve to escape from this fatal town with his army and dash north for Cheshire, via Keynsham and Gloucester?

His cover play was twofold. He spread the word round that his next destination would be Taunton. He deployed his cannon as though to fight a siege and ordered a quick and elaborate fortification of the town, but, as Wade put it, 'only to secure our Quarters and amuse the world'. Richard Goodenough (appointed Paymaster after Dare's death) sent out the royal order to the villages: 'You are hereby strictly charged and commanded in His Majesty's name immediately to summon . . . all the carpenters inhabiting the said hundred provided with axes, hatchets and other instruments belonging to their trade; also 190 labourers, sufficiently provided with sawes, spades, pickaxes, wheel barrows, and hand barrows . . .'

But one member of the Royalist army at least suspected 'his Majesty's' intentions and that was its frustrated Brigadier-General, the future Duke of Marlborough. 'I find by the enemy's warrant to the constables that they have more mind to get horses and saddles than any thing else,' Churchill wrote to Clarendon from Somerton on 4 July, 'which looks as if he had a *mind to break* away to some other place, and leave his foot entrenched at Bridgwater. But of this and all other things you will have it more at large from my Lord Feversham, who has the sole command here, so that I know nothing but what is his pleasure to tell me, so that I am afraid of giving my opinion freely, for fear it should not agree with the King's intentions . . . I see plainly that the trouble is mine and the honour will be another's . . .'[5]

Saturday 4 July saw Monmouth inspecting new remounts and saddlery, supervising the re-shoeing of the army's horses, the servicing of weapons and issue of fresh equipment, the lining up, east of the River Parret, of his supply echelon of forty-two wagons for the move north, and giving the regimental commanders their marching orders. (So he was too busy to give much time to one Bridgwater man, 'the brother of Capt. Silver, Master-Gunner of England', who requested an interview regarding his new invention, 'the arrangement of many musket-barrels, to be discharged at once, sweeping any narrow entrance of the town through which the King's troops might advance'.) He allowed the Tauntonites to go home and say goodbye to their families and sweethearts (and these, almost without exception, returned the following morning). 'God speed!' said the women. 'Monmouth and God with us!' returned the men, for that was their motto now.

Desperate to make up his deficiency in artillery, James sent the troop commanded by 22-year-old Captain Benjamin Hewling to sieze six guns sited for harbour defence at Minehead; and, in one final effort to get the capital's dissidents up in arms, he put Major Manley and his son on the London road. Sunday morning saw him in Bridgwater Castle, which was packed to hear Ferguson, who had laid down his sword in exchange for a gown and clergyman's scarf, rouse the army for the rigorous marches ahead. His text was Joshua, chapter 22, verse 22 : 'The Lord God of Gods, the Lord God of Gods, he knoweth, and Israel he shall know; if it be in rebellion, or if in transgression against the Lord, save us not . . .' Rebellion? Transgression? Not they, but 'the Duke of York' was the sinner . . . Ferguson had the huge, simple audience listening with rapt attention. This was a holy crusade. They were going to fight for God and King Monmouth; this was worth laying down their lives for.

While Ferguson preached, two miles away a certain Mr William Sparke, 'a respectable citizen of Chedzoy and a well-wisher of the Duke of Monmouth', stood on top of the tower of his village church with his spyglass pointing south across the King's Sedgemoor, watching the redcoats encamp at Westonzoyland. Having seen them to their bivouacs, he climbed quickly down and made contact with a herdsman whose employment was on Sedgemoor, an illegitimate – sometimes called Godfrey after his father, and sometimes Newman after his mother – and an ardent Monmouthite. Sparke instructed Godfrey to 'go and spy for the Duke of Monmouth'.

Lord Feversham first chose the more distant Middlezoy for his camp, but, said an army diarist, 'Colonel Ramsay, who was sent before to set out the ground, found a more convenient place* by Weston . . . behind a . . . ditch that runs into the Moor, which they [occupied] in one line, leaving room between their tents and the ditch to draw up. On the left of our foot were our cannon,† fronting the great road that comes from Bridgwater to Weston, and, in the village, which was covered by our camp, were our Horse and Dragoons quartered'.[6]

Feversham's 2,000 infantry, now furnished with the tents, which had reached them at Frome, were divided into five regiments: the First Guards' two battalions (Duke of Grafton), the Coldstream Guards (Lieutenant-Colonel Sackville), Trelawney's (Lieutenant-Colonel Charles Churchill), Dumbarton's (Lieutenant-Colonel Douglas) and the Queen Dowager's (Colonel Kirke).

At the back of the village were the 500 horse under Churchill, with Sir Francis Compton's troop of Lord Oxford's regiment forward on patrol towards Chedzoy, and a Life Guards detachment, under Oglethorp, towards Bridgwater. 1,500 militia, commanded by Lord Pembroke, were placed in reserve, at Middlezoy, two miles southeast. But, as young farmer Godfrey saw, except for the cavalry vedettes, the army at Westonzoyland was in no state of alertness, and many of the soldiers were drunk on cider. The truth was that their French general had little respect for the offensive potential of an enemy composed of peasant irregulars.

After attending the Rev. Mr Ferguson's Castle matins, James, resplendent still in princely purple, Garter star and neatly combed periwig, climbed the stumpy tower supporting St Mary's Church spire – as you can still climb it today – and pointed his glass eastwards. The view (now obstructed by industrial chimneys, trees and houses) then opened clear across the King's Sedgemoor to Weston. To see the white tents and, around them, the scarlet dots of the men he had once commanded, and to know his half-brother, Grafton, and the comrade deputy commanders of his youth – Feversham, the two Churchills, Kirke, Douglas, Sackville and Villiers – were at their head, must have aroused some strange sensations in him. There, three miles away, was the memory of his illustrious Captain-Generalcy, while here below, in Castlefield, was all he represented now, a ragged, ill-armed host of revolutionaries with their backs to the wall, a host which had marched all of 200 miles with him,

*The field chosen for the Royalist camp, Penzoy Pound, was the exact spot selected by both Fairfax, commanding the Commonwealth Army of the West, and Goring, commanding the Royalists, when successively attacking Bridgwater some forty years earlier.
†Commanded by Henry Sheres.

which had lured him, with loving respect, to this fatal Bridgwater.

Ranging his spyglass along the Royalist lines, he noted that the horse were widely separated from the foot, and an idea began to form in his mind. It might be possible to circumvent their artillery, to infiltrate the enemy lines in strength by night, take the cavalry and infantry by two distinct and simultaneous assaults, and so 'prevent their arms coming together'. Why not attack Feversham by stealth, before further reinforcements reached him, then, having routed him, proceed with the current plan and ride to Cheshire?

When he climbed down from the tower, he was told that a Sedgemoor peasant sought an interview. He listened eagerly to Godfrey. The Royalists appeared to have posted no guards nor pickets, the herdsman reported excitedly, and many of them were drunk, or sleeping, their scarlet coats laid out as blankets. The horse were indeed some distance from the foot. Godfrey knew the way across Sedgemoor like the back of his hand, and the paths to Weston. James called a council of war and put his plan to them. It was to surprise the enemy in dead of night, avoiding the guns on the Bridgwater road and any standing patrols that might be watching in this direction by making a detour north of Chedzoy. Godfrey would guide them across Sedgemoor.

A quick discussion followed between Monmouth, Grey, Wade, Holmes, Fowke, Matthews and Basset. The regimental commanders declared themselves unanimously in favour of the change of plan – provided the enemy had not since dug himself trenches and parapets. Godfrey (who, says Oldmixon, 'loved the Duke of Monmouth as much as it is possible for a man to love') was sent to make another inspection, and soon returned. The redcoats were not entrenched. (Apparently the herdsman did not mention the Bussex rhine, that 'convenient ditch', noted by the enemy diarist. But perhaps it was not worth a mention considering he, Godfrey, knew the ditch's 'plungeons', or crossings, and its comparatively dry and fordable places so well.)

Resolved to march that night against Feverham's camp, James climbed the narrow spiral staircase to the top of St Mary's tower again, this time taking with him his senior officers and showing them the enemy's deployment and his own intended route. Indicating the point at which he proposed to broach the redcoats' lines, his glass fell on a battalion of Dumbarton's regiment,* ('by which he had been extremely beloved', and whose men he had especially admired when he was their Captain-General). Instantly recognisable by their white breeches and deep white cuffs, they made him

*Afterwards the Royal Scots.

suddenly afraid: 'I know those men will fight,' he said through tight lips, 'and if I had them I would not doubt the success.' But, as he closed the glass and prepared to descend the church-tower staircase, his regimental commanders were glad to see the dejection give way again to his old jauntiness: 'Why, gentlemen, we shall have no more to do than to lock up their stable doors and seize the troopers in their beds !'[7]

Bridgwater had rarely known such animation as it knew that evening of 5 July, 1685. It was loud with horsemen's boots, scabbards and jingling spurs over its cobbled streets, and with the cheerful speculation of simple countrymen living the lives of temporary warriors in unfamiliar billets and about to take part in a great enterprise (they knew not what). It milled with red-and-yellow-coated militia deserters; it rasped with the sharpening of knives, scythes, pikes and swords; it was busy with the topping of powder-flasks and the cleaning and oiling of firing-pieces; it was filled with admiration for the rebel commander:

> The Duke of Monmouth's at Bridgwater town,
> All a-fighting for the Crown,
> Ho, boys – Ho !

His soldiers took something more than Ferguson's exhortation and blessing with them; they took Dutch courage – cider and 'the fruits of Bridgwater's cellars'. And when they found their company places on the roadside by Castlefield that night many were fuller of it than the King's army were. But the cider did not debauch *them*, it was their native brew; it made them feel ten feet tall. James now broadcast that he was marching to Bristol; the enemy had no wind of his real intention. But they might have done. While the rebel army formed up in their assembly area, a girl 'zealous for the King' stole out of Bridgwater, making her way to the Royalist camp to give away the objective. According to one of Compton's lieutenants, Feversham's officers 'mocked her intelligence, and . . . one who had indulged largely in wine, seized the unhappy maiden and brutally outraged her, and she fled in agonies of rage and shame, leaving the wicked army to its doom . . .' (Or, as Ralph said, 'she kept the secret in revenge for the loss of her honour'.)[8]

Inspired for victory by 'King Monmouth', the ragged ill-armed West Countrymen formed up with a will on the Eastern Causeway, the old Bristol road, at 11 p.m. The Blue Regiment, the Duke's Own, under Nathaniel Wade (Godfrey beside him as guide), made the vanguard, while the White (Matthews), the Red (Holmes, with the stump of his arm only on the mend one week), the Green (Fowke), the Yellow (Basset) and the Lyme Independent Company formed up behind them, a total of 2,500 foot with their company fronts marked by the banners woven by the 'Maids of Taunton'. Grey's 600 horse (deprived of one crack sub-unit, Hewling's troop at Minehead) formed column of troop at the back of the foot, with the four little field-pieces under the Brandenburger, Anton Buyse, bringing up the rear. At 3,000 plus, the rebels had a numerical superiority over the Royalists of about 500. The countersign by which, in the dark, they were to distinguish one another from the enemy, was 'Monmouth and God with us!'

James – his beaver replaced by a helmet now, and with a metal corselet on his breast – detailed distances to be kept between men, horses and sub-units, and gave orders that if any man should make a noise, knock his weapon, be careless with his step, cough or speak, he was to be 'knocked on the head by his neighbour'. Oldmixon watched him leave: 'About 11 o'clock at night I saw the Duke of Monmouth ride out, attended by his Life Guard of Horse, and tho' then but a boy, observed an alteration in his Look, which I did not like . . . Not being able to judge of the Goodness or Badness of his Cause, I ran down with the stream and was one of its well-wishers . . .'[9]

It was James's decision to group the horse in one body. Colonel Matthews, his former aide-de-camp, now commanding the White, urged him to divide them, 'that the charge and conduct of one part might devolve upon some person of courage equal to the critical nature of the duty and the time'. But Grey was still the army's only other nobleman and if James offended him he would probably lose him and his irreplaceable prestige. 'I will not affront my lord,' Monmouth told Matthews firmly; 'what I have given him in charge is easy to be effected.' And so, with Wade's vanguard to set the pace, and his own Lifeguard of Horse riding closely fore and aft of him, James gave the signal for his army to begin its furtive night march.

Since the first mile and a half was over the route they would have marched in flight, if the Royalists saw them it did not greatly matter, for an escape northwards was exactly what Feversham (who, one way or the other, would not move till the morning) was expecting. The King's general had indeed sent Oglethorp with a strong cavalry patrol to report the time and direction of the rebels' departure. But, perhaps owing to the fact that Oglethorp and his men had taken the brunt of the Royalists' scout work during the past ten days and were thus less vigilant than usual, they reported a blank reconnaissance.

Notwithstanding the full moon, the rebel host was concealed by a mist that hung close across the moor. Keeping Chedzoy, a village mostly loyal to the King – and one which he knew to be under-pinned by one of Compton's patrols – well to his right, James had ordered the way to Sedgemoor to be by the muddy, winding Bradney lane and (what is now known as) War lane. Leaving the forty-two baggage wagons at Peazy Farm under a guard, supported by one of the cannon – poised to advance northwards upon the victory – James joined Godfrey in front, and led skilfully over the first drainage rhine, called the Black Ditch. Then he halted to allow Grey to ride forward with the horse and form a parallel column.

The unschooled horses were his greatest liability: the darkness, the nerviness of their inexperienced riders, straining to hear whispered orders, the swirling marsh mist, and the inevitable, continuous concertinaing of the column, would all have contributed to shake the temper of the ill-broken, ill-assorted nags, kicking and shying, often stopping dead in their tracks, and transmitting fear to the troopers, who relayed back their own nervousness. But, con-sidering the whole force numbered more than 600 horses and 3,000 men, all raw levies in a single force, their order and discipline spoke much for James's leadership.

Well on to the open moor now, the smell of peat marsh in their nostrils, the silent army came to the next channel, called the Langmoor Rhine, whose best crossing was marked by a great boulder, the Devil's Upping Stock, or Langmoor Stone. That night the rock was hidden by fog, and Godfrey steered too far east of it. But, after a long agony of suspense, with much blind casting up and down (any moment one of Compton's outposts might have tumbled on the great column), eventually the plungeon was found, and over they tramped. They were only three-quarters of a mile from the Royalist camp now, and the clock on Chedzoy steeple struck one. At this point James sent Grey, accompanied by Godfrey, to the front of the column with the eight troops of cavalry.

But no sooner was the march resumed than the stillness of Sedgemoor was broken by a single shot. One of Compton's blue-coated troopers, glimpsing them through the fog, had raised the alarm.[10]

6–8 July 1685

DISASTER

Spurs hard on, Compton's patrol man galloped back across the Bussex upper plungeon, then down the Royalist battalions' front with a breathless 'Beat the drums, the enemy is come! For the Lord's sake, beat the drums!' Moments later came the drummers' *rat-tat-tat* . . . Not so quickly, infantrymen, with muzzy heads and frantic fingers, buckled on equipment and snatched up and primed their muskets, while eventually, in Westonzoyland, cavalrymen, to the sound of trumpets, saddled, checked their arms, mounted and formed troop.

Monmouth had to take advantage of such surprise as he had won. He told the cavalry commander to race on, attack and fire the village *now*! But, in his dash, Lord Grey left Godfrey behind (or did he dismiss him?). So, a thousand yards on, in horror, the horse reached the dreadful broad Bussex Rhine, the enemy's 'convenient ditch', and knew not where to cross. The plungeon was to the *left*, Grey led *right*, across the Royalists' front, towards the lighted matches of Dumbarton's regiment, the warriors who prompted the Duke's anxious comment on St Mary's tower.

Captain Mackintosh, commanding a company of the regiment, vowing that Monmouth, his old commander, would attack that night, had marked out the ground for his men to stand ready between their tents and the Bussex. (This was the only regiment in Feversham's army to retain matchlocks, the other infantry units being armed with the Dutch-invented snaphaunce, or flint musket.) Grey thought their matches were the lights of Weston, but when he approached them, to his awful dismay, the rhine was still there, wide and deep and soft beneath the clinging mist. The Scots' Commander, Colonel Douglas, challenged them across it: 'Who are you?'

'Horse,' a rebel officer had the presence of mind to reply, 'from the Duke of Albemarle's militia.' Unsuspected, they trotted on.

'Who are you for?' came another challenge, further down the bank, this time from Captain Berkeley, commanding the First Foot Guards' musketeers.

'Monmouth, and God with us!' shouted a rebel officer.

A brief pause. 'Take that with you then!' *That* was the first volley of the dreadful night.

Several saddles were emptied, and the majority of those nervous, untried rebel horses bolted their riders helter-skelter from the rhine to collide with Monmouth's Foot, who were doubling forward to support them. Many of these, believing the army to be already routed, joined in the retreating stampede, leaving the field, never to return. In the chaos of mist and dark and loss of control, there was even a skirmish between the rebel horse and foot, and the panic reached the drivers and guards on the wagons at Peazy Farm, who soon scampered for Axbridge and home. Only one detachment of rebel cavalry was steady enough to engage the enemy – the troop commanded by Captain Jones, a London cabinet-maker. He led his men full tilt at Compton's men guarding the upper plungeon, and put their commander out of action for the rest of the night. With moonlight and the flash of battle on their cuirasses and sword blades, and their chargers steady as rocks, how formidable those troopers of Lord Oxford's Horse must have appeared to Jones's would-be cavaliers, whose mounts were soon sent galloping away in terror.

With the end of the rebel cavalry potential, William Williams heard only this from Monmouth's lips: 'Lost by the cowardice of my Lord Grey!' If only Fletcher of Saltoun had been there! But Although Grey was no Prince Rupert, no Churchill, taking into account that neither the horses nor their riders were trained for the role allotted them, and there was no one to show them the Bussex crossing, Monmouth's accusation was perhaps unjustified.

However the verdicts may differ on that, all agreed that Monmouth himself – dismounted now, infantry officer's half-pike in hand and full of his old courage and vitality – set a fine example, leading forward his column of foot, deploying them on the line of the Bussex, exhorting and inspiring and continuously exposing himself in the front centre. First behind him, Wade's Blue Regiment held their fire, but nerves in the White Regiment, under Matthews, to the left, were at snapping point. His men could not resist the impulse to fire; nor could those of Holmes (the Red) on their left. So a general fusillade began, during which the rebel companies became inextricably mixed in the gloom. Their aim, like the aim of recruits at early 'rapid-fire' practice, was wild and high. But not so the three little iron field-pieces. Under the direction of their skilful artillerymen, the Brandenburger Anton Buyse and his Dutch deputy, they took a heavy toll on the closed ranks of Dumbarton's and the Guards. Did the gunners even then expect to retrieve the situation for the foot?

Perhaps if the infantry had kept advancing and clambered *en masse* over the miry ditch, they might have overrun their enemy in the dark. Bishop Kennet, having spoken to witnesses on both sides, though so: 'Monmouth, as if he had been at the head of regular forces, kept them in too good order. For had he suffered them after the first discharge, to fall on with their other weapons, they would have knocked all their enemies on the head, or have pushed them into the utmost confusion.'[1] But it was not as easy as that. As Wade said, of his battalion: 'I could not get them to advance, so we continued in that station.'[2]

Lord Feversham, who returned from Chedzoy after visiting Compton's patrols an hour or so before Monmouth crept past that village, cannot have been in his bed more than an hour when the alarm rang out, and now (in the hearsay words of the chronicler Oldmixon, then a lad) 'made not so much haste as to forget to set his cravat-string in a paltry little looking-glass in one of the cottages', while Lord Churchill (in Wolseley's description) 'made his presence felt throughout the Royal army'. Determined first to silence Monmouth's midget cannon, the Brigadier-General attempted to have three of the guns on the Bridgwater road moved up to the Bussex, but the ground was too soft for them to be manhandled. Hearing this, Dr Peter Mews, the Bishop of Winchester, a Civil War veteran, who had put up at the Royalist camp for the night ('in case I could be of help'), lent his carriage-horses for the operation; so the King's much superior artillery soon rolled into action.

The Royalist forces were closing for the kill. To reinforce their right flank, which suffered the brunt of the rebels' attack, Churchill brought the Queen Dowager's (under the roguish Colonel Kirke) and Trelawney's (Charles Churchill) behind the three Guards battalions already in action there, and up on their right. Then, at about 2 a.m., when the rebel fire slackened, he led a troop of his dragoons via the lower plungeon, against Buyse's artillery, cutting down or driving away the tattered men who served the guns, while a company of foot followed up to capture them.

Now Feversham bestirred himself: 'My God, these rebels will pay for their impertinence!' He ordered Colonel Villiers, with the main body of the Life Guards and Horse Grenadiers, three troops of dragoons and Compton's troop, across the plungeon – to form line opposite the rebels' right flank, ready to charge when he gave the word, while Oglethorp, whose abortive reconnaissance on the Bridgwater–Bristol road was cut short by the din of the battle, trotted his force behind the Royalist infantry, crossed the upper plungeon and, joining Compton's troop, assaulted Monmouth's left.

But the rebels proved not quite ready for the *coup de grâce*. Inspired all the time by the Duke, their ranks stood resolutely closed. There was a little ammunition left and their scythe-men could still swing and slash to keep the cavaliers at bay. Oglethorp was repulsed. The noises of that famous night persisted : the thunder of hooves on rushy ground, the jingle of bit and bridle, the clash of cavalry sword on peasants' scythe, the ring of pistol and musket fire through the misty, moonlit night, the officers' clipped, nervy shouts and the anguished yells of the wounded, the neigh and snort of chargers, and, overall, the heaving sigh of the King's men grappling with Monmouth's.

Directed by the unerring Churchill, three companies had doubled round by the lower crossing to engage the enemy with musket-fire on the flank, and hand-to-hand in front. It was nearly 2.30 a.m. now. Monmouth's men were desperate : 'Ammunition !' they yelled. 'For the Lord's sake, ammunition.' This was Villiers's moment. Signalled by Feversham, in trotted the Household Cavalry, two ranks line abreast, within pistol range. They made their volley, then drew swords and charged. The rebel groups began to topple.

The enemy was hard on every side. 'Our ranks are broke my lord,' William Williams shouted desperately to his master; 'it is time to flee !' What should Monmouth have done? Stand there and die with his men? Allow himself to be taken? He had given orders to three of his bodyguard to pistol him if the battle were lost, but must have known they would not have the heart for it when the hour came. Although modern historians, from Macauley onwards, have accused Monmouth of leaving the battlefield indecently early, none of the contemporary witnesses, either on his own or on the Royalist side, held that his conduct at Sedgemoor was anything but gallant and selfless. 'Who, of the old Monmouth men', asks Roberts, 'their children, their grandchildren, ever brought any charge of cowardice against the Duke?' Did James reason his moment of flight? (His father had not stayed to die or be captured at Worcester. Now that the result of the fight was known, should he not, as the irreplaceable Protestant Duke, true heir to England's throne and leader in exile of the Old Cause, escape and keep the torch burning? Henrietta would have had him do that.)

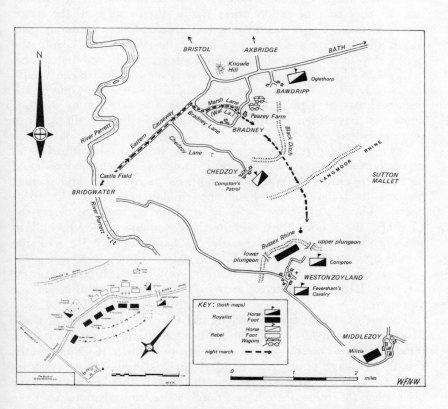

12. Monmouth's Night March, 5–6 July, and the Battle of Sedgemoor,
6 July 1685

While he encouraged his men, behind him more slipped away in flight, to Bridgwater or to the Mendip hills. 'All the world cannot stop those fellows now,' he told Williams, as he watched the enemy's relentless advance. Grey, Dr Oliver, the Duke's surgeon, Anton Buyse and two dozen of the bodyguard came up, waiting for him to go. 'All is lost,' shouted Grey, 'it is time to shift for yourself!' Taking off his helmet and steel corselet, James followed them away from the carnage. Three hundred rebels died in the battle, and another thousand were killed in the pursuit.

As Monmouth and his entourage fled north-west, to be entirely clear of the scene of action, there was a discussion as to the wisest course to take. There was no doubt in Doctor Oliver's mind: 'Sire, this is the farthest you can go without throwing yourself into the hands of your enemies, who are waiting for you all over the country . . . Nobody has heard of our ill-success in those parts [to the West]; let us turn off to the sea coast over against Wales, seize one of the passage boats at Uphill, and get over to the other side, where I know you have friends, among whom you will be safe till you can retire elsewhere.'

Grey upbraided the doctor for offering 'such foolish counsel', and urged James to make for Poole or Lymington. Which advice should he take, to escape to Wales, his mother's native land, and thence, perhaps to Ireland? Or should he emulate his father in 1651, disguise himself, move by night, lie up by day, and sail across the Channel, the sooner thus to rejoin the woman he loved, and in whose company only could he ever be happy again? He took the second option.

'God bless you, sire,' said Oliver, who loved him, as nearly everyone James encountered grew to love him; 'I shall never see you more.'

The escort shifted for themselves and Oliver rode to Bristol, while Monmouth, with Grey and Buyse, headed south, 'designing to get into the New Forest', as the King wrote, 'which if [Monmouth] could . . . have done . . . could have looked on himself as safe, Lord Grey being well acquainted there, and then it would have been easy for himself to have found some embarkation, to have carried him beyond the sea'.[3] After taking a quick mouthful of food with Edward Strode, at Downside, they went on through the evening of 6 July, via Gillingham, to the east end of Cranborne Chase, where they turned their exhausted horses loose, hid their saddles and bridles, and disguised themselves as shepherds. Between Gillingham and Shaftesbury Richard Hollyday offered himself as a guide. A little farther on, meeting Royalist militia search-parties at almost every turn, they decided to split up and make their way individually to the Continent, Hollyday going with Grey, and Buyse with James. The route they were taking must have been betrayed, for Lord Lumley's Sussex militia were combing the area as close as ferrets, and every soldier had been told there was £5,000 waiting for the man, or men, who should find 'James, late Duke of Monmouth'.

At 5 a.m. on 7 July, Grey and Hollyday were seized at Holt Lodge, four miles to the Dorset side of Ringwood. But there was no sign that day of the 'arch-rebel'. At the same time the following morning Buyse was caught in the woods between Fordingbridge and Ringwood. As he told his captors, he had parted with the Duke of Monmouth in the middle of the night, and he took them to the area where he had last seen him (for which information he was spared his life). Ironically, the place he pointed to was on the property of the late Lord Shaftesbury, Monmouth's early sponsor, Dryden's 'Achitophel'.

Amy Farrant, 'a poor woman', had seen two men jump over a hedge just there. It was an enclosed area; Lumley had it cordoned and systematically searched. A militiaman called Henry Parkin spotted the give-away skirt of a man's coat showing among the brackens. Pointing his musket he parted the undergrowth. Two more soldiers came forward, muskets at the ready. The face they eventually woke – from a sleep that made them think him dead – was gaunt, sunk-eyed, ashen and bearded. It could not be the fabulous Protestant Duke, but another rebel.

'Shoot him! let us shoot him!' cried one. But, at the alarm, Sir William Portman, Taunton's M.P., who was assisting Lumley, rode forward and told them not to shoot, but to keep him covered. Searching the scarecrow figure, Portman found the George glinting beneath the peasant's coat.

It is said that Militiaman Parkin burst into tears and reproached himself ever more when he heard who the prisoner was, and that Amy Farrant, shunned and boycotted by her neighbours, 'languished in decay and poverty ever afterwards'.

Two Sussex militia officers, riding hard all day for London, that night informed the King that 'James, late Duke of Monmouth is your Majesty's prisoner'.

30

THE KING'S PRISONER

Searching the prisoner further, Sir William Portman found five books: two on military tactics, another containing 'computes of the yearly expenditure of his Majesty's Navy and Land Forces', a manuscript of 'spells, charms and conjurations', and the carefully kept pocket-book. There were a number of trinkets and lucky charms in James's pockets, too, and some peas, which he had gathered in the fields and would have eaten had he not collapsed in sleep.

He was morally, as well as physically, exhausted. He had nothing left in the world except a heart that was beating for Henrietta Wentworth. For one moment of her laughter, her happy tears, her arms, he would willingly have starved for another week. That and the people's affection was all he wanted: the desire for crowns and power and international prestige had vanished. Through his haze of exhaustion and hopelessness, there was this one tiny glimmer of light: the possibility of life, life that might be shared for another thirty or forty years with Henrietta. Like an animal, driven into the corner of its trap, he would do anything to save the thread of life; anything short of endangering his comrades.

He had been attainted for 'raising arms against his lawful King and for assuming the three Crowns', the consequence of which was death without trial. How often had he listened with terror, hearing the recounting of his grandfather's execution? How many times had he thought of the axe driving into Rusell's and Sidney's necks? He, the man of *joie de vivre*, the man who revelled in living, was as appalled as any man could be at the prospect of losing his life. Did he deserve to die at thirty-six, in the zenith of his years? This adventure had not been his choice: he had been tempted, against his instincts by men who knew he was the only one in the world who could raise and lead a revolutionary army. They had played upon his celebrated generosity. Well, now he had come over and he had done it, and it had failed. It had failed because too many who had lured him from his Netherlands bliss had proved faint-hearted. Those with thinking minds had coaxed him into a situation of mortal peril, then stayed at home like craven dogs.

The West Countrymen, who claimed him as their King, had demonstrated their love for him with a magnificent sacrifice of life and limb and family happiness. But he had wanted only to be their captain, not to wear their crown, which now condemned him. He had been misguided into that by rash, ambitious men like Ferguson and Grey. Nor had he expected to see blood spilled. Those so-called City leaders had advised him that he had only to set foot in England for the common people to rise spontaneously throughout the land, and that he could march safely to Whitehall with nothing more than a switch in his hand, the people and the soldiers loved him so. And thus it might have been, had the lesser leaders not flinched.

What would the people want of him now? That he should be their martyr? On the contrary, surely they would beg him to employ every artifice he knew to get off? For as long as the Protestant Duke lived, the pilot light of liberty shone. What would Holmes and Basset, Matthews and Fowke have him do? Would they not have advised that, as his father's heir, it was his duty to save himself for his people and the Protestant cause if he could? They considered the Catholic king the devil incarnate, who should be tricked as Satan should be tricked. James should go before him on bended knee and offer any promises or excuses that might secure his pardon. Was it too unbearably humiliating? But was it not customary for noblemen to seek pardon of their monarch? Had not his friend, noble Russell, that most upright and unblemished character, pleaded for King Charles's mercy? (And had his father not said, 'I was inclined to have saved him, but was forced to his execution, otherwise I might have broke with the Duke of York.')

His friends would have urged him do all in his power to gain an interview with his uncle – to write him abject letters, to write to his stepmother, the Queen Dowager; to write to the Lord High Treasurer, Rochester; to ask Sunderland, (who wanted to be his Secretary of State) to intercede for him. And, having gained the audience, to kneel humbly before the King, remind him that he was the same flesh as he was and that, if he had him executed, it would be his own blood he would spill. And if at last he began to kindle the ashes of that icy heart, he should promise to be his faithful servant for life; and, if he pardoned him, Monmouth should go across the water and gather his forces again and fight him to the death next time.

When Monmouth had been in trouble in the old days he had always turned to his father to absolve him, to wipe his slate clean. Now, in his helplessness, he was suddenly and starkly conscious, as in some nightmare, that the man in power in Whitehall Palace was not his father, but the uncle who hated him. But since he wanted to live, with a longing such as he had never known before – to live in order to prove what a worthy and useful man he could really be – that uncle must be transformed into his father, his loving, forgiving father. Monmouth is recorded as making only one request of his gaoler during his two days at Ringwood: for pen, ink and paper.

'My Lord,' he wrote to Rochester, 'having some proofs of your kindness when I was last at Whitehall, makes me hope now that you will not refuse interceding for me with the King, being I now, though too late, see how I have been misled . . .' He wrote to the Queen Dowager, who had paved the way for him with the Yorks in the autumn of 1683: 'Madam, being in this unfortunate condition, and having none left but your Majesty that I think may have some compassion of me, and that for the last King's sake makes me take the boldness to beg of you to intercede for me . . .' And he wrote to the King: '. . . I hope I may live to show you how zealous I shall ever be for your service: and could I but say one word in this letter, you would be convinced of it; but it is of that consequence that I dare not do it . . .'

What was that 'one word'? No proof exists. Perhaps it was to disclose the Prince of Orange's designs on the English throne and his complicity in both the recent invasions; or it could have been to betray the double-dealing Sunderland, if he failed to put in a strong word on his behalf. Or it may have been a promise to produce a document or witness proving his legitimacy, and an undertaking to allow the evidence to be kept secret, in exchange for his liberty. Perhaps it amounted to nothing more than words.

Monmouth, Grey and Buyse travelled the four-day journey to London together, closely guarded by four troops of militia, and with Colonel William Legge, sitting beside them, with orders to stab or pistol Monmouth if any attempts were made to rescue him. James remained very dejected, but Grey was in a jocular mood, 'talking of dogs, hunting and racing, etcetera'.[1] They reached Farnham Castle on 11 July and Guildford the following day. During the journey the King sent Ralph Sheldon from Court to meet Monmouth on the road, to report his condition, demeanour and attitude.

'Who are the persons having the greatest credit with the King?' James asked the equerry.

'My Lord Sunderland in the first place.'

'Why then,' exclaimed Monmouth hopefully, 'as I hope for salvation, he promised to meet me! Pray acquaint his Majesty that I will inform him of all my lord's accomplices, whereof I perceive there are some in whom his Majesty puts the greatest trust.'[2]

On 13 July the coaches reached London, where barges waited to convey the prisoners to Whitehall. By chance James's old Court and Tory friend Bruce was there. 'I, coming from the City by water,' he remembered, 'unfortunately landed at the same moment, and saw the Duke of Monmouth led up the other stairs on Westminster side, lean and pale, and with a disconsolate physiognomy, with soldiers with pistols in their hands . . . and I wished heartily and often that I had not seen him, for I could never get him out of my mind for years, I so loved him personally.'[3]

Although the King was fixed in his determination to go through with the death sentence, he had been strongly persuaded by the Queen Dowager to see Monmouth, and, since he was very curious to hear what intelligence the three prisoners might offer, he granted interviews to each. When the people knew this, they were jubilant, for it was an international axiom that no criminal be permitted to set eyes on his sovereign except to receive pardon. 'A King's face', the saying went, 'should give grace.' Meanwhile, as soon as Ralph Sheldon was admitted to the King's closet, on return to Whitehall, Sunderland, who had been hovering outside, pretended some business and followed in. When Sheldon applied for a private interview the King told him that he 'might say anything before my Lord Sunderland'.

'Sire, I am commissioned by the Duke of Monmouth', the equerry started hesitatingly, 'to assure your Majesty that my Lord Sunderland himself was of intelligence with him . . .' During the next tense moments Sunderland (the man who Princess Anne called 'the subtlest working villain that is on the face of the earth') seemed 'extraordinarily struck, so that the King could not but observe it'.

'If that be all he can discover to save his life,' the Secretary of State blurted – 'with feigned laughter' – 'it will do him little good.' (In the event it did Sunderland no harm.)

'Poor Monmouth,' said the King; 'he was always easy to be imposed upon.'[4]

James's spirits remained low. The French Ambassador, seeing him escorted along a Whitehall corridor, remarked that 'his arms were tied loosely behind him and he looked very disconsolate'. While they waited in the so-called 'spy room' of William Chiffinch, Keeper of the Backstairs, where the audience was to take place, James complained of his heavy cold, at which Grey scoffed, saying sarcastically, that his uncle had 'a cure to be applied in a few days'.

Only the Queen, Sunderland, and Middleton, his fellow Secretary-of-State, attended the King during the interviews. No eyewitness account of what passed exists, except the King's comment in a letter to Orange that 'the Duke of Monmouth seemed more concerned and desirous to live, and did behave himself not so well as I expected, nor so as one ought to have expected, from one who had taken upon him to be King'.[5] If that meant he was too abject in his supplication, a kneeling, humble, tearful attitude was just what Charles had prescribed when he sent his son to beg the Yorks' forgiveness in the autumn of 1683. For it was well known that anyone, in York's poor grace, could never hope for forgiveness unless he applied himself with the utmost humility.

Apparently Sunderland had taken Monmouth aside and persuaded him to confine his case to relating the circumstances of his invasion and assumption of the Crown, assuring him that provided he kept silent about their own intrigue, he would do his best to secure a pardon for him.[6] So when his plea was rejected, his eyes would surely have turned across from his uncle to Sunderland, as though to say, 'now it is for you, who were in league with me, to save my life'.

But while there was eventually a reprieve for Grey, who was prepared to divulge names, and for the Brandenberger, who had pointed the way to where James hid in the New Forest, there was to be none for the Protestant Duke himself. The King was adamant. His advice to his nephew was to 'to look to your soul'. England's comment on the interview was that the King should never have granted it unless he was resolved to show mercy. (It was, said Barillon, 'une chose bien extraordinaire et fort opposé à l'usage ordinaire des autres nations'.)

The main London gossip was still about the campaign in the West. 'The Duke of Monmouth', insisted the Tory Sir John Reresby (who was no unqualified admirer of his) 'had, from the very beginning of this desperate attempt, behaved with the conduct of a great captain, as was allowed by the King, who in my hearing, said he had not made one false step'.[7] Charles Bertie wrote proudly to his niece, Lady Rutland, 'all agree that he acted the part of a great general, and charged afoot at the head of his army.' She also heard from Chaloner Chute: 'It is a pity so brave a man, as they say he showed himself in the engagement, should deserve the fate that he is to expect very shortly – it is said without the formality of a trial – and that I wish he had rather been knocked on the head in the engagement.'

So, no doubt, did James, but since he was still alive he was determined to stay so. The Tower of London, where some of his condemned friends had spent their last days, must have been for him the grimmest symbol in the world. His first discharge from those forbidden walls had been at the age of seven, with his mother on 16 July, the day after St Swithin's, in 1656. Pregnani, the astrologer, had once told him that provided he could survive that day, he might 'live to be a great man'.[8] So, as it was now 13 July, the next forty-eight hours were terribly important to him. Perhaps this was his proccupation as he mounted the steps beyond Traitor's Gate between eight and nine o'clock that evening, watched by hundreds of very sad and silent Londoners.

31

13–15 July 1685

MARTYR FOR THE PEOPLE?

Monmouth's children – James, Earl of Dalkeith, eleven years old now, Lord Henry Scott, eight, and Lady Anne, nine – had been locked in the Tower ahead of him, 'to keep them safe until further order', said the King,[1] and their mother had been granted permission to accompany them. Next morning Lord Rochester escorted Anna to her husband's cell. What were their emotions as they faced each other for their first meeting since 1683? It had not been devoid of affection. The Monmouths had been steady companions in the early years and had always shared the love of their children. But their arranged childhood marriage had proved its unnaturalness all too soon. She was so many things he was not: an intellectual, a literary woman, a patron of the arts, and always very decorous in her behaviour. On the other hand she fell far short of his generosity, charm and tenderness, his radiance and his ability to communicate with people in all walks of life.

If Anna was all rectitude now, who could blame her? Had there ever existed 'the least understanding or correspondence between them' – she wanted to know (with Rochester as witness) – regarding his ambition and rebellion against his lawful King? Had she ever shown approval of his conduct during the past five years? How could she ever forgive him for Lady Wentworth? Had she ever 'done anything in the whole course of her life to displease or disoblige him, or ever caused him disquiet, except in two particulars, one as to his women, and the other for his disobedience to the late King'?

On the contrary, James replied, 'you have always shown yourself a very kind, loving and dutiful wife towards me . . . I have nothing imaginable to charge you with, either against your virtue and duty to me, your steady loyalty and affection to the late King, or kindness and affection towards my children . . .' He had never in all his life been seriously culpable of arrogance or pride or inflexibility; he had always sought forgiveness, had constantly promised to mend his ways; yet, being weak, had always stumbled, and, after a few steps, fallen again. But he would never, never, renounce Henrietta; she was his 'wife before God'. Charles Bertie, writing to Lady Rutland two days later, said that James had little desire to speak with Anna, 'for his affections were chiefly set upon my Lady Harriet Wentworth, with whom he confessed he lived these two years as man and wife and thought himself the most happy man in the world, saying the Duchess was imposed upon him when very young'.[2]

Having now abandoned hope of Sunderland's intercession, he decided to submit to the King a full account of the Secretary of State's duplicity. Forty years later Colonel Scott, the Tower Guard commander, a cousin of Anna's, described how his prisoner asked him if he would be prepared to deliver a very personal and important letter to His Majesty. Scott replied that he would have been quite willing to do so, except that 'my orders are not to stir from your Grace till your execution; and therefore I dare not leave the Tower'. James asked if there was another officer who could be entrusted with the errand. Scott named Captain ——, who duly 'promised on his word of honour he would deliver the letter to no person whatever but to the King only'. He went immediately to Court where he was told to await an audience. But Sunderland, who had just been with the King, seeing an officer of the Guards waiting outside the royal closet, asked who the letter was from.

'From the Duke of Monmouth.'

'Give it to me,' ordered the Secretary of State, 'I will carry it to his Majesty.'

'No, my lord, I pawned my honour to the Duke that I would deliver the letter to no man but the King himself.'

'Since the King is putting on his shirt,' said Sunderland – clearly very agitated – 'you cannot be admitted into his closet. But the door shall stand open that you shall see me give it to him.'

As Colonel Scott told his Majesty in exile afterwards, the Captain saw Sunderland's back approach the King, and assumed it was delivered. But the King, of course, knew nothing of it; Sunderland made quite sure of that. ('Colonel Scott, as I am a living man,' said the exiled James II in old age, 'I never saw that letter, nor did I ever hear of it till within these few days.'[3])

The King had first decided that Monmouth should 'suffer the pains of death as a traitor', but was later 'minded . . . to bring him to the scaffold on Tower Hill and then and there to cause his head to be cut and stricken off, and clearly severed from his body; and this execution to be on Wednesday next, the 15th inst, any former judgement, law or commandment to the contrary notwithstanding'.[4] The King wanted the greatest possible audience to see the national hero die. He knew all about the St Swithin's promise, afterwards announcing that he had chosen that day to teach his nephew a lesson 'for giving credit to so vain a prediction; for tho' Almighty God permits such divinations to fall out some times according as they are foretold, yet never to the benefit or advantage of those that believe them'.

Dr Turner, Bishop of Ely, came to James's cell that morning and was joined in the afternoon by Dr Ken (who was afterwards Bishop of Bath and Wells). They prayed with him until late in the night. 'Monmouth was very sincere in his religious professions', as Fox commented, and prayer and supplication, coupled with the new conviction that death was very near, brought him a strength he had probably never known before. Convinced at last that St Swithin's would, after all, be his day of judgement, he shook off his fear and became serene, dignified and nonchalant about all worldly matters, except Henrietta Wentworth. Early in the morning Dr Tennison – vicar of James's parish of St Martins-in-the-Fields and one day to be Archbishop of Canterbury – accompanied by Dr Hooper, joined the two prelates preparing him for the stroke. And when Tennison, to use his own words, 'charged him with his conversation' with Henrietta, James replied, 'I have heard it is lawful to have one wife in the eye of the law and another before God.'

'You should know of the falsehood and ill consequence of such a principle,' said the shocked Tennison.

James shrugged his shoulders: 'Well, but if a man be bred up in a false notion, what shall he do when he has but two hours to live?'

He tried to press a gold watch on Tennison to give Henrietta, but the vicar refused, replying primly, 'I cannot be concerned in any such message or token to her.' With Dr Ken, Monmouth was equally unrepentant: 'I confess I lived many years by all sorts of debauchery. But since that time I had an affection for the Lady Harriot, and I prayed that, if it were pleasing to God, it might continue, otherwise that it might cease. And God heard my prayer. The affection did continue, therefore I doubted not that it was pleasing to God; and that this is a marriage, our choice of one another being guided, not by lust, but by judgement, upon due consideration.'[5]

When he told them he would die a true Protestant, they judged that 'that cannot be so unless you thoroughly believe the doctrine of passive obedience and non-resistance'. As he made no reply, he was refused the sacrament. But, for his children's sake, he drafted and signed a paper renouncing his pretensions to the throne and also declaring that his father *had told him* he was illegitimate, though he was careful not to admit it himself. 'Having declared this', he ended, 'I hope that the King who is now will not let my children suffer on this account.'

He made another statement, referred to on the scaffold as 'the Paper'. According to Bishop Kennet, John Oldmixon and the authors of *Western Martyrology* and *The Whole Glorious Life* – who state that James also spoke the words before execution – this opens with an expression of sorrow 'for what Blood hath been spilt on my account', and goes on to praise the uprising, which was simply 'the very opposing of Popery and arbitrary power', and to condemn 'several most heinous and notorious crimes – such as the unhappy fate of the Earl of Essex and my father of ever blessed memory'.

'I have lived and shall now die in the Faith of this,' Monmouth continued, 'that God will work a deliverance for his People, and then will be discovered the great and horrid and scarcely to be paralleled villainies our enemies have been guilty of. But now you see my case is desperate; yet know that I die a Martyr for the People and shall rather pity the State, that their false and covetous minds have brought themselves and me to, than discover who are the persons concerned in my overthrow, and I heartily forgive all that have wronged me, even those that have been instrumental in my fall, earnestly praying for their souls . . .'[6]

He dressed very carefully that morning, his servant Marshall (formerly in Sir Thomas Armstrong's service) putting out clean stockings and a fresh shirt and lace scarf. He wore a grey cloth suit, lined with black, and a long periwig.[7] Anna, coming with the children to say her last farewell, fell on her knees and begged him to forgive her if she had done anything to offend him, and 'fell into a fainting fit'. James repeated that she had been a very good and dutiful wife and 'begged her pardon for his many failings and offences towards her'. The three children, clinging to him and weeping, listened as he bade his sons obey the King, and his daughter to respect the authority of her mother. His old friend and military secretary, Sir Stephen Fox, then came to the Tower to pay his respects, saying he was 'sorry to see him in such condition', James replying 'and so am I, too, but since it is God Almighty's pleasure, I am going to perform His will'.[8]

At 10 a.m. he stepped into the coach of the Tower's Lieutenant-Governor, accompanied by the two senior prelates, who harangued him the whole way to Tower Hill to be 'particular' regarding repentance for his sin of rebellion. He was bored with them and showed it.

No scaffold had been so heavily defended since his grandfather's execution. By the King's special permission it was covered with mourning. As he approached the steps, followed by Marshall, the churchmen and the Sheriffs of London, he gave the double rank of guardsmen – he was their favourite, too – his debonair wave and smile. Then his eyes found Jack Ketch: 'Is this the man to do the business?' he asked. 'Well, do your work well.'

The audience was enormous, as great as any crowd that had attended an execution since the Restoration. Thousands from the provinces, besides half London, had come to bid their hero farewell, and mourn him. Those who saw James for the first time would have been immediately impressed, not only by his tall figure and gracefulness but also by that kindness of heart he always showed – 'paradise seem'd open'd in his face' in Dryden's words – a manly compassionate face, always responding to all other human life. Of all 'the persons of quality', James was the only one the people knew who was devoid of arrogance and pompousness. No wonder there were 'wailings . . . and sighs and groans that went round the whole assembly'. No wonder the guardsmen felt, as they had never felt before at an execution, that the scaffold might be overrun by the populace.

'My Lord,' one of the prelates addressed him, 'you must acknowledge before the people the Doctrine of Non-resistance . . .'

'I shall say but very little,' James told him; 'I come to die; I die a Protestant of the Church of England.'

His preoccupation was with Henrietta. He raised his voice: 'I have had a scandal raised upon me about a woman, a lady of virtue and honour. I will name her: the Lady Henrietta Wentworth. I declare she is a very virtuous and Godly woman. I have committed no sin with her; and that which has passed betwixt us was very honest and innocent in the sight of God.'

Chaloner Chute was with a friend in the crowd: '. . . and tho' we were a little distance from him we could easily perceive he did not seem to be in any way daunted at the great preparations that were made for his dying . . . He endeavoured very much to clear the Lady Henrietta Wentworth from those scandalous reflections that have been made upon her and said that he could not but make this declaration at his death that she had always lived very virtuously and honourably with him . . . It is said he intimated very much as if he were married to her.'[9] James took a ring from his finger, telling Marshall to give it to Henrietta, while one of the holy attendants contradicted him regarding his relationship with her, adding that it was 'not fit discourse in this place'.

Sheriff Gostlin accosted him 'Sir, were you ever married to her?'

'This is not a time to answer that question,' James told him.

'Sir,' pressed Gostlin, 'I hoped to have heard of your repentance for the treason and bloodshed which have been committed.'

'I die very penitent.'

'My Lord, it is fit to be *particular*,' an assistant chipped in, 'and considering the public evil you have done, you ought to do as much good now as possibly you can, by a *public* acknowledgement.'

'What I have thought fit to say of public affairs is in a paper which I have signed. I refer to my paper.'

'My Lord, there is nothing in that paper about resistance; and you ought to be particular in your repentance, and to have it well grounded. God give you true repentance.'

'I die very penitent,' James told them; 'I die with great cheerfulness, because I know I shall go to God.'

'My Lord, you must go to God in his own way . . .'

'I am sorry for everyone I have wronged,' he said quietly; 'I forgive everybody.'

'Sir, your acknowledgement ought to be public and particular.'

'I am to die. Pray, my Lord, I refer to my paper.'

'They are but a few words that we desired,' said the Bishop; 'we only desire an answer to this point.'

'I can bless God that he hath given me so much Grace' – James said, his thoughts only with Henrietta – 'that for these two years last past I have led a life unlike my former course, and in which I have been happy.'

'Sir, was there no ill in these two years? In these years these great evils have happened, and the giving public satisfaction is a necessary part of repentance. Be pleased to own a detestation of your rebellion.'

'. . . I never was a man that delighted in blood,' James told them; 'I was very far from it, I was as cautious in that as any man was. The Almighty knows how I now die with all the joyfulness in the world.'

'Much may come from natural courage,' said the Bishop doubtfully.

'I do not attribute it to my own nature, for I am fearful as other men are; but I have now no fear as you see by my face; but there is something within me which does it, for I am sure I shall go to God.'

'My Lord, be sure upon good grounds. Do you repent you of all sins, known or unknown, confessed or not confessed . . .'

Not answering, James knelt and prayed 'with great fervency'. They prayed with him, and when he rose they asked if he would not 'send some dutiful message to his Majesty and recommend his wife and children to his Majesty's favour'.

'What harm have they done?' he asked. 'Do it, if you please; I pray for him and for all men.'

A prayer was made for the King, which James did not join in. 'Sir, why do you not pray for the King with us?' asked the Bishop, repeating loudly 'O Lord save the King!'

James paused, thought perhaps for a moment of his children, and answered quietly, 'Amen'. But his concern was to die, the sooner the better. With calm and practical efficiency he began instructing Ketch. He removed his surcoat and cravat. He would wear neither blindfold, he told him, nor cap.

But the assistants had not done with their badgering. A stern, clerical face was at his side again: 'My Lord, you have been bred a soldier; you will do a generous Christian thing, if you please to go to the rail, and speak to the soldiers, and say here you stand a sad example of rebellion, and entreat them and the people to be loyal to the King.'

James was not going to be lured to that; he would not be employed, in his last minutes, as a propaganda agent for the Court: 'I have said I will make no speeches. I will make no speeches. I come to die.'

'My Lord, ten words will be enough.'

It was at this point, certain witnesses said, that he made the 'Martyr of the People' speech, which he wrote in the Tower, and which was probably recorded by Marshall. But, according to the official reports, his next words were only about Henrietta. Taking a little ornate case from his pocket, he handed it to his servant: 'Here, give this to the person to whom you are to deliver the other things.' Then he addressed Ketch with a tip: 'Here are six guineas for you. Pray do your business well. Do not serve me as you did my Lord Russell. I have heard you struck him three or four times. If you give me two strokes I will not promise you not to stir.' He turned again to Marshall: 'Here, take these remaining guineas, and give them to him if he does his work well.' A witness remarked that James 'did all this with as much indifference and unconcernedness as if he were giving orders for a new suit of clothes'.

Ketch, who is thought to have been as strong an admirer of Monmouth as most people in the audience,[10] was thoroughly unnerved by the reminder of his gory treatment of Russell. He must also have sensed the great feeling of resentment against him, as executioner, from the crowd. The soldiers were on edge, too. There had been rumours of a rescue operation. 'One brave old officer, who came over with the Duke', had tried to persuade several of the more spirited sympathisers to form a small party of horse to rescue him from the scaffold, 'but they could not timely be got together'.[11]

I ◊

Two troopes of y Rebells horse cutt of att Carsham Bridge by Coll: Ogilthorpe

a

KNAVE ♣

Ferguson Preaching to the Rebells y Day before y Defeat on Iosh. 22. v. 22.

b

Four of the Monmouth playing cards: (a) The skirmish at Keynsham; (b) Ferguson preaching the day before the battle of Sedgemoor; (c) The rout of the rebels at Sedgemoor; (d) The taking of the Duke of Monmouth

QUEEN ♣

The Defeat of the Rebells 2000 Slayn & their Canon taken

c

III ♠

The Late Duke of M: taken near the L Grey

d

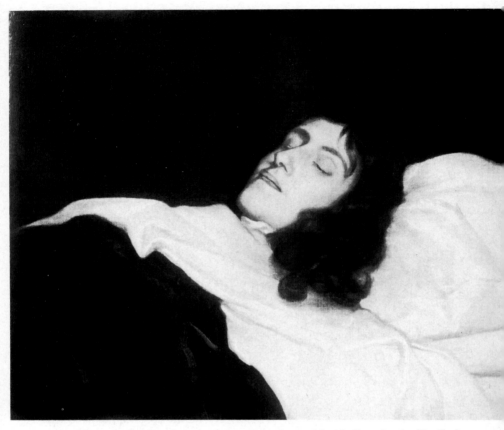

Monmouth, after decapitation, artist unknown (but believed to be Kneller)

James, oblivious of the sea of people feeling so passionately for him, removed his waistcoat and 'threw off' his peruke, to show his father's almost black hair, already greyed at the ends. Again holding up a hand of refusal when offered a blindfold, he prayed for a minute more, then 'with great composure' knelt and fitted his neck and chin into the recesses of the block.

Practical to the end he raised himself on one elbow and looked at Ketch: 'Prithee, let me feel the axe,' he said, drawing his thumb down the blade; 'I fear it is not sharp enough.'

'It is sharp enough and heavy enough,' replied the executioner gruffly, all the time trying to steady himself.

Then, with his neck in the dips again, James heard the churchmen's voices all around him: 'God accept your repentance! My Lord, may God Almighty accept your *general* repentance! Lord Jesus, receive his soul!'

Ketch was shaking now. The first stroke only caught the side of Monmouth's neck and 'he heaved up and his head turned about'. The second made a slightly deeper gash, and he heaved again. The third missed altogether, at which Ketch lost control and threw down the axe, saying, 'God damn me, I can do no more. My heart fails me, I cannot do it!' The furious congregation 'had much ado to forbear throwing him over the scaffold'. A chorus of livid shouting started and they threatened to kill the executioner 'if he did not do his duty better'.

Breast to back and shoulder to shoulder the crowd pressed against the soldiers' halberds. Sheriff Gostlin, just as angry, stepped forward, ordering Ketch to pick up his axe and finish the business. He took three more bad blows, finally resorting to a knife. And, said another witness, 'if there had not been a guard before the soldiers to conduct the executioner away, the people would have torn him to pieces, so great was their indignation at the barbarous usage the late Duke of Monmouth received at his hand . . . There were many that had the superstitious curiosity of dipping their handkerchiefs in his blood, and carrying it away as a precious relic.

The screaming fury against Ketch died away into the bitter sobs of the people's grief; and it only remained for the horses to draw away the black-draped coffin; for the head to be sewn to the body again for the portraitist to paint, for the flagstone to be lifted and the grave dug in the chapel of St Peter ad Vincula in the Tower; and for the obituarists to say their pieces.

'Thus ended the quondam Duke,' wrote Evelyn, 'darling of his father and the ladies, being extremely handsome and adroit, an excellent soldier and dancer, a favourite of the people, of an easy nature, debauch'd by lust, seduc'd by crafty knaves . . . He was a lovely person.'[12]

The author of *The Whole Glorious Life* was more fulsome: 'He was a great General and a person of undaunted Courage, Resolution and Conduct . . . He was all along true and firm to the Protestant interest, as well in as out of Parliament, though abhorring any base way of promoting it. He was all along the People's Darling, whose hearts were entirely his, no man was more beloved, nor no man more deserved it . . .' *The Western Martyrology* concluded that 'No one can deny but he was a great general, a man of courage and conduct . . . The People's hearts were entirely his by Courtesy and Affability, as other persons lost 'em by their Sourness and haughty Pride.'[13]

Let the candid Dr Welwood have the last word: 'Monmouth seem'd to be born for a better Fate; for the first Part of his Life was all Sunshine, though the rest was clouded. He was Brave, Generous, Affable, and extremely Handsome: Constant in his Friendships, just to his Word, and an utter Enemy to all sort of Cruelty. He was easy in his Nature, and fond of Popular Applause, which led him insensibly into all his Misfortunes; But whatever might be the hidden designs of some working Heads he embark'd with, his own were noble, and chiefly aim'd at the Good of his Country, though he was mistaken in the Means to attain it . . .'[14]

There were thousands of people all over England who refused to believe he had gone: 'The Duke of Monmouth is not really dead', one newsheet promised, 'but only withdrawn till the Harvest be over, and then his friends shall see him again, in a much better condition than ever they did yet.'[15] And in the West Country and Scotland his heroic name was handed down from generation to generation.

POSTSCRIPT:
THOSE WE LEFT BEHIND

Henrietta Wentworth, hearing the Bishop of Ely's description of the last scene, 'swooned away' – wrote her old suitor, Lord Bruce – 'and being come to herself told my Lord, "Good God! had that poor man nothing to think of but of me?"' She returned to England in the autumn 'in a most lamentable state of health'.[1] Taking to Toddington a broken heart that no one could mend, she died, aged twenty-six, on St George's Day the following year, and was buried in the village church, where her monument, chipped and battered, still stands. The ancient barony passed into her aunt's family, and Toddington was left empty.

The child which Henrietta is said to have had by Monmouth was brought up in Paris by a Colonel Smyth, a close friend of the Wentworths, and was named James Wentworth Smyth Stuart. He took part in the Jacobite rebellions of 1715 and 1745, and married, as his second wife, in 1739, Maria Julia Crofts, the daughter of Major-General Crofts, Monmouth's son by Eleanor Needham.

Duchess Anna divided her time between Moor Park, Dalkeith and London, until, early in the eighteenth century, she built on to the old castle of Dalkeith to make it her principal home. She lived in great grandeur and insisted upon being served on the knee and styled 'Princess', because, 'from the beginning, she had known that her husband was King Charles's legitimate son'. Three years after Monmouth's death she married the 3rd Lord Cornwallis, by whom she had a son and two daughters. She was a close friend of James II, then of William and Mary, Queen Anne and of George I, whose Queen, Caroline, (said Lady Cowper) 'loved her mightily'.

Monmouth's eldest son, James, Earl of Dalkeith, married Rochester's daughter, Lady Henrietta Hyde. In 1692, in Scotland, his local people 'proclaimed him King at the Cross at Sanquhar'. The title of Monmouth became extinct through the Act of Attainder, and when Anna died, aged eighty-one, in 1732, her grandson, Francis, inherited from her as Duke of Buccleuch. Monmouth's daughter, Lady Anne Scott, died in the Tower, aged ten, a few weeks after her father's execution.

Lord Grey of Werke (still referred to as 'the late Lord Grey' until August), slippery as ever, secured his discharge by disclosing the complicity and hiding-places of many of his fellow rebels, and also by giving Sunderland a bond of £40,000 for interceding with the King. By the autumn he was back in royal favour and dancing at a Court ball. Dutch William, who had long recognised Grey's political skill, appointed him First Lord of the Admiralty and Lord Privy Seal, and created him Earl of Tankerville in 1695. Grey died in 1701, and when the vault where he was buried had to be opened, exactly 200 years later, it was noticed that in his right hand he carried a Dutch clay pipe.

Ferguson, who had never been caught in his life, escaped to Holland after Sedgemoor. He accompanied William at the Revolution and received a comfortable sinecure. But, disillusioned with the new King's authoritarianism and military involvement on the Continent, he became a Jacobite, saying he believed England's hope to be ultimately with the Stuarts, and that King James would learn by his faults. In 1713 it was reported that 'he is yet alive, in great want, and upwards of ninety years, and hath nothing but what he begs'.[2] He died in the following year.

Fletcher of Saltoun, after killing Dare at Lyme, sailed for Spain in Monmouth's frigate, travelled on to Hungary and distinguished himself under the Emperor in the war against the Turks. He then joined the Scottish refugees in Holland, and at the Revolution, returned to his Scottish estates. He was a member of the convention settling Scotland's new government and made an enemy of William, who disapproved of his proposals and policies. Vehemently opposing the Union, he remained a front-rank politician until his death in 1716.

Trenchard and Speke, for whom arrest warrants were issued at the time of the Lyme landing, withdrew to Holland, returning safely to Somerset at the Revolution. Edward Strode, of Downside, Shepton Mallet, who entertained Monmouth during his march to the Avon and again during his flight, was let off with a fine and lived to be High Sheriff of Somerset. Monmouth's chaplain, Hook, who was sent to rouse the London rebels, gave himself up later that summer, turned Catholic and followed the King into exile. Major Wildman became Postmaster-General and 'Sir John', under William.

Argyle was executed at the Market Cross Edinburgh (in the same manner and on the same spot as his father), on 30 June 1685. Colonel Richard Rumbold, who joined Argyle's expedition, was hanged, drawn and quartered ('his living heart being cut out by the executioner and thrown with disdain into the fire'). After making his much-quoted speech from the scaffold: '. . . This is a deluded generation, vailed with ignorance, that, though popery and slavery be riding in upon them, do not perceive it; though I am sure there was no man marked of God above another; for none comes into the world with a saddle on his back, neither any booted and spurred to ride him . . .'

Nathaniel Wade (such an ardent hater of the regime until he was a prisoner) was less noble. After Sedgemoor he escaped with Ferguson and Tyler as far as a house on Exmoor, from which he bolted and was shot in the back as he ran. Recovering from his wound, he gained his pardon, like Grey, by telling all he knew, which included for the King what seemed to be invaluable information about Lord Delamere and other Cheshire dissidents. The King reinstalled him in his native Bristol, of which he became Town Clerk in 1687. He was at the head of the militia when the Kingswood colliers revolted, and was remembered in his city by 'Traitor's Bridge', the place at which he was responsible for firing upon men whose cause, at the head of the Blue Regiment in 1685, he had represented with such distinction.

Fowke escaped and went on to command a regiment under William. Delamere was eventually released from the Tower for lack of evidence, and had the satisfaction of being one of the peers chosen to ask King James to leave the Palace of Whitehall in 1688.

Some 300 rebels died on the field of Sedgemoor and at least three times that number in the pursuit. But what of the prisoners? Feversham's behaviour was exactly the opposite of that of 'gentle Monmouth's' after Bothwell Bridge. He had the first twenty-two rebels he captured hanged from gemmace chains attached to an oak, which became famous as the 'Bussex Tree'. At this point Mew, the Bishop of Bath and Wells, restrained him by pointing out the injustice of hanging men without trial, and 500 prisoners were put under guard in Weston church until escorts could be organised to conduct them to prison. When Feversham was told that a certain young Monmouth officer could perform 'extraordinary feats of agility', he had him stripped and one end of a halter fastened round his neck and the other round that of a wild colt. They were set off at a 'a furious pace' from the Bussex until the colt fell exhausted at Chedzoy, a distance of a mile. But Feversham still had the young officer hanged from the 'Bussex Tree'.

Colonel Kirke (of whose cruelties and excesses in Tangier Pepys wrote such a graphic account) continued the reign of terror, which was to culminate in the autumn in the Bloody Assizes, with mass executions and whippings, transportations to the plantation colonies and crippling fines.

Kirke spent the next few weeks presiding over the summary

hanging of cartloads of men who had been in Monmouth's army or who supported it, and hundreds more who were only suspects. Watching his early victims strung up and in their death throes, with a laugh he shouted 'they shall have music to their dancing', and thereafter, at all his orgies of hanging, he had his regimental horns, fifes and drums playing to drown the cries of the victims and of the bereaved. Among many other acts, he is said to have offered a dead rebel's penis to the fiancée who had pleaded in vain for his life, and to have seduced another, supposedly in return for her lover's life, only to have him hanged from the inn-post where Kirke enjoyed his night of reckoning with her.

Then Judge Jeffreys, who had been busy with his south-east circuit, drove to the west with four senior assistants and with the powers not only of Lord Chief Justice but also of General of the Army in the West. There was no one to defy him, who was himself tortured with gallstones.

'He was perpetually either drunk or in a rage,' said Bishop Burnet. 'He required the prisoners to plead guilty, and in that case he gave them some hope of favour, if they gave him no trouble. Otherwise he told them he would execute the letter of the law upon them in its utmost severity. This made many plead guilty who had a great defence in law. But he showed no mercy. He ordered a great many to be hanged up immediately, without allowing them a minute's time to say their prayers. He hanged in several places about 600 persons . . . his behaviour towards some of the nobility and gentry that were well affected, but came and pleaded in favour of some prisoners, would have amazed one if done by a bashaw in Turkey. England had never known anything like it . . .'

The sarcasm, cruelty and downright injustice of the 37-year-old 'Bloody' Jeffreys will never be forgotten in the West Country. When the septuagenarian Lady Lisle, widow of a regicide and one of Cromwell's lords, came before him at Winchester Castle for harbouring John Hicks and Richard Nelthorp, he browbeat the jury into bringing a verdict of guilty, even though she had sent a servant to inform the magistrates that the two men were in one of her outbuildings. 'If I had been among you, and she had been my own mother, I should have found her guilty,' Jeffreys promised. He ordered her to be burned at the stake and this was only commuted to decapitation on the orders of the King, who was pestered with pleas for mercy. Feversham was one who pleaded for her life, but only because he wanted her estate in exchange. Another old lady, Mrs Gaunt, was burned to death for giving refuge to one of Monmouth's men, although she had not the least idea who the man was.

Colonel Holmes, who had lost a son and an arm commanding the Red Regiment for Monmouth, so impressed the King that he pardoned him and sent him to Jeffreys as an informer. But, ignoring this, Jeffreys promptly had Holmes hanged at Lyme.

At Windsor, on his way back to London, on 28 September, Jeffreys received from the King's grateful hands the Great Seal of Lord Chancellor and the barony of Lord Jeffreys of Wem. When, at the accession of William and Mary, he was clapped in the Tower and taken to task for his evil, his only reply was, 'whatever I did then, I did by express orders; and I have this further to say for myself, that I was not half bloody enough for him who sent me thither'. And, knowing the King's record, one is inclined to believe him.

Matthews, Battiscomb and Tyler were also among those executed at Lyme, near the spot where Monmouth landed. 'Dear countrymen,' Matthews addressed the crowd from his scaffold, 'I suppose we are all of one kingdom and nation, and I hope Protestants. O, I wonder we should be so blood-thirsty one towards another; I have heard it said heretofore that England could never be ruined but by herself, which now I fear is a-doing. Lord have mercy on poor England . . .' Tyler who had read Monmouth's Proclamation at Lyme and at Taunton, spoke in his last moments as well as ever : 'As to the matter of fact for which I die, it doth not much trouble me, knowing to myself the ends for which I engaged with the Duke of Monmouth were good and honourable.'

£3,000 was unavailingly offered for the lives of the very popular Hewling brothers, who were twenty-two and twenty years old. Abraham Annesley, who followed them on to a Taunton scaffold, made one of the most stirring and manly speeches. '. . . Having long since, as a true Englishman, thought it my duty to venture my life in defence of the Protestant religion against Popery and arbitrary power. For this same purpose I came from my house to the Duke of Monmouth's army. At first I was a lieutenant, then a captain, and I was in all the action the Foot was engaged in, which I do not repent. For had I a thousand lives, they should all have been engaged in the same cause, although it has pleased the wise God (for reasons best known to himself) to blast our designs; but He will deliver his People by ways we know nor think not of.'

The light of the Old Cause was snuffed for ever. The King had destroyed his most important challenger. Or he thought he had. Giving an account of Monmouth's execution, Lord Dartmouth told him : 'You have got rid of one enemy but a more dangerous one remains behind.' While his nephew was eliminated, the son-in-law was waiting in the wings.

The good wind was blowing from Holland, where in the same month it was reported that '. . . all those conventicles people do now pray for the Martyr's wife and her children, and say the Duke of Monmouth was a martyr for his religion and that his sons are the right heirs to the Crown, and that the Monmouth party is very great and many in Amsterdam'.[3] Their hearts told them that Monmouth, not York, should have been James II. But, since Monmouth was gone, they opted for the expedient, if indifferent, compromise of Calvinist William and York's Protestant daughter.

How foolish King James had been: if he had spared his nephew's life, but kept him in the Tower, he might have had nothing to fear from his son-in-law.

APPENDICES

A   Circumstantial Evidence on Allegations that Charles II married
        Lucy Barlow
B   Monmouth's Proclamation from Taunton on 20 June 1685
C   Notes and Sources
D   Bibliography
Index

Appendix A

CIRCUMSTANTIAL EVIDENCE ON ALLEGATIONS THAT CHARLES II MARRIED LUCY BARLOW

In the early 1680s John Paterson, formerly Archbishop of Glasgow, wrote in his journal : 'Sr J. Corke told me that the Earl of Newburgh told him that he was witness to King Charles's marriage with the Duke of Monmouth's mother and that Progers and another* were so, too.'[1] Between 1649 and 1654 Charles received several letters from his sister, Mary, Princess of Orange referring to Lucy as his 'wife'.[2] Lucy's maternal aunt, Mrs Gosfritt, vowed she had seen the declaration of the marriage under the King's hand, 'which was taken from her niece in Oliver Cromwell's time'. After William Disney gave evidence at the black box inquiry (into Monmouth's legitimacy) the following note was made : 'this informant further saith that one Mr Gosfritt, a Dutch merchant who lives in the City of London (whose brother married Mrs Barlow's aunt) . . . As he told the informant blaming Mrs Barlow's mother for leaving her daughter abroad in an ill way of living, he said the said Mother to Mrs Barlow reply'd he was mistaken for her said daughter was married to the King. The informant further saith that the said Mr Gosfritt . . . that 'the King was married to the Duke of Monmouth's mother at Liege . .'[3] Lucy, up to the hour of her death, averred it again and again; and her Protheroe grandfather, at least, accepted her statement, for opposite her name in his genealogical tree are the words 'married King Charles ye Second of England'.

James's adoption by the highly principled Queen Henrietta Maria is only credible if one accepts that Lucy was married to her son. Catherine of Braganza treated him as her stepson, and, by the time she was Charles's Queen, it was generally believed in England that the marriage had taken place. In October 1662 Pepys wrote of 'what is whispered that young Crofts (Monmouth's name in childhood) is lawful son of the King, the King being married to his mother'. When the Rev. Peter Bell was in Newgate prison as a political prisoner, in the 1670s, he made the following declaration in a letter to Dr Lake, Chaplain to the Duke of York : 'Mr Werden of Preston having been some years resident at Durham in the Quality of Clerke to his Uncle an Attorney that, had in that time understood of one Mr Forder of Houghton in le-Spring, a Gentleman of 4 or £500 per annum, quondam steward to the late Bishop

*Dr Forder, Dr John Cosin's steward.

of Durham, and his servant abroad when he waited on the King in his Exile, had several times declar'd in Public company, that to his knowledge the Duke of Monmouth was the lawful heir of the Crown of England : for he was present at the Marriage of his Grace's Mother to the King, a Competent time before the birth of the Duke of Monmouth, of which he was, to the discharge of a good conscience, ready to make affidavit before legal authority . . .' Forder 'of Houghton in le-Spring' was steward to Dr John Cosin, the Protestant Chaplain in Henrietta Maria's suite, in 1648–9, and afterwards Bishop of Durham, and the Version of the marriage involving him appears to be the one which most credence was attached.

In 1680, when Monmouth was Whig and Protestant champion, and fresh witnesses came forward to speak for his legitimacy, the Duke of York began a fraudulent rumour that the marriage certificate might be kept in a 'black box' by Dr Cosin's daughter, Lady Gerard, only to have the matter investigated and proved false; then to say, in effect : 'That is that – let us hear no more of the matter.' But the evidence could not be eliminated. Robert Ferguson, in one of his leaflets, wrote : '. . . As all who were abroad with his Majesty at that time knew the Passion the King had for that person [Mrs Barlow]; so some . . . can remember how, through immoderate love for her, being reduced to a condition that his life was despaired of, and the late Queen his Mother, receiving intelligence both of his disease [smallpox], and the cause of it, she consented to his espousal of her, rather than that he should consume and perish in his otherwise unquenchable flames.'[4]

G. D. Gilbert in the appendix ('Lucy Walter') to his revision of Baronne D'Aulnoy's *Memoirs of the Court of England* in 1675, wrote :

We are permitted to quote from a communication we received from the late Sir Frederick Barnewell, dated May 26, 1905 : 'In reply to your letter the following is all I can tell you on the supposed marriage between Charles II and Lucy Walter. A good many years ago the late Sir Bernard Burke, whom I knew very well and who was intimate with the late Duke of Abercorn, told me that he (the Duke) had told him that he had heard from the late Duke of Buccleuch that he one day, looking through the papers in the muniment room at Dalkeith came across a marriage certificate of Charles II to Lucy Walter; that, after considering the matter for some time he decided to destroy it and thereon threw it into the fire and it was burned. I think it was a great mistake as it was a document of historical interest and I believe the Duke of Abercorn was of the same opinion. This is the story as I told it to our mutual friend, Mr W. H. Wilkins.'

Lord George Scott, son of the 6th Duke of Buccleuch, throws further light on this evidence in his *Lucy Walter, Wife or Mistress* (1947) :

. . . a few years ago, the late Sir Hew Dalrymple was looking through some of the Buccleuch papers, of which a good many are both scattered and uncatalogued, and came across the following in manuscript, which he copied carefully : 'The certificate of marriage was found by Henry, Duke of Buccleuch (3rd Duke, b. 1746) and President Hope (Charles Hope, of Granton, Lord President of the Court of Session and Lord Justice-General) amongst some old papers at Dalkeith; and the Duke thought best to burn it. It does not seem clear whether it was the original or a copy of one at Liège where they were married by the then Archbishop of Canterbury. I believe it is supposed that the other copy or original, whichever it was, might be found at Liège if looked for. And it is said Charles II would have acknowledged the Duke of Monmouth as his heir, if it had not been prevented by James II. It is said James never left him on his death-bed, for fear he should then do it . . .'

Finally, in researching at Longleat, I came across the following. In 1878, an eminent member of the British Archaeological and Historical Association, Mr Bloxham, stated that, 'after devoting a great deal of care and attention to the subject of examining many documents, I have arrived at the conclusion that the Duke of Monmouth was the legitimate son of Charles II. He (the Duke of Buccleuch) had a great deal of evidence to show that the King was married to Lucy Walter, otherwise Mrs Barlow.'[5]

Appendix B

MONMOUTH'S PROCLAMATION FROM TAUNTON ON 20 JUNE, 1685

Whereas, upon the decease of our Sovereign Lord Charles the Second, late King of England, &c., the right of succession to the Crown of England, Scotland, France and Ireland, with the dominions and territories thereunto belonging, did legally descend and devolve upon the most illustrious and high-born Prince James Duke of Monmouth, son and heir apparent to the said King Charles the Second; but James Duke of York (taking the advantage of the absence of the said James Duke of Monmouth beyond the seas) did first cause the said late King to be poysoned, and immediately thereupon did usurp and invade the Crown, and doth continue so to doe : We therefore, the noblemen, gentlemen, and Commons at present assembled, in the names of ourselves and of all the loyal and Protestant noblemen, gentlemen, and Commons of England, in pursuance of our duty and allegiance and for the delivering of the Kingdome from popery, tyranny, and oppression, do recognise, publish, and proclaim the said high and mighty Prince James Duke of Monmouth, our lawful and rightful sovereign and king, by the name of James the Second, by the Grace of God, King of England, Scotland, France and Ireland, Defender of the Faith, &c. God save the King.[1]

Appendix C

NOTES AND SOURCES

1

1. BM Add MS 28094 f. 71
2. Clarendon Papers
3. Thurloe State Papers
4. *The Heroick Life*
5. Thurloe State Papers
6. Clarendon State Papers
7. BM Add MS 28094
8. PRO. Flanders Papers, 1658
9. Bishop Floyd
10. Thurloe State Papers, VII

2

1. Wemyss MS, 65
2. From the facsimile in Fraser's *Scotts of Buccleuch*
3. ibid.
4. Clarendon State Papers
5. BM Lansdowne MS, 1236, f. 128
6. Clarendon State Papers
7. Wemyss MS, 65
8. Hartmann, 73; Cartwright, 138
9. Wemyss MS, 65
10. Diary, April 20, 1663
11. *Reliquae Antiquae Scoticae*
12. Booklet: *Establishment of the Duke and Duchess of Buccleuch's servants wages, Burdings, Liveries*
13. Hartmann, *Clifford of the Cabal*, 43
14. Diary, 27 April, 1663
15. Diary, 26 July, 1665
16. CSP (Dom) 12 November, 1664
17. My battle narrative is taken from Lord Sandwich's *Journal*, York's *Memoirs* and CSP (Domestic)

3

1. *Life and Times*, Sept 25, 1665
2. Diary, 15 November, 1666
3. Diary, 26 April, 1667
4. CSP (Dom) 30 June, 1666
5. CSP (Dom) 30 June, 1666
6. Diary, 9 June 1666
7. CSP (Dom) 11 June 1667
8. CSP (Dom) 13 June 1667
9. Diary 21 June 1667

4

1 Hartmann, 197 Cartwright, 251
2 Gilbert, 3
3 de Cosnac, *Memoirs*
4 Montpensier, IV, 66; Choisy, Livre VIII
5 Hartmann, 201; Cartwright, 256
6 Hartmann, 202; Cartwright, 257
7 Hartmann, 202; Cartwright, 207
8 Hartmann, 209; Cartwright, 263
9 Hartmann, 210; Cartwright, 264
10 ibid. 210; ibid. 264
11 Diary, 15 May 1668
12 Hartmann, 212; Cartwright, 265
13 ibid. 217; ibid. 268
14 *Lettres de Mme de Sévigné*
15 Montpensier, Livre IV
16 Arthur, I. 24
17 Arthur, I. 25
18 Diary, 16 September 1668
19 Arthur, I. 83
20 Hartmann, 236; Cartwright, 283
21 Hartmann, 241; Cartwright, 284
22 Diary, 23 November 1668
23 Clarke, I. 442
24 John Downes, *Roscius Anglicanus, A Historical Review of the Stage*, 1660–1706, 29
25 Letter from Lionne (French Foreign Minister) to Colbert (French Chief Minister)
26 Reresby, 149

5

1 Clarke, I, 495 cf. Arthur, I.
2 Burnet, 183
3 B.M. Add MS 27962 T, f. 149; CSP (Dom) 1671, pp. 142, 183
4 CSP (Venetian), 1671, No. 47
5 CSP (Dom), 23 March, 8, 11 and 12 April 1671
6 Arlington Corres.
7 Hamilton, 297–98
8 CSP (Dom), 17 May 1671
9 Le Fleming 1256 (17 October 1671)
10 Diary, 21 October 1671

6

1 CSP (Venetian)
2 Raised 1671. SP (Dom) Car II. Entry Book 24
3 SP FRANCE, Vol. 133, 149; SP (Dom) Entry Book 35A, f. 29
4 London Gazette Order, 18 Feb 1672, sgd by Arlington
5 Mulgrave, II, 29
6 Foxcroft, I, 78
7 Buccleuch MS. I, 503
8 The word is from the Spanish *moquete*, which is derived from *moscas*, the sparks from a light
9 The Spanish *fusil* derives from *focile*, the Italian word for flint
10 A perversion of two Dutch words: *snappen*, to snap, and *Haan*, gun-cock

11 HMC Buccleuch MS, 503
12 Temple, II, 20
13 CSP (Venetian) 1671–71, No 195
14 Montagu MS HMC Report XV, Appx 8, Vol I, 514
15 CSP (Dom) 1672, 291
16 CSP (Venetian), 1671–2, 199
17 *Lettres de Mme de Sévigné*
18 SP France 78, Vol. 133, ff. 189, 194, 196
19 William Perwych Correspondence, 14 May 1672; SP France 78, Vol. 134 f. 8
20 SP 78, Vol. 134, f. 54
21 Longleat MS, Portland Papers, II, f. 252
22 BM, Add MSS 22 878, f. 7
23 Foxcroft, I, 94
24 CSP (Venetian) 1671–2, No. 252
25 BM Add MS 22, 878, f. 7
26 SP (Dom) Entry Book 34, f. 175
27 CSP (Venetian), 1671–2, No. 274
28 BM Add MS 22, 878, f. 129

7

1   Charles Littleton to Lord Hatton
2   SP (Dom) Entry Book 21, f. 120 and Entry Book 34, f. 208
3   SP (Scotland) Warrant Book 2, p. 160
4   SP (Dom) Entry Book 34, f. 205
5   Foxcroft, I, 110
6   Le Fleming MS, HMC 12th Report, 18 April, 1673
7   CSP (Dom) 2 October 1672
8   CSP (Dom) Signet Office, Vol. 8, 301
9   CSP (Venetian) 1671–2. No. 282
10 CSP (Dom) 17 December 1672; CSP (Venetian) 1671–2, 338 and 341
11 Fieffe, *Histoire des Troupes Étrangères au Service de France* 175
12 SP (France) 78, Vol. 137, f. 76
13 SP (France) 78, Vol. 137, f. 87
14 SP (France) 78, Vol. 137, f. 116
15 ibid. f. 112
16 SP (France), 78, Vol. 137, f. 130
17 Alington's account
18 On the evidence of a re-issue of muskets from the Ordnance Stores in London
    later that summer, Cannon in his *Historical Records of the Life Guards*, claims
    that '12 private gentlemen' of that corps took part in the assault. But this
    assertion is not supported by contemporary accounts of the siege. Several
    later authors have been thus misled by Cannon
19 Wolseley, I, 122
20 Perwych Dispatches
21 SP (France), Vol. 137, f. 143
22 Perwych Dispatches
23 Hatton, I, 108
24 SP France 78, Vol. 137, f. 190
25 ibid.
26 ibid. f. 171 and f. 215
27 ibid., 151
28 SP (France) 78, Vol. 137, f. 144
29 ibid., 175
30 Thomas Lediard, *Life of John, Duke of Marlborough*, 25–8

8

1   SP 78, Vol. 137, f. 235
2   Letters to Sir Joseph Williamson, I, 105
3   ibid., 108
4   ibid., 125
5   Hatton, I, 110–11
6   Williamson, Letters, I, 95
7   CSP (Venetian) 1673–5, No. 134
8   Prince Rupert, *Colenbrander* II, 309–10
9   CSP (Dom) Car II, 337, No. 3
10 Mulgrave II, 29
11 Diary, 21 August 1674; cf. CSP (Venetian) 1673–5, No. 376
12 Williamson, *Letters*, I, 119
13 Edward Chamberlayne, *Angliae Notitia*
14 Bridgeman to Williamson (SP Dom Car II, No. 151)
15 Williamson, Letters, II, 72–3. Monmouth was also recommended to go as
    Viceroy to Ireland in succession to Essex.
16 Mulgrave, II, 30–1
17 Burnet, 114
18 Essex Papers
19 Mulgrave, *Memoirs* II, 33
20 ibid., 35–6
21 HMC Report 7, Appx, p. 465
22 'Without doubt the English Queen of Beauty' (Courtin to Pomponne, 21
    September 1676)
23 SP Dom Car II, 360, No. 84; ibid, 376, No. 143; Precedents I, f. 35
24 Le Fleming, 104; Williamson, II, 20
25 SP Dom Car II, 360, No. 84
26 SP Dom, Entry Book 35A, f. 89; cf. Precedents I, f. 35 (similar order to Col.
    Russell)
27 Williamson, II, 11–21; Le Fleming, 104
28 SP Dom Entry Book 43, p. 48; cf. Acts of the Privy Council (Colonial Series)
    No. 1003. (Also with reference to 'all tobacco, planted or sown', Nos 1032 and
    1120; Le Fleming, 117; SP (Dom) 44, Entry Book 28, f. 125; SP (Dom) Entry
    Book 43, p. 48; Longleat MS, Coventry Papers LXXXIII, f. 133; Daniel
    Mackinnon, *Origin and Services of the Coldstream Guards*, 150
29 *The Heroick Life*
30 250 pp. in SP 44, Entry Book 41 (Public Record Office)
31 See Arthur, I, 117
32 Williamson, II, 122
33 SP (Dom) Car II, 464 No. 34
34 Buccleuch MS, I, 329
35 Burnet, 355

9

1   SP (Dom) Car II 395, No. 1 (31 July 1677)
2   Conway Papers; SP Dom Car II, 396, No. 11
3   ibid., Nos 59 and 60
4   SP 44, Entry Book 41, p. 103
5   Fraser, I, 437
6   Burnet, 390; Clarke 490
7   Clarke, I, 494–5
8   SP Dom Car II 403, No. 89
9   Clarke, I, 496
10 SP Dom Car II, Case G, No. 3
11 HMC 15th Report, Buccleuch MS, 236

12 SP 44, Entry Book 52, f. 11; SP (Dom) Entry Book 43, p. 190 SP (Dom) Car II 401 No. 247; Longleat MS, Coventry Papers II, 134, XCIII, f. 17
13 Longleat MS, Coventry Papers II, f. 134
14 Diary, 29 June 1678
15 SP 44, Entry Book 52, f. 17
16 My account of the campaign is taken largely from the official dispatch held in the Public Record Office (SP 44, Entry Book 52, pp. 63–75)
17 Fraser, II, 399
18 SP Dom Car II, 405, No. 244; SP Dom Car II, 406, No. 1
19 Clarke, I, 511
20 ibid., 494–5
21 Longleat MS; Portland Papers, ff. 252–53
22 Bulstrode to Coventry; Longleat MS; Coventry Papers XXXI, f. 316
23 SP (Dom) King William's Chest 3, No. 58

10

1 Ruvigny in Christie, II, 188
2 The word originated at the Green Ribbon Club
3 *The Heroick Life*
4 cf. Pollock, 120–66
5 North, 174
6 cf. Luttrell, I, and Sitwell, 38–42
7 Lords Journals, XIII, 331. See also Chamberlayne, *Angliae Notitia*. Gold Stick, the Court appointment founded and first held by Monmouth, in 1678, is now filled by the Colonels of the two regiments of Household Cavalry, while the subordinate position, now styled Silver Stick-in-Waiting, is held by the Lieutenant-Colonel commanding the whole Corps
8 Dalrymple, I, 312
9 Clarke, I, 531
10 Christie, II, 330
11 Henry Sidney, I, 9
12 Lingard XII, 175
13 Longleat MS Coventry Papers LXXXIV, f. 139
14 Le Fleming, 155
15 *An Historical Relation*, I, 3
16 HMC 15th Report (Savile Foljambe) 129 and 131
17 Ailesbury, I, 35
18 Burnet, 302
19 Christie, II, 313

11

1 Burnet, 312
2 Terry, 15–16
3 Burnet, 313
4 Temple, III, 52
5 Lauderdale, III, 258–9
6 HMC, 15th Report, Appx, Pt V (Savile Foljambe MS), 133
7 North, 81; cf. Ralph, 462
8 Clarke, I, 551–2
9 SP Scotland, Warrant Book 5, 159
10 *The Heroick Life*; cf. *A Further Account of the Proceeding against the Rebels in Scotland*
11 North, 81
12 Ralph, 462
13 Napier, I, 284

14 M'Crie, 109
15 Assessment of Capt. Creighton, (Napier, I, 284); Kirkton put it as low as 2,300 (*Secret and True History*, 466)
16 Lauderdale, III, 170
17 Wodrow, III, 101
18 M'Crie, 472
19 Ralph, 463
20 Son of Sir Thomas Hamilton, of whom Burnet (313) said: 'He was then a lively, hopeful young man, but getting into that company and into their notions, he became a crack-brained enthusiast.'
21 Letters of Hon. Algernon Sidney to Hon Henry Savile (1742 Edition), 94
22 Napier, I, 276
23 Wodrow, 100–101
24 Kirkton, 463
25 Napier, I, 285; Arnot, 120
26 Newcomb
27 Kirkton, 466
28 HMC Appx to 15th Report, Pt IX (Hope-Johnstone MS) 63; this was done through his Scottish agent, Lord Melvill, whose wife later divulged it to the Lords of Articles in Edinburgh (*Acts of Parliament*, Scot. VIII, App, 57–9)
29 Wodrow, III, 105–6
30 Napier 285–6; Ralph 463
31 Kirkton, 466
32 Ralph, 463
33 Napier, I, 286
34 Newcomb
35 Newcomb; Blackader, 242–50; Lauderdale III, 172; Burnet, 314; M'Crie, 478–81; Kirkton, 465–9; Wodrow, 101–10; Arnot, 118–21; Napier, I, 284–97; Terry, 69–84; Tracts (British Museum) 433–7, 443–6; Portland Papers, II, f. 254 Lingard, XX, 435–7
36 Blackader, 249; Arnot, 121
37 Anderson, 152
38 Lauderdale III, 172
39 Wilson, *Poem of the Clyde*
40 Newcomb
41 SP Scotland, Warrant Book 5, 173
42 BM Add MS 23244 f. 18
43 Kirkton, 473
44 Burnet, 314
45 Clarke, I, 568; Terry 81–2

12

1 See Algernon Sidney to Henry Savile, May 1679 (A. Sidney, *Letters*, 52–3)
2 Reresby, 175
3 Temple, III, 55
4 ibid.
5 Burnet, 314
6 SP (Dom) Car II, Entry Book 58, p. 46
7 Macpherson, I, 98
8 Sidney, I, 141
9 Ailesbury, I, 41
10 Sidney, I, 123
11 Clarke, I, 567
12 Temple, III, 72
13 Savile Foljambe, 137
14 Hatton, I, 194

15 Dalrymple, I, 328–9; Savile Foljambe, 138
16 Dartmouth MS
17 HMC, Appx to 7th Report, 474–5; cf. Countess of Manchester to Lady Hatton (Hatton, I, 193)
18 SP 44, Entry Book 41, f. 248
19 HMC. Appx to Report 7, 472

13

1 D'Avaux, II, 24–32
2 D'Avaux, II, 32–4
3 Sidney, I, 156
4 ibid., I, 151
5 ibid., I, 185
6 Somers Tracts, VII, 188
7 Hatton, I, 204; cf. London Newsletter 2 December, in CSP (Dom) 1679, Admiralty Greenwich Hospital I, No. 39; HMC Ormonde MS, IV, 562
8 Forneron 232
9 HMC Appx to 7th Report, 478
10 D'Avaux, II, 35–6
11 Hatton, I, 204
12 Sir Robert Southwell to the Duke of Ormonde (HMC, Ormonde MS, IV, 575)
13 Verney, IV, 264

14

1 Sidney, I, 237
2 HMC, Finch Papers, II, 76
3 Lingard, xii, 241
4 BM Add MS 32095 f. 198 and 200
5 HMC, Finch Papers, II, 76–7
6 CSP (Dom) 26 June 1680
7 Camden Miscellany, XI, 35 (*Some unpublished letters of Burnet*)
8 Ferguson, 115
9 SP (Dom) Car II 413, No. 67
10 CSP (Dom) 26 June 1680
11 Somers Tracts VIII, 197–210
12 HMC, Appx to 7th Report, 498
13 For examples of Chichester's rebellious character, see Tanner MS 148 and 149 in the Bodleian Library; also Coventry Papers, VII, ff. 184 and 194
14 John Kent, *Records and Reminiscences of Goodwood and the Dukes of Richmond*
15 Newsletter, CSP (Dom), 10 August 1680
16 SP (Dom) Entry Book 62, p. 55
17 Admiralty, Greenwich Hospital I, No. 66; CSP (Dom) 7 August 1680
18 *Heroick Life*
19 Old Song, *James Duke of Monmouth* (British Museum)
20 SP Dom, Entry Book 62, 47; Admiralty Greenwich Hospital I, No. 66
21 *A True Narrative of the Duke of Monmouth's Late Journey into the West in a Letter from an Eyewitness thereof to his correspondent in London, 1680* (Bodleian Library); BM Add MS 34362, f. 133
22 BM Add MS 34362, f. 133

15

1 Dalrymple, I, 348
2 Dalrymple, I, 362
3 Reresby (1904 edition 204)

4　Grey, 10
5　Ailesbury, I, 55
6　HMC, Beaufort MS, 83; cf. Christie II, Appx VII, cxvi; Barillon's dispatch to Louis XIV of 28 March
7　Quoted from Christie, II, cxvii
8　Burnet, 328; cf. North, *Examen*, Eachard III, 623; Ailesbury, I, 57
9　Ailesbury, I, 64
10　Eachard, III, 634–5
11　Oldmixon, 667; Russell, II, 6
12　Ailesbury, I, 21

16

1　Hamilton, 271
2　*Heroick Life*
3　HMC Appx. IV to Report X, p. 174
4　Reresby 223
5　*Heroick Life*; cf. HMC Appx 5 to 12th Report (Rutland MS) II, 18 April 1682
6　BM Add MS 28569 (Letters of the Savile and Finch families) f. 36 (W. B. Blathwayt to R. Southwell); cf. Foxcroft, I, 355–6
7　West. (BM Add MS 38847)
8　Appx (Pt IV) to HMC, 10th Report, 173
9　Dalrymple, I, I, 19
10　Dalrymple, I, I, 19; cf. CSP (Dom) September 1682
11　HMC, Appx to 7th Report, 533
12　SP (Dom) Car II, 429, No. 85
13　West, 89

17

1　Sir Charles Littleton to Lord Hatton (Hatton, II, 20)
2　West, f. 89
3　Grey, 19–20
4　West, f. 89
5　Ailesbury, I, 71
6　Burnet, 352; cf. Russell, II, 48
7　Manley, I, III, 330
8　West, f. 93
9　Manley, I, III, 329
10　West, f. 94
11　Wade, f. 267
12　West, f. 94; Russell, II, 24
13　Eachard, III, 699
14　Dalrymple, I, I, 27
15　Burnet, 353
16　Grey, 23–4
17　Grey, 25
18　CSP (Dom) 1678–9 (Army)
19　Vide SP (Dom) Entry Book 41, p. 247
20　Dalrymple, I, I, 31; Cobbett, IX, 609
21　Russell, II, 40–1
22　Wodrow, III, 337
23　Burnet, 354
24　Grey, 32; cf. West, f. 90
25　Cobbett, IX, 610
26　Grey, 32–5. All the rebels leaving records indicate that the tactical planning for the rebellion was made by Monmouth

27 Grey, 37
28 Russell, II, 117
29 Russell, II, 48; cf. Cobbett, IX, 608
30 Grey, 36f; Ferguson, 89
31 Cobbett, IX, 607; Russell, II, 50
32 Grey, 39
33 Cobbett, IX, 609; Russell, II, 51
34 Cobbett, IX, 608
35 West, f. 94
36 Eachard, III, 678

18

1   Grey, 57
2   Ewald, 205 and 275
3   Cobbett, IX, 810
4   Luttrell, I, 239–40
5   HMC, Appx IV, 14th Report, 143
6   Grey 59
7   SP (Dom) Car II 422, Nos 72, 82 and 86
8   Tanner MS 149 (Bodleian Library)
9   Verney, IV, 335; (See also Basil Tozer, *The Horse in History*, 255–6)
10 Oldmixon, 376; Jesse, IV, 19; Luttrell, I, 250
11 Grey, 61–2
12 Reresby (1904 edition), 240
13 Harleian MS, 6845, f. 264
14 Hatton II, 24; Luttrell, I, 265
15 SP Dom Car II 425, No. 105
16 SP Dom Car II 425, No. 150; cf. HMC, 15th Report (Buccleuch MS), 193
17 Luttrell, I, 265
18 Hatton, II, 27
19 Ailesbury, I, 74
20 Burnet, 364
21 Luttrell, I, 264
22 HMC, Appx to Report VII, 481
23 SP Dom Car II, 425, No. 158

19

1   Evelyn, 15 and 22 December 1674
2   HMC Appx to 7th Report, 472
3   ibid., 498
4   Ailesbury, I, 76
5   SP Dom Car II, 425, No. 140
6   Burnet, 373
7   SP Car II 425, No. 19

20

1   Diary, 13 July 1683, p. 410
2   Dalrymple, I, I, 47
3   Russell, II, 74. After the landing of the Prince of Orange, in 1688, James II sent for Lord Bedford and said to him: 'My Lord you are a good man and have a great influence, you can do much for me at this time.' To which Bedford replied: 'I am an old man and can do but little. But I once had a son who could have been very serviceable to your Majesty'. (Cobbett, IX, 684–5).

4   Welwood, 142
5   Foxcroft, I, 399
6   Welwood, 319–23
7   CSP Dom Car II, 433, No. 100
8   Ailesbury, I, 81

21

1   SP Dom, Entry Book 29, 269, 22 July 1673
2   Ailesbury, I, 82
3   SP Dom Car II, 434, No. 88
4   HMC, Appx V to Report XI, 101; Eachard, III, 703
5   Burnet, 373
6   Luttrell, I, 293
7   Welwood, 143
8   CSP, Car II, XXV, 23 and 29
9   cf. Russell, 2, 74
10 Russell, II, 57
11 Eachard, III, 699
12 Ralph, 783
13 Cobbett IX, 902
14 Dalrymple, I, I, 115; cf. HMC, Buccleuch MS, 199
15 Welwood, 322
16 Burnet, 373; cf. Ailesbury, I, 82–3
17 Carte, IV, 654
18 Foxcroft, II, 100
19 Carte, IV, 655
20 Ailesbury, I, 84; Ralph, 791
21 SP Ireland, Car. II. 341, 155 (15 Dec 1683); Burnet, 374; Hatton, II, 41;
    Luttrell, I, 293. Halifax told Sir John Reresby that 'the manner of his
    Grace's being required to sign the document was something hard' (Reresby
    295).
22 HMC, Appx to 15th Report (Dartmouth MS, I, 3)
23 Dalrymple, I, I, 116
24 Burnet, 374
25 Welwood, 144

22

1   Luttrell, I, 303
2   Longleat MS Portland Papers II, f. 257
3   Welwood, 149–50
4   cf. Ailesbury, I, 112
5   SP Dom., Car. II 437, No. 39
6   HMC, Appx V to Report 12, Vol II (Rutland MS), 84
7   Ailesbury, I, 113
8   D'Avaux, III, 8
9   D'Avaux, III, 18, 33, 47–8 and 64–5
10 Dalrymple, I, I, 119
11 Burnet, 374
12 Grey, 70–84; cf. D'Avaux, III, 168
13 Eachard, I, 1043
14 Cobbett, X, 105–23; Hatton, II, 46–7; Burnet, 375–6; Irving, 208–11;
    Oldmixon, 686–7; Ralph, 797–9; Higgon, 269
15 D'Avaux, III, 33–4
16 cf. Burnet, 390
17 M'Crie, 155–9
18 Welwood, 144

19 HMC Report VII, 378; Dalrymple, I, I, Appx. 131; Foxcroft, I, 423
20 M'Crie, 159; Burnet, 391
21 D'Avaux, III, 116–17, 119 and 124
22 Welwood, 144–5
23 M'Crie, 160–1
24 Burnet, 393–4
25 Oldmixon, I, 690
26 D'Avaux, III, 145–6, 149; cf. M'Crie, 165
27 M'Crie, 165
28 D'Avaux, III, 152
29 Burnet, 402
30 Ailesbury, I, 113
31 M'Crie, 165–7
32 Ralph, I, 853

23

1 BM Add Harleian 6845, f. 270
2 D'Avaux, III, 220
3 See Dalrymple, I, 2, 167
4 Fox, Appx (Sir P. Hume's narrative), 18–19
5 Ralph, I, 853
6 Grey, 69–70
7 Roberts, I, 187
8 Grey, 86
9 BM Add MS Harleian 6845, f. 270
10 Welwood, Appx, XV, 323–5
11 Grey, 92
12 Fox, Appx, 12–13
13 Fox, Appx, 15–16
14 Ralph, I, 353
15 Burnet, 404
16 Burnet, 405
17 Ralph, I, 854
18 Ralph, I, 384
19 Eachard, 1065
20 BM Harleian 6845, f. 270
21 HMC, 12th Report, Appx, 392–407
22 Grey, 95
23 HMC, 12th Report, Appx 6, 393–4; BM Harleian 6845, f. 271
24 CSP, Charles II, XXV, 64; cf. Grey, 104.
25 Author of the pamphlet *An Enquiry about the Barbarous Murder of the Earl of Essex*
26 BM Harleian 6845, f. 270
27 Fox, Appx, 37
28 HMC, 12th Report, Appx 6, 395
29 BM Harleian 6845, f. 271
30 Grey, 113–15
31 ibid.
32 Burnet, 405
33 HMC, Appx 6 to 12th Report, 397–9; Grey, 112–16; BM Harleian 6845, 271–2; Burnet, 405
34 Howell, 446
35 HMC, Appx 6 to 12th Report, 397
36 C. F. D'Avaux, III, 172–3. Many of them had been cashiered by William at the King's request. ('The last dismission of his adherents from the Dutch regiments insured [Argyle] of a body of officers, stimulated by the two most powerful of all motives, revenge and want' (Dalrymple, I, II, 171).)

37 Erskine, Journal, 114
38 Grey, 120
39 BM Harleian 6845, ff. 264 and 272; BM Egerton MS 1527, f. 76
40 Grey, 119
41 D'Avaux, III, 199
42 BM Add 1152A, ff. 279–83
43 Grey, 118
44 Clarke II, 40–1; Cartwright, 278–9
45 Fea, *King Monmouth*, 359
46 BM Egerton, 1527, 46–50
47 Eachard, 106–7
48 Ralph, 855
49 D'Avaux III, 154–222; Ailesbury, I, 113–14; Dalrymple, I, II, 174
50 Ailesbury, I, 113–14

24

1   D'Avaux, III, 205; cf. Dalrymple, I, II, 173–74, Hatton, II, 54
2   BM Lansdowne 1152A, f. 275
3   'A certain English captain called Foulkes, whom the King of England caused
    to be cashiered . . . is now a colonel in the Duke of Monmouth's army'
    (D'Avaux III, 253–4).
4   Ailesbury, I, 117
5   Dalrymple, I, II, 186
6   Bodleian. Tanner MS, XXXI
7   BM Harleian 6845 f. 274
8   Fea, 220
9   BM Lansdowne 1152A, f. 237
10 CSP Dom Car II, 427, No. 119 and 431, No. 80
11 King William's Chest I, 2, f. 7
12 Howell, XI, 466
13 Luttrell, 348

25

1   BM Lansdowne 1152A, ff. 269–72
2   Stopford Sackville, I, 2
3   Whiting, 295
4   Coad, 3–4
5   HMC, 3rd Report, 96
6   Stopford Sackville, I, 2
7   BM Harleian 6845, f. 287
8   BM Harleian 6845, ff. 277 (Wade) and 287 (Axe); Dalrymple, I, I, 180–1
9   Whiting, 297
10 Grey, 107
11 Whiting, 298
12 Welwood, 148–9
13 BM Harleian, 6845, f. 278
14 Longleat MS. Portland Papers II, f. 268
15 Axe in BM Harleian 6845, f. 287
16 ibid.

26

1   Luttrell, I, 348
2   BM Add MS 31956, f. 3
3   BM Add MS 31956, f. 3

4   Burnet, 412
5   HMC 5th Report, Appx I, 328
6   BM Harleian 6845, f. 279
7   Ralph, 878
8   HMC 15th Report, Appx I, 328; Ralph, 879
9   Stopford Sackville, I, 12

27

1   Wade in BM Harleian, 6845, f. 279
2   Roberts, II, 21
3   BM Add 31956 f. 4
4   BM Add MS 28,050, f. 47
5   Stopford Sackville, I, 15
6   Paschall in BM Add MS 4162, ff. 123–4

General Sources for the Period 13–30 June, 1685

BM Harleian 6845 (Wade ff. 275–80, Axe, ff. 287–8); Harleian 7006, ff. 184–95; BM Lansdowne 1152A (Williams, f. 237, Parrot, f. 238, Holmes, f. 240, Goodenough, f. 242–5, Tellier, ff. 273–5, Battiscombe, f. 307). Dummer in BM Add MS 31956, ff. 2–5. Luttrell, I, 347–9. Paschall in BM Add MS 4162, ff. 121–4. Whiting, 294–301. Grey, 121–4. Wheeler in *Iter Bellicosum* (Camden Miscellany, XII), 159–62. SP Dom, James II, 2, pp. 7, 13, 17, 24, 25, 28–30, 38–40, 47–9; Entry Book 56, pp. 164, 214, 219, 222–3, 228–9, 233, 236; King William's Chest I, Pt. II, f. 7 and Pt. III, f. 139; SP Ireland 340 p. 95. Thynne Papers, XXII, 168–85; Hatton II, 55–58. HMC Stopford Sackville, I, 1–16. Coad, 3–6; HMC 3rd Report, App; 5th Report, Appx, I, 238; 11th Report (Dartmouth MS) Appx, Pt V, 126–7; 12th Report, II, Appx. V, 89; 13th Report, 97–100; Dalrymple, I, II, 179–82 and Appx, 23–24; Pitman in English Garner, VII; Oldmixon I, 702–3. Pamphlet: *The Whole Glorious Life of James, Duke of Monmouth*, 7–12; Welwood, 146. Burnet, 410–12. Kennet, III, 430–1. Howell, 1023–51. Toulmin, 448–72. Ralph I, 875–80. Roberts, I, 267–338, II, 1–35. Fox, 225–43. Ferguson, 222–33.

28

1   Axe in BM Harleian 6845, f. 288
2   ibid.
3   Paschall in BM Add MS 4162 f. 124
4   Fox, Appx, 109–11
5   Singer (4 July)
6   Stopford Sackville, I, 16
7   Oldmixon, II, 703
8   The incident was also related to Bishop Kennet by a Life Guards captain in 1715 (Kennet, III, 432)
9   Oldmixon, 2,703
10 (see *Western Martyrology*): an enemy of Capt Hucker (Monmouth's host at Taunton) accused him later of firing the shot, but other witnesses disproved this.

29

1   Kennet, III, 432
2   BM Harleian, 6845, f. 281
3   BM Harleian, 6845, f. 295

General Sources for the Period 1–8 July, 1685

BM Harleian 6845 (Wade ff. 280–2; Axe, ff. 288; James II, 289–96); Lansdowne 1152A (Williams, f. 237). Dummer in BM Add MS 31956, ff. 5–7. Paschall in BM Add MS 4162, ff. 124–7. Wheeler in *Iter Bellicosum* (Camden Miscellany XII), 162–3. SP Dom James II, 2, pp. 52–7. Longleat MS, Portland Papers, II, ff. 266–7. Hatton II, 58. HMC, Stopford Sackville, I, 15–19. HMC 3rd Report, 11th Report, Appx. Pt V, 127–8; 12th Report, II, Appx. Pt V, 89–92; 13th Report, 157–9. Clarendon and Rochester, 141–3. Pamphlet, *The Whole Glorious Life*, 12–14. Luttrell, I, 351–3; Dalrymple, I, II, 182–4, and Appx, 24–5. Burnet, 412. Oldmixon I, 703–4. Kennet, III, 431–2. Toulmin, 471–85. Ralph, I, 880–3. Roberts II, 34–108. Fox, 243–50. Ferguson, 233–8. Arthur, I, 185–97. Wolseley, I, 304–8.

30

1   Luttrell, I, 353
2   Macpherson, I, 145–6
3   Ailesbury, I, 119
4   Camden Miscellany, VIII
5   Dalrymple, II, I, 25
6   Ailesbury, I, 119–20; Macpherson, I, 144.
7   Reresby, 270
8   Clarke, II, 40

31

1   SP Dom Jas II, Entry Book 236, 156
2   HMC 12th Report (Rutland MS) Appx, Pt V, II, 94
3   Singer 144–5; cf. Dr Jebb in Camden Miscellany VIII
4   SP Jas II, Entry Book 336, p. 159
5   Eachard, I, 1060
6   Kennet, III, 433; Oldmixon, I, 704; *Whole Glorious Life*, 15; *Western Martyrology*, 197
7   Luttrell, 353
8   HMC 12th Report (Rutland MS) Appx, Pt V, II, 94
9   HMC 12th Report (Rutland MS) Appx, Pt V, Vol. II, 93
10 Oldmixon, I, 704
11 *Western Martyrology*, 188; *Whole Glorious Life*, 16
12 Evelyn, II, 471–2
13 *The Western Martyrology*, 187
14 Welwood, 148
15 Eachard, I, 1067

General Sources for the Period 8–15 July, 1685

Howell, 1066–83; Camden Miscellany, VIII; HMC 12th Report (Rutland MS), Appx, Pt V, Vol II; SP Dom (James II) 254–67; HMC Stopford-Sackville, I, 22; Dalrymple, II, Appx 25–7; Reresby, 270–2; Burnet, 412–14; Kennet, III, 432–3; Oldmixon 704; Pamphlet: *An Account of the Manner of the Taking of, and of what passed at the execution of, the late Duke of Monmouth*; Eachard, I; 1066–7; Ralph I, 883–8; Fox, 249–69; Clarke, II, 34–41; Bell, 269–78; Roberts II, 95–399

Postscript : Those He Left Behind

1   Ailesbury, I, 120
2   Ferguson, 389
3   HMC, Report 7, Appx, 535

Appendix A

1 Fraser, II, 488
2 Thurloe State Papers, I, 665
3 *Information of Mr William Disney, of the City of Westminster taken on oath before the Rt Honble the Earl of Essex and Mr Secretary Jenkins* (BM Add MS 2808417)
4 *Letter to a Person of Honour concerning the King's disavowing the having been married to the D of M's Mother*
5 Longleat MS, Portland Papers, XXXIV, 197

Appendix B

1 Harleian MSS No. 7006

Appendix D

BIBLIOGRAPHY

MANUSCRIPT SOURCES

British Museum
Egerton MS 1527 (Monmouth's pocket-book); Harleian 6845 (including Wade's
and Axe's narratives of the Rebellion) and 7006. Lansdowne 1152A. Additional
MS 19519, 22878, 27962, 28569, 31959, 32095, 34362 (including Dummer's
narrative of the Rebellion) 38847 (including West's confession) and 4162
(including Paschall's narrative of the Rebellion).

Public Record Office
State Papers (Domestic – Charles II and James II)
SP 44
SP (France) 78, 133 and 137
News Letters, France, Vol. 18 (1672–3)
SP (Holland) 84
SP (Scotland) Warrant Book 2
Perwych Papers (Camden Society)
Entry Books 21, 24, 34, 35A, 40, 41, 43, 44, 52, 56, 58, 62

Bodleian Library
Tanner MS 148 and 149

Longleat MS
Coventry Papers VII, XVI, XXXI, XXXII, XXXIV, LXXXIII, LXXXIV,
XCIII, CI
Portland Papers II

Historical Manuscripts Commission
3rd Report, 5th Report, 6th Report (Ingleby MS), 7th Report, 10th Report,
11th Report, 12th Report (Le Fleming and Rutland MS), 14th Report
(Kenyon MS), 15th Report (Buccleuch, Montagu and Savile Foljambe MS)
Beaufort, Stopford Sackville and Ormonde MS, Vols III and IV
Finch Papers, II

OTHER CONTEMPORARY SOURCES

Ailesbury, Earl of, *Memoirs,* I (ed. Roxburghe Club, 1890)
Airy, Osmund (ed.), *The Lauderdale Papers* (Camden Society, 1855)
Airy, Osmund (ed)., *Essex Papers*, Vols II and III

Arber, Edward, *The English Garner*, VII

Avaux, Comte d', *Negociacions*, 4 Vols (1754)

Bulstrode, Sir Richard, *Memoirs and Reflections* (1721)

Burnet, Rt Rev. Gilbert, Bishop of Salisbury, *History of My Own Time* (1708) (1838 edition)

Burns, Rev. Robert (ed.), *History of the Sufferings of the Church of Scotland*, by the Rev. Robert Wodrow, Vols III and IV (1837)

Calendar of State Papers (Domestic) 1661–85

Chamberlayne, Edward, *Angliae Notitiae*. 14th edition (1682)

Crichton, Andrew (ed.). *Memoirs of the Rev. John Blackader* (1823)

Clarendon, Earl of, *History of the Reign of Charles II*, 2 vols (1792)

Clarke, Rev. J. S. (ed.), *Life of James II (From notes left in his own hand)* 2 vols (1816)

Coad, John, *A Memorandum of the Wonderful Providences of God to a Poor Unworthy Creature during the Time of the Duke of Monmouth's Rebellion and the Revolution in 1688* (1894)

Cobbett's *Complete Collection of State Trials*, Vols 8–11

Christie, W. D. (ed.), *Williamson's Letters* (Camden Society, 2 vols, 1874)

Curran, M. B. (ed.), *The Dispatches of William Perwych, English Agent in Paris, 1669–77* (1903)

Dalrymple, Sir John, *Memoirs of Great Britain and Ireland*, 2 vols (1790)

Dalton, Charles (ed.), *English Army Lists and Commission Registers, 1661–1714* (1892)

Defoe, Daniel, *Journal of the Plague Year* (1722)

Downes, John, *Roscius Anglicanus, 1660–1706*

Dryden, John, *Absalom and Achitophel* (Poems of J. Dryden, edited by James Kinsley, I, 1958)

Eachard, Laurence, Archdeacon of Stowe, *History of England*, I (1720)

Forneron, H. *Louise de Keroualle* (ed. S. M. Crawford, 1881)

Fraser, Sir William (ed.), *The Scotts of Buccleuch, II,* (family correspondence and other documents) (1878)

Gilbert, G. D. (ed.), *Memoirs of the Court of England in 1675*, by Baronne d'Aulnoy, (1913)

Grey of Werke, Ford, Lord (Earl of Tankerville), *The Secret History of the Rye House Plot and the Monmouth Rebellion 1685* (first published, 1754)

Hamilton, Anthony, *Memoirs of the Comte de Grammont* (1713) (1930 edition)

Harleian Miscellany (1744–46)

Hatton, *Correspondence of the Family of*, 1601–1704, 2 vols. (ed E. M. Thompson, 1878)

Higgons, Bevill. *Historical and Critical Remarks on Bishop Burnet's History of His Own Time* (1725)

Hinds, Allen B. (ed.), *Calendar of Venetian State Papers*, Vols 37 and 38 (1940)

Howell, T. B., *Complete Collection of State Trials*, 1680–88, Vol II (1811)

Jebb, Dr Samuel (ed.), *Original Letters of the Duke of Monmouth*, in Camden Miscellany, VIII (1883)

Kinloch, G. R. (ed.) *The Diary of John Lamont* (1830)

Kirkton, James, *Secret and True History of the Church of Scotland* (1660–78) (1817)

Locke, Richard, *The Western Rebellion* (1782)

Luttrell, Narcissus. *Brief Historical Relation of State Affairs*, I (OUP edition, 1852)

Macpherson, James, *Original Papers, containing the Secret History of Great Britain* (1775)

Malden, H. E. (ed.), *Iter Bellicosum*, by Adam Wheeler in the Camden Miscellany, Vol XII (1900)

Manley, Sir Roger, *History of the Rebellions in England, Scotland and Ireland*, Book I (1691)

Marvell, Andrew, *Ballads*

M'crie, Thomas (ed.), *Memoirs of William Veitch and George Brysson* (1828)

Montagu, Ralph, *Memoirs*

Mulgrave, John Sheffield, Earl of, *Works*, II (1780)

Newcomb, Thomas, *Defeat of the Rebels at Bothwell Bridge* (1691)

Oldmixon, John, *History of England during the Reigns of the House of Stuart*, I (1730)

Pepys, Samuel, *Diary*

Pike C. E. (ed.), *Essex Correspondence*

Pitman, Henry, Chirurgeon, *Strange Sufferings and Adventures of*, 1689 (English Garner VII, 1903)

Pitt, Thomas, *The New Martyrology* (1689)

Ralph, *The History of England by a Lover of Truth and Beauty*, I (1744)

Reresby, Sir John, *Memoirs* (1734) (ed. Albert Ivatt, 1904)

Rose, Rt Hon. Sir G. H. (ed.), *Selections from the Papers of the Earls of Marchmont*, Vols I–III (1831)

Rose, Rt Hon. Sir G. H., *Observations on the Historical works of the Late Rt Hon Charles James Fox* (1809)

Stepney, Lady (ed.), *Memoirs of Lady Russell and Lady Herbert*, 1623–1723 (1898)

Sévigné, Madame de, *Letters* (1726)

Sidney, Henry, *Diary of the Times of Charles II*, 2 vols (ed. R. W. Blencowe, 1843)

Sidney, Hon. Algernon, *Discourse concerning Government* (1698)

Singer, S. W. (ed.), *Correspondence of Henry Hyde, Earl of Clarendon and Laurence Hyde, Earl of Rochester* (1828)

Somers, Lord, *Tracts*, Vols 7–9. (2nd edition, Walter Scott, 1812)

Sprat, Thomas, Bishop of Rochester, *The True History of the Rye House Plot* (1685)

Summers, Montagu (ed.), *The Works of Aphra Behn* (1915)

Temple, Sir William, *Memoirs*, III (1709)

Tuke, Richard, *Memoirs of the Life and Death of Sir Edmund Berry Godfrey* (1682)

Venetian State Papers, Calendar of, Vols 37 and 38 (Ed. Allen B. Hinds, 1940)

Verney, Margaret M., *Memoirs of the Verney Family 1660–96*, Vol IV (1899)

Welwood, James, *Memoirs of the Most Material Transactions in England for the last 100 Years preceding the Revolution in 1688* (1704)

Wheeler, Adam, *Iter Bellicosum* (in Camden Miscellany XII, 1900)

Whitelocke, Bulstrode, *Memorials of English Affairs* (1682)

Whiting, John, *Persecution Expos'd*, etc. (1691)

Wood, Anthony, *Life of* (autobiography) (1730)

PAMPHLETS

A Letter from a Person of Quality to His Friend in the Country (1674)

Great Victory (1679)

England's Happiness (1679)

An Exact Relation of the Defeat of the Rebels at Bothwell Bridge (1679)

A Further Account of the Proceeding against the Rebels in Scotland since the Arrival of his Grace the Duke of Monmouth in a letter to a Person of Quality (1679)

A True Narrative of the Duke of Monmouth's Late Journey into the West in a Letter from an Eye Witness thereof to his Correspondent in London (1681)

An Account of what Passed at the Execution of the Late Duke of Monmouth (1685)

An Account of the Manner of the Taking of the Late Duke of Monmouth, by his Majesty's Command (1686)

The Whole Glorious Life of James, Late Duke of Monmouth (1708)

Thought to be by Robert Ferguson

Appeal from the Country to the City for the Preservation of his Majesty's Person, liberty, property, and the Protestant religion. (1679)

A Letter to a Person of Honour concerning the Black Box (1680)

A Letter to a Person of Honour concerning the King's disavowing his having been married to the Duke of Monmouth's Mother (1680)

An Historical Record of the Heroick Life and Magnanimous Actions of the Most Illustrious Protestant Prince, James Duke of Monmouth (1683)

SECONDARY AUTHORITIES

Airy, Osmund, *The English Restoration and Louis XIV* (1888)

Anderson, James, *The Ladies of the Covenant* (1851)

Arthur, Capt. Sir George, *The Story of the Household Cavalry*, I (1909)

Ashley, Maurice, *John Wildman, Plotter and Postmaster* (1947)

Ashley, Maurice, *Charles II, The Man and Statesman* (1971)

Atkinson, G. T., *Marlborough and the Rise of the British Army* (1921)

Brett, A. C. A., *Charles II and His Court* (1910)

Brett-James, Norman G., *The Growth of Stuart London* (1935)

Carte, Thomas, *Life of James, Duke of Ormonde*, 4 vols (1851)

Cartwright, Julia, *Madame* (1894)

Christie, W. D., *Life of Anthony Ashley Cooper, 1st Earl of Shaftesbury*, 2 vols (1871)

Clode, Charles M., *Military Forces of the Crown*, I (1869)

Collins's Peerage in England

Dasent A. I., *The Private Life of Charles II* (1927)

Dictionary of National Biography

Ewald, A. C., *Life and Times of Hon. Algernon Sidney*, II, (1873)

Fea, Allan, *King Monmouth* (1902)

Fea, Allan, *The Loyal Wentworths* (1928)

Ferguson, James, *Ferguson the Plotter* (1887)

Fountainhall, Lord, *Historical Notes of Scottish Affairs*, III (1840)

Foxcroft, H. C., *Life and Letters of Sir George Savile Bt., 1st Marquess of Halifax* (1898)

Fox, Rt Hon. C. J., *A History of the Early Part of the Reign of James II*, with an appendix by the Rt Hon. G. H. Rose (1809)

Haile, Martin, *Mary of Modena* (1905)

Haley, K. H. D., *William of Orange and the English Opposition, 1672–74* (1953)

Haley, K. H. D., *The First Earl of Shaftesbury* (1968)

Hartmann, C. H., *Charles II and Madame* (1934)

Hartmann, C. H., *Clifford of the Cabal*, (1937)

Heron, G. Allan, *Lucy Walter* (1929)

Hyde, Montgomery, *Judge Jeffreys* (1948)

Jackson, Canon, article in British Archaeological Association Journal on Monmouth's legitimacy, Vol XXXIV, 197 (June 1878)

Jesse, J. H., *Memoirs of the Court of England during the Stuarts*, Vols 3 and 4 (1840)

Kenyon, J. P., *Robert Spencer, Earl of Sunderland* (1958)

Lingard, John, *History of England, X–XII* (1849)

Locke, Richard, *The Western Rebellion* (1782)

Marks, Alfred, *The Case of Sir Edmund Berry Godfrey* (1907)

Napier, Mark, *Life and Times of John Graham of Claverhouse, Viscount Dundee*, I (1859)

Ogg, David, *England in the Reign of Charles II*, 2 vols (1934)

Pollock, Sir John, *The Popish Plot* (1944)

Roberts, George, *The Life, Progresses and Rebellion of James, Duke of Monmouth*, 2 vols (1844)

Russell, Lord John, *Life of William, Lord Russell*, II (1820)

Ryan, P. F. William, *Stuart Life and Manners* (1912)

Scott, Lord George, *Lucy Walter, Wife or Mistress?* (1947)

Sitwell, Sir George, *The First Whig* (1894)

Terry, C. S., *John Graham of Claverhouse* (1905)

Toulmin, Joshua, *The History of Taunton* (1822)

Trevelyan, M. C., *William III and the Defence of Holland* (1930)

Walton, Col. Clifford, *History of the British Standing Army, 1660–1700* (1894)

Willcock, John, *A Scots Earl. Life and Times of Archibald, 9th Earl of Argyle* (1907)

Wolseley, General Viscount, *Life of John Churchill, Duke of Marlborough, I.* (1894)

Zee, Henri and Barbara Van Der, *William and Mary* (1973)

INDEX

Abercorn, James, 1st Duke of 276

Absolam and Achitophel 120–2, 129–30, 150, 166, 217, 251, 262

Adlam, Capt 230, 232, 235

Ailesbury, Robert Bruce, 1st Earl of 138, 164; Thomas Bruce, 2nd Earl of (*see* Bruce)

Aix-La-Chapelle, Peace of 30

Albemarle, Christopher Monk, 2nd Duke of 38, 98, 119, 141, 209, 213, 218, 221, 222–3, 226, 230, 246; George Monk, 1st Duke of 10, 21, 37

Alberti, Girolamo, Venetian ambassador, *cited* 39, 44, 51

Alford, Gregory, Mayor of Lyme 209, 211, 212

Alington, William, 2nd Lord, Major-General to Monmouth 62–5, 82, 186–8, 189

Althorp (Northants) 20

Amsterdam 46, 47, 49, 57, 115, 192–3, 194, 196–201, 205–7, 236, 272

Anglesey, Arthur Annesley, 1st Earl of 161, 213

Anne of Austria, Queen-Mother of France 27

Anne, Princess (*later* Queen Anne) 55, 79, 114, 166, 168, 255

Annesley, Abraham, rebel 271; Lord 38

Appeal from the Country to the City, An 115

Appleton, Sir Henry 23

Argyle, Archibald Campbell, 8th Earl and 1st Marquess of 151; Archibald Campbell, 9th Earl of xxii, 151, 156, 167, 192, 195–203, 235, 268

Arlington, Henry Bennet, 1st Earl of, Secretary of State 13, 21, 22, 23, 25, 26, 28, 34, 39, 40, 46, 48, 50, 61

Armies: English 21–2, 31, 37, 42–3, 82–5, 240, 245–8; Dutch 46, 47, 49; French 31, 44–6, 47, 56–65; Spanish 84

Armstrong, Sir Thomas: brings news of "Madame's" death 36; member of Monmouth's staff 42, 47; at siege of Maastricht 62; member of Country Party 75; in the St Denis campaign 82–7; at the Battle of Bothwell Bridge 101; returns from Scotland with Monmouth 107–8; is spurned by Charles and York 111; in Amsterdam 115; plots with Ferguson 127; at the Oxford Parliament 134; in Kent with Monmouth 139; sent by Monmouth for *habeas corpus* 145; spying in London 153; ordered by Monmouth to suspend plans for uprising 154; captured in Netherlands 184; tried and executed 184–5; *misc* 261

Artagnan, Capt d' 62–3

Arundell of Wardour, Henry, 3rd Lord 34

Ashill, skirmish at 226

Aulnoy, Baronne d', *cited* 3, 4, 27

Austria, Emperor of 193

Avaux, Jean Antonie, Comte d', *cited* 113, 114, 117, 182–3, 185, 187, 189, 205

Avon, river 226, 228, 230

Axbridge (Somerset) 228, 236, 246

Axe, Rev Thomas 219

Axminster (Devon) 218, 227, 233

Ayloffe, John, lawyer and dissident 147, 196

Bagster, Lieutenant, naval officer 210

Baillie, Robert, *cited* 4

Ball, Henry, civil servant 67

Bamfylde, Col 5

Barillon, Paul de, Marquis de (French Ambassador to London) 93–4, 117, 125, 133, 134, 136, 170, 182, 237–8, 256

Barlow, Francis 14

Barlow, John 3

Barlow, Lucy: parentage and childhood 3–4; changes name from Walters 3; with Charles II, in Netherlands 5–6; travels to London as Royalist agent 6–7; in the Tower 7; is deprived of son 7; dies 8; *misc*, xiii, xxii, 12, 42, 55, 74, 79, 111, 115, 118, 125–28, 216, 238, 250, 275–76

Barnadiston, Sir Samuel 200

Barnewell, Sir Frederick, *cited* 276

Barrington Court (Somerset) 228

Basset, Col, commander of Yellow Regt 223, 227, 230, 241–2, 252

Bath (Somerset) 29, 129, 232

Bath and Wells, Bishop of (in 1680) 129
Battiscombe, Christopher, barrister and
    rebel 199, 271
Beaufort, Henry Somerset, 1st Duke of
    135, 221, 226, 228, 230–1
Bedford, William Russell, 5th Earl of
    135, 169
Bedford House 152
Bell, Rev Peter, evidence of 275
Bennet, Col, champion of Monmouth in
    Parliament 94
Bentinck, Hans Willem (*later* 1st Earl
    of Portland) 79, 206, 212
Berkeley, George, 1st Earl of 156
Berkeley, Lady Henrietta 156, 160
Bertie, Charles, *cited* 256, 259
Birch, Col, champion of Monmouth in
    Parliament 94
Black Box, The 126–8
Black Ditch, The 244
Blackburn 99
Blackheath 57, 67
Blague, Mary 166
Blake, Admiral Robert 220
Blake, Susan, of Taunton, schoolmistress
    220
Blon, Monsieur Le 204
Bloody Assizes 269–71
Bloxham, Mr, researcher, *cited* 277
Bombay 15
'Bond', The 81–2
Bothwell Bridge, Battle of 100–5, 165,
    193, 219
Bourn, Zachary 128
Boyle, Richard 17
Bradford-on-Avon 234
Bradney Lane 244
Bradshaw, John 185
Brandenberg, Frederick William, Elector
    of 56, 193
Bridgwater   (Somerset)   227–8,   236,
    237–43
Bridport, skirmish at 217
Bristol, Earl of 11
Bristol 223, 226, 228–30
Bruce, Thomas, Lord (*later* 2nd Earl of
    Ailesbury) 95, 135, 138, 147, 163–5,
    166, 171, 172, 190, 204, 255, 267
Buccleuch, Francis Scott, 2nd Earl of
    11;   Henry   Scott,   3rd   Duke   of
    Buccleuch   277;   William   Montagu
    Douglas Scott, 6th Duke of 276–7
Buckingham, George Villiers, 2nd Duke
    of 20, 21, 28, 40, 41, 43, 50, 53, 55,
    67–9, 75, 77, 166
Bulstrode, Sir Richard 180, 181
Burke, Sir Bernard 276
Burnet, Rev Gilbert (*later* Bishop of
    Salisbury), *cited* 37, 70, 75, 95, 97,
106, 126, 136, 147, 150, 151, 169,
176, 178, 180, 181, 189, 196, 229,
236, 270
Bussex Rhine, The (Sedgemoor) xxiii,
    240, 241, 245–7
Bussex Tree, The 269
Buyse, Anton, Brandenberg officer 208,
    243, 247, 250, 251, 254

Cabal, The 26, 35, 41, 44
Cambridge, Charles, Duke of 80; James,
    Duke of 20
Cambridge University 13, 33, 69, 72,
    119, 141
Campbell of Cessnock, Sir George 193
Canvey Island 23
Capel, Lord, of Hadham 149
Carbery, Richard Vaughan, 2nd Earl
    of 4
Cartaret, Sir George 19
Castlefield (Bridgwater) xxi, 240, 242–3
Castlemaine, Barbara Villiers, Countess
    of (*later* Duchess of Cleveland) 10,
    11, 12, 24, 28, 166
Catherine (of Braganza), Queen of
    England 10, 12, 14, 73–4, 90, 95, 126,
    164, 253–5, 275
Cavendish, see Devonshire
Chamberlain, Dr Hugh 209
Chard (Somerset) 219, 225–6
Charles II, as Prince of Wales 4; rela-
    tions with Lucy Barlow 5–7; Corona-
    tion of 10; sends for Monmouth 10;
    dialogue with Lady Wemyss 11; on
    Monmouth's   marriage   12;   and
    Monmouth's career 14, 18; declares
    war on Dutch 16; during the Plague
    19–20; during the Fire of London 20;
    during the Dutch raids 22–4; sends
    Monmouth to "Madame" 26; prevents
    Monmouth from joining the French
    Army 28–9; and correspondence with
    Madame   27–30;   on   Duchess   of
    Monmouth's accident 29; and the
    command of the Life Guards 30–2;
    and Fr Pregnani 33; at Dover 34–5;
    and the Coventry Affair 37–8;
    and the Virnill Affair 38–9; and
    Louise de Keroualle 40; raises expedi-
    tionary force 41–2; declares war 41;
    and his children 53; delegates military
    affairs to Monmouth 71; and Lord
    Shaftesbury 73–84; refuses to admit
    Monmouth's legitimacy 79; supports
    marriage of Prince William and
    Princess Mary 79; appoints Monmouth
    Lord-General 80–1; and the Popish
    Plot 89–93; and the Cavalier Parlia-
    ment 93–4; exiles the Duke of York

95; appoints Monmouth, C-in-C Scotland 95; receives Monmouth at Windsor 108; and his illness of 1679 108–9; recalls the Duke of York 109; exiles Monmouth 110–11; his reaction to Monmouth's return 117–19; in *Absolam and Achitophel* 120–2; and the Black Box affair 126–8; health of 128; deplores Monmouth's journey to the West Country 129; and the Oxford Parliament 135–6; arrests College 137; frees Count Königsmark 140; instructs all in Royal service to shun Monmouth 141; institutes *quo warrantos* 142; bans Monmouth from Whitehall 146; and the Rye House Plot 158–61; and his reconciliation with Monmouth 169–71; his rupture with Monmouth 177–8; exiles Monmouth 178; receives Monmouth privately in London 186; his alleged dialogue with Lord Alington 186; orders Duke of York to Edinburgh 187; speculation as to death of 188–9; *misc* xxii, 253–4, 256, 261

Charles V, of Lorraine 78
Charlton, Francis, teacher and rebel 148, 200
Charlton (Sussex hunting establishment) 129
Chaste Nymph, The, by John Crowne 163
Chedzoy (Somerset) xxii, 239, 241, 243–44, 247, 269
Chelsea, Royal Hospital at 78
Chester 144
Chesterfield, Philip Stanhope, 2nd Earl of 23, 119
Chichester (Sussex) 128–9, 139, 157
Chideock (Dorset) 208–9
Chiffinch, Will, Keeper of the Backstairs 89, 255
Chudleigh, Thomas, Envoy at Hague 184
Churchill, Arabella, Mistress of York 70
Churchill, Col Charles, commanding Trelawney's Regt xxi, 226, 240; John, Lord (*later* Duke of Marlborough) xxi, 62, 64–6, 166, 212, 214, 221, 225–6, 228, 232–3, 238, 240, 246–8; Sir Winston 212
Chute, Chaloner, *cited* 181, 256, 262
Clarendon, Edward Hyde, 1st Earl of 4, 11, 15, 21, 24, 26, 28, 127–8, 185; Henry Hyde, 2nd Earl of 92, 238
Clarendon Code, The 210
Clarke, Sir Samuel, Lt-Col R. English Regt 44, 85; William, Quartermaster to Monmouth's troop of horse 22

Cleland, James, Covenanter officer 100
Cleveland, Thomas, 4th Baron Wentworth and 1st Earl of 162–3
Cleves, Duchy of 46, 48
Clifford, Sir Thomas 13, 26, 28, 34
Club Army, The 236–7
Clyde, River 100–5
Coad, John, militia deserter 219, 234
Cochrane of Ochiltree, Sir John 193; Sir George 193
Coker, Edward, Royalist militia officer 217
Colbert, Jean Baptiste 47
Coleman, Edward, secretary to Duchess of York 91–2
College, Stephen 134, 137, 139, 142, 148, 221
Compton, Sir Francis, troop commander, Lord Oxford's Regiment xxiii, 226, 240, 242, 244–8
Condé, Louis II de Bourbon, Prince de 45, 47, 57
Conventicles 81, 96–7, 219, 272
Corke, Sir John 275
Cornwallis, 3rd Baron 267
Cosin, John, Bishop of Durham 126, 275–6
Cosnac, Daniel de, Bishop of Valance 27
Country Party, The 74–5, 77, 79–81, 89, 93, 95, 96, 99, 110, 115, 117, 118, 126–8, 137, 138
Courtenay, Sir William 157
Coventry, Henry, Secretary of State 71, 82
Coventry, Sir John 37–8
Craven, William, 1st Earl of, Colonel, Coldstream Guards 43, 71
Cragg, Robert (*alias* John Smith), rebel courier 198–204, 212
Cranbourne Chase 250
Creighton, Lieutenant, *cited* 101
Creswicke, Squire Francis 229
Crofts, Major-General (son of Monmouth and Eleanor Needham) 70–1, 267; Mary Julia 267; William, Lord 8, 13, 20, 163; Mrs 171–2
Croissy, Charles-Francois Colbert, Marquis de 35
Cromwell, Oliver xxii, 6–7, 9, 127, 149, 151, 163, 185, 210, 273
Crowne, John, playwright 163

Dalkeith and Doncaster, Charles Scott, Earl of, Monmouth's eldest surviving son 178, 258, 267
Dalkeith Palace 267
Dalrymple, Sir Hew 276
Dalrymple, Sir John, *cited* 149

Dalyell, General, C-in-C Scotland 99
Danby, Thomas Osborne, 1st Earl of
(*later* Duke of Leeds) 55, 77, 79, 89,
91, 93–4, 125
Dangerfield, William 117
Danvers, Colonel Henry 200, 201, 203,
212, 213, 230
Dare, Heywood 194, 195, 196, 199, 208,
209, 214, 216, 268; Thomas 216
Dartmouth, George Legge, 1st Lord 110,
126, 159, 271
Dassell, Samuel, Customs officer at
Lyme 209–10, 212
Davis, Moll, actress 37
Defoe, Daniel 218
Delamere, Henry Booth, Lord 144, 200,
213, 269
Denton, Dr 163
Devil's Upping Stock, The (see Lang-
moor Stone)
Devonshire, William Cavendish, Earl of
98, 200, 203
Dieren, Palace of William of Orange
183, 185, 187
Digby, Lord 73
Disney, William, attorney and plotter
7, 75, 198–201, 203, 212, 213, 275
Doesberg, siege of 48
Doncaster, Charles Scott, Earl of
(Monmouth's eldest son) 51, 69
Dongan, Thomas, Major-General to
Monmouth 82
Douglas, Lord 20; Colonel commanding
Dumbarton's xxi, 87, 245
Dounois, Countess, *cited* 4
Dover, Secret Treaty of 34–5, 41
Downes, John, dramatic producer 35
Dryden, John, poet 120–2, 129–30, 166,
251, 262
Dummer, Edward, Royalist artillery
commander 233
Dunbar, Robert Constable, Viscount 38
Dunblane, Lord, Royalist officer 233
Dunkirk 40

Eachard, Laurence, historian, *cited* 184
Eastern Causeway (Bridgwater) 242
Edinburgh 99, 106, 219
Edinburgh Castle 192
Edward IV, King of England 132
Eglinton, Alexander, Montgomerie, 8th
Earl of, under Monmouth in Scottish
campaign 103–5
Eliot, Thomas 40
Elizabeth I ("The Protestant Queen")
115, 151, 162
Elton, John 181
Erskine, William 8
Essex, Arthur Capel, 1st Earl of 69, 75,

109, 115, 135, 147, 149–50, 156, 161,
168–9, 189, 202, 261
Estrées, Admiral d' 57, 68
Euston Hall (Norfolk) 40
Evelyn, John, diarist, *cited* 3, 20, 40,
68, 82–3, 94, 168, 265–6
Evertson, vice-admiral of Dutch Fleet
17–18, 21
Exclusion Bill, The 107, 108, 111, 113,
115, 128, 137, 138, 183
Exeter 40, 131, 212

Falmouth, Lord 17
Fariaux, General de, commandant of
Maastricht 58, 65
Farnham Castle (Surrey) 254
Farrant, Amy 251
Ferguson, Dr Robert ("The Plotter"),
Country Party member 75; in Amsterdam 115; author of *An Appeal from
the Country* 115, 118–19; description
of 126; and the Black Box 126–7; his
plans to assassinate the King 148–9;
flees to Holland 154–5; and the Rye
House Plot 160; plots with Lord Grey
in Netherlands 194; during the
invasion plans 201; deviousness of,
aboard *Helderenberg* 208–9; declaration of, read in Lyme 211; at prayer
219; in Taunton 222–4; preaches
before Battle of Sedgemoor 239; his
later career 268–9
Fergusson, William, Laird of Caitloch
101–2
Feversham, Louis de Duras, Marquis de
Blanquefort and 1st Earl of xxi, 62,
78, 82, 88, 95, 98–9, 109, 163, 226,
228–9, 232–3, 235, 236, 237, 238,
243, 247–8, 269, 270
Fieuliad, Major-General de la 60
Filgrove (Glos) 229
Fitzharding, Lord 219
Fitzharris, Edward 136
Fletcher of Saltoun, Andrew 196, 203,
208, 216, 217, 246, 268
Floyd, Doctor 8
Forde Abbey (Somerset) 131
Forder, Mr, of Houghton-in-le-Spring
275–6
Fordingbridge (Hampshire) 251
Foubert, Monsieur, academy of 140
Four Days Battle, The 21
Fowke, Lt-Colonel, commander of (1)
the White (2) the Yellow Regiment
207, 216, 230, 241–2, 252, 269
Fox, C. J., *cited* 260
Fox, Sir Stephen 119, 261
Fox, Lt-Colonel, commander of the
Yellow Regt 207, 216

Franche Comté 25
Frome (Somerset) 234–6
Frondeurs, The 15
Fuller, Dr William, Bishop of Lincoln 127

Gaunt, Mrs 270
General Point, The 148, 160
George Inn (Lyme) 212, 216
George, Prince of Denmark, Consort of Princess Anne 168
Gerard of Brandon, Lord, (*later* 1st Earl of Macclesfield) 30–2, 117, 144, 153, 157, 158–9, 200; (*later* 2nd Earl of Macclesfield) 98, 144, 200
Gerard, Sir Gilbert 126
Gilbert, G. D., *cited* 276
Gillingham (Dorset) 250
Glastonbury Abbey 228
Gloucester 229, 230, 238
Godfrey, Capt Charles, Life Guards officer 62, 116
Godfrey, Sir Edmund Berry 91–2, 115–16
Godfrey, William, herdsman and guide on Sedgemoor xxii, 239, 241, 244, 245
Godolphin, Sidney (*later* 1st Earl of) 46, 48, 125
Goffe, Father Stephen 5
Gold Stick, appointment of 93, 108–9
Goodenough, Richard, lawyer and rebel 147, 152, 158, 207, 238
Goodwood House 129
Gosfritt, George 82–3, 275; Margaret (*nee* Protheroe). See also Sambourne, 3, 195, 275
Gostlin, Mr, Sheriff of London 262–5
Gouda (Holland) 191, 205
Grafton, Henry Fitzroy, 1st Duke of 233, 240
Graham, Capt John, of Claverhouse (*later* 1st Viscount of Dundee) 97, 103, 105
Grana, Marquess de, Governor of Spanish Netherlands 180, 190
Grandison, Lord 62
Great Fire, The 20, 21, 28
Green Ribbon Club, The 75, 77, 79, 96, 97, 107, 111, 213
Grey of Werke, Ford, Lord (*later* 1st Earl of Tankerville): in the Country Party 75; resigns commission for Scotland 99; host to Monmouth at Up Park 129; at the Oxford Parliament 134; in Kent with Monmouth 139; in the plots of 1682 146–54; scandal of with Lady Henrietta Berkeley 156; at Chichester with

Monmouth 157; during the Rye House Plot 158–60; flees to Netherlands 160; resents Monmouth's neglect of conspirators there 184; escapes when Armstrong is captured 184; plots with Ferguson in Amsterdam 194; during invasion plans 196; appointed to command Monmouth's cavalry 208; at Lyme 210, 216; his cowardice at Bridport 217; in Taunton 220–2; at Keynsham Bridge 230; votes to continue the campaign 235; at Bridgwater 241–3; at Battle of Sedgemoor 245–6, 250; capture of 251; under escort to London 254; at Whitehall 255; his later career 268
Greyfriars, Edinburgh 105
Griffin, Col Edward, Life Guards officer 20, 22, 38, 172
Gwyn, Nell 37, 117
Guildford (Surrey) 254

Hague, The 5, 6, 113–14, 117, 189
Halifax, George Savile, Viscount (*later* Marquess of) 95, 109, 133–4, 141, 143, 169–71, 173, 176–8, 183
Hamden, John (elder) 134, 177; John (younger) 150, 156, 161, 177–8, 199, 200
Hamilton, Anthony (Comte de Grammont), *cited* 39, 70, 139; Robert, Covenanter commander 100–2; William Douglas, Duke of 97; Duchess of 105; Testimony 102; (by Bothwell Bridge) 99–100, 105
Hampton Court Palace 19
Hardy, Dr, of Lyme 234
Harman, Admiral Sir John 68
Harris, Benjamin 119
Hart, Lady 229
Harwich 79, 181, 201
Hatton, Lord 117; Charles, *cited* 116; Christopher, *cited* 67
Hayes, Capt James, Commander of Monmouth's sloop 209
Heeswick, Treaty of 51
Helderenberg, Monmouth's invasion ship 204, 207–8, 210, 216
Henri IV, King of France 25
Henrietta Anne, Princess (see Orleans)
Henrietta Maria, Queen Dowager of England 5, 8, 10, 11, 12, 34, 275
Henry VII, King of England 132, 201; his statute on Kingship 222
Herbert, Lord 139
Heroick Life, The, cited 5, 7, 9, 52, 56, 58, 71–2, 92, 99, 139, 144
Hewling, Capt Benjamin 203, 239, 243; brothers 271

Hicks, John 270
Hill, Ann, maid to Lucy Barlow 7
Hoddesdon (Herts) 159
Holloway, James 147
Hollyday, Richard 250–51
Holmes, Lt-Colonel Abraham, commander of (1) Green Regt. (2) the Red Regt 208, 216, 230, 234, 241–2, 246, 252, 271; Richard, of Chichester 157; Admiral 44
Holt Lodge (Dorset) 251
Hone, William, joiner and rebel 147, 168
Honiton (Devon) 212
Hook, Rev Nathaniel, chaplain to Monmouth 221, 268
Hooper, Dr George 260
Hounslow (Middlesex) 82
Howard, Lady Katherine, ancestress of Lucy Barlow: Sir Philip, Life Guards officer 61; Colonel Thomas 6, 7; of Escrick, Thomas, 2nd Baron 84; of Escrick, William, 3rd Baron 116, 136, 150, 154, 156, 160–1, 168–9, 176
Hucker, Capt John, rebel officer 219–20
Hume, David, Presbyterian Minister 101–2; Sir Patrick (*later* Earl of Marchmont) 193, 195–6, 200
Hunting 33, 79, 129, 139, 164–5, 181
Huntly, George Gordon, 4th Marquis of 62
Hurd, Sarah 220
Hyde, Lady Henrietta 267; (*see* Clarendon)

Ijssel, River 48, 56
Ilchester 130, 221
Inglesby, Sir Henry, *cited* 42
Ireton, Henry 204
Isle of Wight 44

Jeffreys, Sir George, Lord Chief Justice (*later* 1st Baron of Wem) 137, 142, 174–5, 184–5, 270–1
Jenkins, Sir Leoline, Secretary of State 129, 139, 145, 159, 160, 161, 164, 171–3, 181
Jennings, Sarah (Lady Churchill) 141, 166; Lady 221
Jesuits, The 89–90, 128
Jones, Sir Henry 64, 65; John, rebel agent 202, 204; Sir William, attorney-general 81; Capt, rebel cavalry officer 246

Keeling, Josiah, dyer and rebel 148, 159–60
Ken, Dr Thomas, Bishop of Bath and Wells 260
Kennett, Bishop, *cited* 247, 261

Keroualle, Louise de (see Portsmouth)
Ketch, Jack, executioner 169, 178, 185, 262, 264–5
Keynsham 238
Keynsham Bridge, skirmish at 228–30
Killigrew, Sir William 19
King's Evil, The 132, 144
Kingswood Colliers, The 269
Kirkby, Christopher 89
Kirke, Moll 70, 166
Kirke, Colonel Percy xxii, 42, 226, 228, 237, 240, 247, 269–70
Kneller, Sir Godfrey 3, 129
Konigsmark, Count John 140–41

Lake, Dr, Chaplain to York 275
Lalec, Herr, Governor of Sluys 84–85
Lambert, Major-General John 10
Langley, Col Roger 113
Langmoor Rhine 244; Stone xxiii, 244
Lauderdale, John Maitland, 2nd Earl of and 1st Duke of 11, 13, 26, 41, 67, 69, 81, 96–101, 105, 107, 108, 119
Law of Brabant, The 25
Lediard, Thomas, biographer of Marlborough, *cited* 65
Legge, Col William 82, 254; (see Dartmouth)
Leicester, Robert Sidney, 2nd Earl of 4, 175
Lely, Sir Peter 3
Lesley, David, Scottish artilleryist 102
Leveson-Gower, William 144
Lichfield 144
Liège xxii, 127, 273
Lille, Fortress at 56–7
Linlithgow, Lord 97, 98; under Monmouth in Scotland 101
Lisle, Dame Alice 270
Littleton, Sir Charles 83, 85, 117, 161
Liverpool 144
Livingston, Lord, under Monmouth in Scotland 102
Lock, Matthew, Secretary at War 43
Lockhart, Sir William 60, 61, 65
London: Arlington Garden 111; Aldersgate 134, 146, 152; Bedford House 152; Blackheath 57, 67; Bow St. 37, Chancery Lane 74, 115, 126; Charing Cross 13, 116; Covent Garden 4, 201, Essex St. 161; Exchange, the 151, 152, 213; Fleet Bridge 152; Greenwich 19; Hedge Lane, Monmouth's house in 38, 116, 129, 140, 152; Haymarket 37–8; Horse Guards 151 Hyde Park 21, 31–2, 140; Lambeth 153; Leadenhall St. 204; Lincoln's Inn Fields 38, 200; London Bridge 152–3; Ludgate 148, 152; Newgate

152; Newgate Prison 174, 184; Northumberland House 152; Primrose Hill 91; Road to Reading (Piccadilly) 140; St James's Park 111; St James's St. 140; St Martins-in-the-Fields 91, 141; St Paul's 148; Snow Hill 152; Soho Square 129, 158; Somerset House 7, 91; Southwark 71-2, 153; Suffolk St. 37; Temple Bar 116, 200; Thanet House 134, 137, 146; the Tower 151, 152, 154, 160, 161, 168, 174, 186, 256-61; Tower Hill 259, 261-5; Tyburn 79; Wapping 146, 153, 154; Westminster 153; Whetstone Park 38; Whitehall Palace 12, 13

Longleat (Wilts) 129, 140
Lopping Point, The 148, 160, 169
Lorge, Major-General de 60, 61, 64
Lorraine, Philippe, Chevalier de 27, 28
Louis XIV, King of France 10, 21, 25, 26, 33, 34, 40, 41-52, 54, 56-65, 77-8, 82, 108, 115, 117, 125, 136, 157-8, 182, 205, 229, 237
Louvois, François-Michel, Marquis de, French Minister for War 44-5, 48, 51, 110
Lovelace, Lord 135
Lowestoft, Battle of xi, 16-18, 165
Lully, Jean-Baptiste 30, 45
Lumley, Richard, Lord (*later* 1st Earl of Scarborough) 251
Luxembourg, François Henri de Montmorency, Duke of, Marshal of France 78, 82, 83-8
Lyme (Dorset) 198, 209-18, 227, 271
Lymington (Hants) 250

Maastricht, Fortress of 47; siege of 57-65, 111, 165, 186; siege re-enacted at Windsor
Macauley, Lord, *cited* 248
Macclesfield, see Gerard
Mackintosh, Capt, Company commander, Dumbarton's Regt 245
Madrid 46
Manchester, Edward Montagu, 2nd Earl of 20
Manderville, Robert Montagu, Viscount 23
Manley, Isaac, rebel 239; Major John, rebel 239
Mar, Lord, under Monmouth in Scotland 101
Marie-Thérèse, Queen of France 25
Marshall, servant to Armstrong, then to Monmouth 261-2, 264
Marshall, Blank, Cromwellian spy 8
Martinet, Colonel 44, 45

Marvell, Andrew 38, 41
Mary I, Queen of England 192
Master of the Horse, appointment of 69, 72, 119, 131, 214
Matthews, Lt-Col Edward, commander of (1) Red Regt (2) White Regt 194, 200, 207, 217, 230, 241-3, 246, 252, 271; Mrs, wife of above and dau. of Armstrong 184-85
Mayn, Major of Monmouth's Regt of Horse 101-2
Mazarin, Armand-Charles, Duc de 27
Mead, Mary, of Taunton 220; Mr, of Essex, rebel leader 202, 203
Medway, The, Dutch ships in 23
Melville, George, Earl of 78, 101, 195
Mendip Hills 25
Meuse, River 46, 47, 48, 57, 60, 62
Mew, Dr Peter, Bishop of Bath and Wells (*later* of Winchester) 247, 269
Middleton, Mrs 70
Middlezoy (Somerset) 239-40
Minehead (Somerset) 239, 243
Mocenigo, Piero, Venetian Envoy 33
Molière, Jean-Baptiste 30
Monmouth and Buccleuch, Anna Scott, Duchess of: proposed as wife for Monmouth 11; marriage 12; expenses 13; with King and Lady Castlemaine 24; dancing accident 29; her ambitions for Monmouth 69-70; Evelyn on 94; Henry Sidney on 94; understands Monmouth's problems 118; travels to Paris 129; friendship with Duchess of York 141-2; her house searched, 1683 161; and Lady Wentworth 166; intercedes for Monmouth 171; prevents his sale of the Manor of Spalding 204; sees Monmouth in the Tower 258, 261; later life 267
Monmouth and Buccleuch, James Scott, Duke of: birth of 5; in London with his mother 7; is taken from his mother 7; is educated in Paris 8; travels to England 10; his titles discussed 11-12; his marriage 12; appointed Knight of the Garter 13; expenses of 13; early relationship with his father 14; at the Battle of Lowestoft 15-18; during the Plague 19-20; during the Fire of London 20; with Lord Oxford 21; first regimental command 22-3; patrols coast during Dutch scare 23; stays with "Madame" 26-30; is appointed Captain-Commandant of the Life Guards 30-2; his further appointments 33; speculation as to becoming Prince of Wales 34; at Dover 34-5; and the Coventry affair 37-8;

and the Virnill affair 38–9; at review of French Army 40; at Newmarket 40; appointed to command expeditionary force (1672) 42–3; raises Royal English Regt 42, 46; in Paris 47; marches to join the French 48; at sieges of Zutphen and Doesberg 48; heads English delegation at Heeswick 50–1; honoured by Louis 52; his status in England (1672) 53–4; further appointments 54; takes Test 55–6; is appointed supreme English commander (1673) 56; at the fortress of Lille 56–7; at siege of Maastricht 58–65; again honoured by Louis 65; his reception on return to England 67; his friendship with York 68–9; appointed Master of the Horse 69; first rupture with York 69–70; and Eleanor Needham 70–1; appointed to co-ordinate the Army 71; suppresses Weavers' Riots 71; and the Southwark fire 71–2; his duties as Captain-Commandant of Life Guards 72; his other roles 72; becomes patron of the Country Party 75; under Luxembourg in Lorraine (1677) 78; plans for Royal Hospital, Chelsea 78; at marriage of William and Mary 80; strengthens forces in Netherlands 80; is promoted Lord-General 81; as commander in 1678 campaign 82–5; at the Battle of St Denis 86–8; as counter-insurgency commander 92–3; investigates death of Sir E. B. Godfrey 92; disbands the army in Flanders 93; organises fire-fighting at Middle Temple 95; as Lord High Chamberlain of Scotland 96–7; is appointed Commander-in-Chief, Scotland 98; proceeds to Edinburgh 99; in Bothwell Bridge campaign 99–106; reports to King at Windsor 108; his reaction to York's return 109; is dismissed from posts and exiled 110; sails to Netherlands 111; in league with William of Orange 113–14; returns to England 116–17; his emotional conflicts 118–19; subject of Dryden's verse 120–2; and the Black Box affair 125–8; at Chichester 128–9; tours the West Country 129–32; speaks in the Lords 134; at the Oxford Parliament 135–6; stands surety for Shaftesbury 138; in Kent 139; investigates Thynne's murder 140; his altercation with Lord Halifax 141; his tour of the Midlands 143–5; is arrested at Stafford 145; is forbidden to enter Whitehall 146; is at variance with Shaftesbury 146–7; plans insurrection 147–54; orders all plotting to be suspended 154; succeeds Shaftesbury as revolutionary leader 156; in Chichester with Lord Grey 157; wins International Plate (1683) 157–8; hides in London after Rye House Plot is revealed 161; flees to Toddington 161; is harboured by Lady Wentworth 162–4; his superstitious tendencies 165, 167; his religious Faith 167; is pardoned by King 169–74; begs Yorks' forgiveness 174; is subject of the nation's rejoicing 174; is requested as witness by Algernon Sidney 175; rupture with the King 176–8; is exiled again 178–9; is granted colonelcy of a Spanish regt 180; is befriended by William of Orange 182–3; returns secretly to England 185–6; his reaction to his father's death 189; returns to Spanish Netherlands 190; travels to Gouda with Lady Wentworth 191; states his position in writing 194–95; his dialogue with Sir Patrick Hume 195; plans invasion of England 196–204; raises money to equip invasion 204; his relationship with Lady Wentworth 205; informs William of Orange of final plans 206; sails from the Texel to Lyme 207–10; in Lyme 210–12; strengthens his cavalry 215–16; his action on the death of Heywood Dare 216; and the skirmish at Bridport 217–18; marches to Taunton 218–19; in Taunton 220–4; marches to the Avon 227; organises the scythe companies 227; decides against attacking Bristol 228–30; at the Fight at Philips Norton 233–4; holds Council of War at Frome 235; exhorts his men at Frome 236; at Shepton Mallet 237; in Bridgwater 237–43; plans his night march xxi, 241–3; marches to attack Westonzoyland xxii, 243–4; at the Battle of Sedgemoor 245–50; his flight and capture 250–1; his reflections in captivity 252–3; writes appeals 254; is escorted to London 254–5; is interviewed by James II 256; is confined in the Tower 258–61; sees his wife and children 258, 261; is interviewed by clergy 260–1; on the scaffold 261–5

Monoux, Lieutenant, of Lord Oxford's Regt 226

Mons 165

Montagu, Lord 128; Ralph (*later* Duke

of Montagu) 43, 45, 46, 93–4, 133, 139
Montal, General 62
Montbrun, Charles Henri de Bellegarde, Marquis de 29, 62
Montespan, Françoise-Athénaïs, Marquise de 30
Montpensier, Anne Marie Louise, Duchesse de, "La Grande Mademoiselle" 27, 30
Montrose, James Graham, 3rd Marquis of, under Monmouth in Scotland 104
Moor Park, Rickmansworth 178, 181, 202, 204, 267
Moore, Sir John, Lord Mayor of London 142, 158
Morangle, Marquise de 29
Morbecque, Marquis de 65
Moselle, River 46, 48
Mulgrave, John Sheffield, Earl of (*later* Duke of Buckingham) 68, 69–70, 78, 119, 189
Musgrave, Miss, Taunton schoolmistress 220
Muskerry, Lord 17

Nantwich (Salop) 144
Needham, Eleanor 70–1, 161, 267
Nelthorp, Richard 147, 270
Newburgh, James Livingstone, Earl of, witness to Lucy Barlow's marriage 275
Newmarket 33, 40, 90, 159, 165, 181
Nijmegen 183, 185; Peace of (1678) 86–8
Nokes, Mr, Actor 35
Norfolk, Thomas, 6th Duke of 39, 55
Northumberland, Algernon Percy, 10th Earl of 4, 140; George Fitzroy, 1st Duke of 53

Oates, Titus 89, 91–3, 110, 120, 137, 184
O'Brien, Capt Charles, Life Guards officer 38, 62, 64
Ogle (see Thynne)
Oglethorp, Major Theophilus, Life Guards officer 100–5, 172, 226, 230, 240, 243, 248
Old Bailey, The 137–8, 168
Oldmixon, John, historian, *cited* 189, 237, 241, 243, 247, 261
Oliver, Dr William, surgeon to Monmouth 250
O'Neile, Col Daniel, equerry to Charles II (*later* commanding Lord Oxford's Regt) 6, 7
Opdam, Admiral in Dutch Fleet 17
Orange, William, Prince of (*later*

William III) 42, 74; takes command in Holland 48; character of 49; floods his country 49; marries Mary of York 79–80; at Battle of St Denis 86–8; his dialogue with Monmouth (1679) 113–14; visits Windsor 139; his friendship with Monmouth (1683–85) 182–3, 185, 187, 189–90, 206; sends Bentinck to James II 206; offers support to James II 232
Orange, Prince William of (William the Silent) 49; Princess Mary of (*later* Mary II) 55, 79–80, 109, 113, 114, 166, 182–3, 187; Princess Mary of (Princess Royal of England, sister of Charles II) 5, 6, 10, 42, 134, 216, 275
Oratorian College, Colombes 8, 10
d'Orleans, Gaston, Duc 177; Henrietta, Duchesse ("Madame") 10, 12, 26–30, 34–5, 40, 47; Philippe, Duc ("Monsieur") 10, 26, 27–30, 34–5, 60
Ormonde, James Butler, 1st Duke of 15, 53, 78, 95
Osborne, John, Lieut, Monmouth's troop of horse 22
Ossory, Thomas Butler, Earl of 20, 78, 82, 86–7, 92, 166
Oxford, Aubrey de Vere, 20th Earl of 21, 22, 39, 43, 114
Oxford University 13
Oxford 20, 132

Parcet, Elizabeth, sufferer of King's Evil 132
Parker, Capt John, Horse Grenadiers 230
Parkin, Henry, Sussex militiaman 251
Parret, River 239
Parsons, Major, rebel officer 235
Paschall, Rev Andrew, rector of Chedzoy xviii
Paterson, John, Bishop of Glasgow 275
Paton, Sir Richard, rebel leader 202–4, 230
Peazy Farm (Somerset) 244, 246
Pedwell Plain (Somerset) 237
Pegge, Catherine (*later* Lady Green) 53
Pemberton, Sir Francis, Lord Chief Justice 168–9, 175
Pembroke and Montgomery, Thomas Herbert, 8th Earl of 226, 228, 235, 240
Penn, William 149
Pensford (Somerset) 228
Pensoy Pound (Somerset) 240
Pepys, Samuel, diarist: on Monmouth's arrival at Court 10; on Monmouth's marriage 13; on Monmouth's installation as KG 13; on a river journey 14;

on a Court ball 14; on the King's fondness for Monmouth 16; on Monmouth's activities in 1667 23; on King with Duchess of Monmouth 24; on Monmouth's Captain-Generalcy of the Life Guards 32; on speculation about Monmouth's advancement 10, 12, 34, 275; at re-enactment of siege of Maastricht 68; on Colonel Kirke 269

Perwych, William, secretary at Paris embassy, *cited* 48, 64, 65
Phelips, Colonel Sir Edward 218
Philip IV, King of Spain 25
Philips Norton, The skirmish at 233–4
Plague, The Great 19, 28
Player, Sir Thomas 147
Plymouth, Charles Fitz-Charles, Earl of 53, 78
Plymouth (town of) 40
Pomponne, Simon Arnauld, Marquis de 50–1
Poole, 235, 250
Portman, Sir William 251, 252
Portsmouth, Louise de Keroualle, Duchess of 40, 93, 119, 125, 133, 170, 189
Portsmouth (Hampshire) 16, 40, 153, 226
Prance, Miles 91–2
Pregnani, Abbé, Theatine priest 32–4, 257
Prideaux, Sir Edmund, of Forde Abbey 131, 209, 213, 214
Progers, Edward, witness to Lucy Barlow's marriage to Charles 7, 273
Protheroe, Elenor, 4; Elizabeth 3, 4; John 3, 4
Pym, John 134

Quo warrantos 142

Racing, horse 14, 33, 40, 128, 132, 139, 145, 157, 165, 181
Radnor, John, 1st Earl of 111
Ralph, historian, *cited* 105, 191, 196, 242
Ramsey, John, Sergeant-at-Arms 145; Colonel, Royalist officer 239
Red Lion, The, Taunton Inn 213, 220
Regiments: Life Guard of Horse (Life Guards) 21, 30–2, 37–8, 41, 72, 79, 80, 93, 104, 119, 169, 172, 215, 226, 228, 229, 230, 240, 247–8; Royal, of Horse (Earl of Oxford's) 21, 36, 42, 99, 214, 225, 240, 244–8; King's Own Royal, of Dragoons (Tangier Horse) 214, 225, 233, 247; The Horse Grenadiers 226, 228, 230, 233; Duke

of Monmouth's, of Horse 42, 98, 103–4; King's, of Foot Guards (Grenadiers) 21, 163, 165, 240, 246–7; Duke of Albemarle's, of Foot Guards (Coldstream) 21, 240, 247; The Queen Dowager's of Foot 214, 225, 226, 240, 247; The Royal English (Duke of Monmouth's) 42, 46, 48, 98; The Holland (Royal East Kent) 84; Lord Dumbarton's (*for* Lord George Douglas's, *later* The Royal Scots) 42, 240, 241–2, 245–7; Lord Roscommon's 42; Sir George Hamilton's 42; Trelawney's 240, 247; Prince Rupert's, of Horse 23, 30; Scottish Foot Guards 102–4; Marquis of Atholl's Foot 103–4
Reresby, Sir John 35, 95, 107–8, 134, 140–1, 256
Rhine, River 46–8
Rich, Rev, vicar of Chard 225–6
Richardson, Capt, keeper of Newgate Prison 184
Richmond, Charles Fitzroy, Duke of 54, 141
Richmond and Lennox, Charles Stuart, Duke of 28, 38–9; Frances Stuart, Duchess of 20, 28
Ringwood (Hampshire) 251, 254
Rivers, Thomas Savage, 3rd Earl 144
Roberts, George, *cited* 248
Roche Castle 3, 4
Rochester, Henry Wilmot, Earl of 20, 38; Laurence Hyde, Earl of 164, 170, 185, 213, 253–4, 258
Rochfort, Major-General de la 60
Rockingham, Edward, 2nd Baron 61
Roe, John, of Bristol 178, 230
Rohanez, Major-General de 60, 64
Roper, Squire, Master of Monmouth's hounds 129
Ross, Thomas, tutor to Monmouth 8, 16
Rotterdam 190, 200
Rouse, John, rebel 147, 168
Royal Charles, The (Flagship) 17
Rumbold, Richard, maltster and rebel 148, 159, 196, 268
Rumsey, Colonel John, rebel 147, 149, 160
Rupert, Prince 15–17, 20, 22, 31, 34, 38, 40, 43, 53, 55, 57, 68, 74, 246
Russell, William, Lord: member of the Green Ribbon Club 75; his attack on Lauderdale 97; resigns Scottish Commission 99; at the Oxford Parliament 135; during the plots of 1682–83 147, 149–50, 153, 156; arrested 161; trial and execution of 168–9; *misc* 252–3, 264

Russell, Lady 168–9; Colonel John 20, 43, 117
Rutherglen Testimony, The 102
Rutland, Countess of 181, 256, 259
Ruyter, Admiral Michael Adriaanzoon De 15–17, 21, 57
Rye House Plot 159, 170–1, 192

Sackville, Lt-Col (Coldstream Guards) xxi, 240
St Albans, Charles Beauclerk, Duke of 54
St Denis, Battle of 86–8
St George's Chapel, Windsor 13, 214
St James's Fight 21
St Mary's, Bridgwater 238, 240–1, 245
St Peter ad Vincula, Chapel of, in Tower 265
St Swithin's Day 7, 205, 257, 260
Salisbury 20
Salisbury, Bishop of 189
Salisbury (Wilts) 20
Sambourne, Margaret (nee Protheroe), aunt of Lucy Barlow 127
Sambre, River 46
Sandwich, Edward Montagu, 1st Earl of 17–18
Sanquhar, Cross at 267
Savile, Henry 109
Saxham Hall (Suffolk) 20
Schalland, Count 85
Scheldt, River 83, 88
Schomberg, Count 53, 61, 68
Scott, Lord Francis, grandson of Monmouth 267; Lord George, son of Monmouth 119; Lord Henry (*later* Earl of Deloraine), son of Monmouth 178, 258; Lady Anne, daughter of Monmouth 178, 258, 267; Col, Commander of Tower Guard (1685) 259; Mrs 220
Scroggs, Sir William, Chief Justice 133
Sealed Knot, The 36
Sedgemoor 228, 239–42, 244
Sedgemoor, Battle of xxi–xxii, 245–50
Sedley, Catherine, mistress of York 70
Severn, River 226, 230
Sévigné, Marie de Rabutin-Chantal, Marquise de, *cited* 47
Shaftesbury, Anthony Ashley Cooper, 1st Earl of : member of the Cabal 26; tricked by the King 41; emerges as leader of Country Party 55; his career 73; his political scheming 73–4; President of the Country Party 74–5; and Monmouth's appointment as Lord-General 81; committed to the Tower 77; and the Popish Plot 89; President of the Council 95; and the Scottish revolt 97–9; and the Exclusion Bill 107; is deprived of Presidency of Council 111; celebrates Queen Elizabeth's birthday 115–16; his faith in Monmouth 119; in *Absolam and Achitophel* 120; and his "brisk boys" 128; host to Monmouth in Dorset 131; and the Exclusion Bill 133–4; at the Oxford Parliament 134–6; in the Tower again 137; his *Agreement with the People* 142; exhorts Monmouth to lead Midlands rising 144; complains to Grey about Monmouth 146; moves to Wapping 146; as revolutionary leader 146–50; refuses collaborate with Monmouth 153; flees to Netherlands 154–5; death of 155; Margaret, Countess of 91; (Dorset) 250
Sharp, Dr James, Archbishop of St Andrews 97, 106
Sheldon, Ralph, equerry to James II 254–5
Sheppard, Thomas, rebel 147, 154, 160
Shepton Mallet (Somerset) 228, 236–7
Sherborne (Dorset) 226
Shere, Henry, Royalist artillery commander 226
Shrewsbury, Alice Maria, Countess of 28, 40; Charles Talbot, 12th Earl of 55, 163; Francis Talbot, 11th Earl of 28
Shute (Somerset) 218–19
Sidney, Col Algernon 149, 156, 170, 174–5, 177, 252; Col Henry (*later* Earl of Romney) 84, 94, 113–15, 117, 133, 170, 175; Col Robert 125
Silver, Mr, of Bridgwater, inventor 239
Silver Stick, appointment of 93
Skelton, Sir Bevil, Consul in Netherlands 181, 203, 207
Slingsby, Colonel Sir Arthur 7, 8, 11–12; Capt 62
Smith, Aaron, rebel 148, 156, 175; "Madame", friend of Lord Argyle 192
Smyth, Colonel 267; Sir William 162
Smyth Stuart, James Wentworth (son of Monmouth) 205, 267
Snaphaunce (musket) 245
Snow Hill (*see* London)
Solebay, Battle of 48
Somerset, Charles Seymour, 6th Duke of 141, 213, 219
Somerton (Somerset) 238
Southampton, Charles Fitzroy, Earl of 53; Thomas, Wriothesley, Earl of 15
Southwell, Sir Robert, Clerk of the Council 92
Spalding, Manor of, property of Mon-

mouth's 204
Sparke, William 239
Speke, George 130–2, 151, 209, 213, 216, 221, 268; John 216, 219, 236
Stafford, Thomas Howard, Viscount 135; (Staffs) 145, 185
Stamford, Lord 200
Strangways, Wadham, Royalist militia officer 217
Strode, Edward 228, 250, 268; Sir William 131, 209, 213, 228
Sunderland, Robert Spencer, 2nd Earl of 20, 94, 109–10, 115, 119, 125, 170, 188, 208–9, 219, 230, 232, 253–6, 259, 268; Dorothy, Dowager Countess of 125, 175
Sydenham, Sir John 131
Sydenham Mead (Glos) 229

Tangier 15, 71
Taunton Dene 144, 157, 198, 216, 217, 219–25, 226, 227, 237, 238–9, 271
Taylor, Silas, civil servant 23
Tellier, Capt, rebel officer 207
Temple, Sir William, Ambassador to the Hague 25, 46, 108–10
Tender Consciences, Declaration of Indulgence for 54–5
Tennison, Dr Thomas, vicar of St Martins-in-the-Fields (*later* Archbishop of Canterbury) 260
Thanet, Thomas Tufton, Earl of 163
Third Dutch War, The 41
Thompson, Councillor 161
Thorald, Anthony, customs officer of Lyme 212
Thynne, Lady Elizabeth (*for* Countess of Ogle, *later* Duchess of Somerset) 140–1; Sir Thomas 95; Thomas, of Longleat (Tom O'Ten Thousand): member of the Green Ribbon Club 75; resigns Scottish Commission 99; host to Monmouth 129–31; as *Wise Issachar*, of Dryden's verse 129–30; murder of 140–1; mourned 216, 221
Toddington (Bedfordshire) 161–7, 267
Toddington Oak, The 167
Tonge, Dr Israel 89
Tower of London, The (see London)
Townshend, Horatio, 1st Viscount 40
Trenchard, John (*later* Sir), rebel officer 151, 153–4, 157, 177, 209, 213, 268
Triple Alliance, The 25, 30, 41–4
Tromp, Admiral Cornelis van 68
Tunbridge Wells 139
Turenne, Henri, Vicomte de, Marshal of France 15, 25, 28, 45, 47, 48, 56, 57, 71, 229
Turner, Dr Francis 260, 267

Tye, Thomas, Port Surveyor of Lyme 209
Tyler, Capt Joseph, of Bristol, rebel 211, 228, 269, 271

Up Park, Lord Grey's Sussex home 129, 157, 160
Ure, James, of Shargaton, *cited* 100, 102
Utrecht, Treaty of 49–51

Valera, Don 190
Vauban, Sebastien Le Prestre de, military engineer 47, 56–60
Veitch, Rev William, *cited* 186–9
Vendôme, César, Duc de 50
Venner, Lt-Col Samuel, commander of the Blue Regiment 207, 209, 216, 217, 230
Verney, Edmund, *cited* 119; John, *cited* 111; Sir Ralph 163
Vernon, James, secretary to Monmouth 60, 65, 67, 69, 71, 81, 82–8, 101, 111
Versailles 28, 30
Vic, Sir Harry de 12
Villa Hermosa, Duke of, Governor of Spanish Netherlands 84
Villiers, Major-General Edward, Life Guards Officer 62–3; Major-General to Monmouth 82; commanding Life Guards at Sedgemoor xxi, 247–8
Vincent, Capt, rebel commander of musketeers 233
Virnill, Peter, parish officer, Lincoln's Inn 38
Voltaire, Jean de, *cited* 44

Waal, River 48
Wade, Lt-Col Nathaniel, commander of the Blue Regt xxii, 75, 147, 149, 160, 192, 196, 198, 199, 200, 204, 207, 210, 211, 214, 217–9, 222, 230, 232–4, 238, 242–3, 246–7, 269
Wakeman, Sir George 90, 110
Walcot, Lt-Col Thomas, rebel officer 147, 149, 155
Waldeck, Count de, Dutch commander 86–8, 182
Wallasey 144
Walter, Elizabeth, mother of Lucy Barlow: Justus, brother of Lucy Barlow 4, 6; Richard, brother of Lucy Barlow 4; William, father of Lucy Barlow 3; Mr, cousin of Lucy Barlow 127
Walters, Mr, pilot of *Helderenberg* 216
War Lane 244
Warbeck, Perkin 132
Warminster (Wilts) 236
Washington, James, factor to Monmouth 191, 204
Watson, Capt Edward, Life Guards

officer 61; Capt Francis, Life Guards officer and ADC to Monmouth 61, 62; Capt Lewis, Life Guards officer 61

Weavers' Riots 71

Welch, John, Covenanter officer 101; coachman to Monmouth 161

Wells (Somerset) 219, 228, 237

Welwood, James, *cited* 124, 169–71, 172–4, 176, 178–9, 180, 187–8, 194, 266

Wemyss, Margaret, Countess of, mother of Duchess of Monmouth 11–12; David Erskine, 2nd Earl of 10, 12

Wentworth, Henrietta, Baroness, of Nettleside 161; harbours Monmouth at Toddington 162–7; joins Monmouth in Netherlands 180–3, 188; raises money for invasion 204; parts with Monmouth 205–6; and Feversham 229; subject of Monmouth's thoughts in the Tower 258–60; her name spoken by Monmouth on the scaffold 262–4; hears of Monmouth's execution 267; her son by Monmouth 267, death of 267; Philadelphia, Lady 162; Thomas, 5th Baron 162–3

Werden, Mr, of Preston, witness to alleged marriage of Lucy Barlow 275

West, Robert, barrister and rebel 142, 147, 160; cited 142, 146, 148 149, 154

Western Martyrology, cited 261

Westonzoyland (Somerset) 239–40, 245, 249, 269

Wharton, Philip, 4th Lord 75, 77; Thomas 157

Whigs, The xi, 79, 94, 95, 117, 134, 168–9, 171, 176, 189

Whitehall (see London)

White Lackington (Somerset) 130, 213

Whiting, John, a Quaker 218, 220–2

Whole Glorious Life, The, cited 261, 266

Wildman, Major John (*later* Sir John), rebel officer 75, 116, 147, 199–204, 212, 213, 230, 268

Wilkins, W. H. 276

Williams, William, servant to Monmouth 178, 212, 246, 248, 250

Williamson, Sir Joseph, Secretary of State 23, 27, 29, 46, 67, 69, 71, 81, 82

Witt, Cornelis De, Dutch statesman 21, 25, 42, 44, 48, 49

Woburn Abbey (Beds) 168

Wolseley, Field-Marshal Viscount, *cited* 247

Worcester, Henry Somerset, 3rd Marquess of (see Beaufort); Battle of (1651) xxii, 9, 107, 163, 165, 238, 248

Wren, Sir Christopher 32, 78

Wrington (Somerset) 218

Yard, Robert, Civil Secretary 67, 68–9

Yonge, Sir Walter, of Colyton 131, 209

York, Anne Hyde, Duchess of 55, 127, 185; James, Duke of (James II): his alleged comments on Lucy Barlow 3; escapes Roundhead wardens 5; is dismissed to the Hague 5; his concern at Monmouth's elevation 11; his early military training 14–15; at Battle of Lowestoft 15–18; on King's intention to become a Catholic 34; his own Catholicty 34; backs Monmouth's appointment to command expeditionary force 43; declines Test 55; at the re-enactment of Maastricht 68; his fondness for Monmouth 68–9; first rupture with Monmouth 69–70; marries Mary of Modena 73; opposes marriage of his daughter to William of Orange 79; opposes Monmouth's appointment as Lord-General 80–1; quotes Monmouth on Battle of St Denis 88; is exiled 94; persuades the King to make public declaration on marriage 94–5; commences series of letters to William against Monmouth 95; complains of Monmouth's unbridled power 98; returns secretly to England 110; his triumph at Monmouth's exile 110; leaves Edinburgh for London 125–6; and the Black Box Affair 126–8; is shipwrecked on return 141; speculates on Shaftesbury's death 155; and the Rye House Plot 158–61; pardons Monmouth 173–4; recommends Monmouth serve term in Tower 174; expresses satisfaction at Sidney's execution 175–6; resists King's reconciliation with Monmouth 176; triumphs in Monmouth's second exile 178; is ordered to Edinburgh by Charles 187; and death of Charles 188–9; brands Monmouth as traitor 189–90; receives news of Monmouth's invasion 212; his counter-measures 213–14; sends Ralph Sheldon to meet Monmouth 254; interviews Monmouth 256; issues order for Monmouth's execution 259–60; and the Bloody Assizes 271; Mary, Duchess of (Mary of Modena) 70, 80, 114, 141, 163, 174, 256

Zeeland, plans for invasion of 53, 57, 67–9

Zutphen, siege of 48

Zuyder Zee 49

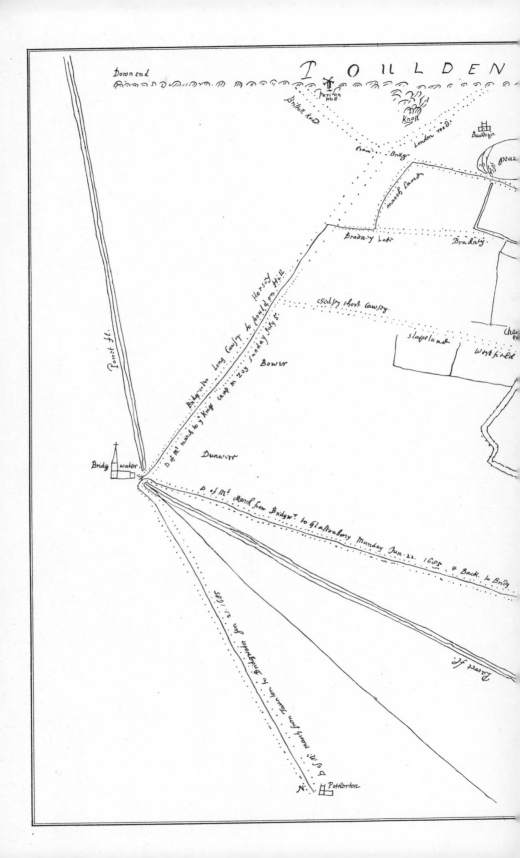